*T*he return of Eastern and Central Europe to true independence, following the collapse of Communist rule, has reanimated an enormous number of historical and cultural issues largely dormant since the disasters of World War II.

Conflict and Chaos in Eastern Europe analyzes five of the most important of these issues: the legacy of the Habsburg Empire; the "cultural faultline" of Bosnia-Hercegovina; the disputes over the region of Macedonia; the tensions between Hungary and Romania over Transylvania; and the instability of Poland's eastern borders.

Cutting through the tangle of nationalist propaganda that obscures so many of Eastern Europe's historical problems, Dr. Hupchick has produced an intriguing and evocative book that greatly enhances our understanding of this fascinating, but highly unstable, part of the world.

For a note on the author, please see the back flap

CONFLICT
AND CHAOS
IN EASTERN EUROPE

Also by Dennis P. Hupchick

THE BULGARIANS IN THE SEVENTEENTH CENTURY:
Slavic Orthodox Society and Culture under Ottoman Rule

THE PEN AND THE SWORD:
Studies in Bulgarian History by James F. Clarke *(editor)*

CULTURE AND HISTORY IN EASTERN EUROPE

CONFLICT
AND CHAOS
IN EASTERN EUROPE

Dennis P. Hupchick

St. Martin's Press
New York

ISBN 0-312-12116-4

Library of Congress Cataloging-in-Publication Data

Hupchick, Dennis P.
    Conflict and chaos in Eastern Europe / Dennis P. Hupchick.
    p. cm.
    Includes bibliographical references and index.
    ISBN 0-312-12116-4
    1. Europe, Eastern—Politics and government. 2. Former Soviet
republics—Politics and government. I. Title.
DJK42.H86 1995
947—dc20
                                                    94-38207
                                                        CIP

Interior design by Digital Type & Design

First Edition April 1995:
10 9 8 7 6 5 4 3 2 1

For My Mother,
ETHEL J. HUPCHICK

▦ CONTENTS ▦

◼ LIST OF MAPS ◼

◈ PREFACE ◈

The essays included in the earlier volume, *Culture and History in Eastern Europe* (St. Martin's Press, 1994), present a broad conceptual framework for understanding the dramatic events that have swept through Eastern Europe and Western Eurasia in the past half decade. Unlike most current analyses of those developments that regularly appear in our media, which address them from strictly political or economic viewpoints, the analytical approach taken in *Culture and History* delves deeper to examine the more fundamental cultural and historical forces constantly at work, either consciously or subconsciously, among the inhabitants of those regions. Some readers initially may react with a pang of skepticism to such a premise—on the surface, it appears to lack the social-scientific paraphernalia that we Westerners demand of analysis, such as the mathematical models that political scientists and economists hold dear. This is understandable. While in our Western predilection for science history has sometimes been translated into statistical analysis (of such things as tax rolls, voter registrations, property deeds, business ledgers, and a plethora of other recorded listings, including telephone books) and dubbed a "social science," culture mostly has been relegated to "the arts," or those areas of human endeavor that, although oftentimes interesting and emotionally valuable, are considered of lesser account in the universal scientific scheme of things. *Culture and History* takes a somewhat different but consistently logical tack regarding both of the subjects in its title.

Simply stated, culture is the unique common perception of reality shared by a particular group of people (a society) that is shaped by the group's physical and human environment. Out of that fundamental sense of reality springs all of a society's accepted norms, within which every aspect of the members' human existence is institutionalized and thus preserved, developed further, and handed down to succeeding generations. Therefore, culture is the most intrinsically deterministic factor in human social life. It exists on two levels: the micro, which we Westerners today call nationality (or, at least, ethnicity) and which we commonly define primarily by language; and the macro, which we know as civilization and which is best expressed by a highly sophisticated, institutionalized religion or philosophy (or both) that is shared among a number of member microcultures. History is the study of civilizations' internal and external developments and interactions over time on both the macro- and microcultural levels. All human activity, both individual and group, is molded at the time it occurs by the contemporary state of culture held by those involved. Thus both culture and history operate in symbiotic and simultaneous fashion in human societies and play a joint fundamental role in all places at all times.

There are in Eastern Europe three civilizations—Western European (Catholic/Protestant Christian), Eastern European (Orthodox Christian), and Islamic (Muslim)—containing among them at least seventeen major nationalities in total. The key to understanding the events of 1989 and later, which ended the Communist era in Eastern Europe, lies in grasping the nature of their realities and how they interrelate with one another on both levels of culture. This is precisely the task that *Culture and History* undertakes.

In every sense of the word, *Conflict and Chaos in Eastern Europe* is a sequel to *Culture and History.* The following essays constitute case studies illustrating the concepts presented in the earlier volume. In fact, when the idea for this project was originally broached to the publisher, it was envisioned as a single book divided into conceptual and case-study halves. Happily, St. Martin's felt two volumes worked better than one. In this, the publisher truly knew best.

The essays in *Conflict and Chaos* take a general survey approach to their individual topics and, perforce, paint their illustrative images in broad strokes. An attempt has been made to keep the technical jargon to a minimum, in an effort to aid the interested general reader or student in following the lines of the narratives and in understanding their thrusts. Having three civilizations, seventeen major nationalities, at least seven forms of religion, two separate alphabets, nineteen states, and four empires to deal with, Eastern Europe is complex and confusing enough as it is, without being complicated by incomprehensible language. Since the essays found in this collection are individually written entities, some repetition of ideas and information among them, and with those in *Culture and History,* should be expected. Often the repetition is intentional to aid the informational purpose of this volume.

Just as the essays in *Culture and History* were written without the benefit of dedicated research, but drew on previous years of study, research, firsthand experience, and teaching, so too are those in *Conflict and Chaos.* But while the earlier volume was created in somewhat of a stream-of-consciousness approach, with little recourse to notes or specialized texts, the essays in the present volume make use of assorted classroom and lecture notes, a few general studies, and occasionally a specialized text. *Culture and History* contained no notes to the text of the essays but included an additional essay on further readings. The publisher requested that the essays in *Conflict and Chaos* contain notes. Since nearly all of the material presented in the narratives is generally well-known among specialists, and since few truly specialized works were consulted, most serve to point out useful readings dealing with specific subjects treated in the texts. In addition, a select bibliography has been provided. Because, as in the earlier volume, the envisioned audience for *Conflict and Chaos* is assumed to be English-speaking general readers and students, works listed in both the notes and in the bibliography are written in English. Regarding the apparent arbitrary limitation in scope of this decision, it should be mentioned that those who can read foreign languages will find plenty of non-English materials cited in the notes and bibliographies of works listed herein.

I wish to thank wholeheartedly the two manuscript readers and critics—Tom Bigler and Robert Heaman—from Wilkes University, who played an important role in giving final shape to the essays in *Culture and History,* for graciously agreeing to serve in those capacities once again. I deeply appreciate their willingness to tolerate my impositions on their time, and I hold their comments and criticisms in great respect. Harold Cox, also from Wilkes University, who produced the maps and provided valuable assistance in preparing the manuscript of *Culture and History* for publication, not only repeated his expert efforts on the present volume but he outdid them. He has my sincere gratitude. I also would like to recognize and thank Simon Winder, the senior editor at St. Martin's Press who oversaw this project through both of the volumes, and who provided valuable encouragement, support, and creative input the entire way. Finally, special thanks are due my wife, Anne-Marie, who tolerated all my mental preoccupation and my hours of monasticlike seclusion in front of a computer.

Dennis P. Hupchick
WILKES-BARRE, 1994

◩ NOTE ON PRONUNCIATION ◩

In the texts of the following essays, an attempt has been made to retain the native spelling of most proper names and foreign terms, except in the case of languages using non-Latin alphabets, when either a phonetic transliteration of the phonics (for Bulgarian and Russian) or the Latin-based Croat form (for Serbian) are used. Some more well-known proper names (for example: Prague, Sofia, Warsaw, Moscow, and Belgrade) are given in their common forms rather than in their native spellings. A guide to the simple phonetic pronunciation of certain foreign letters is as follows.

á (Hungarian, Czech, Slovak): . . . . .as a in *a*h
c (in all cases *except* Turkish), ţ (Romanian): . . . . .as ts in bea*ts*
ch (Polish, Czech, Slovak),
    h (Bulgarian, Serb, Croat, Turkish): . . . . .as ch in Ba*ch*
cz, ci (Polish), č (Serb, Croat, Czech, Slovak),
    ć (Serb, Croat, Polish), cs (Hungarian), ç (Turkish): . . .as ch in *ch*ur*ch*
dj (Serb, Croat), gy (Hungarian), c (Turkish): . . . . .as dzh in ba*dge*
é (Hungarian): . . . . .as long a in b*a*y
ě (Czech): . . . . .as ye in y*e*t
ę (Polish): . . . . .as nasal eln in h*elln*ight
ğ (Turkish): . . . . .as silent h in o*h*
i, í, ý (in all cases), yi (Hungarian): . . . . .as ee in sw*ee*t
j (in all cases *except* Romanian): . . . . .as y in *y*et
ł (Polish): . . . . .as w in *w*on
ń (Polish): . . . . .as soft n in k*n*ew
ó (Hungarian): . . . . .as long o in s*o*
ö (Hungarian): . . . . .as ur in p*ur*ge
š (Serb, Croat, Czech, Slovak), sz, ś (Polish),
    s (Hungarian), ş (Romanian and Turkish): . . . . .as sh in *sh*eet
sz (Hungarian): . . . . .as s in *s*ay
u (in all cases), ó (Polish): . . . . .as oo in z*oo*
ü (Turkish, Hungarian): . . . . .as yoo in mil*ieu*
ŭ (Bulgarian), ă (Romanian), ı (Turkish), ë (Albanian),
    ö (Hungarian): . . . . .as short a in b*u*t
w (Polish, German): . . . . .as v in *v*ery
x (Albanian): . . . . .as dz in bu*ds*
y (Polish, Russian, Czech, Slovak), î (Romanian): . . . . . . .as short i in *i*t
ž (Serb, Croat), ř (Czech, Slovak), zs (Hungarian),
    j (Romanian), ż (Polish): I .as zh in mea*s*ure

AUSTRIA-HUNGARY IN 1914

-•-•-•-•-•-•-• International borders
━━━━━━━━━ Border of Austria-Hungary
----------- Border of Kingdom of Hungary
··············· Major regional borders

0 50 100 150 200
|___|___|___|___|
Miles

MARRIAGES AND DIVORCES

● ○ ●

Post-1989 events in Eastern Europe have brought a number of sweeping changes to a world we had grown accustomed to taking for granted. One of the more dramatic changes brought about by the fall of European communism has been the reconfiguration of the political map of Eastern Europe and Eurasia, with the disappearance of states that most twentieth-century Westerners long took for granted as natural political realities—the Russian/Soviet Empire, Czechoslovakia, and Yugoslavia. They were replaced by a number of smaller ones, most of which either never existed before, except in the minds of certain groups of nationalists or religionists (such as Slovakia, Slovenia, Moldova, Belarus, and the Central Asian states of the former Soviet Union), or had enjoyed some previous independent existence in the often-distant past that various nationalist groups continuously used prior to the end of the cold war as justification for the survival of their political programs (notably Ukraine [Kievan Russia], Croatia, Bosnia, Serbia, Montenegro, the Czech Republic [Bohemia], and the Georgian and Armenian states of the formerly Russian/Soviet-controlled Caucasus).

Then again, the West actively interceded in the process of state reconfiguration in the case of the Baltic republics, doing so in the name of political and national morality, through overturning a German-Soviet pact prior to World War II that disrupted the previous Versailles effort at European mapmaking responsible for the creation of the three republics in the first place. Of the three Baltic states, only Lithuania existed as a state before the end of World War I; the others—Estonia and Latvia—must be classified in the ranks of those new post-1989 states without an independent past (except for two brief decades following the Versailles settlement).

Western perplexity, on the one hand, and intervention, on the other, in reshaping the European and Eurasian map at the close of the cold war illustrates certain important characteristics of the Western European sense of political reality. In the first place, the West considers the world political map to be determined by its own dictates. When we speak of redrawing the map of Europe and Eurasia, we, of course, actually are talking about modifying political cartography that originally was drawn by the victorious Western Great Powers (specifically, Britain, France, and the United States) during the peace negotiations at Versailles (1919–21) ending World War I. They decided the contours of the political borders for the postwar states of Europe (especially for those in the Eastern regions), Western Eurasia, and West Asia. No matter that those decisions were based on the political and economic self-interests of the Western victors, once the borders were drawn they became political reality because their Western creators had the muscle to enforce their wills. The Western powers institutionalized their configuration of the world by founding, first, the League of Nations (minus the participation of the United States) and then, following World War II, the United Nations (led by the United States). These organizations were intended to legitimize the Western-imposed political settlement of states shaped along the lines of the West's nation-state principles by making state borders inviolable through a set of international laws created in the nation-state image.

One of the underlying factors in the development of the cold war rested on the Soviet-led Communist world's rejection of the West's power to dictate political cartography. Ideally, communism was ideologically opposed to the fundamental precepts that supported Western political culture—self-interested liberalism and democracy, industrial capitalism, and the nation-state. By being so, communism of necessity repudiated inviolate state borders. So long as the threat to Western European political culture remained theoretical, the West, though wary, could afford to act on the world's stage as it wished. Once Lenin and his Bolsheviks successfully made communism a political reality in Russia after 1921, fighting off a halfhearted Western intervention against them in the process, the West was forced to voice its claim to worldwide political dominance in a more circumspect fashion than at Versailles. Conflict could only result, finding its ultimate expression in the post-1948 cold war.

Fortunately for the West, communism in reality proved far less philanthropic and effective, and far more imperialistic and tyrannical, than in the ideal. For all of communism's blustering rhetoric in praise of universal human social and economic solidarity and condemnation of human divisiveness caused by capitalism, nationalism, and the nation-state, events following 1989 have demonstrated that European communism only served to perpetuate the political map created by the West at Versailles. Without the iron-fisted conservative domestic policies of Soviet and European satellite Communist governments, more intent on preserving a strong ideological front against Western capitalism than on living up to internationalist ideals, artificially created states such as Yugoslavia and Czechoslovakia most likely would have fallen apart at their national seams decades ago. By delaying the inevitable dissolution, the Communist era only pressurized the simmering internal divisions in such states, ensuring their more rapid and volatile disintegration once Communist control ended.

The doomed experiment in communism on the European political stage served to provide the West with a new opportunity to reevaluate its role in dictating world political mapmaking by demonstrating the potential dangers inherent in creating and maintaining artificial nation-states.

In reality, Versailles Eastern Europe never reflected the Western ideal of each nation-state truly representing the interests of its total population. While taut- ing the Wilsonian principle of national self-determination of peoples, the victorious Western architects of post-World War I Europe made cynical use of that doctrine in their mapmaking to mold the borders of old and new states created at Versailles to their own interests. We all are familiar with the catastrophic results of Versailles regarding the victors' mistaken efforts to punish the Germans for the Great War. By redrawing the borders of Germany in such a way as to cripple German industrial potential (by placing the Ruhr-Rhineland under French occupation) and to limit the country's demographic base (through leaving thousands of Germans stranded within newly created states, such as in Austria, Czechoslovakia, and a resurrected Poland), the Versailles settlement violated the West's own avowed nation-state ideals and furnished the Germans with valid national grievances within the very context of Western European political culture. They eventually chose to rectify their national humiliation through Adolf Hitler and his Nazis, bringing on World War II and its sequel, the cold war.

But the Versailles settlement defiled the nation-state precepts of Western European political culture in deeper and more subtle ways than in the obvious German example. Western recognition of state borders in Eastern Europe could not be separated from the victors' shortsighted policy of rewarding those peoples regarded as allies and of punishing those who were the losers in World War I. In determining the map of postwar Europe, the Western powers played loose with the publicly proclaimed moral ideal of national self-determination as the framework for nation-state cartography. The victors favored the claims of "friendly" nationalities; those of "enemies" were granted short shrift or ignored completely. Nowhere in geographical Eastern Europe did the national territorial claims of any one people go uncontested by those of another. The Versailles political mapmakers resorted to public polls (plebiscites) to adjudicate border disputes among "friends" in some kind of seemingly equitable fashion, but similar conflicts between allied and "enemy" peoples were almost always judged in favor of the former, often with their most grandiose nationalistic territorial pretensions completely satisfied. The borders of the East European nation-state winners at Versailles—Poland, Czechoslovakia, Yugoslavia, Romania, and Greece—were determined at the direct expense of equally valid, but disregarded, nationalist claims of nation-state losers— Germany, Hungary, and Bulgaria.[1]

That there could be winners and losers in drawing the borders of European states pointed to an innate but unrecognized fallacy in Western European political culture concerning nation-state nationalism. The course of human history, whether in Europe or anywhere else, militated against neat territorial divisions in terms of exclusive regions of habitat among different neighboring groups of peoples. Even in Western European states, whose societies had experienced centuries of native microcultural development within relatively consistent and recognized borders (such as France, Spain, and England), significant subcultures with strong variant ethnic traditions could be found inside their borders. The fact that history shaped most of those Western divergent groups into subcultures, and not into fully independent microcultures, colored the West's perception of political realities in terms of the nation-state concept. In geographical Eastern Europe, microcultural development of the various human societies took place over long periods of time in which those societies were merely components of larger, multicultural imperial states, whose borders bore no specific relation to any one of them in particular. Within the far-flung frontiers of the Habsburg, Russian, and Ottoman empires, there were few internal boundaries to confine neighboring groups of people, which resulted in the widespread territorial mixing of different societies and their microcultures that were in contact with one another. By the time Western nation-state precepts were applied to them at Versailles, no truly national borders could have been drawn, even if the mapmakers had been as objective in their determinations as possible. But the mapmakers were consciously unobjective in their work, and they openly admitted as much when, primarily as a public relations ploy, they established a League of Nations commission in Geneva to arbitrate the just but disregarded claims of the many national minorities created by their decisions.

Furthermore, the settlement of Versailles contradicted one of the important components in the very nature of the Western European nation-state political culture. Nationalism and the nation-state represented the West's complete rejection of artificially and arbitrarily constructed countries that were a political legacy of the Middle Ages. In adopting nationalism and in denouncing unrestricted monarchism as the "natural" bases for state-building, the West declared as "unnatural" the combination of different nationalities within common borders merely for the benefit of an elite governing class, whose only loyalties were to itself. Prior to the advent of nationalism and the nation-state in the West, monarchs freely acquired territories through wars or marriages with little regard for the ethnic (eventually national) character of their populations. This was especially common in geographical Eastern Europe, where native monarchies died out by the late fourteenth century and where foreign ruling houses thereafter came and went in an almost unbelievably confusing game of musical royal thrones.

One of the politically significant results of World War I was the final elimination of anational, monarchical statehood in Eastern Europe. In fact, in his famous "Fourteen Points," American president Woodrow Wilson had proclaimed this as a primary war aim on the United States' entry into the conflict. Wilson's declaration served to inflame the national aspirations of numerous nationalities within the borders of the enemy Central Powers (thus helping undermine their military potential) and to force his allies to accept national self-determination of peoples as the avowed basis for the later Versailles peace. Wilson, like most Americans at the time, was naive when it came to high-level international politics, and he was easily circumvented by his more experienced and pragmatic colleagues at the peace conference, who did not share his idealistic scruples regarding the nature of the nation-state when it came to furthering their own national agendas. True, the old anational political structures were dismantled, but, unfortunately, the new states created in their wake were constructed more to ensure both the prolonged punishment of the defeated Central Powers and the political and economic interests of the Western Great Powers in Eastern Europe than to uphold Wilsonian ideals.[2]

In attempting to preclude any resurrection of concerted challenges to the victorious Great Powers' dominance in European affairs by the defeated Germans, Hungarians, and Bulgarians, the Versailles mapmakers violated the precepts of their own nation-state political culture by sanctioning the creation of states artificially encompassing disparate nationalities—Czechoslovakia (Czechs, Slovaks, Germans, Hungarians, and Ukrainians), Yugoslavia (Serbs, Croats, Bosniaks [Bosnian Muslims], Bulgaro-Macedonians, Albanians, Hungarians, and a smattering of others), and Romania (Romanians, Hungarians, Germans, Bulgarians, and Turks).

The victors at Versailles were cognizant of the awkward national makeup of those new states. The original names of two were hyphenated, either literally or figuratively: Czecho-Slovakia and the Kingdom of Serbs, Croats and

Slovenes. (The name Yugoslavia [meaning "Land of the South Slavs"], emerged only in 1929 by decree of the state's Serb king Aleksandr I [1921–34], who also proclaimed a royal dictatorship in a move designed to squelch the centripetal national aspirations of non-Serb nationalities, especially of the Croats and of the Bulgaro-Macedonians, in his multinational state.) After Versailles, and virtually until the post-1989 disintegration of those two states occurred, the West stubbornly refused to admit publicly the contradiction their recognition posed to the essence of Western European nation-state political culture by glibly speaking of "Czechoslovaks" and "Yugoslavs" as if such creatures existed as authentic nationalities in their own right. By placing their own political interests into the forefront of their mapmaking, the victorious Western Great Powers at Versailles willfully sanctioned new states just as arbitrary in national makeup as the former enemy state they dismantled in the name of the nation-state principle. That former enemy had been an important and accepted player on the European political power stage for centuries past—the Habsburg Empire.

>‡< ‡>‡

When in 1914 it initiated the hostilities with Serbia that would escalate into the war that eventually brought about its total destruction, the Habsburg Empire (in its final political manifestation, Austria-Hungary) was already a political anachronism in Europe. Nearly all of the European Great Powers with whom it shared the international stage were states firmly predicated on the principles of nationalism and of the nation-state. The lone exception was the Russian Empire, but even it had managed to concoct a hybrid form of "Russian" nationalism within its borders by the force of its autocratic central governing institutions firmly grounded in Byzantine-created Orthodox political culture, which maintained tight control over the empire's far-flung territories and disparate nationalities. So deeply rooted in Russia was that Eastern European political culture that, even though tsardom was overthrown during the course of World War I, the Russian Empire survived the devastation of that war, two revolutions, and a subsequent civil war to emerge virtually unscathed as a state (the Soviet Union)—grounded on a new ideology, to be sure—which continued to be identified internationally as "Russia" until its dismemberment in 1991.[3]

Misfortune for Habsburg survival lay rooted in a modern Western European political culture that did not provide the ruling elite with an accepted mechanism for establishing effective, centralized autocratic authority over the territories and populations it governed—"divine right" was utterly rejected. The Habsburg Empire essentially was a holdover from the Middle Ages that had managed to survive the Reformation, the Enlightenment, the rise of liberalism, and, for the extent of a century, the advent of nationalism through a series of deft but stopgap political compromises and partial adaptations. Yet from its rise to prominence in the early sixteenth century to its total collapse in 1918, the nature of political authority in the Habsburg state remained medieval—the "God wills it" principle. The actual power of the Habsburg monarch was effectively limited by a system of political checks and balances posed by the state's multicultural aristocracy, on whom the ruler depended for bureaucratic, fiscal, and military support in governing. The aristocrats exerted their political muscle through various regional assemblies (diets) that represented the interests of the nobility inhabiting a patchwork of assorted distinct territories within the empire.

All of the territories, with their disparate populations, had been acquired by the Habsburg monarchs through the traditional medieval means of direct inheritances within the family, wars with neighboring monarchs, elections by local nobles, or marriages into other ruling houses. No matter the method of acquisition, the process was haphazard and drawn out, taking little notice of the ethnic and cultural diversity of the various populations wedded to the authority of the house of Habsburg. Throughout the four centuries of its existence, the Habsburg state essentially constituted the personal patrimony of the ruler and his family. The basis for its existence lay in the acceptance by the nobility and the population within each of the various, ethnically diverse territories of the Habsburgs' hereditary right to the office of supreme political authority. In the final analysis, loyalty to the house of Habsburg served as the cement that held the essentially medieval state together into the twentieth century. That such fragile political mortar succeeded for over three hundred years, dissolving only after nearly a century of nationalistic hammering by assorted ethnic groups within the empire's population, speaks volumes for the strength of tradition in human societies and cultures.[4]

Though we rightfully may wonder at the longevity imparted to the Habsburg state by royal tradition, we also must admit that entrenched traditions are often two-edged swords for the societies that hold them. While they may provide a strong sense of human continuity, security, and pride, they also may act as obstacles to those societies' adaptive abilities in facing changes in their human environments.

Consider, for example, the case of the Ottoman Empire in Europe. From its establishment and rapid expansion in the Balkans during the fourteenth and fifteenth centuries until its apex in the sixteenth, the Ottoman state was perhaps the strongest, most efficient in all of Europe. The Ottomans' centralized government and their great wealth (principally based on the Turks' role as middlemen in the crucial overland and Indian Ocean East-West trade routes) were envied by the monarchs of all the Western European states. Their near-invincible military forces, anchored on the iron-disciplined Janissary standing infantry units with their supporting artillery corps, were feared and emulated by their European enemies. To the Turks themselves, the underpinning moral mortar for Ottoman strength lay in Islamic political, economic, and military traditions that were centuries old and believed divinely ordained. When in the seventeenth century their Western Christian enemies evolved new, highly effective gunpowder-based small arms and the military tactics to maximize their potential, the Turks were reluctant to adapt. By the time they decided to give up the traditional bow, arrow, and blade weapons and tactics that had proved so successful through centuries past, it was too late—the West had won a tech-nological military advantage that it never relinquished.

Fifteenth- and sixteenth-century Western shipbuilding and navigational technologies permitted the Western European states to circumvent the Turks and establish direct trading contacts by sea with India and the Far East, as well as to open new sources of goods and precious metals in the Americas, which ultimately undermined commercial profits and caused rampant inflation in the Ottoman Empire. Such developments rendered the old Central Asian overland trade routes, which the Ottomans controlled at their western terminus, secondary for Western Europe. As for the sea routes, the Turks' naval capabilities, tra-ditionally geared to short Mediterranean, Red Sea, and Persian Gulf traffic, proved inadequate in stopping Western naval dominance in the Arabian Sea and Indian Ocean. By the late sixteenth century British and Dutch navies roamed the eastern seas almost at will.

Politically, the Reformation and the religious wars that it spawned resulted, by the seventeenth century, in the rise of young, dynamic regional monar-chical states in Western Europe that were able to consolidate the resources of their respective territories under increasingly efficient central authority. At the same time, the traditional foundations of the Ottomans' strong centralized gov-ernment—the slave administration controlled by an all-powerful sultan and the integration of their large, diverse non-Muslim subject populations through the *millet* system of religious identity, which permitted them a good deal of local autonomy under their ecclesiastical leaders—were disintegrating under pres-sures exerted by economic and military fossilization and a near-progressive degeneration in the abilities of successive sultans. Yet until the nineteenth cen-tury, the Muslim ruling establishment in the empire adamantly refused to consider initiating governmental reforms that involved disbanding institu-tions sanctioned by Islamic traditions. By that time the government's political ineptitude, the rising internal anarchy, and the empire's economic helplessness had precluded any but the most drastic of remedies from having even a chance of success and had forced the non-Muslim European subjects to seek their futures by adapting what they viewed as superior Western nationalistic values. The Ottomans never proved willing to take drastic enough reform measures, so their non-Muslim European subjects, married to the empire by force centuries before, divorced themselves by force from Ottoman rule over the course of the nineteenth and early twentieth centuries. After Ottoman defeat in World War I and the dismantling of the Turks' West Asian Arab provinces by the Versailles mapmakers, a militant group of Turks led by Mustafa Kemal (Atatürk) broke completely with tradition, adapted to Western European nationalist nation-state political realities, created a secular Turkish state in Anatolia, and consigned the hapless remnants of the Ottoman Empire to history's dustbin.[5]

Medieval Western European political traditions played a similar role within the Habsburg Empire, helping to bring on it a similar fate.

⊷ ⊶

The Habsburgs were the last to emerge of a series of royal houses that vied for possession of the thrones governing the medieval states of Central-Eastern and Northeastern Europe during the fourteenth through early sixteenth centuries. For most of that period, French-Italian Anjous, German Luxemburgs, and Lithuanian Jagiełłos dominated the royal leadership in Poland, Bohemia, and Hungary. They enjoyed a curious interrelationship through marriage alliances that caused the various thrones to pass mostly among themselves. For example, in the early fourteenth century the Luxemburgs came to Bohemia as the ruling house; by the end of that century they had acquired the Hungarian throne, replacing the Anjous, who, in turn, had gained power in Hungary at the time the Luxemburgs had originally entered Bohemia. Sigismund of Luxemburg (King of Hungary [1385–1437] and King of Bohemia [1419–37]) succeeded as Hungarian king Louis the Great (1342–82) of Anjou (who, by the way, also had acquired the Polish throne [1370–82] and whose daughter, Jadwiga, married Władisław V Jagiełło [1386–1434], establishing the Jagiełłonian dynasty in Poland). Sigismund ultimately was elected Holy Roman Emperor (1410–37) of the Germans.

Though to the modern observer such confusing and anational political leadership makes little sense, in the medieval context it was seen as quite normal. Only the aristocracy of the states had any stake in political affairs, since it was the warrior-landowning class that upheld the state structure itself. The state existed expressly to maintain or advance the interests of the nobles, and it mattered little to them whether their liege-king was of similar ethnicity to themselves, so long as he ruled in a way beneficial to their vested interests. For this reason the nobles, who retained a certain amount of elective power regarding the choice of their rulers, whether real (as in the case of Poland) or formal (as eventually in the Bohemian and Hungarian instances), tended to accept outsiders more readily than one of their own, in the generally held belief that they could manipulate foreigners more easily, thus weakening the rulers' effective authority and strengthening their own. Whether in Poland, Bohemia, Hungary, or even in the Holy Roman Empire, if the ruler personally was unable to exert sufficient power over the state's landed aristocracy to found a family dynasty, the nobility would usually seek out the weakest available royal candidate as his successor. Having no effective voice in the political process, the masses of the population were forced to accept as their rulers those chosen by their self-interested noble masters.

The Swiss-German house of Habsburg was a relative latecomer to the dynastic games of the East European states. The family started out as obscure minor German aristocrats within the Holy Roman Empire holding lands in the eastern regions of what is today Switzerland. The Habsburg rise from obscurity began in 1273 when Count Rudolf of Habsburg was chosen Holy Roman Emperor (1273–91) by the princely German Electors of the empire to thwart the bid for supreme power within Germany advanced by the strongest single ruler of all the empire's component states, the Czech king Otakar II Přemysl (1253–78) of Bohemia. The weaker German princes had no desire to elect a powerful emperor; they feared he would curtail their individual authority by consolidating and centralizing the empire. They turned to Rudolf because of his very obscurity and perceived weakness as a prince. From such a miserable situation sprang a great European imperial dynasty that would last until 1918, long after the houses of the princes who elected Rudolf had passed into political oblivion.

Although until 1437, and the death of Emperor Sigismund, Habsburgs would alternate on the Holy Roman imperial throne with Luxemburgs, Bavarians, and Nassauans, Rudolf, the first Habsburg emperor, set the official policy that ultimately would secure the throne permanently for his house as well as create a vast family empire separate from the Holy Roman Empire itself. Rudolf expanded the family's dynastic possessions by taking advantage of a medieval imperial privilege: When the regional princely throne of Austria, centered on Vienna, fell vacant, it reverted to the emperor for redisposal. Rudolf promptly handed Austria to his son. The Grand Principality of Austria was established as the new heartland of Habsburg possessions, and further lands in Central-Eastern Europe were brought under the authority of Vienna in similar fashion during Rudolf's reign.[6]

Throughout the fourteenth century, even during periods when the Habsburgs were out of imperial power, the family continued to enlarge its lands and to maintain claims on the imperial throne in Germany through deft political marriage alliances with the houses of Luxemburg and Anjou. The marriage of Albrecht II of Habsburg to the daughter of Emperor Sigismund cemented the family's imperial dreams. Albrecht succeeded his father-in-law as emperor (1438–39), thereafter, until the Holy Roman Empire was abolished by Napoleon in 1806, the imperial throne never again passed out of Habsburg hands. Yet the beginnings of the Habsburg imperial monopoly were anything but auspicious. Albrecht's successor, Frederick III (1440–93), was embroiled in complex and militant dynastic conflicts with German Luxemburgs, Lithuanian Jagiełłos, Czech Poděbradys, and Hungarian Hunyadis over the thrones of Bohemia and Hungary, to which past marriages had furnished the Habsburgs with claims. The foreign and domestic problems facing Frederick grew so mountainous that, at one point, he found himself besieged by his own people in Vienna; during that time it was said he was forced to eat rats to survive.

It was precisely during this apparent nadir of Habsburg imperial fortunes that the family implemented an aggressive, effective, and ultimately highly successful foreign policy of marriages that, in little less than half a century, transformed the Habsburgs into the wealthiest and most politically powerful ruling house in all of Europe.

⚔ ⚔

The late fifteenth century was a time when centralized, regional monarchies were replacing the political hodgepodge of feudal states in Western Europe. In France the "Spider King," Louis XI (1461–83), was rivaled for the royal title by the powerful and wealthy duke Charles the Bold of Burgundy (1467–77), who headed a potent Anglo-Burgundian alliance that defeated Louis in battle several times. The duke had no son—only a daughter, Mary. In the midst of his own travails, Emperor Frederick managed to marry his son and successor, Maximilian (emperor, 1493–1519), to the Burgundian duchess. Maximilian, known in history as "the Last Knight," was an outstanding Habsburg—he wrote books, he was handsome, and he had a way with the ladies. He was also impoverished at the time of his wedding (1477), but Mary brought with her the vast riches and lands of the Burgundian house (to which Maximilian became heir through the marriage), giving a sense of reality to the rather pretentious Habsburg family monogram that Emperor Frederick had fashioned: A.E.I.O.U. (*Austriæ est imperare orbi universo*, or, *Alles Erdreich ist Oesterreich unterthan*—loosely translated: "Austria rules over all the world").[7]

The Burgundian coup was but the first of successful Habsburg marriages bringing to the house increased territorial possessions and riches. The second proved spectacularly more so, both in terms of family wealth and of authentic political power. Maximilian and Mary had a son, Philip the Fair, who died too early to rule as emperor but married as the imperial heir apparent before his untimely death. His spouse was Joanna, daughter and heiress of the Spanish monarchs Ferdinand and Isabella (1474–1504), who by sponsoring the voyages of Columbus opened to Spain the riches of the New World. The fruits of discovery fell into the hands of the fortunate couple, who produced two sons, Charles and Ferdinand. Between them, the brothers ultimately came to share the largest and wealthiest political inheritance in Europe.

Prior to the Burgundian and Spanish marriages, the Habsburgs held Austria and the Holy Roman emperorship (which was a title with only titular authority); through the marriages, the family acquired new lands and resources—new bases of real power—that changed the empty imperial title into a strong political reality. Drawing on their vast resources, the Habsburgs were able to exert their will on all those living within the orbits of the Holy Roman Empire and of Spain. No other European royal or princely dynasty had the wherewithal to compete directly with the family on its own terms. Within only a few decades the Habsburg possessions had multiplied and the family had risen to the apex of European political power.

But greatness had its costs, as elder brother, Emperor Charles V (1519–56), soon discovered. After years of constant pressure in attempting to wield effective authority over his far-flung territories, ranging from the continents of the Americas, through Spain, Naples, Milan, and the Netherlands, to the Holy Roman Empire and Austria, and in the face of continuous political and military conflicts with England, France, German Protestants, and the Ottoman Empire, Charles concluded that the Habsburg possessions were unmanageable by a single head of the family. He abdicated the German imperial and Spanish royal thrones and divided the family patrimony between eastern and western lands, giving his brother Ferdinand I (emperor, 1556–64) the former and his son Philip II (king, 1556–98) the latter. Philip presided over the decline of Spanish Habsburg fortunes in the West, caused by his religious fanaticism and expensive but fruitless warfare with Protestant England and Catholic France. The eastern branch of the divided Habsburg patrimony retained the imperial title and the core possessions of Austria. It was this eastern branch that continued to carry the Habsburg legacy into the twentieth century as an essentially Central-Eastern European Great Power.

By the time Ferdinand I was elected emperor, he had already started Habsburg expansion beyond the patrimonial Austrian lands. His wife, Anna, was the sister of Louis II Jagiełło, king of Bohemia and Hungary (1516–26), who was killed in 1526 on the battlefield of Mohács in a futile effort to stem the invasion of Hungary by the Ottoman Turks under Süleyman I the Magnificent (1520–66). As the brother-in-law and only direct male heir of Louis, Ferdinand won election to both vacant crowns following the debacle. Neither election, which directly stemmed from his marriage to Anna, was without its problems.[8]

The Kingdom of Bohemia was one of the seven important states within the Holy Roman Empire holding the privilege of electing the emperor, and it was the only one among them with the royal status of kingdom. It possessed a long and proud history within the German world of Central Europe, despite the fact that its nobility and its population were predominantly Slavic (Czech-Moravian). During the fourteenth century a Luxemburg king of Bohemia, Charles I (1346–78), had been elected emperor as Charles IV (1347–78), elevating his capital of Prague to one of the major political and cultural centers in Europe. The university founded in that city in 1348, which bore his name, was the first east of the Rhine River and grew into the intellectual center for all of Central-Eastern Europe. From its halls emerged Jan Hus (1371–1411), who provided Europe with the earliest example of the revolutionary effects involved in linking ethnic identity with religious reform. The Czech Hussite Movement that rocked the Holy Roman Empire and the late feudal papal order in Western Europe during the fifteenth century found its inspiration in Prague a hundred years before Luther sparked the similar but more successful Protestant Reformation. The kingdom's nobility were proud of Bohemia's past political and cultural roles and cherished their ethnic self-identity acquired through the Hussite Movement.[9]

When Ferdinand stood for election by the kingdom's nobility in 1526, acceptance by three regional aristocratic diets was required. Those of Moravia and Silesia elected him as hereditary king, but that of Bohemia proper, centered on Prague and jealous of its perceived traditional rights, refused, retaining its free elective privileges regarding the throne. From that moment on it became a major goal of the Habsburgs to gain hereditary right to the Bohemian throne and to overcome what essentially was only a personal union of the kingdom with the growing Habsburg family empire. At the end of the Schmalkaldic War (1546–47), in which a league of imperial German Protestant states unsuccessfully attempted to throw off Habsburg imperial rule, Ferdinand was able to impose the Habsburg hereditary right to rule Bohemia on the Czech nobility as punishment for their fence-sitting during the conflict. The Czech aristocrats, unhappy with that turn of events, seethed for seventy years, looking for ways to regain the right to freely elect their king.

As the seventeenth century opened, the Habsburgs furnished the Czech nobility with the opportunity they sought. The Jesuit-led Catholic Counter-Reformation was in full swing, but Emperor Rudolf II (1576–1612) felt personally uninvolved with religious matters. He was perfectly willing to grant the Protestant-leaning Czech aristocracy of Bohemia a Patent of Religious Toleration in 1609, pressed on him by Protestant Transylvania's siding with the Turks in the war then being pursued by the Habsburgs in the Balkans. But Rudolf's successor, Matthias (1612–19), ignored the patent. He had no heir, and his successor was Ferdinand II of Styria, a cousin and a known unscrupulous, pro-Catholic fanatic. The Czechs wished to avoid Ferdinand as their king at all costs. In 1618 the Bohemian estates tried to negotiate with Matthias over the question of Ferdinand II's succession, but the talks got nowhere. In frustration, members of the Czech nobility threw two imperial envoys then in the Prague castle out of a third-storey window, along with one of their secretaries. All three survived—the German Catholics later claiming that it was a miracle demonstrating the truth of their faith over that of Protestantism; the Czech Protestants declaring that accumulated dirt and feces in a dung heap located under the window cushioned their fall. (It was also said that the miserable secretary, splashing one of his masters with dung as he landed, excused himself, for which courtesy he later was ennobled and rewarded with the title of baron.)[10]

This defenestration of Prague led to the outbreak of the Thirty Years War (1618–48) when the Czechs, anxious over Habsburg retaliation, turned to the Protestant Union in Germany, led by Frederick Elector Palatine, a Calvinist and the son-in-law of English king James I (1603–25), whom they elected Bohemian ruler in violation of Habsburg hereditary right. Frederick moved into Bohemia, where he managed to reign briefly (1619–20). Meanwhile, the hated Ferdinand II attained the imperial throne (1619–37), withstood two Protestant attacks on Vienna, and in 1620 invaded Bohemia, where his forces crushed the Protestants at White Mountain, just outside Prague. The war thus sparked between the Catholic Habsburgs and Protestant Europe quickly spread to the rest of Germany for its remaining twenty-eight years, but as far as Bohemia was concerned, it was over decisively.

The Battle of White Mountain left the Czech nobility utterly defeated. Its consequences drastically reshaped Czech society and history. The traditional Czech aristocracy was uprooted, with many of its members either killed or forced into exile. Their place was taken by an alien Catholic nobility implanted into Bohemia by the Habsburgs from other regions of Germany, from Spain, and from Italy. Most of the newcomers spoke German as their primary language, thus elevating it to an equal footing with Czech in the kingdom. They joined a growing German common population, which had begun colonizing the mountainous northern and western frontier regions as early as the twelfth and thirteenth centuries as miners, as well as an already significant German urban population. With such a large minority of Germans in the state, cultural pressures on the native Slavic language were intense. In fact, by the end of the eighteenth century, foreigners visiting Bohemia thought it was a German land.[11]

In 1627 a new constitution was created for Bohemia that transformed its position within Germanic Central Europe. Bohemia's status as an independent state within the Holy Roman Empire vanished; it became, instead, directly integrated into the family patrimony of the Habsburgs under the guise of a fictional political autonomy. The formerly Slavic state in Germany became a Germanized Slavic possession of the ruler, with an aristocratic assembly that played no important political role other than to rubber-stamp the will of the Habsburgs. The seat of government was effectively transferred from Prague to Vienna, where it eventually was merged directly into the Austrian administration. Bohemia would remain wedded to the interests of the Habsburgs until the nineteenth-century rise of nationalism among the still Slavic common classes set the stage for its divorce from its domineering German political spouse in 1918.

Turning to the second problem involved with the marriage of Ferdinand I to Anna Jagiełło, the Hungarian election following the disaster of Mohács was contested by a large segment of the Magyar nobility of Transylvania, who advanced one of their own, János Zápolya, as rival monarch with Ottoman Turkish backing.

Prior to their defeat by Süleyman the Magnificent, the Hungarians had successfully faced the Islamic threat from out of the Balkans for over 150 years. Their continuous struggles with the Turks in the Balkans provided Europe with many of its most daring and effective military crusaders, such as János Hunyadi. The state of Hungary was strategically located as Western Europe's frontier buffer against the powerful Ottoman Empire in the Balkans. It was centered on the Pannonian Plain and the Transylvanian Plateau of the Danubian Basin, which placed it squarely across most of the northern boundary of the Balkan Peninsula. The 1102 personal union of the Croatian royal throne to that of Hungary extended the borders of the state westward to the Adriatic Sea and involved the Hungarians in the Balkan affairs of Bosnia and of Hercegovina. (The latter name is derived from the Hungarian princely title of its fourteenth-century governors—*herzog.*) Thus all roads for further Ottoman expansion into Europe led through Hungary. The crucial geographic situation forged among the Hungarian nobility an intense perception of themselves as the heroic frontier defenders of Western European civilization against the growing specter of Islamic incursion.

The highly militant and strongly traditional Hungarian aristocrats clung tenaciously to their perceived feudal rights and actively resisted all attempts by their monarchs to consolidate central authority in the state. Following the reign of

King Matthias Corvinus (1458–90), his Jagiełłonian successors were kept weak and the power of the large Hungarian magnates rose, causing increased internal instability. Lacking any kind of support from the royal authority, the common rural and urban populations in the state were left to the not-so-tender mercies of their noble lords, who were free to exploit them with unbridled impunity. Peasant uprisings erupted against the imposition of serfdom (at a time—the early sixteenth century—when that institution was all but dead in the rest of Western Europe), which the nobles mercilessly crushed. At the same time, the cities in Hungary were thrown into decline because of continuous aristocratic efforts to revoke their autonomous privileges. The debacle of Mohács was the result of the magnates' reluctance to subordinate themselves to the direct authority of the unfortunate young king Louis II. They left him in the lurch to face the Turks with a small, mostly foreign, mercenary force; by so doing they sealed the fate of their crippled state.[12]

With the threat of the Turks still dangling over their heads following the battle, the Hungarian nobility refused to agree on a successor to Louis and broke into two factions. Each staged its own royal election; one wing voted for the Habsburg Ferdinand while the other elected one of their own, János Zápolya, a Transylvanian magnate. To retain the throne of Hungary, both rival monarchs were forced into vassalage to the powerful sultan Süleyman, who briefly was content to let the contest for royal authority between the two keep the traditional Hungarian enemy weak. But realizing that it was only a matter of time before Habsburg resources would prevail in reconstructing a strong European defense, the Turks successfully invaded the divided state in 1541. Hungary was trisected: A narrow strip of northern and western Hungary (known as Royal Hungary), which included part of Croatia and Slovakia, remained in Habsburg hands; the central, Pannonian region, with the rest of Croatia, was incorporated directly into the Ottoman Empire; and Transylvania, ruled by Zápolya's successors, was proclaimed an autonomous principality under Turkish suzerainty.

For the next century and a half, the Habsburgs consolidated their hold on Royal Hungary and waged intermittent warfare with the Turks over Pannonia. Meanwhile, the Hungarian nobility in Transylvania, taking advantage of the autonomy granted them by dependent status to the Ottoman Turks, who gave them free rein within the principality in return for their role in foiling Habsburg ambitions, forged their state into a powerful anti-Habsburg force during the religious wars in the sixteenth and seventeenth centuries. Many of the Transylvanian Hungarian nobles converted to Calvinism or Unitarianism, further demonstrating their continued refusal to accept Catholic Habsburg rule. Under the powerful Báthory princely house Transylvania increased its political and cultural influence in Eastern Europe during the second half of the sixteenth century. István Báthory, Transylvanian prince (1571–86), was elected to the Polish throne in 1576. The apex of Transylvania as a Hungarian cultural and political center came during the reign of Prince Gábor Bethlen (1613–29), whose alliance with the anti-Habsburg forces in the Thirty Years War made Transylvania a vital player in general European politics.

The decline of the Ottoman Empire in the seventeenth century opened the door to the Habsburgs for making good on their claims to the Hungarian lands of Pannonia and Transylvania that lay outside Royal Hungary. Emperor Leopold I (1658–1705), having settled pressing European matters that had diverted Habsburg attention from the Turkish-Hungarian problem in the past, found himself at last free to deal decisively with the Turks over possession of Hungary. Fending off an Ottoman siege of Vienna in 1683, the Habsburg forces countered with an all-out offensive that expelled the Turks from Pannonia and delivered Transylvania into Leopold's hands. With the Treaty of Sremski Karlovci in 1699, the Turks henceforth were confined mostly to regions south of the Danube. Twelve years earlier, in 1687, Leopold had compelled a grateful Royal Hungarian nobility to declare the Habsburgs hereditary rulers of Hungary. Transylvania was not united with Royal and Pannonian Hungary. Through a separate imperial diploma issued by Leopold in 1691, it was placed directly under the authority of the Habsburg ruler as an independent royal principality.

Leopold initiated a policy of repopulating devastated Hungary with foreigners. His Italian and German aristocratic military officers were rewarded for their successful war efforts with lands in the newly won Hungarian regions. The decimated common population was augmented with Serb, Swabian, and French peasant colonists. This caused a reaction among the proud, native Hungarian nobility that erupted into a rebellion lasting from 1703 until 1711. At its close the Habsburgs agreed to respect the political and social rights of the Hungarian nobility by recognizing the Hungarian diet, their representative political organ. From that time on the Hungarians were able to maintain officially their unique sense of self-awareness and to defend their self-interests within the Habsburg Empire, in blatant contrast to the fate of the Czechs. While the governing aristocracy of Bohemia was Germanized and its political organ (diet) removed from Prague to Vienna, the Hungarian nobles won recognition from their Habsburg rulers and the continued right to govern themselves and their lands from the seat of their diet, first in Pozsony (Bratislava) and then Budapest (after 1848). The Hungarians' position within the Habsburg Empire was further reinforced in 1723, when the Hungarian diet ratified the Pragmatic Sanction of Emperor Charles VI (1711–40), which permitted the imperial and royal Habsburg succession to proceed through the female line. It was cemented in 1741 when, in return for immunity from taxation, the Hungarian nobility enthusiastically supported Empress Maria Theresa (1740–80) in the War of the Austrian Succession started by Frederick II the Great (1740–86) of Prussia over possession of Silesia.[13]

The Habsburg marriages into the two kingdoms of Bohemia and Hungary resulted in two very different sorts of political spouses. One (Bohemia) was rendered meek and subservient to the will of the dominant partner; the other (Hungary) remained proud, willful, and able to demand respect and special considerations from a partner that was considered little better than an equal.

Habsburg marriages also created a sprawling, ethnically diverse state that represented the personal patrimony of the ruling house. This family empire essentially was a medieval construct that, with the resolution of the Hungarian relationship under Maria Theresa and the acquisition of Polish Galician lands in the partitions, acquired its final form in the late eighteenth century. Although it was commonly referred to as "Austria" by its European contemporaries, because the Habsburgs were technically the princes of the Austrian lands (which included present-day Austria, Slovenia, and the northeast regions of Northern Italy), the Habsburg family state encompassed lands and peoples far beyond the Germanic Austrian heartlands—Bohemia (including Moravia), Hungary (including Croatia-Slavonia and Slovakia), Transylvania (including Vojvodina and Bukovina), and Galicia (including Kraków [Cracow] and much of Little Poland).

This Habsburg family patrimony must not be confused with the Holy Roman Empire, over which the Habsburgs presided from the sixteenth century until its demise in the early nineteenth. The two states remained separate. Habsburgs were habitually elected emperors of the Holy Roman Empire, while they served as hereditary princes and kings in the various lands of the family patrimony. Only the Austrian and Bohemian lands of the latter were members of the former. Needless to say, some confusion in terminology resulted from the dual political reality caused by the medieval nature of Habsburg rule. Technically the Habsburg imperial title was valid in approximately half of the family patrimony. Although the Habsburgs continued to use their traditional imperial title after Napoleon forced the dismantlement of the Holy Roman Empire in 1806, that title held for their Austrian and Bohemian lands alone, in which they also continued to hold the old titles of Austrian prince and Bohemian king. The Habsburgs ruled their Hungarian lands as kings only, not as emperors. So long as the Habsburg family state existed on essen-

allied states, then the other allies could be called on to intervene militarily. They could coordinate their policies, as well as mediate any disputes that might arise from conflicting policies, through periodic meetings (congresses) of representatives at the highest levels of government.[14]

This swan song of the old political order in Europe lasted thirty-three years and never functioned entirely as planned. The congress idea lasted little over a decade before it collapsed after both England and France, greatly concerned over the undesirability of potential foreign intervention in their internal affairs by majority vote of the allies, opted out. More significantly, judicial repression, police surveillance, and censorship (then as now) could not destroy or effectively hinder the spread of ideas considered dangerous to the state, ideas that the victorious monarchies themselves had been forced to foster in the first place to raise the mass armies that eventually brought them victory in the wars against the French. In post-Vienna reactionary Europe liberalism and romantic nationalism spread among the populations of the Western European states despite the repressive efforts of the monarchical governments on the Continent. With the outbreak of the 1848 revolutions in France, in the Germanys, and in the Habsburg Empire, the old order was forced either to compromise with the rising tide of liberal democratic nationalism and transform itself into one grounded in constitutional government along those lines or to resist the new political forces, making the fewest concessions possible, and thus preserve itself by force. In France and Prussia the decision was made in favor of compromise and transformation. The Habsburgs opted for resistance and sealed their eventually unhappy ultimate fate.

While liberal democratic nation-state nationalism was seen as a threat to traditional political order by all of the continental European monarchies, it was potentially fatal to the Habsburgs. At least in France, Prussia, and Spain, as well as in most of the smaller regional kingdoms, the monarchs ruled relatively homogeneous ethnic and cultural populations that helped ease the transition from "divine right" to liberal constitutional rule. They had the English constitutional monarchy to serve as a precedent, if not a model. When the populations of France and the Germanys rose up in antimonarchical revolutions in 1848, compromise on the part of the old order became inevitable. Although monarchism was finally swept away in France by the upheavals of that year (the brief later imperial interlude of Louis Napoleon [1852–70] was a hollow exception), in most European states the monarchs found it expedient to link themselves to nation-state nationalism by accepting liberal constitutional political forms to preserve their thrones.

Only the two multiethnic, multicultural European Great Powers—Russia and the Habsburg Empire—refused to compromise with the tidal wave of liberal,

tially medieval terms following 1806, the name "Habsburg" or "Austrian" Empire was valid. But the birth of modern Western European political culture—nation-state nationalism supported by liberal democracy and industrial capitalism—signified by the French Revolution and the Napoleonic wars—against which the Habsburgs had fought determinedly—spelled the opening of the final act in the drama of Habsburg political existence.

It seems somewhat ironic that the final political consolidation of the essentially medieval Habsburg Empire occurred during the second half of the eighteenth century—a time when the rest of the Western European world was about to begin jettisoning the last remaining traces of medievalism. The Habsburgs were thus woefully out of sync when the French Revolutionary and Napoleonic wars forcibly changed Western European political culture for good. Perhaps this helps explain the less-than-glowing performance of the Habsburg military effort during those conflicts. It certainly hindered the Habsburgs' political impact. An imperial title over medieval patrimonial lands carried far less respect and authority among brother Western Great Powers than had the old imperial title over all of Germany, even though the actual political authority of the Habsburg (Austrian) emperor within his patrimonial state far exceeded in effectiveness the politically empty Holy Roman imperial position in Germany. To compensate for the decline in perceived political prestige, as well as to bend all of their remaining actual European political influence toward preserving their anachronistic existence, the Habsburgs led the reactionary efforts of the victorious European monarchies to suppress liberal and national movements in Europe following the Congress of Vienna in 1815, which ended the wars with revolutionary and imperial France. It was no accident that the last but futile effort to stem the tide of liberal democracy and romantic nationalism was born in the Habsburg capital and became associated with the name of the Habsburg chancellor Klemens von Metternich (1809–48).

It was Metternich, a man of old-order political insight and forceful character, who shaped the post-Napoleonic wars policy of the victors meeting in Vienna. A creature of an outdated political system, his only answer to the powerful liberal and nationalistic ideologies of the French Revolution was to turn back the political clock by autocratic force. He managed to convince the Habsburgs' allies, especially Prussia and Russia, that monarchism could be defended from liberal democracy through the exertion of autocratic authority by means of repressive legislation, increased police enforcement, and strict media censorship. If these should fail to stamp out liberal threats in any of the

constitutional, and national sentiment in Western Europe, because attempting to do so would have meant their demise. In any case Russia, while a major player in general European affairs and simulating a certain amount of Western European culture, at heart was not a member of the Western European world. It was a Eurasian state. Its Eastern European cultural traditions did not lend themselves to compromising the ruler's imperial authority. Though many of the Russian military aristocracy had returned from the Napoleonic wars infected with liberal ideas, they were a distinct minority in a ruling elite that was separated by a wide social chasm from the Russian masses, who were doggedly devoted to their native Eastern European culture in all of its aspects, including the political. The non-Russian masses in the population were mostly Central Asian Turkic Muslims or Orthodox peoples of the Caucasus, who were far removed from any of the cultural developments occurring in Western Europe. Given the opportunity to play a liberal role in governing the state, those non-Russians would have separated themselves from their Russian overlords swiftly, taking well over two-thirds of the Russian Empire's territory with them. Only the autocratic authority of the tsar and the military force he commanded held the empire together.

On the other hand, the Habsburg Empire was firmly ensconced in the Western European world. Members of its disparate regional populations had participated actively in every stage of the West's cultural development, from the late feudal through the Enlightenment. Its diverse human and natural resources unified under the direct authority of its ruling house—a traditional source of strength in the past—posed a growing danger to its continued existence in an age of nation-state nationalism. The prolonged wars with the French had affected the Habsburg Empire's military classes just as had been those in Russia. But in the Habsburg case the military was composed of elements from all of the state's varied subjects. Unlike the Russian example, the Habsburg military effort had proven singularly unsuccessful in most of the wars, causing many affected by the new national-liberal ideas to question the benefits of continuing the traditional political order unchanged. Hungarians, Croats, Czechs, and other regional populations had served their monarch faithfully throughout the ordeal of the French wars only to experience postwar judicial repression and censorship as their reward. In the minds of the Habsburg rulers, very little would be needed to transform the various regional populations in the state into dangerous national factions demanding political autonomy or even independent nation-states of their own. Thus any compromise whatever of Habsburg political authority posed a mortal threat to the existence of the empire. Habsburg fears were validated by the events of 1848.

❧ ❧

The upheavals within the Habsburg Empire during 1848 and 1849 can be viewed as the beginning of public family quarrels that eventually would lead the various ethnic-national populations wedded to the monarchy to file divorce proceedings by 1918. Just as such difficulties between human spouses possess fermentation periods before they openly explode, so too did the domestic problems within the empire.[15]

The family feuds that would tear at the Habsburg patrimonial state in the nineteenth century had their origins in the reign of Maria Theresa's son and heir, Joseph II (1780–90). An adherent of the Enlightenment, Joseph attempted to create a state similar to the contemporary European regional monarchies out of the medieval conglomeration of territories and peoples under his rule by instituting reforms aimed at centralizing the empire's government in Vienna. Among Joseph's social, political, and economic initiatives was his attempt to introduce German as the common administrative language. His reforms provoked a cultural reaction among the various non-German populations in the empire, whose aristocracies and intellectuals turned to emphasizing their local rights, traditions, and cultures. Upon Joseph's death, most of his reforms were revoked by his successors, Leopold II (1790–92) and Francis I (1792–1835). To mollify the rising fears concerning Germanization, the imperial authorities established a chair of Slavic languages at the University of Vienna (1791), thus giving semiofficial sanction to the cultural validity of the empire's non-German subjects. Although the Habsburgs did not realize it, this move was the turning point in their political fortunes. From that moment on, national consciousness among the varied non-German populations of the empire surged.

The Hungarians, with their long-standing resistance to absolute Habsburg control, were willing recipients of Enlightenment and Romantic concepts. They were the first of the empire's non-German populations to take effective advantage of the imperial recognition of local languages. Since the eleventh century the literary language of the Hungarian nobility had been Latin, no matter whether its members ethnically were Magyar, Slovak, Croat, or any of the other various groups existing within the borders of the Hungarian kingdom. Only the Hungarian aristocracy of Transylvania had made extensive use of the native Magyar language. Beginning in the 1770s with a literate Hungarian guards officer in Vienna, György Bessenyei, who came into contact with French Enlightenment ideas, a movement toward replacing Latin with Magyar gradually spread among the Hungarian nobility, reinforced by reaction against Joseph II's Germanization efforts. By the 1840s the native language movement had turned liberal and nationalist but split between two factions. The moderate wing, led by István Széchenyi, called for the complete overthrow of traditional aristocratic leadership in favor of liberal institutions and partnership with non-Magyars in a multicultural Hungary remaining within a progressively reformed Habsburg Empire. The moderates were opposed by a radical wing led by Lajos Kossuth, who demanded immediate liberal reforms favoring the traditional aristocracy and complete independence for the historic kingdom of Hungary—including Slovakia, Croatia, Transylvania, and the Vojvodina—as an exclusively Magyar nation-state. In 1848–49 the radical Hungarian nationalists emerged as the dominant leaders within the country, leaving the Habsburgs no choice but to retain control over them by force.[16]

The Czech answer to the reform attempts of Joseph II was Panslavism, born in Prague and directly nurtured by the creation of the Slavic language chair at the University of Vienna. Initiated in 1792 by Josef Dombrovský, a Czech Catholic priest, Panslavism was a scholarly, intellectual, and highly romantic movement among Slavic philologists in the empire, whose research traced their linguistic history back to the time before the Slavs divided into the three main language groups of eastern, western, and southern. Supported by the German romantic Johann von Herder, romantic Slav linguists in the Habsburg Empire stressed the common origin of all Slavic languages and the supposed brotherhood of all Slavic peoples, whether subjects of the Habsburgs or not. They looked toward a future when all of the Slavs would be equally united in a Great Slavic confederation, which would naturally be shaped around Russia, the only independent and powerful Slavic state existing at the time. Among the culturally repressed Czechs Panslavism acted as a tonic, especially after František Palacký's multivolume history of the Czechs, published in the 1830s and 1840s, gave the Czech people a glorious past. The Panslav Czech intellectuals in Prague soon attracted the attention of linguistically related Slovak intellectuals, such as Pavel Šafařík and Jan Kollar, who moved to Prague and added their voices to the rising Panslav chorus of Greater Slavic unity. Under Czech literary influences, the Slovaks began cultivating their own native language, thus giving rise to the idea that they were somehow closely related to the Bohemian Slavs despite their centuries-long association with the Hungarians. Herein lay the root of the later Czecho-Slovak idea.[17]

Among the Croats, the incorporation of much of their territory into Napoleonic France as the Illyrian Provinces (1809-13) opened the door to direct exposure to liberal and national concepts in their most militant form. They possessed a strong aristocracy that had been politically active in the affairs of the Hungarian diet and provincial administration prior to the coming of the French, and their native literary language could be traced back to the thirteenth century. Reverting to Hungarian authority after the Illyrian interlude, the

Croats retained the national ideals bestowed on them by the French. By the 1830s and 1840s, Panslav influences among the increasingly nationalist Croat aristocracy resulted in the emergence of the South Slav movement in Croatia, often called the Illyrian Movement, intellectually fed by Ljudevit Gaj. Advancing the myth that the ancient Illyrian populations of the Balkans were actually Slavs, the Croat nationalists held that, because of their own history (they could claim one of the oldest Slavic states in Europe, second only to the Bulgarians), their culture (they were full members of Western Europe and not repressed by a foreign, Islamic civilization, as were the other Slavs in the Balkans), and their political capabilities (they had retained an important, autonomous voice in Hungarian political affairs since their union with Hungary in 1102), they were superior to all other Slavic peoples in the Balkans and rightfully deserved to lead any future Balkan Slavic confederation that might emerge as the result of Panslavic success.[18]

When the French, fed up with their "shopkeeper" monarchy established in 1830, overthrew King Louis Philippe (1830–48) in February 1848, their revolution sparked revolutionary uprisings in various German states and in the Habsburg Empire calling for the establishment of constitutional governments in place of the imperial traditions of the past. Pressurized by the continental monarchies' post-Vienna Congress policies of reactionary repression, radical liberalism swept through Central and Central-Eastern Europe, its goal the overthrow of the aristocratic political order personified by Metternich. The March riots that erupted in the streets of Berlin and Vienna; the nationalist revolutionary assemblies that quickly convened in Frankfort, in Budapest, and in Prague; and the Panslav Congress staged by the Czechs in Prague struck a telling first blow to the monarchies of Germany and Austria, which initially were shaken enough to grant liberal concessions to the various assemblies. Metternich resigned and fled the Habsburg Empire.[19]

The tide began to turn against the revolutionaries in June when the Habsburg military crushed the Czech nationalists in Prague, along with the Panslav movement, which, unfortunately, had been drawn into the nationalist conflict in spite of its overtly intellectual nature. In that same month the Croats declared their independence from Hungary and Baron Josip Jelačić led a Croat invasion of Hungary with Habsburg blessings. The Hungarians responded by intensifying their demands for self-rule and by unsuccessfully invading Austria proper in October. Vienna, again wracked by revolutionary agitation, was bombarded into submission to Habsburg authority and its radical revolutionary leadership executed.

Habsburg emperor Ferdinand I (1835–48) abdicated in December. His successor, Francis Joseph (1848–1916), considering himself free from any constitutional promises his predecessor had made to the revolutionaries, led the Habsburg counterattack against the Hungarians, the last remaining revolutionary force in the empire. A constitution that ensured the highly centralized auto-cratic authority of the Habsburg emperor, despite the window dressing of a rep-resentative state diet and a responsible ministry, was promulgated in March 1849 for the empire as a whole. The Hungarians thereupon proclaimed their complete independence from Habsburg rule and set out to create a nation-state of their own. Kossuth was elected governor-president by the Hungarian diet, and laws were promulgated discriminating against the non-Magyars in the Hungarian population. Wracked by Serb and Romanian revolutionary move-ments from within, and by Austrian and Croatian military invasion from with-out, independent Hungary collapsed in August when Tsar Nicholas I (1825–55) of Russia sent troops against the Hungarians in support of his fel-low imperial autocrat. (The Hungarians have never forgiven the Russians for this act.) By year's end, Hungary was firmly back in Habsburg hands and the monarchy had weathered the revolutionary storm.

Habsburg medievalism had managed to survive its first serious threat from mod-ern nationalism with only minor compromises of imperial authority. Success stemmed in large part from the imperial government's ability to take advan-tage of an intrinsic weakness of nationalism—its inherent divisiveness. Time and again Habsburg success resulted from playing off one nationalist group against another. Austrian Germans crushed the Czechs. Germans, Croats, Serbs, and Romanians were combined to defeat the Hungarians. Croats were used to subdue the Viennese Germans. The diverse ethnonational makeup of the empire's population made anti-Habsburg unity difficult to achieve but, con-versely, offered the imperial authorities a ready tool for defeating the revolu-tion in detail. The events of 1848–49 had demonstrated an important political reality: Nationalism was not liberal, despite the alliance of liberals with nation-alists that characterized the upheavals. Nationalists had little tolerance for con-stitutionally guaranteeing the rights of others who did not belong to their own particular ethnonational group. In a truly nationalist world, war, oppres-sion, and persecution could be the expected lot of national minorities.

Unfortunately (and ironically) for the Habsburgs, it was German national-ism, and not the national aspirations of their non-German subjects, that actu-ally undermined the continued existence of the medieval state that they controlled. The 1848 Revolution among the Germans represented the attempt of an allied liberal and nationalist front to create a single, constitutionally united

Germany out of thirty-nine disparate monarchical states. Because the Frankfort Assembly, established by the revolutionaries to draw up the necessary constitution, spent too much time debating the issue of a united Germany's nature after the initial successes won by the revolution in its early stages, the monarchical authorities were able to regain control and to put down the revolution. The various rulers of the German states did not want to disappear totally from history. This was especially true of the Hohenzollerns of Prussia. Prussia had a tradition of being a European Great Power. Prussian king Frederick William IV (1840–61) refused the crown of a "Germany" offered him by the revolutionaries of Frankfort in 1849, and the revolution ended with the forced reversion to the status quo ante in the following year. If a German nation-state was to be constructed, it would be so through the will of its monarchs.[19]

The burning question for the Habsburgs was determining just how they fit into the new German nationalist picture. They had held the crown of the Holy Roman Empire of the German Nation for centuries, which had included such non-German areas as Bohemia and had excluded important German lands, such as East Prussia. It was obvious that the German revolutionaries of 1848 were intent on creating a German nation-state and not a new German empire. The Habsburgs still enjoyed the titular German imperial title of emperor, but they actually led only the South German Catholic states, such as Bavaria and Austria. The German states to their north were Protestant, and the cultural separation was reflected in the political thinking of the liberal-nationalist revolutionaries who had turned to Lutheran Prussia in their constitutional efforts at Frankfort, making the unification of Habsburg lands with a new nationalist Germany a difficult matter for South Germans. Compounding the problem for the Habsburgs was the issue of Bohemia. It had been an important component of the old Germanic Holy Roman Empire but was non-German in nationalist terms. When the Frankfort revolutionaries invited the Czech Panslav activist Palacký to participate in their deliberations for a united Germany, he refused because he felt himself a Czech and not a German.[20]

The practical nationalist results of 1848 among the Germans was the development of two separate conceptions regarding the nature of a future German nation-state. On the one hand, there was the traditional, medieval idea of Greater Germany, which would have included all territories historically linked to German identity, including the Catholic South German lands of the old Habsburg-led Holy Roman Empire. On the other, there emerged the Lesser Germany ideal, which accepted the loss of certain traditional German lands— those in the Habsburg Empire—to build a strong German nation-state from among areas that were closely related culturally through Protestantism and almost exclusively German in ethnic makeup. The Frankfort revolutionaries toyed with both concepts but eventually settled for the Lesser German solution before their demise. The Habsburgs, bound by their imperial traditions, naturally would have opted for the Greater German approach if seriously forced to compromise with German nationalism. They never were faced directly with the need to make that decision—it was made for them by Otto von Bismarck, chancellor of Prussia (1862–90), in 1866.[21]

Bismarck decided the question between Greater and Lesser Germany in favor of the latter through a series of wars that created a German nation-state centered on Protestant Prussia. By maneuvering the Habsburgs into a disadvantageous alliance for his Danish war in 1864, Bismarck intentionally set the stage for a second conflict with his outmoded ally in 1866. Prussian victory over the Habsburgs at Königgrätz (Sadowa) was decisive, and the terms of the peace treaty that followed forced the losers to give up their Italian possessions and effectively excluded them from any further direct involvement, or even influence, in the affairs of northern Germany, which in 1867 Bismarck swiftly unified into a constitutional confederation of the German states under Prussian leadership. In 1870 Bismarck's defeat of France crowned his militant solution to the German nationalist problem with the proclamation of a unified German nation-state, encompassing the short-lived German confederation, from the mirrored halls of conquered Versailles.

Humiliated in war and unable to cow rabid Hungarian nationalists at home, who constantly and actively resisted the harsh treatment meted out to them by the imperial authorities following 1849, the Habsburgs were forced to come to grips at last with the realities of their medievalism. They worked out a political compromise with the only consistently powerful nationalist group in the empire—the Hungarians—in an attempt to preserve some semblance of real state strength in European Great Power politics, by making a governing partner of the most dangerous internal threat they faced. For all practical purposes, the Great Compromise *(Ausgleich)* of 1867 created virtually two separate states from the lands of the Habsburg Empire—Austria, which included Bohemia and Slovenia, and which continued to be governed directly by the Habsburgs as patrimonial possessions, and Hungary, which comprised the historic lands of the medieval Crown of St. István (Pannonia, Slovakia, Croatia, Vojvodina, and Transylvania) claimed by the Hungarian nationalists, and which was internally governed by the Hungarian diet meeting in Budapest. Both halves were held together by the accepted rule of the Habsburg monarch—emperor of the family patrimony and king of Bohemia in the Austrian half, king alone in the Hungarian. Further bonds were provided by the retention of control over crucial military, foreign policy, and financial matters common for both in the hands of the imperial government in Vienna. In effect, the *Ausgleich* legally recognized the Habsburgs' inability to continue ruling in arbitrary sixteenth-century imperial fashion a multinational state in a nineteenth-century European world that was being rapidly transformed by nationalist nation-state political reality.[22]

Once again the Habsburgs survived the pressures of rising modern nationalism by making the fewest concessions possible. In compromising with the Hungarians, the monarchy managed to preserve the borders of its ancient state and an outward semblance of continued political strength by conciliating and supporting the most cantankerous bride in its increasingly fractious harem of peoples. But there was no disguising the internal political weaknesses of the empire in its Austro-Hungarian form. The compromise could not help but agitate the less fortunate non-German and non-Hungarian nationalities within the state, whose aspirations had been ignored. In the Austrian half, the Czechs were left discontented, since they could rightly lay claim to historical justifications for special recognition by the monarchy equal to those advanced by the Hungarians, and the Austrian Germans had every reason to regret the loss of their perceived right to leadership in the larger empire. The Habsburgs turned over those nationalities inhabiting the Hungarian half to the not-so-tender mercies of the Hungarians, who looked upon their share of the empire as an essentially Hungarian nation-state and proceeded to act accordingly.

Since the majority of the non-German and non-Hungarian nationalities fell within the borders of the Hungarian half of the state, the xenophobic Magyarization policies of the governing nationalists intensified the internal instability of the newly reshaped empire to an extreme never before experienced. Particularly rankled were the Croats, who had determinedly battled the Hungarians in 1848 and 1849 on behalf of the Habsburgs in vain hopes of winning imperial gratitude for their national cause. By cutting an expedient deal with one nationalist faction in their population and then committing themselves to preserve it at all costs, the Habsburgs had created a plethora of increasingly strident nationalist movements that threatened to undermine the continued existence of the empire from within. Just as had the 1848 revolutions, the compromise again demonstrated that nationalism and liberalism were essentially incompatible in the best of circumstances, but were positively dangerous for a multinational state.

✧ ✧

Besides the internal restructuring, Bismarck's solution to the German national question forced the Habsburgs to switch their foreign policy priorities from Germany and Italy to the Balkans. With the door to a strong Western European presence closed to them, the only avenue left open for justifying their continued status as a European Great Power lay in the south, where a declining Ottoman Empire was already in the advanced stages of terminal political illness.[23]

Immediately across the Habsburgs' southern borders, by 1830 the Serbs had managed to carve out an autonomous principality for themselves centered on Belgrade. The Greeks had won independence from the Turks in the southern Balkans at the same time, thanks to English, French, and Russian assistance. Wayward Serb Montenegrins, secure in their remote mountain fastness, proved a constant thorn in the side of the Ottoman authorities still holding the Sandjak of Novi Pazar and Albania. Since 1828 Russian troops had established a protectorate over the Ottoman satellite Romanian principalities of Wallachia and Moldavia. All told, the nineteenth-century Balkans were in a state of near-perpetual turmoil.

The Russian Empire considered the Balkans its most important field of European foreign policy. Control of the peninsula would open the Bosphorus and Dardanelles straits for Russian naval access to the Mediterranean, making its warm-water Black Sea ports usable for international military and commercial operations. Moreover, Russia was greatly attracted to Istanbul, the Ottoman capital and the fabled Constantinople of Byzantium, to validate its claims to "Third Rome" leadership in the Orthodox world as successor to the Byzantine Empire. Neither the English nor the French could afford to permit Russia to attain its goals in the Balkans, which would have resulted in grave threats to their respective imperial ambitions in India and West Asia. Their imperial interests forced them to prop up the faltering Ottoman Empire in an effort to thwart any expansion of Russian influence beyond the limits of the Black Sea.

Russia was a traditional friend and ally of the Habsburgs. Since the eighteenth century the two empires had waged war together on the Muslim Turks in the Balkans. They had fought Napoleon as allies, and had forged the post-1815 reactionary regime at Vienna. In 1849 the Habsburgs had no compunction about calling on the Romanovs to help crush the Hungarian Revolution, thus saving their empire. The two were, in essence, imperial peas from the same premodern political pod, although the Habsburgs were far less autocratic in nature because of their Western European political culture.

But the post-1848 situation in German Europe changed the relationship between the two. The Habsburgs, attempting to salvage their influence among the Germans, were drawn closer to Prussia, while Russia, infected by its own version of Panslavism—Slavophilism—grew increasingly anti-German in its European foreign policy outlook. That the Habsburgs and Russia were drifting apart became evident during the Crimean War (1854–56). Tsar Nicholas initiated Russian military operations against the Turks in the traditional manner—

by invading the Ottoman Empire through the Romanian Principalities—expecting Habsburg support. Nicholas, however, blundered in believing the Habsburgs would return the favor done them in 1849. Instead of support, the Habsburgs, whose recent military alliance with Prussia required a strong anti-Russian stance, sent him an ultimatum to evacuate the Balkans. When Nicholas pulled out of the principalities, Austrian forces moved in to ensure he did not return. For the rest of the war, the Russian military was bottled in the Crimea, where Russia eventually was defeated by the combined forces of England, France, and the Ottoman Empire. The role of the Habsburgs in the war laid the basis for a lasting antagonism between them and the Russians that would prove catastrophic for both, as well as for Europe.[24]

Their mutual animosities were intensified by the Russo-Turkish War of 1877–78 and its aftermath in Berlin. The Russians were intent on pursuing their imperialistic goals in the Balkans under the guise of punishing the Turks for massacring thousands of Bulgarians following a futile Bulgarian nationalist uprising in 1876. Freed to wage war by a wave of British anti-Turkish public opinion that tied the hands of the pro-Turkish Disraeli government, they sought out a preliminary oral agreement with the Habsburgs that gave Russia a free hand against the Turks in the eastern Balkans in exchange for the Habsburgs' right to occupy regions in the western half of the peninsula. The Russians met with overwhelming military success in the resulting war, nearly reaching the walls of Istanbul and forcing the Turks to relinquish nearly all of their remaining holdings in the Balkans. The Russians organized this area into a large Bulgarian state intended to serve as a Russian puppet dominating the strategic heart of the region. England immediately threatened military intervention to save its Ottoman buffer state. A new war was prevented only by Bismarck, who in 1878, seeing an opportunity for the newly created Germany to display international muscle, invited all of the Great Powers to Berlin for a congress to solve the crisis peacefully.

At Berlin the Habsburgs denied that they had made any oral agreement with Russia regarding the division of the Balkans. Faced with the united opposition of the Western Powers, Russia was forced to return any territory it had conquered and its Bulgarian puppet state was split apart, with much of it (especially Macedonia) returned to direct Ottoman control. The princes of Serbia and Romania, both of whom had aided Russian military efforts during the war, were granted recognition as kings of states completely independent of the Turks. Finally, in a decision that would prove most fateful for Europe and the Western world in general, the Habsburgs were permitted to occupy the Turkish provinces of Bosnia and Hercegovina—the very regions granted them by the supposedly nonexistent verbal agreement made with the Russians prior to the war. In attempting to prevent a European-Russian conflict, the Berlin congress unwittingly sowed the seeds of World War I by rewarding the pathetic Habsburg attempt to demonstrate continued Great Power status through Balkan expansion.[25]

Master of *Realpolitik*, Bismarck was aware that Berlin had intensified Habsburg-Russian animosities to the point of potentially dangerous conflict. His first response was to forge an alliance of the two German powers, Germany and Austria-Hungary, in 1879. He then attempted to shape a more general alliance of the three emperors of Germany, Russia, and Austria-Hungary, who found common ground in their shared possession of Polish lands resulting from the late eighteenth-century imperial larceny of the partitions. Yet even after that imperial league was solidified in 1881, tensions among the three continued. Both Germany and Russia treated their subject Polish populations badly, whereas the Habsburgs, forced to make concessions to liberalism and nationalism by the Hungarians, took the opposite approach, thus increasing their frictions with autocratic Russia, since Habsburg Galicia became a "home away from home" for Ukrainian nationalists intent on throwing off Russian domination. The growing liberalism of Austria-Hungary (in 1907 the Habsburgs were the first European government to grant its population universal male suffrage) led to the eventual downfall of Bismarck's Three Emperors' League.[26] To his credit, Bismarck realized its fragility from the start—in 1882 he concluded the Triple Alliance among Germany, Austria-Hungary, and Italy.

When Bismarck was expelled from office in 1890 by Kaiser William II (1888–1918), German-Russian foreign policy alliances collapsed, and Russia, needing outside investment for its tardy industrialization, moved closer to France, which was willing to provide seemingly unlimited loans in return for political support against Germany. French loans led to the 1894 secret alliance between the two powers that finalized the web of international treaties that divided the European states into two opposed camps: the Austro-German (the Central Powers) and the Franco-Russian (the Entente). Italy and England, on the peripheries of the alliances, were eventually drawn into the system on opposite sides—Italy unsteadily with Germany; England with France and Russia. By the opening of the twentieth century, peace among the European Great Powers was maintained by a balance of power achieved through the two mutual defense treaty blocs, which operated much as nuclear deterrence did following World War II—prevent war by making it abhorrent to contemplate.

The alliance system might have worked had it been restricted to the Great Powers alone. But it was not. Lesser states were drawn into the system under the assumption that their participation would strengthen the international balance. So it was that Russia, having lost its Bulgarian puppet and most of its direct influence in the Balkans at Berlin, eventually turned to Serbia as an alternative Balkan ally. The Habsburgs' occupation of Bosnia-Hercegovina had the opposite result of that intended. Instead of weakening Serb nationalistic ambitions, it intensified them. The Serbs viewed the two provinces as natural regions for expansion. By marrying the provinces to the empire through what might be considered a form of shotgun wedding, the Habsburgs created an intractable Serb enemy in the Balkans. At first wary of Habsburg might, the Serbs gradually overcame their initial fears and, as a result of a coup of 1903, in which the pro-Habsburg Serb king Aleksandr Obrenović (1889–1903) was butchered by his military officers and the pro-Russian Petr I Karadjordjević (1903–21) installed in his place, Serbia moved firmly into the Russian camp.

Open animosities between the Habsburgs and the Serbs first erupted in the "Pig War" (1905–7), a tariff conflict begun by the Habsburgs to force Serbia into a more amenable position. (Austria-Hungary was the leading market for Serb pork products, one of the small country's primary industries.) Serbian antagonism turned to hatred of the Habsburgs in 1908, when, as a result of a deft piece of international diplomacy, the Habsburgs tricked the Russians into accepting outright Habsburg annexation of occupied Bosnia-Hercegovina, restraining their Serb allies' reaction, and then receiving absolutely nothing in return. In response, the Serbs founded organizations to spread pro-Serb nationalist propaganda in the lost provinces, the most dangerous of which was the Union or Death Society (also known as the Black Hand).

Internal nationalist tensions within Austria-Hungary conspired to transform the annexation of Bosnia-Hercegovina into the opening curtain for the death scene of the Habsburgs. By 1908 the Hungarians dominated Habsburg foreign policy. Now that the Habsburgs were forced to look to the Balkans as their primary arena of foreign policy, such a development was logical. Their Hungarian ruling partners possessed abiding national interests in Balkan affairs stemming from centuries-old involvements in Bosnia, Hercegovina, northern Serbia, and the two Romanian Principalities. Moreover, large numbers of the national minorities living within the borders of the Hungarian half of the empire were Balkan peoples—Croats, Serbs, and Romanians. The empire's Balkan imperialist policies thus concerned the Magyars directly. Southward territorial expansion into the peninsula raised burning national issues regarding their subordinate minorities. Acquisition of Bosnia-Hercegovina brought increasing numbers of Croats and Serbs into the empire who could magnify the already strained national tensions within the Hungarian-controlled half. It also created fear and distrust in Serbia, especially, and in Romania, both of which lay immediately across the southern and eastern borders from the Hungarians, and whose own nationalist contentions included the eventual incorporation of all their conationals existing within the Hungarian borders of Austria-Hungary. Ultimately, the annexation of the two provinces raised a serious threat to the continued existence of Austria-Hungary because of the Hungarians' national interests. That threat became one of the crucial underlying causes and, as it turned out, the immediate cause of World War I.[27]

Viewed from hindsight, the elimination of the Habsburgs from Germany, the *Ausgleich* with the Hungarians in 1867, and the turn toward a Balkan foreign policy that directly involved only the interests of their Hungarian partners made the Habsburgs' final disappearance from Europe inevitable. This combination of events finally opened the door to the nationalist dangers within the empire. In conjunction with the militant national aspirations of the small, independent Balkan states to their south, these developments conspired to bring on the destruction of the medieval Habsburg monarchy.

Emperor Francis Joseph found himself in a peculiar position for an early twentieth-century head of state. He was not a national ruler of a national empire. Instead, the state he governed was merely the representation of a dynasty that crossed all territorial-national boundaries within its borders. Only loyalty to the House of Habsburg served to cement the disparate parts of the empire together. Following the Compromise of 1867, the various ethnic-national groups in the ramshackle state looked to the emperor for satisfaction of their rising national aspirations, but his hands were tied by commitments to his Hungarian partners and intricate constitutional matters governing relationships between himself and the various peoples under his rule, as well as among the groups themselves.[28]

In the Austrian half of the empire, Habsburg problems were mostly of a constitutional nature. There the emperor's greatest political headache was caused by the Czechs, who laid claim to historical constitutional rights rooted in the medieval Bohemian state (the "Crown of St. Vaclav"). But the political reality of Habsburg victory at the Battle of White Mountain in 1620 had killed Czech chances of becoming a "Second Hungary" in the now-dualistic empire by reducing Czech constitutional rights to a fiction. The presence in Bohemia of large numbers of Germans, who were an integral and important element in the population distributed generally throughout the region, further complicated the Czech problem—Czechs and Germans could not be divided geographically with ease. Unlike the Hungarians, who had won a large measure of constitutional independence within the empire through past armed, bloody resistance to Habsburg domination, the Czechs had remained mostly passive following their defeat in the early seventeenth century and thus emerged in the twentieth in a subordinate position. Their only hope for national rejuvenation lay in following the dualistic formula created in 1867 and having the emperor apply it additionally to Bohemia. Faced with total assimilation into a German-dominated Austrian half of the empire, the Czechs strove for constitutional parliamentary democratic policies that would expand the limited rights of the Bohemian crown into a constitutionally autonomous and relatively separate Bohemia similar to Hungary after the compromise. The emperor could not attempt to satisfy Czech national demands without endangering the position of his Hungarian partners, whose various national minorities most likely would demand similar national compensation.[29]

In the Hungarian half of the empire, national matters were far more serious than in Austria. The Magyars were utterly committed to preserving the status quo of the *Ausgleich* that gave them exclusive national rights and control over their area. They pursued an anti-minority policy that often crossed over into outright persecution. In Transylvania Hungarians dominated the governing aristocracy in partnership with the resident urban Germans, who thus posed no threat to Magyar control. The predominantly peasant Romanian population was weak and divided. A minority of them were Uniates—former Orthodox Christians who had united with the Roman Catholic church by agreeing to a few important compromises in their original doctrine—and the Uniate church had joined the Hungarian establishment. The rest remained Orthodox and relegated to second-class citizens under the Hungarians. They looked not to the Romanian state across the border with Transylvania but to the emperor in Vienna to find support for their national aspirations within the empire and to counteract Magyar oppression. Never having possessed a historical state of their own to use as a precedent, the Romanians' hopes were more futile than those of the Czechs in Austria.

Even more so were those of the Slovaks. They were the least influential minority in the Hungarian half of the empire. For close to a thousand years the Slovaks had existed as docile peasant subjects of the Magyars. Those Slovaks who had risen to prominence within Hungary had done so by acculturating themselves into Magyars—speaking Hungarian and adopting Hungarian dress and mores. Following the Turkish conquest of Pannonian Hungary in the sixteenth century, Slovakia became an important part of Habsburg Royal Hungary, and its principal city, Bratislava, served as the seat of the Hungarian diet from that time until 1848. The Slovaks possessed vague cultural and historical ties to the Czechs—linguistic, primarily, with a hazy ninth-century historical connection to the Czech state of Greater Moravia—and had first expressed them openly in the Panslav movement of the late eighteenth and nineteenth centuries. The fact that the Czechs lay in the Austrian and the Slovaks in the Hungarian half of the empire, and that the boundaries between them were more cultural than historic, complicated any real attempt to forge closer ties. Left isolated from the only other ethnic-national group that could have lent them any sort of real support, the Slovaks were the most culturally persecuted of all the minorities in the Hungarian sphere.[30]

The Croats posed the chief national minority problem for the Hungarians. Frustrated in their bid to win independence from the Magyars following their pro-Habsburg actions in 1848 and 1849, the Croats were forced to make a constitutional deal with the Hungarians after the *Ausgleich* of 1867. In the following year a compromise agreement was forged between the leaders of the two peoples that reflected political-national realities. The Croats were forced to accept continued Magyar rule over Croatia in return for limited representation in the Hungarian diet. Croat local administration in Croatia, where few Hungarians lived, was assured. But the compromise satisfied nationalists on neither side. The radical Hungarian nationalists continued to demand direct Magyar control of Croatia as part of the historic "Crown of St. István," while Croat nationalists pressed for complete independence from Hungary, holding up, as did the Czechs, the 1867 Compromise as a model for creating a tripartite empire. Occupation of Bosnia-Hercegovina in 1878, whose populations contained significant numbers of Croats, intensified the agitation of the Croat nationalists. The provinces' 1908 annexation served only to heighten their nationalistic demands.[31]

Tragic events in the late nineteenth century reduced the succession to the Habsburg throne to the nephew of Francis Joseph, Archduke Francis Ferdinand. Relations between the two men were strained. The old emperor could not countenance his heir's morganatic marriage and personally treated the couple abominably. The heir apparent, in return, detested the doddering emperor and made no secret of his determination to renounce him and the imperial system he had constructed by radically restructuring the empire after he attained the throne. Francis Ferdinand nurtured a personal hatred for the Hungarians, whom he blamed for the growing internal national instability of the Habsburg state, and he was determined to cut them down to manageable size by forging a tripartite, and possibly even a quadripartite, empire. Counting on the various national minorities' traditional loyalty to the imperial house, who until his time had tended to envision their futures solely within the context of a continued Habsburg Empire, the archduke publicly expressed his willingness to recognize the Czechs of Bohemia as equal partners with the Magyars in his planned revamped state, and he spoke openly of forging a fourth partner—the Croats—out of a future Habsburg "Illyrian" (Croat-controlled) Balkan dependency.

Little did the archduke realize that he and his policies would be the instruments of the Habsburgs' downfall. It was obvious to all, both within and without the borders of Austria-Hungary, that Francis Ferdinand was on the verge of transforming the essentially medieval Habsburg Empire into a workable modern, multinational state to the national disadvantage of the empire's Hungarians and its Serbian and Romanian neighbors. This was worrisome most especially to the Serbs in Serbia, who stood to have their national ambitions regarding Bosnia-Hercegovina definitively thwarted. Black Hand terrorist operations in Bosnia were intensified and Bosnian Serb guerilla groups, such as Young Bosnia, were secretly armed and instructed by highly placed officials in Belgrade. In one of the most imbecilic political gaffes committed by a government's military and foreign policy staffs in modern European history, Francis Ferdinand—the single most dangerous individual for Serb nationalist pretensions at the time—was permitted to tour the empire's Bosnian military installations in 1914, with a scheduled visit to Sarajevo, Bosnia's capital, on 28 June—the anniversary of the Serb national disaster at the Battle of Kosovo Polje in 1389. No Habsburg action could have been more insulting to Serbian national pride than his visit on that day.

Security in Sarajevo was lax, though the archduke's visit had been publicized well in advance and all knew that the Serbs were agitated over the event. Even so, the Serb-armed Young Bosnians who intended to carry out the assassination of the hated Habsburg at first bungled the plan. It was purely accidental that Gavril Princip, one of the youthful plotters, actually managed to pull off the deed in the end. He was on his way home resigned to the failure of the plot when, suddenly, the car carrying the archduke and his wife out of town mistakenly turned the corner on which Princip happened to be standing. The driver, realizing his error, stopped the vehicle and attempted to back it out into the intersection. In that brief instant, Princip stepped forward, pulled a pistol, and shot to death both the archduke and his wife. With Princip's gunshots there began a rapid chain of events leading to the outbreak of World War I and the end of the Habsburgs.[32]

⫷   ⫸

World War I came as an accident, starting with Princip in Sarajevo, that nobody in Europe desired. Rulers of all the Great Powers and their diplomatic agents tried hard to head it off, yet war erupted. Relieved of fears regarding their position within the empire by the archduke's assassination, the Magyars in the Habsburg foreign ministry saw their opportunity to squelch the threat of Serb minority nationalism by thrashing decisively upstart Serbia in what was believed to be a manageable, localized war. Such a conflict would have posed no danger to Europe, if had been possible to keep it contained. It was not. The weblike system of alliances forged in Bismarck's time, to which both Austria-Hungary and Serbia were a part, precluded all efforts to prohibit the proliferation of military action once Habsburg troops crossed the border into Serbia in July 1914. The Serbs were Russia's allies in the Entente Alliance, and the only way Russia could support Serbia by the terms of their treaty was to threaten Austria-Hungary with first an ultimatum and then military mobilization. Once Russian mobilization occurred, Germany was obliged to mobilize in support of its Central Alliance ally, Austria-Hungary, which, in turn, forced France to follow suit according to its treaty with Russia. Given the nature of the opposing alliances and the expenses involved, military mobilization meant that combat could not be averted, no matter the frantic efforts of rulers and diplomats. Within a little over a month of the tragedy in Sarajevo, the European world found itself embroiled in total war.

The details of the war need not concern us here. The conflict was never confined to the Balkans and Austria-Hungary never achieved swift victory over Serbia. Neither did the quick knockout-blow victories sought by all the other participants materialize once the fighting became general in Europe. The war settled into a grueling and horrendously costly conflict, in which ultimate victory went to the side that could best survive the astronomical costs in human lives, material resources, and socioeconomic pressures that the fighting charged all of the contenders. It comes as no surprise that Habsburg Austria-Hungary, the least unified and internally stable participant, lost—fatally.

Austria-Hungary's military efforts in the war were less than resounding. The initial conflict with Serbia, which was expected to be swift, dragged on into 1915, with a number of humiliating reverses before the Serb forces and their king were driven over the Albanian Alps to the Adriatic, from which they were evacuated by the British first to Corfu and then to Thessaloniki. Following Italy's defection from the Central to the Entente Alliance, a military front against Austria-Hungary opened along the Isonzo River region in its alpine northeast. It resulted in a series of battles, characterized by military ineptitude common to both sides, that the Habsburg forces eventually managed to lose. On the eastern military front against the Russians, Austria-Hungary fared little better. The empire's troops needed German bolstering to preserve their tactical integrity. By 1917 Habsburg emperor Charles I (1916–22), who succeeded Francis Joseph, was aware of the disaster for his empire that loomed on the horizon should the Central Powers be defeated. His sincere efforts to pull the empire out of the war before it was too late were stymied by his German allies and by the growing intransigence of his enemies to accept anything less than total victory over the Central Powers as a whole.

A major factor in the Entente's refusal to pursue separate terms with Austria-Hungary was the consideration they began to give to the national desires of a number of emigré representatives of minority groups from within the empire for nation-states of their own. At first, such support was guided by military considerations alone. The various ethnic components of the Habsburg military forces on the whole fought loyally for their ruler through the early years of the war, but their morale began to flag as the war dragged on and defeats multiplied. Encouraging future hopes for their national aspirations was one way to weaken fatally a key member of the enemy alliance. With the entry of the United States into the conflict on the Entente's side in 1917 and Wilson's pronouncement of his "Fourteen Points," encouragement was transformed into publicly avowed goals. The transformation resonated among the national minorities in Austria-Hungary, tolling the death knell for the Habsburgs in Europe.

At the outbreak of general warfare, nationalist leaders of various ethnic groups from within the empire had made their way to the West, where they actively pursued agendas aimed at creating independent nation-states for their peoples in place of the multicultural, anational Habsburg state.

In late 1914 the Czech Tomáš Masaryk fled Bohemia for France, where he was later joined by Edvard Beneš. The two soon developed a political program calling for the unification of Bohemia-Moravia with Slovakia and the creation of an independent Czechoslovakian nation-state. They were joined by a Slovak nationalist living in France, Milan Štefánik, and together, in 1916, they established a Czechoslovak National Council in Paris. At first, they made little headway with the Entente allies, who were then more concerned about surviving the war's maelstrom than with matters regarding the future dismemberment of postwar Austria-Hungary. But the indefatigable propagandizing of the two Czechs among emigré Czech and Slovak groups, particularly in the United States, and among the leaders of the Entente states eventually paid off. Overcoming the Slovaks' suspicions that the more nationalistically advanced Czechs sought to dominate any new united state, the work of the two ardent Czech expatriates helped forge a 1915 agreement in principle between Czech and Slovak groups in Cleveland. That success was followed in 1918 by a more concrete arrangement regarding a future united Czechoslovak state, presided over by Masaryk, signed in the Schenley Hotel in Pittsburgh (now the University of Pittsburgh's student union). When by 1918 the Entente allies had concluded that Austria-Hungary indeed would be dismantled at the end of the war, and that the Czechs required a reward for the mass defection of their troops serving among the enemy forces on the Eastern Front following the initial 1917 revolution in Russia, the Pittsburgh Agreement provided them with a political framework for the new Czechoslovak nation-state that they would create at Versailles—it simultaneously was the official bill of divorce from the Habsburgs for the Czechs and Slovaks and their license to wed each other.[33]

While Croat troops generally fought well for the Habsburg war effort during the early stages of the war in continued hopes for a tripartite reorganization of the empire at its end, a small number of Croat nationalists, led by Ante Trumbić and the Dalmatian Franjo Supilo, were enamored with Serb-inspired ideas concerning the creation of a Yugoslav state in the Balkans. When war came, Croat and Serb nationalist emigrés established a Yugoslav Committee in London, which contacted the Serb government-in-exile on Corfu in 1916. Both the exiles and the Serbs were greatly disturbed by the Entente allies' offering Dalmatia, among other Adriatic regions, to Italy the previous year in return for that country's entry into the war against Austria-Hungary. Their common concerns led to a 1917 meeting of Trumbić and Supilo with Nikola Pašić, the Serbian royal prime minister, and other representatives of the Slovenes and the Montenegrin Serbs on Corfu. There a joint declaration was signed, proclaiming that Serbs, Croats, and Slovenes formed a single nation that desired a single nation-state under the Serb Karadjordjević dynasty.

Agreement among the participants in the Corfu Declaration had not been easy—the Croats were wary of Serb intentions and the Slovenes more so. Neither's representatives were certain that they actually voiced the majority opinion among their respective conationals. As it turned out, in 1918 the total collapse of the Habsburg military and its allies in the Balkans left the Serbs in command of the only effective forces in the region, and, despite a weak Croat effort at resistance, the Serbs were able to occupy the territories claimed under the Corfu Declaration. For all intents and purposes, Yugoslavia was created. The Croats grudgingly divorced the Habsburgs and remarried their poor relatives, the Serbs. As for the Slovenes, most of whom were Germanized to the point of being "almost German," in a plebiscite in 1920 approximately half chose to remain with the new, Versailles-created Austrian nation-state rather than join the overly South-Slavic Kingdom of Serbs, Croats, and Slovenes (the official name for Yugoslavia until 1929) shaped on Corfu.[34]

Regarding the lowly Romanians of Hungarian-dominated Transylvania, they possessed no major emigré nationalist organization. The Transylvanian Romanian nationalists were supported by their independent conationals in Romania, which lay across the Carpathian Mountains to their east and south. The nationalists in independent Romania held different, Greater Romanian nationalist views than did those in Transylvania, shaped by a Byzantine-Ottoman historical tradition completely foreign to the latter. In 1916 the Entente allies secretly offered heretofore neutral Romania all of Transylvania, including Banat, for entering the war against the Central Powers. Romania did so by invading its secret prize but was soundly and humiliatingly trounced by Habsburg defense forces, after which the country resumed its former neutrality. But that stance proved merely a waiting game to see which side would ultimately crumble. In late 1918, when it became obvious that Austria-Hungary was facing utter defeat, Romania once again invaded Transylvania, secure in the knowledge that there would be little or no resistance. Transylvanian Romanian nationalists thereupon immediately proclaimed their independence from Habsburg rule at Alba Iulia, and the victorious Entente peacemakers proclaimed the divorced Transylvania's wedding to Romania final at Versailles.[35]

The collective bills of national divorce issued in 1917 and 1918 represented a death warrant for the old political order in Central-Eastern Europe. The Habsburg multicultural, anational, essentially feudal empire ceased to exist. With it disappeared any truly stable basis for multicultural harmony in the region in the face of multinational discords.

Far from bringing peace and tranquility to the peoples of the former Habsburg Empire, Versailles succeeded in sowing the seeds of future nationalist turmoil in geographical Eastern Europe. By shortsightedly holding to punitive measures as the overriding motives in their mapmaking, the war's victor Great Powers managed to create new states that were nearly as artificial, in strictly nationalist terms, as had been the one that they dismantled. Moreover, all of the states that emerged from Versailles, whether truncations of former ones—such as Hungary and Austria—or completely new ones—such as Czechoslovakia, Yugoslavia, and Greater Romania—were politically and economically weak. These facts throw a suspicious light on the underlying motivations of the Versailles mapmakers, who appeared not only to favor nationalist friends in their decision making but also purposely determined to ensure that former friends and foes alike would be little more than dependent client states, submissive to the victors' own greater national interests. In the end, the Versailles settlement proved founded on false pretenses: The losers in World War I managed to instigate a second such conflict even more devastating than the first; the Versailles European Great Powers lost their position to the United States and the Soviet Union, whose own national interests alone maintained the small, relatively weak, Versailles-created East European Habsburg successor states; and, ultimately, the artificial nature of those states was demonstrated by the internal nationalist discord that erupted within them once the cold war between the two new superpowers ended.

Before Versailles, a state of Czechoslovakia had never existed. It possessed no historical precedents or traditions. The state's Versailles borders joined together two parts—Bohemia-Moravia and Slovakia—that, with brief exceptions, had been separate since at least the tenth century. Masaryk's Pittsburgh Agreement with American Slovak emigrés, which was the biggest factor in his nationalist reputation and earned him the first presidency in the new country, formed the basis for a state that essentially was created on the basis of a hyphen—two separate parts and peoples joined together to shape one, supposedly unified state. Soon after Czecho-Slovakia became a political reality, Slovak nationalists began insisting that they had been taken in by Masaryk. Of course, the Czech nationalists denied those claims, but political realities inside the new state only tended to confirm the Slovaks' awkward position in the arrangement from the start.[36]

It was impossible to create a unitary state consisting of two equal halves out of halves that were actually unequal. The Czechs, with their Bohemian heartland, possessed a long history of participation in the political life of the Habsburg Empire. Bohemia's capital city, Prague, which became almost automatically the capital of the new state, had been a cultural and intellectual center for all of Central-Eastern Europe since the fourteenth century. It was the home of Panslavism, which formed the earliest expression of modern nationalist thought among both the Czechs and the Slovaks. Despite their subordinate position under the Habsburgs, the Czechs had maintained a political voice in the imperial diet in Vienna. On the other hand, the Slovaks, who had existed under Hungarian rule for close to a thousand years, had played no political role in the Hungarian portion of the old Habsburg Empire and had had no voice to speak of in the Budapest diet. They had grown highly Magyarized over time because that was the only avenue open to them for advancement. So Magyarized had they grown that, during the long period of Ottoman control over much of Hungary in the sixteenth and seventeenth centuries, the Hungarian diet met in the Slovaks' chief city, Bratislava, and Trnava in Slovakia existed as the leading Hungarian cultural center and seat of the Hungarian Catholic church's prince-primate, the archbishop of Esztergom.

The unequal differences that separated the two national partners in the new Czechoslovak state were apparent in any number of areas. While Czech Bohemia was heavily industrialized, urbanized, and liberal-minded, mountainous Slovakia remained agriculturally primitive, backward, and conservative. The Czechs were nominally Catholics but were not devoted particularly to the church, except to a national, Hussite version of Catholicism. The Slovaks were strongly Catholic. Because of their social and religious development, the Czechs tended to be secular, materialistic, and anticlerical in character, which fostered a predilection for socialism among them. (In the interwar years of the 1920s and 1930s, the percentage of socialists in Czechoslovakia was higher than in any other European country.) The less socially developed but more religious Slovaks, on the other hand, were more open to leadership by the clergy, who traditionally filled the ranks of the Slovak nationalists.[37]

It seemed inevitable that the Czechs, from their capital at Prague, would play the leading role in government, economics, and education within the new Czechoslovak state. But the differences that existed between themselves and the Slovaks could not help but create suspicion on both sides, with most of the suspicion stemming from the lesser partner, the Slovaks. By the time Adolf Hitler set out to obliterate Czechoslovakia from the map of Europe in 1938 and thus lay open Central-Eastern Europe to direct German domination, the unbalanced Czech-Slovak relationship had led to the rise of a nationalist Slovak separatist movement seeking a new divorce from its domineering Czech partners. Soon after the Munich sellout, an independent Slovakia was proclaimed, but its independence was based on Nazi German support, and it lasted only as long as did its fascist ally.

Additional national and economic conditions exacerbated the internal tensions intrinsic to the Czech-Slovak relationship. The Versailles mapmakers included a third ethnonational group of people within the borders of Czechoslovakia—the Ruthenians. All the unequal comparisons that were made regarding the position of the Slovaks relative to that of the Czechs was true for them to a greater degree. Lying in the extreme eastern corner of the state, they possessed no historical connections to the Czechs whatsoever, since they were geographically separated from them by the Slovaks. They, like the Slovaks, had been long associated with the Hungarians, and their territory was even more mountainous and backward. The Uniate-Catholic church organization in Ruthenia was basically controlled by Slovaks and provided the basis for the Ruthenians' nascent sense of nationality, since it cut them off from the ethnically related Ukrainians to their east and north. Unfortunately, it also laid them open to Slovak cultural-nationalist claims that they were essentially Slovaks. While the Slovaks complained that they were forced to accept an inferior role in the workings of their new country, at least they had a role to speak of. The Ruthenians, faced by overwhelming Czech dominance and by Slovak nationalist claims, were reduced to virtual nonentities in Czechoslovakia. During the closing years of World War II, Soviet agitation among them prepared the way for their direct incorporation into the Soviet Union in early 1945 as part of Ukraine.[38]

Less welcome than the Ruthenians in Czechoslovakia but far more troublesome were the large and outwardly disgruntled Hungarian and German minorities left inside the new state's borders by the Versailles settlement. Significant numbers of ethnic Magyars inhabited a broad swath of territory in the south of Slovakia along its entire border with post-Versailles Hungary. In 1919, before the Trianon agreement deciding the fate of Hungary at Versailles was finalized, and in the midst of the turbulent and short-lived Bolshevik takeover of Béla Kun, Hungary briefly invaded and occupied a large portion of Slovakia. Only the advance of Romanian troops into the heart of Hungary from the southeast forced the Hungarians to relinquish the conquered territories, caused the collapse of Kun, and led to the installation of a chastised Hungarian government that was willing (though extremely reluctant) to sign the final peace treaty in 1920. The almost 740,000 Hungarians left inside the Slovak portion of Czechoslovakia after Versailles never accepted their transformed position in Slovakia—from dominant majority in old Hungary to fearful minority in the new state, afraid for its continued cultural identity—and they persisted in embracing a strong sense of Magyar nationalism, in march-step with their conationals on the opposite side of the border. When Hitler set about dismembering Czechoslovakia following the Munich sellout in 1938, the Hungarians of Slovakia proved to be his ready accomplices. In the First Vienna Award later that year, Hitler turned over the Hungarian-inhabited area of Slovakia to Hungary, which held it only until the close of World War II, when it subsequently was returned to reconstituted Czechoslovakia.[39]

Even more instrumental in Hitler's destruction of Czechoslovakia at Munich were the Germans in Bohemia, who inhabited a long belt of territory in the mountainous Sudet, Ore, and Bohemian Forest border regions, which collectively came to be known as the Sudetenland. Directly across the Versailles-imposed frontier lay defeated and nationalistically frustrated Germany. Although the Masaryk-Beneš Czechoslovak government made honest attempts to integrate their economically important German minority into the new state, the Sudeten Germans eventually succumbed to the frenzied hysteria of Nazi German ultranationalism and became willing tools of Hitler in his successful efforts to destroy the country. The Sudetenland was attached to Germany for the duration of World War II, but it was returned to post-1945 Czechoslovakia, as were Slovakia and Hungarian Slovakia. Soon thereafter President Beneš, in pursuing his own form of "ethnic cleansing"—the forced expatriation of minorities known as the Košica Program—managed to force out those Germans who had not already fled voluntarily from the country. He was less successful in "cleansing" the Hungarians from Slovakia because the 1948 Communist takeover put a stop to such activities before the anti-Hungarian effort had gathered a full head of steam.[40]

Economically, the new Czechoslovak state faced the same problem as did the newly created Austria—they both possessed large industrial-commercial heads without internal markets to serve as bodies. One of the strengths of the old Habsburg Empire had been the natural economic system that a politically unified Danubian Basin provided. The metal, mineral, and timber resources of the surrounding mountain regions complemented the agricultural, crafts, and manufacturing products of the plains and valleys. A conveniently converging riverine system of communications centered on the Danube, supplemented by man-made road and railroad networks, linked together the various subregions of the basin and created thriving natural commercial and industrial centers— Vienna, Prague, and Budapest—that depended on and benefited from resources and markets scattered throughout the basin. The borders of the new, mostly mutually suspicious Habsburg successor states in the region cut through the natural lines of communications, making Czechoslovakia and Austria, the two industrialized states, economically top heavy and cut off from direct access to their natural markets in the basin, while agricultural Hungary faced a similar problem from the opposite economic direction. Despite all of the political tensions that existed among them as a result of the Versailles settlement, they were forced to negotiate workable trade agreements out of economic necessity. In essence, these agreements were less than successful attempts to restore the virtues of a unified Danubian market—a market that the Habsburg Empire had provided for centuries past.[41]

After experiencing four decades of continued marriage to the Czechs under communism, the Slovaks finally took the opportunity of that ideology's European fall between 1989 and 1991 to divorce themselves from their dominant Czech state partners and establish a small but weak nation-state of their own. The new Slovak nation-state, still heavily agricultural, was strapped with the additional economic liability of a small artificial, obsolete, and uneconomical heavy industrial sector created by the former Communist regime to cater to the ideological and weapons needs of the now-dead cold war.

In Yugoslavia the Croats and those Slovenes who had decided not to stay with Austria soon found that their concerns over remarrying themselves to the Serbs were valid. To their dismay they discovered that their Balkan partners were truly products of an Eastern European civilization that was foreign to their Western European sensibilities. The Serbs lost no time in organizing the state as a veritable centralized nation-state under strong Serbian royal control. Both the Croats and the Slovenes envisioned the political structure of the state in more liberal-democratic and federalist terms that would grant them significant local autonomy. Neither of the two highly Westernized peoples was happy with the thought that the Serbs—who to their minds were cultural inferiors, whose royal house stemmed from glorified, illiterate pig farmers a century earlier—intended to play the role of dominant partner in a highly centralized state. While the Slovenes were able to maintain somewhat of a low profile in terms of political opposition to the situation because Croatia separated them from direct contact with the Serbs, the Croats, by their very geographical position next to Serbia, were forced to play the leading oppositional role.[42]

Croat nationalist opposition exploded into extremism under Serb king Aleksandr I, who particularly was intent on consolidating the state under his central authority. When Croat boycotts of elections and parliamentary proceedings initially failed to win political concessions from the Serbs, the Croats, led by Stjepan Radić, eventually entered the political process and won seats in both the parliament and the royal cabinet after 1924. But after Radić was fatally shot in the parliament's chamber by a radical Serb in 1928, the Croats withdrew their political participation in Belgrade, demanded a new federal constitution, and established their own separatist government in Zagreb, Croatia's capital. In response the next year, Aleksandr proclaimed a royal dictatorship, dissolved the nationalist Croat political party, and arrested Croat national leaders. The country was renamed Yugoslavia and administratively reorganized on a purely geographical basis in an effort to eliminate all traces of historical-national divisions. A new constitution was issued in 1931, which essentially rigged any political participation in favor of the Serb-dominated royal government, and Croat and Slovene oppositional leaders continued to be arrested.

Out of this unbalanced cultural-national situation there arose among the Croats an extremely radical, ultranationalist terrorist organization—the *Ustaše*. It forged close relations with outside Hungarian and Italian fascist leaders and internal Yugoslav Macedonian terrorists. From its headquarters in Hungary in 1934, the *Ustaše* masterminded the assassination of King Aleksandr in Marseilles. Less radical Croats offered to cooperate with Prince Pavel, the regent of the dead king's young successor, Petr II (1934–41), but he reneged on his promised political concessions to them, thus tilting Croat opposition back once again toward the extremists. This trend was further reinforced in the more strictly cultural sphere when, in 1937, Paul's regency government dropped a project to grant wider privileges to Roman Catholics (that is, to Croats and Slovenes), according to a concordat made with the Vatican, following widespread disturbances instigated by Orthodox groups and Serb radicals who opposed any such arrangement.

Rising Croat opposition, reinforced by a growing democratic movement among more farsighted Serbs, led to serious discussions with the royal government in 1938 and 1939 regarding conciliatory moves to relieve the national-political pressures building in the country. Royal dictatorship was ended

and plans laid for federalizing Yugoslavia, with the Croats to receive full autonomy in cultural and economic matters. Croat leaders even were readmitted into
the royal cabinet. But this progress came to an end in March 1941, when a successful military coup against Pavel and his pro-German policies placed the
youthful Petr on the throne. Ten days later Hitler invaded Yugoslavia, with the
help of his Italian, Hungarian, Bulgarian, and Romanian allies, and crushed
the Yugoslav forces in less than two weeks. He then established a friendly Croat
Ustaše government to hold the country while he went about prosecuting his
invasion of the Soviet Union.[43]

The Serbs have never forgotten the depredations inflicted on them by the
Ustaše during World War II. To both the Serb royalist *četniks* and Tito's
Communist partisans, the extremist Croat puppet government became the
supreme enemy. At the war's end, Tito vented his wrath on them (though he
was a Croat himself) and their wartime atrocities through mass executions of
Croats, whether *Ustaše* or not, and later by perpetuating the traditional Serb-
Belgrade domination within the supposedly federalist, but Communist, state
that he forged. Croat nationalist resistance to the covert punitive situation led
to the reemergence of *Ustaše* terrorist activities in the 1970s, which reached
as far afield as the United States.

As for the Slovenes, their small numbers, isolated geographic location relative to the main Croat-Serb conflict, and industrial economic importance spared
them from the brunt of national antagonistic attention. Yet they, as Western
European Roman Catholics, suffered from the same cultural-political biases
of the dominant Serbs. Given no choice but to remain within Tito's
Communist Yugoslavia by force of partisan arms, the Slovenes managed to
parlay their economic development in return for being spared the retribution
meted out to the Croats. As a result, Slovenia grew into the primary industrial
force driving the economy of Communist Yugoslavia. Following the death of
Tito in 1980, as the country slipped inexorably into economic decline and internal intranational conflict, the Slovenes were looked to by all the other national
groups as the only possible saviors of a continued unified Yugoslav state. When
they failed to cure the mushrooming economic crisis of the late 1980s and early
1990s, the Slovenes were the first to decide in 1991 that they would be better
off divorcing themselves from both the Croats and the Serbs and going it
alone in their own independent nation-state. All other non-Serbian cultural-
national groups in the country that were free to do so—Croats, Bosniaks, and
Macedonians—soon followed their lead, and Yugoslavia quickly disintegrated into its ethnonational components, nearly all of which attempted to recon-
stitute themselves as independent nation-states.

⊀ ⊳

By 1 January 1993, with the official separation of Slovakia from the Czech Republic, the artificial Versailles map of Central-Eastern and Southeastern Europe that had replaced the Habsburg Empire was torn up. The states of the friendly "winners" in World War I, with the exception of Romania, fragmented into smaller nation-states that were, however, more valid in terms of true national self-determination of peoples. Whether these states possess the internal strength and resources to maintain their existence in the face of powerful political-economic forces alive in today's Europe, or to withstand nationalist claims on some of them held by other states in the region, is a question that will be answered only in the course of time. It is interesting, however, that the earliest moves on the part of all the new, post -1989 Central-Eastern European successor states to shape a chance for continued survival tend to infer the reestablishment of the decades-lost sense of economic and political security that once was furnished by their ex-spouse—the Habsburg Empire. Almost the first international act of post-Communist Hungary was to establish closer ties with Austria. The Czech Republic, Slovakia, Croatia, and Slovenia all quickly forged economic, cultural, and political agreements in assorted combinations with Austria, Hungary, or Germany. If one were not cognizant of the troubled nationalistic past of the region, one might be tempted to think optimistically that the future of Central-Eastern Europe lies in the reconsolidation of a federalized Danubian Basin—a Habsburg Empire "by any other name"—that would be heavily influenced by developments taking place in the European Union. For that future to occur, a much-needed marital reconciliation among the old partners on new, postnationalist grounds would be needed.

THE TRANSYLVANIAN QUESTION

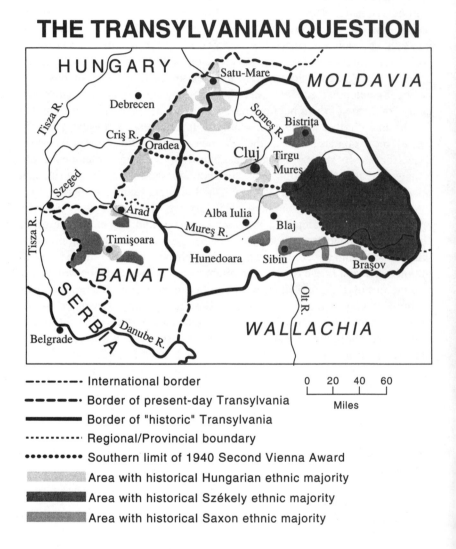

-------- International border
------- Border of present-day Transylvania
━━━━━━━ Border of "historic" Transylvania
············ Regional/Provincial boundary
•••••••••• Southern limit of 1940 Second Vienna Award

Area with historical Hungarian ethnic majority
Area with historical Székely ethnic majority
Area with historical Saxon ethnic majority

0   20   40   60
Miles

TRANSYLVANIA: THE
UNDEAD QUESTION

● ○ ●

hanks to Bram Stoker's *Dracula,* an ingeniously chilling piece of Gothic horror, and to scores of Dracula films ranging from the abominable to the exceptional, the name "Transylvania" has acquired something of a mythical aura in the mind of the average Westerner. It seems to conjure up images of dark, forlorn castles perched precipitously on craggy, forested mountain cliffs that are perpetually swathed in lowering mist and rain. Lightning and thunder are far more common than sunlight. Evil exudes from every tree trunk, rock, and bush. There are no colorful flowers, no babbling brooks, no lush green meadows; only bristling briars, raging rapids, and fuming bogs. The people who inhabit this intimidating landscape are mostly cowed, aged, and frightened peasants who dwell in ramshackle huts and wear worn, odd-looking clothes. Those few who are not numbered among the huddled masses are suave, well-dressed but menacing, heartless characters who live in the forbidding castles and who are obviously the sources of the peasants' fears. Because of such imagery, many Westerners think that Transylvania exists only in the minds of fiction writers and filmmakers.

Many express surprise when they learn that Transylvania actually exists. It is a real region in Central-Eastern Europe, today about the size of Kentucky, and one of the three component provinces of Romania. Far from the exotic, exaggerated images of fiction, Transylvania's landscape and inhabitants are in aspect "normal" for the continental climate that they enjoy. Its mountains, rolling countryside, rural villages, and urban skylines are more photogenic than foreboding. Its people look little different from the others—Hungarians,

Germans, Romanians, Czechs, and Slovaks—who inhabit less romanticized regions of Central-Eastern Europe. Yet for all of the ordinariness that seemingly characterizes authentic Transylvania, the realities of life for its residents are not quite "normal"—not now and not for some centuries past.

History has shaped Transylvania into one of the seismic epicenters along the human fault separating Western and Eastern European civilizations. Just as in the eastern confines of Poland to the north and in Slavonia to the south, the two Europes disquietingly intermingled in Transylvania for centuries. Whereas civilizational friction proved almost continually explosive in Poland and intermittently so in Slavonia, its character in Transylvania has been one of lengthy compounding pressures mostly below the surface. Only once did those pressurized forces erupt dramatically into the open—at the end of World War I—and their aftershocks rocked the region for over two decades. When the eruption ended, the civilizational friction once again subsided into deep, underground rumblings, beginning to build up pressure anew. The lone major flaring of the human fault in the region has come to be termed the "Transylvanian Question," and although it currently is not blazing openly, all indications are that the forces that fed it, both civilizational and national, are far from dead.

The Treaty of Trianon, signed on 4 June 1920, officially ended World War I for Hungary. It provided for the annexation by allies of the victorious Entente powers—the new winner nations created at Versailles—of various regions formerly under Hungarian rule. Trianon gave the historical principality of Transylvania, and more, to Romania. Herein lies the crux of the Transylvanian Question. The Western European Hungarians claimed that this act constituted a crucifixion of the Hungarian nation-state because Transylvania had been an integral part of Hungary for a thousand years. On the other hand, the Eastern European Romanians justified their claims to the region by advancing their own historical arguments that emphasized the continuity of a majority Romanian population in Transylvania for an even longer period of time, dating back at least to the second century and the ancient Dacian Kingdom. These claims were mutually exclusive. No common denominator could lead to a workable compromise.

When drawing the postwar map at Trianon, the victorious Versailles peacemakers, absorbed in the principle of favoring national self-determination for allied peoples, had little compunction in rewarding the Romanians for their less-than-decisive military efforts during World War I through satisfying their full claims to the region. By doing so, the victors created a Hungary that has ever since sought redress of this perceived national humiliation. This situation led the Hungarians into the arms of Adolf Hitler at the opening of World War II, despite the fact that Romania also was allied to that same Nazi dictator. In a 1940 dictate of expediency intended to smooth over the feud between his two valuable allies, Hitler offered the only attempt ever advanced at a compromise solution to the Transylvanian Question in the guise of the Second Vienna Award. Yet the award disregarded the substance of each people's claims and thus was doomed to failure from the start.

Following World War II both Romania and Hungary were incorporated into the Soviet-led Communist system of East European buffer states against the capitalist West, and overt Hungarian irredentist demands for Transylvania were inhibited greatly by obligatory outward adherence to Marxist internationalism and socialist solidarity. But Hungarian nationalist claims on the region continued to simmer below the surface inside Hungary, while expatriate Hungarians never ceased campaigning actively for the revision of Trianon's terms regarding Transylvania. The Romanian nationalist, anti-Hungarian policies in Transylvania of Nicolae Ceauşescu during the late 1970s and throughout the 1980s proved more than even the "brother" socialist Hungarian government could accept without public protest, but to little avail. Finally, the courageous stand of László Tökés, a Hungarian pastor in the Banat city of Timişoara (Temesvár, in Hungarian), against Ceauşescu's policies sparked street demonstrations that quickly escalated into the 1989 Christmas Revolution that toppled the regime. Before the first political dust raised by the change in government had settled, the Hungarians of Transylvania, whose street demonstrations had opened the way for the revolution in December, were being beaten by Romanians on those very same streets the following March. Three Hungarians died. The Transylvanian Question, and the cultural-national animosities that it encompasses, did not.

◄⧖ ⧗►

In historical terms, Transylvania has not been a single, unalterable geographical region. There have, in fact, been three chronologically successive Transylvanias, all in the same general area of Central-Eastern Europe but with varying boundaries. The first and earliest existed as the Roman military province of Dacia. Emperor Trajan (98–117) conquered the region in 107 after two hard-fought campaigns against the native Dak peoples, after whom Trajan named his newly won territories. His incorporation of the conquered lands north of the Danube River as a military defensive position against northern Gothic barbarians, protecting the provinces of Upper and Lower Mœsia, which lay south of the river, represented the first attempt to extend the borders of the Roman Empire beyond those established by Emperor Augustus (31 B.C.–A.D. 14).

Roman Dacia's geographical frontiers were well defined to the north, east, and south by the horseshoe-shaped ramparts of the Carpathian Mountains, whose two open prongs jutted to the northwest and west, respectively. Although this range has often been referred to as the Carpathian Alps, the chain was of medium-average height by alpine standards and easily accessible by deep-river passes. The highest Carpathian peaks lay in the south, where they reached almost 8,000 feet. The area within the bend of the Carpathians was a series of rolling upland plateaus formed by small, low mountain chains running north and south at right angles to the southern Carpathian arm. The westernmost of these highlands was the Bihor range, but it did not form the frontier of Roman Dacia in that direction. Instead, Trajan pushed the western border onto the Pannonian Plain, which was a Trans-Carpathian extension of the Great Eurasian Plain. (The exact limits of the province's western and northwestern border on the plain are unknown.) The southwestern border of Roman Dacia rested on the Danube in the area of the present-day Serbian province of Vojvodina and the Romanian Banat region.

The Roman presence in Dacia lasted for some 160 years, during which time the troops stationed in the province were under constant pressure from the Gothic barbarians of Northern Europe. In essence a large salient protruding northward from the main frontier defense lines in the Balkans, Dacia's lengthy borders lay exposed to attack from three sides. Maintaining the army in Dacia proved a costly affair, taxing both the human and material resources of the empire. Ultimately, the strain proved too much, especially in terms of the manpower needed to keep the military units up to strength—there seems to have been a chronic and continuous shortage of troops to man the region's defenses adequately. In an effort to consolidate the empire's northern defenses, Emperor Aurelian (270–75) decided to abandon the exposed province in 271, and the troops stationed there were withdrawn south of the Danube.

The second Transylvania was "historic" Transylvania. It was formed by the Transylvanian Plateau, which was the upland area lying within the bend of the Carpathians and bounded in the west by the Bihors. The Hungarians, who considered this region an integral part of their state for close to a thousand years, gave it the name Transylvania. Slightly smaller than the state of West Virginia, this was the Transylvania that existed as a historical fact from the time the Magyars (Hungarians) began moving into the region in the eleventh century until 1918. The actual name Transylvania first appeared in the seventeenth century when Latin was adopted as the official administrative language of the Royal Hungarian diet within the Habsburg Empire. The word was the Latin translation of the old Magyar term for the region—*Erdély*, meaning "Beyond the Forest" (namely, the Bihors, which were heavily wooded hills). The majority

Romanian population in the region called it *Ardeal,* which was derived pho-
netically from *Erdély,* while the German residents of "historic" Transylvania
named it *Siebenburgen,* probably after the seven fortified towns that they
founded and inhabited. (It is this second, "historic" Transylvania that will receive
most of the attention in the following pages.)

The third, and present, Transylvania closely resembles the first. It includes
all of "historic" Transylvania, with the addition of the Banat area in the southwest and the Maramureş area in the north. Because it was created by the
Versailles treaty ending World War I and annexed to Romania, this third
manifestation of the region might properly be termed "Trianon" Transylvania.

Four ethnic (eventually, national) groups constituted the population of "historic" Transylvania—Magyars, Székelys (related to the Magyars), Saxons
(Germans), and Romanians. The first three of these peoples developed as member societies of Western European civilization; the latter were East Europeans
and comprised the numerical majority of the region's inhabitants. Over centuries of historical development there evolved a confused territorial intermingling and dispersion among the four peoples and, thus, between the two
civilizations. Once Western European nation-state political culture emerged
as the dominant factor in shaping political reality in the minds of all
Europeans, whether Western or Eastern, the demographic situation in
Transylvania prevented the Trianon treaty ending World War I in the region
from reaching a boundary settlement equitable for both the West European
Hungarians and the East European Romanians. The centuries-old civilizational
frictions in the region between the two were channeled into the more narrow
but readily understandable sphere of national animosity, leading to the open
eruption of the Transylvanian Question on the general European political stage.

To comprehend the human cultural dynamics that drove the Transylvanian
Question in its elemental Hungarian-Romanian form, it is necessary to understand the historical background of all four of the ethnic-national groups com-
prising the region's population.

The Magyars did not begin to populate the Transylvanian region actively
until the eleventh century. These Turkic, Asiatic warrior nomads arrived on
the Pannonian Plain of Central-Eastern Europe around the year 896 after suffering the fate of all their nomadic predecessors—strong demographic pressures pushing them westward exerted by other nomadic peoples to their east
(in this case, the Turkic Pechenegs [also known as Patzinaks]). Using
Pannonia as their base, the Magyars conducted wide-ranging, violent, and

continuous raiding operations into Western Europe, which struck such terror into the minds of their Germanic victims that they were quickly equated to the legendary Huns of Attila and called Hungarians. Ever since, the Magyars have been known to their neighbors in the West by that name. Following their decisive military defeat in 955 by the German Holy Roman Emperor Otto I (936–73) in the Battle of the Lech, the Magyars turned to consolidating their hold on the Pannonian Plain and forging a stable, settled tribal state.[1]

The conversion to Roman Catholicism around the year 1000 of King Vaic, more commonly known as St. István I (1000-38), followed by that of his warrior aristocracy, was a watershed in Hungarian history. This action brought recognition of the Hungarian Kingdom by the leading powers in Western Europe—especially the pope and the Holy Roman emperor—as a member of the medieval Western European community of states. Its monarch István was accepted as an equal among those in the West, with his position solidified through the bestowal of a royal crown by Rome in 1000. With their adoption of Roman Catholicism, the Magyars definitively reoriented their culture from that of a Central Asiatic tribal society to that of a Western European civilized people. For leading the way in this crucial evolution, István was canonized a Catholic saint in 1083.

Joining Western European civilization, however, did not eliminate totally the military threats facing the Magyar state. On the contrary, it may have intensified them. No longer concerned with possible extermination as barbarians at the hands of their Western neighbors, the Magyars' membership in the Western European civilized community of peoples transformed them into the easternmost border defenders of the Western world against further barbarian incursions from the east. In this role, István quickly came to realize the strategic importance of the Transylvanian region. Its eastern and southern wall of mountains made it a natural fortress against the waves of Asiatic nomads that were fast following in the wake of the Magyars. In the early years of his reign, István conquered Transylvania from its local ruler, Gyula (in Romanian, Gelu), whose ethnicity—Hungarian or Romanian—is still a matter of dispute and lies at the very core of the Transylvanian Question. No matter Gyula's ethnic character, István brought "historic" Transylvania into being through his conquest and incorporation of the region into his Magyar lands.[2]

For two centuries following the conquest, the Magyars consolidated their hold on Transylvania. Fortresses were established, Catholic religious orders were founded, and a bishopric was created at Alba Iulia (in Hungarian, Gyulafehérvár; in German, Karlsburg). Members of the Árpád Hungarian royal family served as the dukes or governors of Transylvania through nomination by the Magyar kings, but the region's distance from the royal capital in Buda provided too enticing an opportunity for those royal governors to flaunt their independent authority, making a permanent governing post for Transylvania that would be subordinate to the will of the ruler a necessity. After 1260 a new office, that of *vajda* (in Romanian, *voivode*), a military and administrative post filled through appointment by the king, was established to govern the region, which by then was officially recognized as a province of the Hungarian Kingdom. Over the same period of time, ethnic Magyars gradually but steadily moved into Transylvania and settled. Their numbers initially were sparse, so the Hungarian kings turned to outside peoples for help in colonizing and defending the region.

The earliest of those colonists and defense troops were the Székelys. Their ethnic origins remain obscure, and various theories regarding them have been advanced. One hypothesis attributes to them a Hunnic origin; another postulates that they are descendants of the Turkic Bulgars or Avars; a third declares them Magyars. There are also a number of conflicting subtheories. In any event, no matter what their distant ancestral origins, the Székelys quickly assumed the Magyar ethnic outlook and became a Magyarized people.[3]

By the twelfth century the Székelys were firmly established in the extreme eastern and southeastern corner of Transylvania within the Carpathian bend. They possessed a strong sense of tribal patriotism, traces of which existed as late as 1918, and they looked on the non-Székely Magyar population of the region as latecomers and less "Magyar" than themselves. Culturally and politically, the Székelys formed a compact cluster of Magyarphones in southeastern Transylvania, organized into eight "seats" (*széks,* from which they derived their name) and ruled by a count holding direct authority from the Hungarian king. Because of their position as border guards with military obligations to the state, they were exempted from taxation, just as were the traditional Magyar nobility. Over time, this fiscal privilege successfully led the Székelys to claim noble status as a group, and they officially came to be ranked by the Hungarian government among the so-called sandal, or lower, Magyar nobility. Originally members of the Székely communities held their lands in common and avoided large feudal estates. In many ways, the Székely petty nobles resembled the original German *Junker* class of East Prussia.

Despite their uniform aristocratic status, by the mid-nineteenth century the mundane state of the Székelys was far from noble and egalitarian. Over time, those who through circumstance had acquired large tracts of land in the countryside had assimilated into the dominant Magyar aristocratic class, while those who had not could barely be distinguished from the common Magyar peasants in their way of life. Yet those essentially poor Székelys retained a stubborn sense of class arrogance through their possession of dusty charters of nobility, which they jealously guarded in their rural hovels and which they could produce at will to prove their superiority over their common neighbors.

The Hungarian census of 1910 listed a Transylvanian Székely population of some 460,000 persons, who constituted over 50 percent of the Magyar inhabitants and approximately 16 percent of the province's total population.[4]

A second group of people used as Transylvanian colonists and soldiers by the Magyar state was the Saxons. "Saxon" was the name commonly given to the German inhabitants of the region as a whole, though they all did not originate in Saxony. A great many of these German colonists actually immigrated into Transylvania from the Moselle-Rhine region. Invited into Transylvania by King Géza II (1141–62) in the mid-twelfth century, the Saxons swiftly established seven fortified cities to serve as both the foundations and the administrative centers for their colonies. As had been the Székelys, they were granted privileged exemption from taxation and permitted a large measure of self-government by the Hungarian authorities in return for frontier duty. By the first half of the thirteenth century, the Saxon colonization was completed.[5]

At that time an additional Germanic element entered the Transylvanian scene—the Teutonic Knights. Invited by King András II (1205–35) to settle and to guard the southeastern border of Transylvania in the area of Braşov (in German, Kronstadt; in Hungarian, Brassó), this crusading warrior religious order, having been expelled from the Holy Lands, was eager to find a new home. In 1211 the king granted them a charter of privileges in the area of their settlement, which ultimately was extended to all of the Saxon colonists, that excluded all subsequent newcomers from having a share in them. But the relationship between the Knights and the Hungarian crown soon soured. When the pope attempted to use the militant religious order to gain direct control over the area they inhabited, András drove them out in 1225. Their Transylvanian sojourn proved an interesting footnote to the history of Western Europe since, following their expulsion from the region, the once-again homeless and restless military order accepted a Polish Piast invitation to crush the Baltic Prussian tribes threatening Poland. After successfully accomplishing that task, they settled in the conquered territory, adopted the ethnic name of the people they had all but exterminated, and founded the Prussian German state that evolved ultimately into the leading force in Germany.[6]

The Saxon settlements were scattered throughout all of Transylvania. A heavy concentration of their towns and villages lay in the area between the Mureş and the Tîrnava Mica rivers in the southeast. Others settled Braşov and its surrounding countryside in the far southeast, as well as in and around Bistriţa (Bistritz) in the northeast. Although geographically dispersed, the Hungarian royal charter extended to them as a group forged a small but unified ethnic community jealous of its privileges. It was organized into nine "seats," the chief among them being Sibiu (Hermannstadt, in German; Nagyszeben, in Hungarian). Two districts within Transylvania were recognized as Saxon—Bursenland, with Braşov as its administrative center, and Nösenerland, governed from Bistriţa. The Saxons called the region of their colonies *Siebenburgen*, commonly thought to refer to the seven German castles built in the area, but the name may have derived from that of the fortress erected in Sibiu, which was known as Sibin Burg. The Saxons eventually became the major owners of commercial enterprises established in virtually every urban center in Transylvania. Their commercial preponderance in the province was challenged only by a growing Jewish population, which flourished particularly after the Napoleonic wars.[7]

Of all the primary ethnic groups living in Transylvania, reliable pre-1910 population figures exist only for the Saxons. (Perhaps this is because they alone never figured prominently in the historical ethnonational controversy that eventually flowered into the Transylvanian Question itself, since they were recognized as a separate but important minority by both of the main contenders, and they themselves tended to support the party that held sway at any given time.) In 1468 they numbered about 80,000. Continual warfare during the sixteenth and seventeenth centuries involving the Habsburgs, the Ottoman Turks, and the various protagonists of the religious wars in Europe, combined with some assimilation into the Transylvanian Magyar aristocratic leadership, resulted in their slight demographic decline to about 76,000 by 1713. By the end of the eighteenth century the Saxon population had rebounded to 120,000; and by 1910 they reached nearly a quarter of a million, constituting 8 percent of the province's total inhabitants.[8]

By the end of the twelfth century nearly all of the agricultural land in Transylvania was owned or occupied by Magyars, Székelys, or Saxons, all of whom were members of mainstream Western European civilization, as expressed through their Roman Catholicism until the coming of the Reformation in the sixteenth century. (Even after that development, their Protestantism was deeply rooted in traditional Western Catholic thought.) The land outside their control—the more highland or heavily forested areas—was occupied by the fourth ethnic-national group in Transylvania's population, a considerable number of whom also joined the many poor Magyar (but not Székely) peasants working as serfs on the landed possessions of the others. These were the Romanians.

The origin of the Romanians is such a controversial point and plays such a crucial role in Romanian nationalism that a discussion of it is more appropriate within the confines of our later examination of the Transylvanian Question itself than in a general overview of the Transylvanian Romanian population. It is reasonably certain that the Romanians in the twelfth and thirteenth centuries occupied approximately the same territory that they do today, but in smaller numbers. The earliest extant reference to them as inhabitants of southern Transylvania dates to 1222.[9] They held almost nothing in common with the other ethnic groups living in the region. While the Magyars, Székelys, and Saxons were culturally developed and Western, the Romanians existed on the level of a more primitive tribal society and were Eastern. Their Orthodox Christian faith placed them squarely within Eastern European civilization, sprung from Byzantium as opposed to Rome, and definitively set them apart from their Catholic (later also Protestant) neighbors. Although they spoke a bastardized form of Latin, until the late seventeenth century they used the Cyrillic, rather than the Latin, alphabet in their primarily religious literature and celebrated their liturgy in Church Slavonic, reflecting the earlier medieval cultural and political dominance over them enjoyed by the Bulgarians to their south. Adding to their separateness was the Romanians' lack of a native aristocracy that could compete for the sort of privileges enjoyed by those of all the other Transylvanian ethnic-national groups. What Romanian nobles there were had been assimilated rapidly into the Magyar or Székely aristocratic classes because of the personal gains that membership offered—a charter recognizing their nobility, tax exemptions, and landed estates.

From the earliest mention of Romanians in Transylvania in the thirteenth century until 1918, they remained essentially a peasant people. This status meant that, until the seeds of Western-style nationalism began to take root and to bloom during the eighteenth and nineteenth centuries, a great many Transylvanian Romanians were resigned to a position of serfdom as bad as, and often worse than, that imposed on the peasants of other Western European regions during the darkest period of the Middle Ages. Although numerous Magyar peasants also were tied as serfs to the landed estates in the province, so general was the Romanians' presence within the serf ranks that their ethnic name—Vlahs (sometimes Germanized as Wallachs)—commonly became used by others as a synonym for "peasant" or "serf." ("Romanian" actually is an artificial term that first appeared in the mid-fourteenth century.) Yet the equation of "Romanian/Vlah" with "serf" was misleading and inaccurate. A large number of the region's Romanian inhabitants were, in fact, mountain shepherds, woodsmen, and the like, who could not be tied to the soil as serfs. But whether serf or not, the Transylvanian Romanians received no social or political privileges from the authorities who governed the province.

The Romanian population in Transylvania grew rapidly after the thirteenth century, and by the eighteenth it was definitely the single largest in the region. In 1804 the Romanians accounted for 50 percent of the total Transylvanian population. By 1910 their share had risen to 55 percent.[10]

Because of their generally low social position and their lack of any noble class that could claim recognition by the authorities, the Romanians were looked down upon by the other ethnic-national groups in Transylvania, who despised them for their foreign Orthodox culture and ignored them politically. The cultural and political inferiority of the Romanians of Transylvania was graphically illustrated by the alliance known as the Union of the Three Nations, the basis for the Transylvanian governing constitution created in 1437, in which the Magyar, Székely, and Saxon leaderships divided legal political authority in the region among themselves. Eventually they legally recognized only the religious faith held by their own followers. The Romanians and their faith were expressly excluded from participating in that important governing arrangement.

⊀ ⊁

A peasant revolt, led by discontented, poor Magyars and including large numbers of Romanians, broke out in Transylvania in 1437. The political repercussions resulting from the ensuing civil disturbances formed the foundation for Transylvania's governing constitution until well into the nineteenth century—the Union of the Three Nations (Unio Trium Nationum). This union was an alliance among the landed Magyar aristocracy, the Székely petty nobility, and the Saxon urban population forged both to maintain control over and to defend themselves against the province's peasant masses, Magyar and Romanian alike. While the term "nation" played a prominent role in the alliance, it was used in the late-medieval sense of denoting an aristocratic-privileged class rather than nationality in terms of our modern understanding. Transylvanian society was split among ruling elites, who constituted a minority in the total population, and peasant masses, who were in the demographic majority. It was a traditional Western European feudal division. The nobility despised and distrusted the peasantry, who were seen as posing a perpetual threat to the aristocracies' position of power, while the peasantry viewed all nobles with equal distrust, considering them their common oppressors. Strict lines of modern national consciousness did not appear in Transylvania until 1848.

Nationhood in the feudal Transylvanian sense was determined by a certain group's possession of a charter issued by one of the Hungarian kings. The royal charter specified that group's privileges and tax exemptions. Only a group holding such a charter could justify its claim to nobility. The Magyar aristocracy did not need to possess specific charters since they were the class in power within all of Hungary. Their dominant status rested in the Golden Bull of 1222, which guaranteed an aristocratic role in government, that was forced from King András II by the powerful military and administrative retainers ("servants of the king") on his royal patrimonial lands at a time when a true aristocratic class was just beginning to coalesce in Hungary. Although the bull at first was valid only on lands outside those possessed by the original Magyar clans and those held by outsiders invited into Hungary and granted privileges, by the fifteenth century the Magyar nobility as a whole successfully claimed its prerogatives in full. In Transylvania the Székelys, considered Magyars by all concerned, shared in the general Magyar claims to rights under the Golden Bull, while they also possessed specific charters verifying their special privileges. Although holding no claim to Magyar privileges, the Saxons held various twelfth-century charters signed by King Géza II, but the most important of such covenants dated from 1224—the Golden *Freibrief*—which András II had issued to them. In it, the Saxons were granted the right to self-government and sole control over the lands encompassed by their colonies. It also freed them from all government tolls, dues, and military obligations.[11]

Once the peasant uprising was put down in 1438, the three allied privileged classes were able to install themselves as the legal representative coalition for all of Transylvania. The lengthy lines of communications between the province and the Hungarian royal capital at Buda left Transylvania virtually an independent entity within Hungary, governed by the royally appointed *vajda* and a diet composed of representatives from the three privileged, feudal "nations," who held faithfully to the union so long as it benefitted their own individual interests. One of the first acts taken by the united privileged "nations" was to deprive the peasants of virtually all of the few rights they had previously enjoyed.

Unfortunately for the Romanians, without an aristocratic leadership, they were not considered worthy of possessing the status of "nation" in the eyes of both the Hungarian royal government and of the other feudal "nations" of Transylvania. This was the avowed reason for their exclusion from the 1437 union.

It seems ironic that two of the greatest Hungarian national figures from the fifteenth century—János Hunyadi and his son Matthias Corvinus—were scions of a noble family that probably was of Romanian origin (the Hunedoaras). Hunyadi was a powerful south Transylvanian frontier lord who won his first major victory over the Ottoman Turks in 1437. From that moment until his death in 1452, his exploits earned him the honor of being considered Hungary's most famous and successful military commander. In 1441 he defeated an Ottoman attempt to capture the Hungarian fortress of Belgrade, following which, for two successive years, he led Hungarian invasions deep into the Turkish-held Balkans. After forcing Sultan Murad II (1421–44, 1446–51) to sign a peace treaty at Edirne in 1444, the pope and the Byzantines prevailed on Hungarian king Władisław I Jagiełło (1440–44) to break the agreement and attack the Turks. Hunyadi reluctantly obeyed, but the renewed campaign ended disastrously for the treaty-breakers at the Battle of Varna. Four years later, in 1448, Hunyadi was again utterly defeated at the hands of the Turks in the Second Battle of Kosovo.[12]

In 1458 Hunyadi's fifteen-year-old son Matthias was elected king of Hungary (1458–90). He distinguished himself as a soldier, a statesman, and a patron of the arts. Earning the title of Corvinus ("the Just"), Matthias strengthened the power of the crown vis-à-vis the Magyar nobility and made Hungary the dominant power in Central-Eastern Europe for the period of his reign. Among his many achievements were the creation of an effective standing mercenary army, a famous law code issued in 1486, and the founding of a voluminous library housing valuable illuminated works by noted Italian Renaissance artists. His prolonged struggles against Czech king Poděbrady (1458–71) and Holy Roman emperor Frederick III (1440–93) resulted in his acquisition of the Bohemian crown in 1470 and of much of Lower Austria, including Vienna in 1485, which Matthias thereafter established as his capital. Despite his successes, however, he was unable to realize his ultimate political goal of leading a united European campaign into the Balkans against the Ottoman Turks before his death at the age of forty-seven.[13]

Following Matthias's death, most of his work in cementing a strong, centralized Hungarian monarchy was undone during the succeeding reigns of two weak Jagiełłonian kings, which culminated in the overwhelming Hungarian military disaster at Mohács in 1526 inflicted by the Turks, the Magyars' perennial enemies. The debacle at Mohács had important repercussions for Transylvania. Its *vajda* at the time, the Magyar aristocrat János Zápolya, was elected to the vacant Hungarian throne by his fellow Transylvanian, as well as by a number of Pannonian, Magyar nobles in direct opposition to the Habsburg Ferdinand I, who was the choice of the remaining Pannonian Magyar and Croatian aristocracy. The civil war that erupted between the two factions ended in 1528 with Zápolya's defeat, despite support from the Turks. By the peace ending the war, Zápolya was recognized as ruler over those lands that he held, including Transylvania, for as long as he lived, but following his death the undivided crown was to fall into Ferdinand's possession. Zápolya then placed himself under Ottoman vassalage, thus ultimately sparing Transylvania the horrors of Turkish occupation when the Turks resumed their incursions deeper into the heart of Central-Eastern Europe in the 1540s.

Within twenty-five years of Zápolya's death in 1540, Transylvania emerged
as a principality independent from the direct authority of the Habsburg-held
Hungarian crown, ruled in virtual absolute fashion by its traditional *vajda,* who,
though forced to renounce any claim on the royal throne, enjoyed semiindependent status as a vassal of both the Habsburg Hungarian kings and of the
Ottoman Turkish sultans. (This dual vassalage was unique in Europe during
the sixteenth and seventeenth centuries.) All traditional Hungarian law continued to be followed scrupulously within the principality's borders. Moreover, the coalition of the "Three Nations" retained its legal representative
monopoly under the *vajda* as before. Except for two brief periods during the
sixteenth century, when foreign princes won control of the office by force (the
Habsburg Ferdinand I [1551–56] and the Romanian Wallachian prince Mihai
Viteazul [1599–1600]), the *vajdas* were Magyars for as long as Transylvania
maintained its singular semiindependence. Despite occasional clashes
between Magyar plainsmen and Székely mountaineers, the two class partners
generally were united under the patronymic of "Magyars" and, with Saxon
support, formed a common front against the predominantly Romanian peasantry. While most of Pannonian Hungary was incorporated directly into the
Ottoman Empire after a series of successful anti-Habsburg military campaigns carried out in the early 1540s by Sultan Süleyman I the Magnificent
(1520–66), essentially nominal dual Turkish and Habsburg suzerainty permitted
the dominant Transylvanian "nations" to continue as they had before 1526,
and even to expand their prerogatives.

The period of Transylvanian semiindependence between 1526, when Zápolya
laid the foundations for its emergence as an autonomous principality, and 1699,
when the Treaty of Sremski Karlovci definitively expelled the Turks from
Hungary and placed the principality under direct Habsburg control, can be considered the apex of Transylvania's history. Under its great *vajdas* Gábor Bethlen
(1613–29) and György I Rákoczi (1630–48), Transylvania enjoyed a "Golden
Age," in which it ranked as one of the Great Powers in all of Europe. That achievement was linked directly to the Protestant Reformation, during which the principality came to play a leading role in the Thirty Years War (1618–48) as a
European Protestant power.[14] Tied to that phenomenon was the final development in the unique cultural-political constitutional structure of the principality—
the merging of "four accepted religions" with the Union of the Three Nations.

⚔ ⚔

The Protestant Reformation entered Transylvania soon after Lutheranism first
entered Hungary just prior to the Mohács debacle. Because the Lutheran faith

was protected by Mary, the unpopular queen of King Louis II Jagiełło, who died in the battle, it proved unattractive to most Hungarians and was confined predominantly to the Saxon colonists in the principality. It was spread among them by Johann Honterus of Braşov.[15] From the Saxons, Lutheranism was diffused among most of the non-Romanian (Orthodox) inhabitants of the region by the 1540s, except among the large Magyar landowners, who remained Roman Catholics. By the mid-1560s Calvinism had entered the Transylvanian religious scene and had attracted the adherence of most Magyars living in the principality. Calvinism's rejection of centralized lines of authority tying all of society to the person of the monarch sat well with the Transylvanian Magyar nobles, who continuously resisted any efforts to subordinate them to the will of the Habsburg-controlled Hungarian crown.[16] Also by that time, the Saxons had established a separate Lutheran church of their own.

Meeting in diet at Turda (in Hungarian, Torda) in 1564, the representatives of the Three Nations issued a law granting Calvinism and Lutheranism rights of worship equal to that enjoyed by Roman Catholicism in Transylvania and proclaiming freedom of worship for all three religions throughout the principality. In addition, each was granted rights to equal representation in the principality's central administration, self-government in religious matters, and justice for its adherents before the law. The clergy of each were given the same rights and privileges as those enjoyed by the recognized nobilities. This decree of religious toleration was remarkable for Europe at the time. Autonomous Transylvania became the first state to espouse legally the principle of toleration in a European world wracked by sectarian intolerance and violence. In effect, the decree of 1564 created a constitutional addition to the older order of the Three Nations by broadening it to include recognition of the "three accepted religions."

But in the same year that the Turda diet forged its decree of religious toleration, a new Protestant religion made its appearance in Transylvania among the Magyar Calvinists living in and around Cluj (in Hungarian, Kolozsvár; in German, Klausenburg), and it quickly began to spread, especially among the Székelys. Spawned by Italian and Polish antitrinitarian influences, this indigenous faith—Unitarianism—caused numerous and lengthy debates among the representatives of the three "nations" and "religions." When the *vajda,* János-Zsigmond Zápolya (1559–71), converted to Unitarianism, the diet of Tîrgu Mureş in 1571 felt constrained to elevate that sect to the position of fourth "accepted religion."[17]

The legal institution of "four accepted religions"—Roman Catholicism, Calvinism, Lutheranism, and Unitarianism—reduced all other faiths practiced in Transylvania to a tolerated, but not "accepted," status, thus lacking any legal rights. Moreover, clergy of merely tolerated faiths received no privileges, as did those of the four accepted religions. Despite the remarkable expression of religious toleration that the principle of "acceptance" involved, its benefits did not extend to the numerous Orthodox Romanians in Transylvania, or to the far less numerous Jews and Armenians found as merchants in some of the principality's towns. By excluding these faiths from the decree of legal recognition, the accepted religions principle essentially left the existence and condition of their adherents to the fickle pleasure of the ruling *vajda* and of the Three Nations. As it turned out, this was both positive and negative. When István Báthory, a staunch Roman Catholic, gained the office of *vajda* (1571–86), he definitively capped the propagation of additional recognized faiths by declaring the 1571 Tîrgu Mureş decree fixed for all time. He then proceeded to bring in the Jesuits and led the Catholic Counter-Reformation in Transylvania, ultimately succeeding in winning back to the Roman faith large numbers of Protestant Magyars. Báthory, a true Transylvanian Magyar, scrupulously upheld all of the laws of the principality and did not infringe on the accepted religions and Three Nations principles of the constitution.

While Báthory prevented any proliferation of Protestant sects from gaining legal recognition in the principality, his cementing of the Three Nations and the four accepted religions as the definitive framework for the Transylvanian constitution worked against the hapless Romanian majority in the region's population. Soon after Báthory's successes, the nations and the accepted religions came to coalesce—Magyars became identified with Roman Catholicism and Calvinism; Székelys with Unitarianism; and Saxons with Lutheranism. This development brought to the surface the cultural animosity that actually underlay the apparent feudal sociopolitical division of Transylvanian society since the thirteenth century. If the Three Nations alone had constituted the essential element in the constitution, then feudal legacies would have been adequate in justifying the Romanians' exclusion from the legal structure of authority. But the legal identification of "nations" with "accepted" Catholic and Protestant religions in the Transylvanian constitutional system, and with the Orthodox Romanians still excluded, illustrated a much deeper motivation driving those in authority.

More than merely representing the "haves" exerting their dominance over the "have-nots," the merging of the Union of the Three Nations and the four accepted religions institutionalized Western European civilization's claims to superiority over that of Eastern Europe in Transylvania. By entrenching the sociopolitical dominance of the numerically smaller Western European population over the numerically larger Eastern European, this inequitable constitutional arrangement laid the Orthodox Romanians open to treatment as inferiors in virtually every way. The ruling nations viewed them as "vagabonds, outcasts, thiefs, whores and savages."[18] Most Romanians, for their part, never sought to be assimilated into the ranks of their Western oppressors.

In 1699 Sremski Karlovci officially ended the unique semiindependent status of the principality, but this had been terminated realistically eight years earlier, in 1691, when Habsburg emperor Leopold I (1657–1705), having the Turks on the run militarily, entered the city of Buda in Pannonian Hungary and made good on Habsburg claims to the royal crown of all Hungary. In December of that year he issued the *Diploma Leopoldinum,* officially confirming the rights of the Transylvanian nations and accepted religions, and recognizing the autonomy of Transylvania as an imperial Grand Principality. As a result of Leopold's diploma, Transylvania once again was nominally placed under the direct authority of the Hungarian crown, now indisputably worn by the Habsburg ruler. In practice, however, the principality retained its own diet, administration, and judicial system.

Since under the imperial diploma the Transylvanian constitutional system remained intact, the Romanians' lack of political and legal representation in the principality compelled them to turn to the Orthodox church—the institutional expression of their East European culture—as the most important force in their civil and spiritual lives.

An Orthodox church organization had been functioning in Transylvania since the fourteenth century. By the fifteenth, it was governed by an archbishop seated in Alba Iulia, who was, in turn, under the overall jurisdiction of the metropolitan of Bucharest, located in the Romanian principality of Wallachia to the south of Transylvania. The political and financial situations of the Transylvanian church were precarious. It was not included among the accepted religions, so it shared none of their rights and privileges. Because it owned little land with which to support its clergy, churches, and schools, the Transylvanian Orthodox church generally possessed insufficient economic resources for meeting its mostly rudimentary needs. The clergy usually were literate in the Church Slavonic literary language used by the church, but they received little formal training beyond memorizing the Orthodox liturgy, parts of prayer books, and instructions for performing basic priestly duties. Most parish priests were indistinguishable from their peasant parishioners, since, not enjoying official recognition, they were subject to the same labor services owed the landowners in the areas where they lived and worked. During any given week, the Romanian Orthodox priests worked in the fields just as did the other Romanian peasants. The shared lifestyle of both clergy and parishioners fashioned a strong bond between them that resulted in the priests exerting extraordinary political and spiritual influences in their villages. It was into this setting among the Romanians that Emperor Leopold, for political reasons, sought to interfere.[19]

⚜ ⚜

The traditional method by which the Habsburgs maintained their centralist control over the widespread, multiethnic domains under their rule can be summarized in one singular maxim: divide and rule. As the lands of Hungary were being liberated from the Turks by his armies, Leopold came to realize that he was going to have difficulty keeping the traditionally independent-minded Magyar nobility in check under his rule. Leopold was a farsighted monarch in that respect. In 1703 the Magyar nobles rose in revolt against him. Though he died two years later, and the uprising continued under his successor, Joseph I (1705–11), Leopold had to face and to deal with the agitation leading up to it. In searching for allies to support him against the growing Magyar threat in the years immediately preceding the revolt, Leopold hit upon the idea that the Transylvanian Romanian masses might serve as a serious counterthreat to the unruly Magyar nobility if they could be brought directly under Habsburg control. Leopold's problem lay in achieving control over the Romanians. The solution arrived at cut to the core of the civilizational nature of the sociopolitical division in Transylvania.

Plans for enticing the Orthodox Romanians to forsake their native faith and join the Roman Catholic church were laid in Vienna, Leopold's capital, in the latter years of the seventeenth century, while the war against the Ottomans in Hungary was still raging. The idea of uniting Orthodox Christians with the Roman Catholic church under papal authority was not original: It had existed in the Catholics' minds since the fifteenth-century Council of Florence first raised the issue as the price the Orthodox Byzantine Empire had to pay for Western aid against a rising Ottoman Turkish menace. In 1596 at Brest, the Catholic Swedish Vasa ruler of Poland forged a Catholic-dominated union with some of his Orthodox Ukrainian subjects. In the Habsburg Empire itself, the Orthodox Carpatho-Ruthenians (some claim them as Ukrainians) of northeastern Hungary had been joined to the Roman Catholic church in the 1648 Union of Uzhgorod (Ungvár, in Hungarian). Should similar plans succeed in Transylvania, the Romanians would look to Leopold as a friend and benefactor, since the Habsburgs were the traditional European champions of Rome. Given the hapless conditions of the Romanians under the Transylvanian constitutional arrangement, they would have no choice but to do so. The union of Orthodox Romanians with Roman Catholicism would have a dual positive result. The Romanians would not only become useful allies of the Habsburgs, but the union would also partially fulfill the traditional goal of Rome to recapture authority in the Orthodox East, a goal that the Catholic Habsburgs shared concerning the empire over which they presided. But grand ideals aside, such a union would give Leopold the mass Romanian pawns he sought in his struggle to central- ize imperial control over the recalcitrant Magyar nobility of Transylvania.[20]

Habsburg unionist plans focused on the higher Orthodox clergy in the prin- cipality. Although those men lived modestly, they enjoyed a higher standard of living than did the Orthodox parish priests. They resented the fact that they were discriminated against by the privileged nations and the accepted religions. Their discontent was counted on as a major factor in ensuring the success of Catholic Habsburg plans for the church union. Leopold placed the actual efforts for implementing the plans into the hands of the Jesuits, who had returned to Transylvania in 1693 after a forced absence of nearly a century. Their skill and learning would prevent the region's Protestants from gaining Romanian converts in attempting to counter the Catholic scheme. Although the Jesuits were charged with transforming the religion of the Orthodox masses as Leopold's imperial agents, they were not to interfere with the exist- ing social or political structure of Transylvania. The emancipation of the Romanian serfs was not considered. Heading the Jesuit effort was Hungarian cardinal Lipót Kollonics, a Hungarian aristocrat whose pro-Habsburg sympathies already had won him notoriety as an important anti-Magyar imperial official in Leopold's government bureaucracy.

The Jesuits directed their main efforts at the Romanians' Orthodox clergy, since to have concentrated on converting the masses would have proven a lengthy and difficult process. Pamphlets were distributed among the higher church officials, in which the insignificance of the differences that separated Catholic from Orthodox was stressed. Essentially four principal dogmatic differences had served as barriers between the two major wings of Christianity since at least the eleventh-century Great Schism (1054), although problems over them had sur- faced as early as the ninth. Known as the Four Points, these differences were: Catholic acceptance of the Roman pope as the supreme head of Christianity on earth (the Orthodox recognized only the overall authority of the collective Christian high clergy meeting in ecumenical councils); the use of unleavened (Catholic) or leavened (Orthodox) bread in the sacrament of holy communion; the Catholics' belief in the existence of Purgatory (the Orthodox did not); and perhaps the most important difference, the Catholic modification of the Nicæan Creed, the supreme expression of true Christian belief, that redefined the Third Person in the Trinity (the Holy Spirit) as proceeding from both the Father *and* from the Son (Christ)—the infamous *filioque* clause. (The Orthodox accepted the original wording, which defined the Spirit's procession from the Father alone.)

Kollonics handled the problems involved with the Four Points skillfully, explaining to the Orthodox prelates that accepting Catholic views on these issues actually required little change in the religious life of the average Orthodox Romanian. He emphasized that their canon law and liturgy would remain unchanged, and he assured them that Romanian priests would be permitted to marry, as before. In any case, the theological subtleties of the Four Points meant little to the average Orthodox priest and his peasant parishioners.

All in all, acceptance of the Four Points, which constituted union with Rome, seemed a small price to pay for the benefits it would bring to the church and its clergy. The disgruntled high Orthodox hierarchy in Transylvania assumed that union would automatically elevate them to an accepted religion as a component of the Roman Catholic faith, with all of the rights that acceptance entailed. Also, it logically should bestow on them the recognized privileges enjoyed by those of all the other accepted religions. By a seemingly slight compromise of their Eastern European cultural ideals, unionist Romanians would share in all the benefits that Western superiority offered, while continuing to remain essentially East European.

The deft arguments of Kollonics and his Jesuit followers won over the high Transylvanian Romanian Orthodox clerics. In February 1697, on behalf of himself and of his clergy, Metropolitan Teofil of Alba Iulia announced the unanimous acceptance of the Four Points and the union of the churches. He also publicly demanded the same rights and privileges for his clergy as those enjoyed by the "accepted" Roman Catholics—a significant event since it marked the first formal political demands raised by Transylvanian Romanians. In October 1698 Teofil's successor as metropolitan, Atanasie Anghal, along with over a thousand Romanian clergymen, signed the official Act of Union at a highly attended synod in Alba Iulia. Through an imperial diploma issued in February 1699, Leopold granted the unionist Romanian clergy—called Uniates—the same rights and privileges as those of the Roman Catholic clergy, exempted them from compulsory labor services and tithes to the Magyar landowners, and provided for supporting their metropolitan and parish churches. The Transylvanian diet, whose ratification of the diploma was required before it could be enacted as law, initially opposed it, but Leopold's threat of armed intervention forced the irate nobility to yield to his wishes. At a church synod in September 1700 (the largest ever held in Transylvania), the union of the churches was concluded formally, although a second imperial diploma from Leopold, issued in March 1701, was needed to alleviate Metropolitan Atanasie's fears over potential interference in the union by the Transylvanian nobility.[21]

By the time the unionist plans succeeded in part, Leopold seems to have lost confidence in the union's usefulness in his political struggle against the

Magyar nobility. Uncertain whether the Uniates would docilely comply with the role he imagined them playing on behalf of Habsburg interests, Leopold severely restricted their autonomous rights by placing them under the direct ecclesiastical authority of the head of the Hungarian Catholic church, the prince-primate archbishop of Esztergom, who thus acquired a decisive voice in Uniate affairs. Roman Catholic domination of the Romanian unionists that this arrangement signified caused friction between the two church partners from the start. The upper Uniate clergy, questioning the wisdom of their decision to join with the traditional Roman cultural enemy, were of two minds in the matter.

Church union did not automatically elevate the Romanians to fourth "nation" status in Transylvania. The Three Nations considered the principality's constitution inviolate as it stood. Leopold's pro-Uniate diplomas of 1699 and 1701 did not confer "nationhood" specifically, since that action would have represented a violation of the Transylvanian constitution. Only a vote of the principality's diet could do so, and the diet's member nations jealously adhered to Báthory's actions that fixed the number of nations at three in perpetuity. Though forced to "accept" the Uniates within the general framework of Roman Catholicism, they refused to recognize those ignoble, peasant Easterners as a new nation equal to themselves. Only the threat of force had led them to compromise their traditions regarding accepted religions, but they drew the line at nationhood. If Leopold seriously wished otherwise, he would have to defeat them in war. This, of course, was precisely what the emperor was trying to avoid by pursuing the union efforts in the first place. Some of the Uniate hierarchy realized this, but most looked to Vienna and the imperial court as a friendly ally. They failed to realize that the Habsburgs would be receptive to their appeals only when the interests of the monarchy were served, and that the ruler had no thoughts of considering them the equals of their dominant Roman Catholic ecclesiastical authorities—they were inferior, culturally foreign Eastern tools of one side in an exclusively Western power struggle.

Despite the harsh realities of the Uniates' true situation, the imperial diplomas validating the church union provided the Transylvanian Romanians with a constitutional basis for pursuing further political activity in the principality. At first, this was confined to the Uniate clergy alone, but by the end of the eighteenth century members of the lay population were embracing the sociopolitical issues raised by the union.

The fact that the Uniates represented the first crack in the traditional exclusionary sociopolitical defenses of the privileged nations in Transylvania must be considered important. As an instrument of Habsburg centralist aims in the principality, the Uniates ultimately proved a failure. But as pioneers of a Romanian ethnonational awareness, they were immensely successful. The privileges granted the upper Uniate clergy ultimately raised the standards of Romanian education, which lay in the hands of the church, financed seminaries and printing presses, and established connections between the Transylvanian Romanians and the West.

The immediate advantages to the Transylvanian Romanians resulting from the union of the churches were cultural. Through the upper Uniate clergy, state money was invested in Romanian education, especially on the seminary level. In 1754 an exclusively Uniate religious center was founded in Blaj, which swiftly grew from a small village into a thriving urban center, with a cathedral, a monastery, and numerous schools. The town served as the major focal point of Romanian Uniate cultural activity in Transylvania. Its Romanian-language secondary schools were the earliest in the principality. There also was established the first Romanian printing press in 1738. Later the Blaj press became a principal instrument of the Romanians' ethnonational awakening, issuing in 1780 the first Romanian grammar printed in the Latin, rather than in the Cyrillic, alphabet. Moreover, Roman Catholic schools and colleges throughout Transylvania were opened to Uniate Romanian students, the most talented of whom were eligible for scholarships to study abroad in the West.[22]

One of the most significant fruits of the church union for the Romanians of Transylvania was the possibility for Uniate clergymen to study at Catholic seminaries in the West. A program to send Uniate students to the College for the Propagation of the Faith in Rome was started in 1738 and lasted until 1779, when it was discontinued by Emperor Joseph II (1780–90). Many of those who participated in the study-abroad programs offered through the Uniate opening emerged as the vanguard in spreading ethnonational consciousness among the Romanians in Transylvania. None was more influential than the eighteenth-century Uniate bishop, Ion Ionchentie Micu.[23]

Micu was a product of that newly opened opportunity. He was educated in a Jesuit seminary in Nagyszombat (today Trnava, in Slovakia). That city was then the center of Hungarian learning. A university established there in 1635 was the ancestor of the future University of Budapest. During the period of Ottoman control over Pannonian Hungary in the sixteenth and seventeenth centuries, Nagyszombat had served as the seat of the archbishop of Esztergom. Steeped in Hungarian culture, Micu's obvious abilities led to his appointment as bishop in 1730 at the direct intervention of Emperor Charles VI (1711–40).

The new bishop viewed the Leopoldine diplomas granted to the Uniates as vehicles for the political emancipation of the Romanian peasantry in Transylvania; thus he worked zealously for the peasants' conversion to the union so that they could be covered by the provisions in those documents. It was he who established the Blaj Romanian cultural center out of lands that he personally held as the Transylvanian Uniate bishop. Micu actively pleaded before the Transylvanian diet and the imperial court in Vienna for the Romanians' recognition as a nation. No distinction was made in his mind between Uniate and Orthodox in that regard. When his attempts to gain political satisfaction failed with both the diet and Empress Maria Theresa (1740–80), who nevertheless patronized the Romanian press in Blaj in an effort to promote the church union among the Romanians, Micu left Vienna for Rome in late 1744 without imperial permission. This cost him his influence at court, and he never again returned to Transylvania. In 1751 he resigned his office of bishop, and he died in a Roman monastery in 1768.

Micu's contribution to the development of Romanian ethnopolitical consciousness was fundamental. He was the first to formulate a broad program of political and social action aimed at emancipating the Romanian peasants of Transylvania and raising them to the status of nationhood. His disciples, who carried on his legacy, were later termed the Transylvanian Latinist School. Micu often was given credit for "discovering" the Latin origins of the Romanian language. While in Rome, he was purported to have noticed that the bas-reliefs on the antique Trajan's Column, erected in the second century by that emperor to commemorate his conquest of Dacia, portrayed the ancient Dacians as wearing hats similar to those worn by Romanian peasants in Micu's time. Whether the story is apocryphal or not, Uniate Latin scholars studying in the West slowly developed an ethnopolitical doctrine based on their philological studies, as related to their native Romanian language. These men traced the Romanian vernacular to roots lying in the imperial Latin used during the second- and third-century period of Roman occupation in Dacia. Their scholarly studies led them to conclude that the lowly Romanians were actually the indigenous inhabitants of Transylvania, directly descended from the Daks, whom Trajan had defeated and who were subsequently Romanized. That being the case, then all of the other non-Romanian peoples living in the region—the Three Nations—were later interlopers.[24]

Further eighteenth-century political developments in Transylvania placed those nascent ethnonationalist Uniate scholars and followers of Micu at a disadvantage. In 1762 Maria Theresa issued an imperial patent that officially defined the constitutional organization of Transylvania in favor of the traditional Three Nations and four accepted religions arrangement. It was one of many ways that she demonstrated her continued official gratitude to the Magyar nobility for their recognition of her as ruler in 1741 and for their active support in both the past War of the Austrian Succession (1740–48) and, more important, in the Seven Years' War (1756–63), which was then raging. In her patent, Maria Theresa ruled that the Orthodox church had a recognized status inferior to that of the Uniates', and that both ranked below that of the four accepted religions. The ruling had great impact. Many Romanian Uniates renounced their affiliation and returned to Orthodoxy. Since neither of the two religions was proving advantageous regarding the conditions of their lives in Transylvania, they preferred to adhere to the faith that most closely expressed their native, centuries-old worldview. Despite all the acculturational efforts of the Western European Habsburgs, in the end, the Romanians by and large chose to remain Eastern Europeans.

꘏ ꘏

The high hopes that both the Habsburgs and the Romanian Uniate clergy entertained regarding the church union were never realized. By the mid-eighteenth century, Romanian defections from the Uniates' ranks seemed to indicate to Habsburg officials in Transylvania that the union had failed. The Horia Rebellion in 1784 made this a certainty in their eyes. It was obvious that the Romanians viewed the union only as a road to recognized nation status. Those hopes were dashed with Micu's earlier failures before the Transylvanian diet and the imperial court, and with the atrocities associated with the peasant uprising led by the Romanian serf Vasile Nicola, better known by his nickname, Horia. That affair was linked directly to the reform efforts of Habsburg emperor Joseph II.

In some respects, Joseph was a friend of the Transylvanian Romanians. They looked on him as an ally in their efforts to overcome the prejudices of the nations and accepted religions. His sympathy for the plight of the peasants stemmed from his plans to centralize and modernize the Habsburg Empire, and not from any particular soft spot in his heart for the Romanians. Joseph was a creature of eighteenth-century political concepts summarized by the term "Enlightened Despotism." His enlightened ideals included religious toleration, just treatment for all—nobles and peasants alike—under the law, rationalism in government, and the abolition of serfdom, which he considered both morally evil and out of date and an obstacle to profitable agricultural development. In 1783 he issued a preliminary decree emancipating the serfs of Transylvania. Unfortunately, it did nothing to check the underlying causes of the peasants' miseries: the nobles' increasing hunger for land and the crushing financial duties owed by the peasants to the state and the landowners. Expecting Joseph to go easy on the peasant rebels because of the preliminary decree, Horia stirred up his revolt in the following year, only to discover that Joseph was just as dedicated to the principle of law and order as he was to peasant emancipation. The rebellion was decisively crushed and Horia was brutally executed.

But the Horia incident did have one positive consequence: Joseph took a hard look at the situation of the Transylvanian peasants and then issued a second, final, emancipation decree in 1785. In it the peasants were granted personal freedom and the right to acquire and to dispose of property, especially land. Landlords were forced to keep strict account of dues and services rendered to them by peasants, and the jurisdictional authority governing such relations was removed from the local authorities and placed into the hands of agents of the central, Habsburg government. Unfortunately for the peasants, the decree turned over no land to them, so they were freed only to find themselves tenants of the landowners, obliged to pay their rent by the same means as they had before—tithes, dues, and services.

As far as religion was concerned, Joseph tolerated both the Uniates and the Orthodox. He attempted to raise the latter to a level of development equal to that of the former by planning a system of Orthodox schools. In 1781 he proclaimed an Edict of Toleration for Transylvania. By its terms Orthodox subjects were no longer barred from public office because of their faith, and they were granted equal treatment under the law. The edict eventually succeeded in undermining further the Uniate church in Transylvania, since large numbers of its adherents returned to the Orthodox faith. Joseph, of course, had not intended this to happen, so he countered with a new decree in 1782 that declared attempts to persuade Roman Catholics or Uniates to join the Orthodox church illegal and subject to severe punishment. Furthermore, should a Catholic or Uniate decide to convert voluntarily, without outside persuasion, a mandatory six-week course in Catholicism was required before that person could be received into the Orthodox church or be buried by an Orthodox priest.

Beyond serfdom and religious intolerance, Joseph sought a revolutionary transformation in the political nature of the Habsburg Empire. He was filled with an intense dislike of both the nobility and the clergy, whose landed properties and fiscal privileges he viewed as detrimental to a modern, enlightened state. Such a state required unity under a strong, central governing authority. Thus he instituted a sweeping reform program aimed at: breaking the various regional centers of authority and replacing them with his own imperial administration, cemented together through the universal use of German as the official administrative language; establishing a uniform, state-run educational curriculum in the empire, permitting learning in local ethnic languages but stressing German throughout; confiscating church-held lands, especially those attached to the seats of bishoprics and to monasteries, so as to transfer revenues from the church to the state; reforming taxes to maximize state revenues; as well as others in similar veins. His policies were well intentioned, for the most part, but proved severe and inconsiderate in practice. By attempting to modernize his empire swiftly, Joseph succeeded only in raising near-universal opposition to his government and to his person.[25]

The Romanians received few tangible gains from Joseph's centralizing reforms. By the close of his reign, the Transylvanian Magyar nobles were in revolt against them, and the nations generally ignored the regulations safeguarding the lot of the peasants. Before his death in 1790, Joseph was forced to repeal all of his reforms except those abolishing serfdom and establishing religious toleration. Ironically, though his efforts failed, Joseph's reign significantly strengthened the Habsburg monarchy by giving it a sense of regeneration and vitality. Moreover, his efforts made a lasting impact on the minds of those subjects in the empire who were not members of the aristocratic elites. The relationships between those two classes would never be the same after him as they had been before. For good or ill, a return to the pre-Josephine situation within the empire was unthinkable.

On the accession of Emperor Leopold II (1790–92), the Three Nations again returned to complete power in Transylvania. Romanian intellectuals there, most of whom were Uniate clergymen or products of Uniate cultural centers, sent a list of proposals to the new ruler in Vienna. That list, known as the *Supplex libellus Valachorum* (Representation/Petition of the Free Romanians), expounded a broad political program for the Transylvanian Romanians. In it the intellectuals, speaking on behalf of both Uniate and Orthodox, demanded constitutional equality for their people on an official par with the Three Nations. The *Supplex* included proposals that they thought would lead to the gradual incorporation of Romanians into the Magyar-dominated political oligarchy that controlled the principality through the diet, and they called for the end of anti-Romanian discriminatory practices in Transylvanian political and social life. The Saxons, beginning to fear the rising chauvinism evident among the dominant Magyar nobility, lent the Romanians tentative support.[26]

The *Supplex* marked the initial public emergence of a Romanian sense of what today can be called national consciousness. The process that led up to it was one that evolved out of the cultural frictions between societies representing the two European civilizations. It acquired definite shape through the Uniate experiment. Within a century of the Uniates' establishment, the Eastern European Romanians were transformed from a mute society of serfs and shepherds subservient to the will of Western European regional masters into a vocal class expressing "national" aspirations. The intellectual and cultural traditions forged by the Uniates became the foundation on which the modern, nineteenth-century Romanian nationalists would build, first in Transylvania and, from there, in the two Romanian principalities of Wallachia and Moldavia beyond the Carpathians.

In a process beginning with reaction to the reform efforts of Joseph II, building through events surrounding the French Revolutionary and Napoleonic wars, and maturing during the postwar period of official government repression under the impact of the Romantic Movement, modern nationalism emerged among the various ethnocultural groups within the Habsburg Empire by the fourth decade of the nineteenth century. Given their lengthy and successful resistance against Habsburg attempts to reduce them to docile, subservient subjects, the Magyar nobility were the first to manifest a sense of national consciousness in modern terms. Of those groups, the Magyar nation in Transylvania perhaps was the most developed. Unlike those of the Pannonian and Slovakian regions of Hungary, the privileged Magyars in the principality had retained the administrative use of their native Magyar language (while the others had officially adopted Latin), had refused to accept Habsburg rule after Mohács, and had managed to play an important, though technically semiindependent, role in major Western European affairs throughout the following 160 years. Even after the Habsburgs had gained direct control over Transylvania in 1699, the great anti-Habsburg rebellion of 1703–11, led by Ferenc II Rákoczi (Transylvanian *vajda*, 1704–11), and the concessions later wrung from Emperor Charles VI and Empress Maria Theresa in return for supporting their political policies, placed the Transylvanian Magyar nobles in the forefront of Hungarian national development. As we have already seen, that same period also led to the awakening of an ethnonational awareness among the lowly Romanians of Transylvania through the agency of the Uniate Movement, which had an unintended influence on all Romanians in the principality, whether partners to the union or not.

The Revolution of 1848–49 brought the essentially cultural friction between the Western Magyars and the Eastern Romanians into the open, cloaked in the mantle of conflicting nationalisms.

In the events over the two decades leading up to the revolution, Transylvania lay relatively quiet while important national developments occurred among the Pannonian Magyars. A liberal and national movement rapidly emerged, led by István Széchenyi. An individual moderate in his views, Széchenyi was primarily concerned with Hungarian economic and cultural matters. He envisioned a future Hungary economically developed along Western European lines. This would require the complete overthrow of all latent feudal vestiges, including noble privileges, and maintaining Hungary's unique position within a rejuvenated, progressive Habsburg Empire, which he saw as a large and potentially profitable economic unit. Since Hungary historically was a multicultural, multiethnic state, Széchenyi felt that it would be a grave mistake to alienate the non-Magyars by attempting to satisfy Hungarian national aspirations alone. Within his nationalist scheme for the future, multicultural toleration would assist economic well-being. Eventually, the non-Magyars would realize the benefits accruing from this arrangement, and they would willingly adopt Magyar nationality. He initiated his active political program in 1825 by using Magyar, instead of Latin, for the first time in the Hungarian diet.[27]

Opposition to Széchenyi's moderate program soon appeared. Led by Lajos Kossuth, the more radical Magyar nationalists demanded immediate reforms that would create a truly liberal Hungary completely independent of the Habsburgs. Kossuth's vision of the new Hungary was that of an exclusively Magyar nation-state, with no recognition of the national rights of its non-Magyar citizens. Through the radicals' newspaper that he edited, founded in 1841, Kossuth spread his chauvinistic propaganda and won numerous followers by his violent verbal attacks on the Habsburgs and on the non-Magyars living in the Hungarian lands. While Széchenyi and the moderates advocated an evolutionary approach in constructing a new Hungary, Kossuth and the radicals called for revolutionary measures. As the decade of the 1840s progressed, support among the Magyar nationalists perceptibly swung from the moderates to the radicals.[28]

Caught in the middle between the two nationalist wings was Ferenc Deák. Intellectually closer to the moderates than to the radicals, Deák called for a middle course, in which Hungary would be assured of an autonomous position within the Habsburg Empire as well as a modern, liberal parliamentary government. He played on the common interests held by both nationalist wings— extending the use of the Magyar language and retaining Magyar political dominance over the non-Magyars—to build a certain bipartisan liberal following.[29]

Elections for representatives to the lower house of the Hungarian diet in 1847 returned a majority of liberal-minded gentry. Deák proceeded to unite various liberal factions behind a compromise reform program, known as the Ten Points. Among the standard liberal policies advocated by Deák's program— responsible government, popular representation, freedom of the press, religious liberty, the right of public assembly, universal equality before the law, universal taxation, the abolition of serfdom with compensation to the landlords—there also appeared the political incorporation of all Transylvania into Hungary. The diet's lower house accepted the Ten Points, but the upper, composed of some 130 of the largest Magyar landowners, certain church prelates, and high officeholders, rejected them, thus forcing negotiations with the imperial government. By early March 1848 those talks had reached deadlock, when news of the February Revolution in France reached Budapest, sparking action by the Hungarian radicals. The news tipped the balance of nationalist support from Deák's centrists and Széchenyi's moderates over to them, and Kossuth immediately delivered a daring speech denouncing the reactionary regime established at the Congress of Vienna in 1815 and demanding responsible government for Hungary. His boldness inspired street demonstrations in Vienna that led to violence and clashes with imperial troops. The Revolution of 1848 in the Habsburg Empire had begun, and the radical Magyars were its vanguard and most outspoken proponents.[30]

With revolutionary fervor building, in mid-March the Hungarian diet's lower house adopted Deák's Ten Points, and they, thereafter known as the March Laws, essentially became the new Hungarian constitution. Although the upper house continued to oppose the program, Emperor Ferdinand I (1835–48) accepted it, as well as further Magyar demands, making Hungary an all but independent state, tied to the empire only through a personal union of the Habsburg emperor as Hungarian king. But having gained many of their nationalist objectives, the Magyars quickly learned that what was good for them was also considered equally as good by the non-Magyars living in the historic Hungarian lands. The Croats clamored for separation from Magyar rule and militantly moved to back up their nationalist claims; the Slovaks joined the Czechs in their Panslav efforts at the Prague Panslav Congress; and the Transylvanian Romanians raised demands for recognized rights under the newly adopted union of the principality with the rest of Hungary.

As revolutionary activity spread throughout the length and breadth of the Habsburg Empire and the German states, continuing into October, the radical Magyar nationalists made no secret of their desire to see the empire completely dismantled. Ferdinand unleashed Croat troops under Josip Jelačić in an invasion of Hungary, but they were defeated by the Hungarians. The victors, in turn, proceeded to invade Austria and advanced to within sight of Vienna before being turned back. In the midst of those heady events, the Transylvanian Romanians were forced to devise a strong nationalist program for themselves or risk losing completely any possible national recognition.

At the opening of the revolution in March, most Romanian intellectuals were in sympathy with the liberal views of the Magyar moderates and centrists as expressed in the March Laws. But the union of Transylvania with the rest of Hungary, and the obvious continued political dominance of the Magyars in that new situation, made the creation of a Romanian national organization imperative. Led by Simion Bărnućiu and Aron Pumnul, the Romanians attempted to call a Romanian national congress to accomplish that task, but they soon discovered that, although the March Laws ideally guaranteed freedom of public assembly in Hungary, in Transylvania the old Magyar-dominated political system remained in full force. Despite intimidation from the Magyar authorities, the first-ever Transylvanian Romanian national public assembly took place in April 1848. It resulted in the Romanians' movement from docilely accepting the union of the principality with Hungary to actively struggling to preserve Romanian national identity through autonomy within Hungary. Both Uniate and Orthodox were united in their dedication to the national program, though the Uniates successfully demanded that continued loyalty to the Habsburg house be made part of the national agenda.

At a second political assembly held just outside Blaj in May, thereafter known as the meeting on the Field of Liberty, the nationalist Transylvanian Romanian intellectuals and church officials expounded their national program, which they intended to submit to Emperor Ferdinand for approval. Its sixteen points included: recognition as an independent nation; the use of the national name "Romanian" instead of the ethnic one of "Vlah" or "Wallach"; proportional representation in the diet and in all government posts; the official use of the Romanian language in matters pertaining to Romanians; "acceptance" of the two Romanian churches on a basis equal to those already accepted, and their complete jurisdictional independence; abolition of serfdom, without landlord compensation; economic freedom; state support for Romanian schools at all educational levels; the standard liberal personal and group freedoms (press, assembly, and such); equitable taxation; a new constitution for Transylvania; and the postponement of the union of Transylvania with Hungary until the national political demands of the Romanians were met. These sixteen points, asserting the rights of Romanian self-determination in all human spheres of activity, became the fundamental framework for modern Romanian nationalism in the principality.[31]

The dominant Magyar liberals in Budapest refused to accept the Romanians' national program. Instead, they demanded that the Romanians relinquish their national goals and adopt those of the Magyars alone. Having taken that stance, they thereafter gave the Romanians little or no serious consideration. After all, Ferdinand had already sanctioned the union of

Transylvania with Hungary, and the Romanians were lowly, no-account peasants, who, furthermore, were not even Westerners but holders of an Eastern culture that they deemed inferior to their own. By the time they started to take the Romanians seriously in 1849, it was too late to conciliate them or to save the Magyars' revolution.

In December 1848 Emperor Ferdinand abdicated and was succeeded by Francis Joseph (1848–1916). The young monarch did not feel bound by any promises made to the Hungarians by his predecessor, and he was determined to bring those recalcitrant subjects back under his full imperial authority. Losing little time, Hungary was invaded by his military forces in January 1849 and Budapest was quickly occupied without a fight, but the Hungarians drove them out the following month. Thereupon, the emperor had the Austrian governing assembly dissolved and, in March, promulgated a new constitution for the empire as a whole, including Hungary, which was written by his powerful military adjunct, Felix Schwarzenberg. That document created a highly centralized government, a representative imperial diet, and a responsible imperial ministry. The emperor served as a provisional autocrat until the situation within the empire stabilized enough for the constitution to be implemented. There was no doubt that the new law was intended to goad the Hungarians into doing something rash. They did not disappoint the new emperor.

With that new turn of political events, the radical Magyar nationalists finally gained completely the upper hand in Hungary. In April the Hungarian diet proclaimed an independent Hungarian Republic, with Kossuth elected its governor-president. By that time, the Habsburgs' continuous military efforts against the Hungarians, though proving generally unsuccessful, were being aided in Transylvania by what amounted to a civil war pitting Romanians, led by Avram Iancu and assisted by Saxons, against Magyars and Székelys. The Romanians had moved beyond their sixteen-point national program to one demanding an autonomous Romanian national state within Transylvania. They had also established direct relations with Francis Joseph, who, thankful for their help against the common enemy, lent them a certain amount of limited support but no concrete promises.

The Hungarians' resistance proved so dogged that, in June 1849, the emperor was forced to accept an offer of military intervention from Russian tsar Nicholas I (1825–55) to help suppress the revolution. Caught in a pincers between invading Habsburg forces, including the anti-Hungarian Croats, from the west and Russian troops from the northeast, the Hungarian revolutionaries were forced into Transylvania with their backs against the proverbial wall. Simultaneously, a nationalist uprising against Hungarian rule erupted among the Serbs in Vojvodina. In desperation, the Magyars turned to the Romanians with offers to satisfy some of their national aspirations if only they would cease their resistance in the principality, the last bastion of Hungarian defense. They were rejected. Overwhelmed, the Hungarians were decisively defeated near the Banat town of Timişoara in August 1849, and the great Hungarian Revolution was finished. Kossuth fled the country for Turkey, and at Arad, in Banat, nine Hungarian revolutionary generals were hanged and four were shot.

What jubilation the Romanians may have felt regarding the outcome of the revolution was soon staunched by Habsburg policies. Dependency on foreign troops to overcome nationalist opposition to the imperial government caused a reassessment at the highest imperial level. In an effort to regain the position of a serious European Great Power, which had been shaken by the revolution, Francis Joseph was determined to centralize the empire by suppressing all nationalist movements, friends and foes in the revolution alike. A vigorous policy of Germanization was instituted. The Schwarzenberg constitution was suspended in 1851, and the empire was divided into five administrative districts ruled by German officials, who were backed by imperial troops and responsible directly to Vienna. Transylvania, Croatia, and Vojvodina-Banat became separate provinces, and their Romanian and Slavic inhabitants, who had been loyal allies in the recent revolution, were subjected to the same antinational fate as were the rebellious Magyars. This repressive, centralizing policy came to be known as the Bach System, after the imperial minister of the interior who carried it out, Alexander Bach.[32]

Despite such efforts, the Habsburg Empire continued to slide from Great Power status in a European world that was being transformed by nation-state politics. In October 1860 the emperor overthrew the Bach System and issued a diploma establishing a new federal constitution that gave wide autonomy to the various recognized "lands" under an imperial diet with limited powers. The Hungarians, realizing that this would remove permanently Transylvania, Croatia, and Vojvodina-Banat from their own land, opposed the diploma and demanded the restoration of their 1848 constitution. Francis Joseph thereupon issued a patent in February 1861 "interpreting" the previous diploma but actually advancing a new imperial constitution, which gave the German middle classes—the mainstay of the empire in the emperor's eyes—a disproportionate representation in a new bicameral imperial diet. Again the Magyars refused to accept the patent, and renewed negotiations with the emperor over the constitutional arrangement of the empire dragged on into 1866. By that time the Habsburgs had been overwhelmingly defeated by Bismarck's Prussia and decisively expelled from future German affairs in Europe. Desperate to salvage some semblance of continued strength as a European Great Power through forging lasting internal stability at any price, the imperial government was forced to come to terms with its most militant and intransigent national population. In October 1867 a compromise was reached with the Magyars. The empire was divided in half, with the Magyars receiving complete control over all the lands and peoples they historically claimed as forming part of the Hungarian Kingdom under the constitutional system they had devised in 1848. The rest of the empire fell to Austria, where the Germans were to dominate politically under the terms of the 1861 February Patent. The two virtually independent halves were loosely tied together by a personal union of the monarch and by common ministries of war, foreign affairs, and finance. The radically reorganized state was renamed Austria-Hungary and often referred to as the Dual Monarchy. In both halves the ruler—emperor in Austria, king in Hungary— governed through responsible ministries.[33]

While the Compromise *(Ausgleich)* of 1867 was seen as a victory for Magyar nationalism—the Magyars swiftly began governing their half of the empire as a veritable Hungarian nation-state—it was a major defeat for the non-Magyar populations inhabiting the territories placed under Magyar control. The new system officially terminated the long-standing autonomy of Transylvania. The unification of the principality with Hungary was the Romanian nationalists' worst nightmare. Yet, surprisingly at first, it seemed that, despite unification, the nightmare would not materialize.

The Hungarian Nationalities Law passed in 1868 augured well for the future of the non-Magyar national minorities in Hungary. It was the brainchild of József Eötvös, a liberal-minded Magyar statesman. He believed that the political and social aspirations of the non-Magyar nationalities in Hungary could be recognized and satisfied by granting them the same rights as Magyars under the law, permitting them to organize and operate their own schools and religious institutions, giving them a share in central and local governments, and furnishing them with unimpeded freedom to develop culturally and politically. The law on nationalities that he managed to have passed granted all of those things, but prohibited the non-Magyar nationalities from forming distinct territorial units within Hungary or from organizing nationally based corporations of any kind.[34]

Eötvös may have been a liberal but he was also a Magyar nationalist, who considered Hungary a unitary Magyar nation-state. The strict prohibition of non-Magyar national territorial units and corporations made his approach unworkable in the highly charged nationalist atmosphere within multinational Hungary. Non-Magyars found the Eötvös program unsatisfactory. But like it or not, faithful implementation of the Nationalities Law by the Magyars most probably would have averted the fatal nationalities problem Hungary faced until 1918.

For the Romanians in Transylvania, it is unlikely that the plan could have been implemented in an unbiased manner. The dominant Magyar politicians there were steeped in traditional cultural antagonism against them, and that feeling had been fanned into nationalist bigotry by the Romanians' anti-Magyar actions during the Hungarian Revolution. The liberal spirit of Eötvös found little sympathy among them, and that which may have been grudgingly accepted was soon abandoned. In Transylvania the period between 1867 and 1918 was one of near-constant cultural warfare, disguised in nationalist forms, conducted by the politically dominant Western European Magyars against the politically subservient Eastern European Romanians.

A policy of Magyarization was begun through which the Magyars hoped to assimilate the Romanians artificially. All inhabitants were required to have a knowledge of the Magyar language. This was reflected actively in the educational sphere. In the 1880s Magyar was made the compulsory language of instruction in the state schools. The state-run educational system did not teach any minority languages.

Magyarization also had an impact in the political sphere. By the late 1880s only 2 percent of close to a thousand officials employed in the more important branches of the Hungarian government were Romanian, and they were the lower-grade officials. In 1887 there was one Romanian deputy in the Hungarian diet, representing 2.5 million Romanians. When the lone Romanian later resigned, he was sent to prison for two years because of the passionate nature of his resignation speech. Soon after, in 1894, the Romanian National Party of Transylvania—founded in 1881 and the only political organization representing the Romanian minority in the country—was dissolved because the Magyar government pronounced it unconstitutional. By the outbreak of World War I in 1914, there were only eight Romanians among a total of 413 deputies in the Hungarian diet—in a country where only 54 percent of the total population spoke Magyar natively—at a time when 55 percent of Transylvania's population was Romanian. Since ballots were open in elections, voters were intimidated from casting pro-Romanian ballots. Government troops often were used against opposition parties and nationalities, and electoral bloodshed was common.[35]

The Magyar nationalist leadership manipulated the state judicial system against their counterparts among the non-Magyars. Political trials of non-Magyar national leaders became commonplace events. Many of the Transylvanian Romanian leaders were publicly ostracized for treachery, arrested, tried, and imprisoned on the slightest of charges. Just as in most cases of such repressive measures, the trials only served to create national martyrs and helped feed the fires of anti-Magyar sentiment among the minorities in the country.

A telling example of the deep-seated cultural animosity toward all other nationalities, whether Romanian or not, held by the radical Magyar nationalists who controlled Hungary during its final period of imperial existence was the answer given by a late-nineteenth-century prime minister to a question put him by a deputy in the diet: Why were non-Magyars not taught their national histories in the state schools along with that of the Hungarians? His reply: That was impossible, since there were no "national" histories other than of those who were Magyars in Hungary (!).[36] Such shortsighted chauvinism ultimately proved fatal for the Hungarians when they were defeated decisively in World War I.

Less than a month after the November Armistice ended the bloodletting of the Great War, Romanian nationalist leaders from Transylvania and Banat assembled in the Transylvanian town of Alba Iulia. On 1 December 1918 they voted for a union of those two regions with the Kingdom of Romania. True to their reputation as opportunists, the Transylvanian Saxons threw in their lot with the Romanians when it became obvious that the Magyars had lost the war. The Eastern European Romanians who had been adrift inside Western Europe for centuries had taken the definitive step of joining their independent cultural and national brothers on the far side of the Carpathians. For good measure, they brought part of Western Europe—the territory of Transylvania, with its numerous Western European Magyar and Saxon inhabitants—with them.[37]

From the time that the *Supplex libellus Valachorum* was presented to Leopold II in 1790 until the early twentieth century, Transylvanian Romanian nationalism basically had been aimed at gaining the same rights and privileges as the Three Nations enjoyed both within the principality and the Habsburg Empire as a whole. No active liaison was carried on between the Transylvanian nationalist leadership and their counterparts in the Romanian Principalities. This was so despite the fact that Romanian nationalism itself had originated among the Transylvanians, thanks to Uniate cultural and intellectual activities, whose Latinist-Roman traditions had filtered over the Carpathians into the principalities by means of economic and cultural (Orthodox) links and awakened the Romanians there. Few Romanians from either side of the Carpathians, however, seem to have given much consideration to the real differences that existed between their two nationalist traditions.

While the Transylvanian Romanians were struggling to gain recognized parity with other nationalities and social reform within the Habsburg Empire, those of the principalities, under heavy French influence, were concerned mainly with blotting out the Greek Phanariote legacy of their Ottoman past and looking to build a Greater Romania. During much of the pre-1914 Romanian nationalist period, most of the Transylvanians had no interest in the Greater Romania ideal.

Even after the 1867 Compromise, only a handful of Transylvanian Romanians sought closer relations with their Trans-Carpathian conationals. Most aimed at winning a national partition deal with the Habsburgs similar to that won by the Magyars. Moreover, at its core, Transylvanian Romanian nationalism was based on a policy of social reform for an essentially egalitarian society, which was incompatible with the highly aristocratic and essentially feudal form of nationalism that existed in the Romanian Principalities.[38]

Romanian King Karl I (1866–1915) started agitation among the Transylvanian Romanian nationalists for union with his kingdom before the outbreak of World War I. By signing the Triple Entente in 1883, he hoped to gain Transylvania in return for his participation. He thereafter began making anti-Magyar public attacks aimed at gradually separating Transylvania from Hungary through the efforts of its Romanian nationalists. Although the Magyar government did its best to suppress Karl's nationalist agitation efforts in the principality, Habsburg crown prince Francis Ferdinand, who despised and distrusted the Magyars, made secret promises to Karl involving the cession of Transylvania to Romania if Karl agreed to join his country to the Habsburg Empire. By the time war erupted in 1914, Karl's agitation among the Transylvanian Romanians was highly developed but largely unsuccessful.[39]

In 1916 the Romanians launched a militarily futile invasion of Transylvania. Their decisive defeat effectively knocked them out of the war until its late stages in 1918, when they seized the opportunity offered by a collapsing Austria-Hungary and again invaded the principality against little real opposition. This action proved the deciding factor in bringing about the Alba Iulia Assembly and the union of Transylvania to the Romanian Kingdom. When the war's victorious Great Powers sat down in Versailles' Trianon Palace to decide the fate of defeated Hungary in 1920, they recognized a fait accompli and awarded Transylvania to Romania as part of the settlement, comfortable in their self-assurance that the ideal of national self-determination of peoples had been served. On the ground itself, Hungarian military exhaustion (resulting from the war and the 1919 battles fought against the Slovaks and Romanians during the ill-fated Bolshevik regime of Béla Kun) and the Romanian military presence (they had even captured Budapest in suppressing Kun) ensured that the Trianon decision was implemented.[40]

⋈ ▷

Trianon's international sanctioning of the Alba Iulia resolutions, which proclaimed the union of Transylvania with Romania, brought what came to be known as the Transylvanian Question to center stage in intra-European foreign affairs.

By the terms of the treaty, Hungary was stripped of almost two-thirds of its former, "historic" territories, over which it had ruled for close to a millennium. With the territorial losses there went also over 50 percent of the country's former inhabitants, including a significant minority of Magyars. These reductions essentially created the situation that the Magyar nationalists had been demanding all along—an ethnically homogeneous Magyar nation-state, in which over 90 percent of the population belonged to the ruling national group. Yet the nationalistic Magyars declared the cost prohibitive and the process wholly unfair. They considered the Trianon borders of Hungary utterly artificial and imposed by force, and they became the most outspoken proponents of revising the Versailles Peace settlements in Europe. Their nationalistic slogan, *"nem, nem, soha"* (no, no, never), relative to accepting the Trianon borders as final, reverberated continuously and publicly throughout the country over the decades leading up to World War II.

The passionate, sometimes close to fanatical, opposition of the Magyar nationalists to the Trianon settlement serves as a good illustration of the cultural nature of Western European nation-state nationalism, with its innate human dangers. Nationalism linked solely to common ethnicity is meaningless. A Western-style nation-state is not the political manifestation of a particular group of people alone. Together nationalism and the nation-state encompass much more. They require linking a unique history that took place within a precise territory to a particular group of people. Without these two additional historical and territorial ingredients, there can be no nationalism or its political nation-state incarnation. Since nowhere in Europe, and especially in geographical Eastern Europe, have particular groups of people existed over time in territories completely isolated one from the other, nationalist conflicts among them are endemic. There is just too much historical and territorial overlap. Problems always exist regarding where to draw nation-state borders, and why. All parties involved in the process possess their own unique demographic, historical, and economic justifications—and only rarely do national neighbors agree with each other completely.

Thus, though Trianon Hungary ideally was as ethnically homogeneous as any nationalist could have desired, it was flawed as a true Magyar nation-state because it failed to include territories, also inhabited by Magyars, that had played continuous and important roles in the thousand years of Magyar history in Europe. For the Hungarians, Trianon was a blatant violation of Western European nation-state political culture and a national humiliation of the first order. Territories that formed parts of Hungary for centuries had been cut away by force and incorporated into neighboring, mostly newly created, nation-states that were anything but friendly to the Magyars. The Magyar nationalists' violently vocal and persistent reaction against the terms of Trianon caused fear among their neighbors, who had all benefited from large slices of former Hungarian territory handed to them by that treaty. In a series of agreements signed among themselves in 1920 and 1921, Czechoslovakia, Yugoslavia, and Romania, counting on French support, banded together in a political-military alliance bloc, termed the Little Entente, aimed at common protection against Hungary. Although the Great Powers took the alliance seriously for some years as a guarantor of regional stability, it had little practical results and succeeded only in further entrenching national bitterness between the two sides.[41] Frustrated in their revisionist claims and hemmed in on all sides with avowed national enemies, the Magyar nationalists slipped further to the political right during the 1930s, eventually tying themselves closely to Adolf Hitler's radically revisionist Nazi Germany.

While the Magyar nationalists ardently sought to reclaim all the territories and populations torn from "historic" Hungary by Trianon, no loss was more galling to them or more fervently disputed than that of Transylvania. Their attempts to gain international redress regarding the former principality began at Versailles in the negotiations leading up to the final treaty. They were actively continued through the Minorities Question Section of the newly constituted League of Nations' Secretariat, as well as through the national and international print media. The Magyar nationalists' unwillingness to let their Transylvanian cause subside from international notice forced the Romanian nationalists to respond in kind. The incessant public dispute between them soon became known as the Transylvanian Question. It lasted as an open diplomatic and media sore until Hitler attempted to force a compromise solution on the two sides in 1940; thereafter, the end of World War II and the subsequent submergence of both contending parties beneath the tide of communism hid the conflict below the surface of Soviet-imposed international socialist brotherhood.

Although from 1919 until 1940 both the Magyars and the Romanians poured mountains of statistical data relating to demographic, economic, and political issues into supporting their respective arguments, the heart of both sides' cases justifying their conflicting claims on Transylvania was historical. Summarized succinctly, the issue essentially centered on who entered Transylvania first, and how they developed the region for their group interests from that time on. The Versailles peacemakers actually had little interest in arguments over historical origins regarding Transylvania—they were already predisposed to favor their Romanian allies because of more immediate war-related commitments—but after the ink was dry on the Trianon Treaty the international community proved a more susceptible general audience. Viewed in as objective a fashion as possible (and this is difficult, since virtually everything written concerning Transylvania is highly biased toward one or the other side), the Magyars seemed to have advanced the sounder historical case, which was: From the eleventh century on, Transylvania was an integral part of Hungary; it was under Hungarian rule from the start, and it possessed a Western European culture. The start was King István I and all the territory that constituted his kingdom—lands collectively termed the Crown of St. István. While radically Magyar nationalist assertions that the lands falling under the crown were indivisible and that virtually all lands in which Magyars ever trod since István were Magyar for eternity may be considered extreme, their historical arguments concerning Magyar claims to Transylvania in particular had merit.

According to the Magyar case, when István moved into Transylvania in the early eleventh century, soon after his conversion to Roman Catholicism, and established it as an eastern defensive bulwark for his kingdom, the only occupants were a few Magyars who had settled there rather than with the main group in Pannonia. They were swiftly brought under István's control. Because the region was virtually uninhabited, troops to man the mountain defenses first had to be brought from Pannonian Hungary. Over the following two centuries, the numbers of the original Magyar frontier defenders were augmented by further Magyar immigrants and invited Székely (close Magyar relatives) and German (collectively called Saxon) colonists. By being the first European people to establish direct and continuous rule over an essentially uninhabited Transylvania, and then colonizing it, the Magyars claimed the territory as an integral part of their ancestral homeland in Europe. No evidence existed for the presence of Romanians in Transylvania prior to the thirteenth century, which indicates that they were latecomers to the region relative to the Magyars, and that they were seminomadic pastoralists who had slowly filtered across the Carpathian Mountains from their Balkan homelands in the south. That they were traditionally known as Vlahs, and that large numbers of wandering shepherds bearing the same name were to be found throughout the Balkans, helped support the Magyars' contentions. Furthermore, the Transylvanian Romanians held to the Orthodox version of Christianity, whose center also lay in the Balkans and the Byzantine Empire. The rest of the Magyar historical argument basically retold the story of Transylvania after Mohács, stressing the seminal part it played as the citadel of Magyar freedom during the Ottoman Turkish period as well as the region's role as last stronghold for the Magyar nationalists during the 1848–49 Hungarian Revolution.[42]

In terms of nineteenth- and early twentieth-century Western European nationalism, the Magyars' historical claim on Transylvania was both strong and just. They were able to augment it with equally sound geographical and economic reasoning. Geographically, Transylvania was surrounded on three sides by mountains, which constitute natural borders for the region. On its fourth, the western side, it lay open to the Pannonian Plain of Hungary, into which all except one (the Olt River) of its primary lines of communication flowed. Thus, Transylvania and Pannonia formed a geographical unit. This unity was reflected in the natural economy. Transylvanian trade and rich natural resources followed the geographical lines of communication westward to Pannonia, and the products of the two regions complemented each other— Transylvania sent its lumber, ores, and minerals to Pannonia in exchange for Pannonia's foodstuffs and manufactured goods. It had been that way for centuries. The Magyars claimed that severing the ties between the two regions amounted to crass economic disruption and possibly eventual ruin.

The Romanians' initial argument was predicated solely on their traditionally enjoying the demographic majority in Transylvania. It soon became apparent that a purely numerical justification for Romanian possession of the region could not stand up objectively against the Magyars' strong claims. The Romanians were forced to make a viable historic case to counter that of the Magyars.

To refute the Magyars' claims that they had formed the first political organization in Transylvania, the Romanians advanced the Dacian or Daco-Roman theory first expounded in the eighteenth century by Transylvanian Uniate intellectuals studying in the West. Very simply, the theory went as follows: Before Roman emperor Trajan conquered the region, Transylvania was the seat of a Dak state. Termed "Dacians" by the Romans, the conquered people intermingled with the occupying Romans for the 160 years the region served as an imperial province. When the Romans abandoned Dacia, they left behind a numerous indigenous Dak pastoral population that had become Latin-speaking. Those Daco-Romans weathered the numerous storms of invasion by Germanic and Asiatic intruders—various Goths, Huns, Avars, Bulgars, and finally Magyars—who swept through the region over the course of the fifth through ninth centuries, only to emerge under the Magyars as the modern Romanians. They survived by hiding in the densely forested mountains until the dangers had passed. When, with the coming of the Magyars in the ninth century, the invasions ceased, the fugitive Romanian inhabitants gradually moved down from their highland asylums into the lowlands; some eventually wandered southward into the Balkans, where they remained as the nomadic Vlahs. Thus the Romanians, and not the Magyars, were indigenous to Transylvania. The

Magyars were the latecomers who had usurped control of the region from its rightful population by force.[43]

This Daco-Roman theory of Romanian origins has been questioned by Magyar nationalists and third-party scholars alike. Except for the fact that the Romans had conquered the region of Transylvania from Daks and then turned it into an imperial province, every point involved in its argument has been contested. No historical sources have yet been uncovered supporting the contention of the Romanians' survival in the mountains during the long period of extremely fluid and disruptive Germanic and Asiatic intrusions. The theory rests mostly on the purely philological studies of the Transylvanian Uniates, who discovered that their native language was basically Latin in structure and phonetics, and on the presumed resemblance of headgear between that worn by eighteenth-century Transylvanian Romanians and that of second-century Daks as depicted on Trajan's Column in Rome. Nineteenth-century Romanian nationalists glibly drew a connection between the two and began calling themselves Romanians instead of their ethnic name, Vlahs. Out of that unsubstantiated connection, the Daco-Roman theory was born. So tenuous has it been from its inception that even past noted Romanian historians discredited the argument.[44]

If the Daco-Roman theory is laid aside, the Romanian historical case for Transylvania amounted to the region's role as fountainhead for modern Romanian nationalism itself. The Uniates had created a cultural and intellectual tradition in the eighteenth century that had filtered across the Carpathians into the principalities and had awakened the Romanians living in them. To the Romanian mind, it seemed only just that the region that had spawned and led the rise of nationalism among them should form part of a Romanian nation-state. But again, the logic of the argument was flawed, since it failed to account for the distinct differences in the nature of the nationalisms between the region and the principalities.

In terms of countering the Magyars' geographical and economic cases, the Romanians once again found themselves at a disadvantage. Their only course lay in weakening their opponents' arguments, since they could not be utterly discredited. Attempting to undercut the Magyar notion of geographical unity, the Romanians asserted that the Bihor Mountains, which directly faced the Pannonian Plain, could furnish as good a western boundary for the region as did the Carpathians in the other directions. They argued that, economically, the Magyars' two natural riverine lines of communication between Transylvania and Pannonia were actually unnavigable except for rafts, and that the region's system of roads was not centered on Budapest but on the Romanian Principalities through seventy-six passes in the Carpathians. By implication, therefore, the mountain borders oriented Transylvania's economy to the south and east, rather than to Pannonian Hungary in the west.[45]

Despite their weak historical, geographical, and economic arguments, the Romanians enjoyed a single advantage in the post-World War I Transylvanian dispute with the Magyars—the victorious Great Powers had ruled in their favor at Versailles—and that factor decisively overrode all others. Having favored the Romanians on the Transylvanian issue as part of an overall policy of punishing defeated enemies for the war and of crippling their capabilities for causing future wars, England, France, and their assorted postwar allies stubbornly refused to make any major modifications of their Versailles decisions. They politely listened to the Magyars' numerous arguments brought before the League Secretariat's minorities section, sometimes publicly spoke of reconsidering certain points in the Trianon Treaty, and then did nothing. Eventually their tenacious adherence to the Versailles settlement backfired because the rise of revisionist Nazi Germany proved that the very policy on which the system rested was fatally flawed.

It came as no surprise that the Magyar nationalists, rejected by the League upholders of Versailles and its Trianon corollary, allied themselves to Hitler, the most vocal and effective European adversary of the Versailles settlement. Ironically, the Romanians, who had every reason to support the status quo imposed by Versailles, also gravitated into Hitler's German camp as a result of long drawn out internal political and economic turmoil caused by rabid anti-Semitism and deep class conflicts that were expressed through contentious native fascist, Christian Rightist, and peasant movements, as well as of a German-Romanian economic treaty (1939) that had bailed out Romania's faltering economy. As it happened, Hitler needed both Hungary and Romania to secure his plans regarding a German-dominated Eastern Europe. A faithful Hungary would ensure that Central-Eastern Europe remained subservient to his will, since the Hungarians were known to be itching for the chance to revise the Trianon borders with their neighbors by force, and he alone had the power to keep them at bay. Romania was a source of much-needed petroleum supplies, which Germany lacked, and a potential source for manpower when Hitler finally turned his attentions toward the Soviet Union.[46]

Unfortunately, those two useful allies were at loggerheads over the issue of Transylvania. In fact, following Hitler's June 1940 victory over France and his subsequent forcing of the Romanians to relinquish Bessarabia to the Soviets, as stipulated in the 1939 Ribbentrop-Molotov Pact, the Hungarians were on the verge of invading Romania and conquering Transylvania by force. Desperate to head off the conflict, which could threaten the precious Romanian oil fields, and with no troops available in the region to intervene, Hitler decided to mollify the Magyars by imposing a compromise solution to the Transylvanian Question. On 30 August 1940, after negotiations ordered by Hitler between Hungary and Romania had failed, their ambassadors were summoned to Vienna. Without discussion, a partition of Transylvania was dictated to them by Hitler, his minister Joachim von Ribbentrop, and Italy's foreign minister, Count N. G. Ciano. Known as the Second Vienna Award, the dictate gave the northern two-fifths of Transylvania, including the Székely region in the extreme southeast, with a population of some 2.5 million people (52 percent of whom were Magyars), to Hungary.[47]

Although Hitler considered the matter settled, and the two protagonists had no choice but to accept his dictate, the Vienna solution solved nothing. Besides the fact that the partition of the region made no geographic, economic, or political sense, neither the Magyars nor the Romanians considered the award anything but a temporary settlement that would be worked out in full once Germany won the war. Its immediate result was the disaffection of both German allies, whose cultural-national hatred for each other was only intensified by the acquiescent face they were forced to wear in public. Unfortunately for the Magyars, the award was nullified by the German defeat in World War II. Romania, true to its World War I form, defected again at the end of 1944 to the anti-German allies and received all of Transylvania as a reward.

With the end of the war, the Communist conquest of both Hungary and Romania effectively put an end to the Transylvanian Question as an open intra-European issue. Moscow, through Comecon, imposed "international socialist solidarity" throughout most of the East European region that ultimately fell under its sway in the years following 1948. Transylvania disappeared from the pages of the international news media, as the world turned its attention to matters involved in the cold war: the 1948 Berlin airlift, and Tito-Stalin split; the 1956 disturbances in Poland and the even more dramatic Hungarian Uprising; the 1960 Sino-Soviet split; the 1968 Warsaw Pact invasion of Czechoslovakia; and the 1980 Soviet invasion of Afghanistan and the Solidarity Movement in Poland. Yet the conflict between Western European Hungarians and Eastern European Romanians in Transylvania had not ceased; it merely went underground, where it has continued to simmer ever since.

The Transylvanian cultural-national conflict continues to simmer below the surface because, far from solving the problem in the region, Trianon did little more than reverse the situations of the two major protagonist populations.

A Magyar dominance over Romanians was replaced by a Romanian dominance over Magyars. What followed makes a sad commentary on the ability (or willingness) of groups of people to heed important and useful lessens taught by history.

It seems startlingly ironic that peoples who have suffered extended, often centuries-long, periods of cultural-national discrimination at the hands of other peoples seem to forget how terrible a fate that truly is once they succeed in attaining a position of dominance over others. Former national minorities usually prove as bad, if not worse, to their own minorities, and especially so if those minorities were formerly the national majorities who persecuted them when they were in power. The only lessons taught a people by oppression, it seems, is how to oppress in their turn when given the opportunity to do so. This is another of the many negative by-products of nationalism and the nation-state. And if the national animosities also reflect civilizational differences, the situation is intensified. One need only consider the state of affairs between Serbs and Muslims in Bosnia; Greeks or Bulgarians and Turks in Thrace; Jews and Arabs in Israel and the Occupied Territories; Lithuanians, Latvians, or Estonians and Russians in the Baltics; Armenians and Azerbaijanis in Nagorno Karabakh; among many examples, to realize the dangers inherent in such situations.

By the terms of Trianon, the territory of Transylvania given to Romania housed approximately 5 million inhabitants. Of those, some 57.5 percent were ethnic Romanians, while Magyars and Székelys together constituted about 25.5 percent and Germans around 10.5 percent. The remaining population was composed of small groups of Jews, Bulgarians, Serbs, Ruthenians, and a smattering of others.[48] In governing the province, the Romanians were to prove just as chauvinistic and shortsighted regarding the non-Romanian minorities as the Magyars had been in the past.

At first, after Trianon took effect, the Transylvanian minorities, especially the Magyars, hoped that the historical and cultural differences, and often strained relations, that existed between the Romanians of Transylvania and those of the old Romanian Principalities of Wallachia and Moldavia (often called the Regat) would preserve them from ultranationalistic Romanian control. But this hope quickly proved in vain. The minorities were socially and economically stronger than the native Romanians, who, in turn, viewed that situation as posing a threat to their cultural-national superiority within the nation-state. Their reaction was to implement programs that would weaken the minorities and strengthen themselves.

Forced to sign the Minorities Treaty, which the Versailles peacemakers had made a prerequisite for all the friendly recipients of territories cut out of the old Habsburg enemy, the Romanian government in Bucharest responded by eliminating Transylvanian Romanian governing institutions and placing the province's administration into the hands of officials from the Regat. Minority officials were systematically weeded out of their posts through special job evaluation tests. Once the administration of the province was safely under central control from Bucharest, the educational system was attacked; schools became tools for Romanianizing the Transylvanian minorities, with Romanian-language classes receiving the most attention by the teachers. Numerous church and private schools were seized by the government, and many others were closed on the most specious of pretexts. There then followed systematic personal attacks on minority individuals and local communities. Beatings and imprisonments of non-Romanians became commonplace. A few reports of such conduct reached the world outside Romania; especially telling were those written by American Unitarians investigating the conditions of non-Orthodox churches in Transylvania. In one Unitarian report, when a Romanian army officer was told that coercion and suppression of schools and other minority institutions would be ruinous to Transylvania, he was quoted as replying: "Better a ruined province which the Romanians own than a prosperous one owned by others."[49] Published official responses by the Romanian government to such reports proved weak and unconvincing.

Romania's oppressive treatment of minorities in Transylvania most often went unnoticed by the outside world because of the sugary facade of the country's laws. The 1923 constitution was a model of liberal-democratic ideals. It guaranteed minority rights, proportional representation in government, and freedom of religion, education, and national organization for all peoples in the state. The law itself was good; its enforcement was not. Romanian officials bullied the minorities living in their respective districts and showed utter contempt for the laws they were sworn to uphold. At first, the corruption that permeated the Romanian government proved useful for the minorities, who found that bribery could help have the laws enforced. But as time went on, and the older generation in politics died out, their younger, more efficient, and yet more chauvinistically nationalist replacements not only cut down on corruption but increased the injustices toward the minorities.[50]

The Agrarian Reform begun in 1920 also was an outwardly progressive policy that was used as a means to discriminate against non-Romanians in Transylvania. The reform was certainly needed in the Regat, where traditional feudal great landowners literally lorded it over the abjectly poor peasant masses. In Transylvania it was given a different twist. It proved to offer an excellent means for depriving the minorities of their much-needed land. Traditionally, the religious denominations supported themselves through the profits derived from the lands they owned. Likewise, the school system of Transylvania was denominational, and also was supported by the churches' land profits. By expropriating church lands and handing them over to mostly Romanian peasants, the government both weakened the national aspirations of the minorities, which were intimately linked to their denominational faiths and their related schools, and, at the same time, gained direct control of minority education. Thus the Agrarian Reform was a financial, spiritual, and, perhaps most important, cultural blow to the non-Romanian—Western—minorities in Transylvania.[51]

This discriminatory situation played a leading role in keeping the Transylvanian Question alive throughout the interwar period in Eastern Europe by providing the Magyars with the ammunition to keep up their strenuous efforts at obtaining revision of Trianon. Following World War II the Romanians' anti-Magyar policies continued, but the Hungarians were placed in an ideological straitjacket by Soviet-enforced East Bloc solidarity in publicly responding to the situation. Anti-Communist Magyar emigrés attempted to keep the issue alive in the international media from their refuges in Western Europe and North America, but it was given low priority and little serious attention by a world preoccupied with the superpower politics of the cold war.[52] Finally, the extreme cultural-national anti-Magyar policies of Ceauşescu in the late 1970s and throughout the 1980s proved more than the socialist Hungarian government could tolerate in silence. With the coming of glasnost and perestroika in the Soviet-led East European world, the Hungarian government and various Hungarian intellectuals and nationalists openly protested in 1988 against Ceauşescu's plans for bulldozing Hungarian villages in Transylvania and the forced relocations of their populations into high-rise cities in regions outside the province. Persecution of Magyar Calvinist and Unitarian churches, repositories of the Magyars' senses of cultural and national self-identities in Romania, resulted in open street demonstrations in December 1989 that sparked the Romanians to overthrow the Ceauşescu regime and bring an end to Communist control—at least technically—over the country.

But the reforms that followed the fall of Ceauşescu soon were shown to be similar to those that came after Trianon. The Christmas Revolution meant change for the benefit of Romanians, not for the minorities. The Magyars learned that lesson within three months of the revolution they had inspired, when their demonstrations for equal rights under the new "reforms" resulted in police crackdowns and the deaths of Magyar demonstrators. Once again repression ruled in Transylvania, and that repression has continued. The cultural-national conflict that has plagued the region for centuries thus continues to seethe, waiting either for some dark moment in the international scene to spring to life once again or for some courageous leaders, Magyar or Romanian or both, to overcome cultural-national hatreds and formulate truly enlightened, tolerant political structures that recognize the cultural value of all sides involved in the issue by transcending narrow nation-state mentalities.

THE MACEDONIAN QUESTION

Current international borders
Historic Macedonian boundary (Bulgarian claim)
Approximate Greek claims
Approximate Serbian claims
Approximate area claimed by Greece and Serbia

0   10   20   30   40   50
Miles

MACEDONIAN MISCHIEFS

● ○ ●

In 1993 the United States sent a small detachment of troops into the former Yugoslav republic of Macedonia. The publicly avowed purpose of their dispatch was participation in a United Nations effort to prevent the warfare raging since 1992 in the Bosnian and Hercegovinian territories of former Yugoslavia from spreading deeper into the Balkans.

The immediate problem was that the Serb-Muslim conflict appeared likely to spill over into Serbia's southern province of Kosovo, which lay directly north of the Macedonian border, where Muslims enjoyed a huge demographic preponderance but the small Serb minority maintained its political and social control essentially through armed force. Tensions between the two peoples had risen in Kosovo throughout the 1980s, beginning with Muslim student demonstrations in 1981, and had erupted into outright violence in 1989, when the ultranationalist Serbian government of Slobodan Milošević curbed the autonomous status of the province and brought it under direct Serb control. The fundamental East European (Orthodox)–Islamic (Muslim) civilizational conflict that characterized the Serb-Bosniak warfare in Bosnia-Hercegovina was intensified in Kosovo by the additional explosive factor of nationalism. The Kosovo Muslims were ethnically Albanian and could look to the neighboring nation-state of Albania for inspiration in their resistance against Serb nationalist pressures (unlike the Muslims of Bosnia-Hercegovina [Bosniaks], who were ethnically mixed Serbs and Croats). The Orthodox Serbs considered Kosovo the medieval birthplace of the Serb nation—the site of Raška—and thus indispensably and perpetually a part of any Serb nation-state, no matter the ethnic composition of its population.

Muslim Albanians were not confined to the Serb province of Kosovo in the former Yugoslavia but also were found within the confines of Macedonia. Like Kosovo, Macedonia's western neighbor was Albania, and a significant Albanian population inhabited regions within its western and northwestern borders. Although a certain amount of tension was expressed between the Muslim Albanian minority and the Slav majority when Macedonia declared its independence from Yugoslavia in 1991, this soon was soothed by the establishment of a multiethnic governing cabinet, which gave representation to the Albanians and even to the Muslim ethnic Turks living in the new state. Calmed though they may have been by the political arrangement, tensions between Muslims and Christians in Macedonia did not disappear, nor did the national affinity of the Muslim Albanians toward their conationals in Albania and, perhaps more important, in Serb-dominated Kosovo.

It was within the cultural-nationalist Muslim Albanian-Orthodox Serb context of Kosovo that the United Nations, with a high profile given to the participation of a few hundred United States troops, intervened in Macedonia in 1993 with "peacekeeping" military forces. Smarting somewhat from a perceived lack of leadership and will among the international community regarding the human rights debacle in Bosnia-Hercegovina, the United States drew its "line in the sand" on the northern border of Macedonia facing Serbian Kosovo. American public opinion regarding the move was mollified by official statements that, though the size and risks of the intervention were small, the benefits were great. By taking up positions some two hundred miles southeast of Sarajevo, the focus of virtually all Western media attention, the small American military contingent was safely removed from both the fighting on the ground in Bosnia-Hercegovina and intense media attention, while their very presence served to guarantee peace in the center of the Balkans by deterring any future spread of the cultural-ethnic violence, especially should it erupt again in Kosovo. The government's case for the American intervention thus emphasized low risk to American lives and high gains in keeping the Bosnian conflict localized. As a result, there was little serious public questioning in the United States of the Macedonian intervention, and it received brief and routine notice in the American media.

A rather obvious question regarding the United States' small military intervention in Macedonia could have been raised publicly, had the public not been ignorant of the region's history. The necessity of intervention itself could not have been doubted—it was a needed preventive measure against a very real danger (which still exists). Rather the nature of the potential danger posed by Macedonia and the possible risks involved in facing it required honest questioning. There were a number of generally known intimations that the

Macedonian intervention might not prove so risk-free in the long run as the government's public justifications implied. One came from the fact that, unlike the other breakaway states of former Yugoslavia, Macedonia did not receive speedy international recognition of its independence. Only Bulgaria, soon followed by Turkey, immediately extended this acknowledgment to the newly proclaimed state in 1991. Highly vocal Greek opposition, centered on the "Greekness" of the name "Macedonia" itself, prevented UN recognition of an independent Macedonian state until early 1993, when it was finally admitted to its own seat only by means of a technicality regarding its official name as the "former Macedonian republic." Following the UN step, independent Macedonia began to receive formal recognition from individual states within the international community, including the United States.

Another hint that Macedonian intervention might not be as simple as publicly implied formed part of the official U.S. government explanation of its motives. While emphasizing that the intervention would help keep the fighting in the former Yugoslavia localized in Bosnia-Hercegovina, it was added, usually in a somewhat perfunctory fashion (a technique that often succeeds in diverting serious media scrutiny), that failure to do so ultimately might result in the outbreak of hostilities over Macedonia involving all of the Balkan states, as well as Turkey, which, in turn, could lead to civil war within the North Atlantic Treaty Organization (NATO) because Greece and Turkey, both NATO member states, would align themselves on opposite sides. Despite the obviously catastrophic scenario painted by such a statement, there was surprisingly little public demand for an elaboration as to why it was a likelihood and what the U.S. role would be if the intervention failed in its objectives and such a conflict did erupt. Relieved that American lives were not being placed into immediate jeopardy in Bosnia-Hercegovina, the general public in the United States blithely accepted an American military intervention in Macedonia, a region with a recent history so volatile and filled with such explosive violence and vitriolic nationalist passions that it earned the title of "powder keg of the Balkans."

⊁⊀ ⊁⊀

Between the years 1870, when the Ottoman Turks granted recognition of a separate Bulgarian Orthodox church organization within their empire, and 1948, when Tito's split from Stalin effectively ended the last efforts at constructing a viable South Slav political federation, the "Macedonian Question" was one of Europe's most burning and consistently violent national problems. While the intrinsic civilizational conflict between Orthodox Eastern Europe and

Islam played an important role in the earlier period of the Macedonian may-
hem, the problem essentially centered on deep-seated factional clashes among
three East European societies—Bulgarians, Greeks, and Serbs—each struggling
to create for themselves a modern, Western European-style nation-state in a
region only slightly larger in size than the state of Vermont, where they lay
in such close geographical contact with one another that their ethnic frontiers
intermingled. So confused was the ethnic picture of Macedonia, and so nationally xenophobic were the efforts of all three parties in the dispute over its ownership, that most of the region's Orthodox inhabitants eventually opted to assume
a completely separate ethnic identity—that of Macedonians—in hopes of
finding escape from the constant pressures on them to bend to the national wills
of the main contenders. Thus a fourth player—one that had never truly existed
before the late nineteenth century—entered the nationalist fray, further com-
plicating an already complex problem.

Since modern European Romantic nation-state nationalism demands historic
and linguistic continuity within a given territory, all of the sides laying claim
to some or all of Macedonia as an integral part of their nation-states were forced
to advance justifications for the righteousness of their assertions. In true
Romantic fashion, they all traced their claims back to some distant pre-
Ottoman Turkish Balkan past, whether ancient or medieval. Also in line with
Romanticism, none of the contenders for Macedonia was above creating fictional elements to fill gaps in the more verifiable historical record of its argument, usually with the express purpose of refuting specific claims made by one
or more of the other players in the nationalist dispute. As a result, virtually every
point raised by all of them in their historical arguments became a matter of
intransigent dispute.

It could not have been otherwise. As all good historians know, history
itself is not a matter of immutable facts, cut in stone and forever unchanging.
Instead, it is essentially a matter of interpretation of known facts, changeable
with the advent of new facts or interpretive perspectives. So long as the
method of interpretation of the facts is flexible enough to account for newly
uncovered facts, but consistently objective, the resulting history at least can
be considered viable. The major problems in history nearly always stem from
disputed interpretations of known facts—what was the meaning of these or those
things or events, or why did they come about as they did—rather than from
the facts themselves. Any process so utterly dependent on human interpretation grounded in honest objectivity as is history lays itself open to misuse and
corruption. Nineteenth-century Western European Romanticism not only
founded the modern forms of interpretive historical study by its emphasis on
discovering the origins of European peoples, but it also guaranteed that his-

tory became one of the most important and dangerous political tools available, once it was linked with nationalism and the nation-state. Nationalistically biased historical interpretations of the past, and even outright fabrications of pasts that possess no objective proofs, have become the sources of conflict among disparate nations and the justifications for the crassest of national policies. The interpretive nature of history thus points to an innate, humanly disruptive flaw in the nationalist nation-state political culture that the West has given to the rest of the world. The Macedonian Question provides one of that flaw's most telling examples.

The nationalist quagmire that Macedonia became was rooted in the late-nineteenth century conjunction of two historical developments in the Balkans. First there was the inexorable reality of Ottoman Turkish decline. In the fourteenth and fifteenth centuries the Turks had stormed out of their Anatolian homelands and conquered nearly all of Southeastern Europe, destroying or incorporating in the process all of the then-existing Orthodox East European states in the region—the Byzantine Empire, Bulgaria, the Morea, Serbia, Bosnia, and the Romanian Principalities. As a theocratic Islamic state, the Ottoman Empire imposed on its subjugated Christian peoples a sociopolitical system that erased official recognition of group identity along ethnic lines in favor of religious criteria. Through the institution of the religious *millet,* Christian and Jewish subjects were administered directly by the church hierarchies of their respective faiths and granted a certain amount of autonomy by their Turkish masters regarding cultural expression and local self-government. So long as those non-Muslims did not denigrate or impinge on the dominance of the rulers' Islamic precepts and paid the taxes, both regular and extraordinary, levied on them by the Muslim government, they were free to worship in their faiths openly, to conduct native cultural activities, and to control their mundane local affairs. No matter where they might live within the general confines of the Ottoman state, non-Muslims were identified and governed strictly by their respective *millet* organizations. With no ethnic or territorial restrictions operative within the empire, non-Muslim ethnic groups often lived intermingled with one another, especially in the border areas that separated the traditional native habitats of differing ethnic groups.[1]

So long as the Ottoman Empire remained both internally and externally strong, the lot of its non-Muslim subjects was far less onerous than that experienced by subjects of analogous status in Christian European states of the time. They enjoyed official religious toleration, freedom from serfdom, local self-government, and the benefits of trade and commerce. Gifted and ambitious non-Muslims, no matter the social position into which they were born, had the opportunity to rise in Ottoman society as far and as rapidly as their talents and skills afforded, though this usually required them to compromise their faith and forgo their personal freedom (which, within the context of Ottoman realities, proved a small price to pay for the vast political power and personal wealth that were the possible rewards). But when Western European technologies, especially in weaponry and transportation, brought a halt to Ottoman expansion and under-cut its economy beginning in the second half of the sixteenth century, the com-plex internal structure of the Turkish state, which was predicated on continuous military victory against foreign enemies and on control of the main East-West trade routes, began to unravel. Over the course of the seven-teenth and eighteenth centuries, the empire experienced a progressive break-down in law and order: The once-vaunted Ottoman military gradually crumbled into ineffectiveness and anarchy; the authority of the central gov-ernment declined; inflation ran rampant; corruption permeated all sociopolit-ical institutions; and Muslim religious xenophobia emerged. All of this had a deleterious effect on the lives of the empire's non-Muslim subjects, especially Christians, who increasingly bore the brunt of the internal decline through exor-bitant taxation; arbitrary and violent attacks by Muslim authorities, anar-chists, and fanatics; and infringements on both their personal and their local political freedoms.[2]

After nearly two centuries of increasing internal Ottoman disintegration, the second historical development involved in the Macedonian Question came into play within the empire—the non-Muslims' importation of Western European concepts of nationalism and the nation-state. Two of the primary contenders for Macedonia—the Greeks and the Serbs—were also the earliest of the Ottomans' non-Muslim subjects to be exposed to nationalism. The third—the Bulgarians—formulated their national aspirations later and, in the process, sparked the Macedonian Question.

⟶⟨ ⟩⟶

Almost from the very beginnings of their subjugation by the Turks in the fif-teenth century, the Greeks enjoyed a certain privileged station within the Ottoman world that was unique among all the empire's non-Muslim sub-jects. This was partly explained by the respect that the Turks held for the Byzantine Empire that they had destroyed, which in its final years was virtu-ally a Greek state, and partly by the Turks' lack of skills and inclination in fields lying outside those expressly involved in the pursuit of land warfare and in

Islamic cultural activity. When the Turks captured Constantinople in 1453 and Greek Morea soon thereafter, they recognized that their newly acquired Greek subjects possessed a highly developed and sophisticated culture (which the Turks soon set to imitating in efforts aimed at assimilating various of its elements into their Islamic culture) and long-standing commercial, economic, and naval skills (which the Turks found extremely useful). In creating the Orthodox *millet* in 1454, Ottoman sultan Mehmed II the Conqueror (1451-81) placed that largest and most important non-Muslim administrative imperial institution in the hands of the Greek Patriarchate of Constantinople, which essentially gave that Greek patriarch more secular power than the office had ever enjoyed under the Christian Byzantine Empire. In his efforts at transforming the formerly Christian imperial capital of Constantinople into the Muslim imperial capital of Istanbul, Mehmed spared the captured city from sacking and invited the Greeks in the city's population to remain—eventually turning over to them a living quarter of their own, the Phanar (lighthouse) district, that, significantly, lay along the shore of the city's thriving commercial harbor, the Golden Horn.[3]

Possessing a history that stretched back to ancient times, the Greeks' peninsular and island environment had shaped among them a culture that was highly adapted to seafaring and maritime commerce. The Greek residents of the Phanar, collectively known as Phanariotes, many of whom were scions of old Byzantine nobility and merchant families, and the Greek merchants of Thessaloniki soon established their hold over Ottoman maritime commercial and military activities. Ottoman naval military forces, which until the seventeenth century ruled the eastern Mediterranean Sea, essentially were manned by Greek sailors (along with a few North Africans), and the supreme naval commander was nearly always a Greek. Greeks dominated the Ottoman merchant marine until the early decades of the nineteenth century, and they were able to extend their commercial activities even to land-based endeavors, easily overcoming competition from Jewish and Armenian traders. Although the mass of Greek peasants and shepherds who inhabited the mainland Greek peninsula remained as poor and as downtrodden as those of their non-Greek Bulgarian, Serbian, or Romanian *millet* compatriots, by the eighteenth century the Phanariote and Thessaloniki Greeks essentially controlled the domestic and international economic life of the Ottoman Empire, and they constituted its wealthiest single group of non-Muslim subjects.

Phanariote and Thessaloniki Greek wealth and knowledge of worldly affairs outside the confines of the empire brought them influence and power. Their unique position enabled them to monopolize the office of Greek patriarch, the single most important non-Muslim religious-political post, since it controlled the Orthodox *millet* and represented all of the Orthodox Christians in the state, whether Greek or otherwise, to the Turkish central government. Only they of all the non-Muslims had the financial wherewithal to pay the huge bribes to Turkish authorities necessary for acquiring the patriarchal office, as well as for all of the subordinate church offices in the upper Orthodox hierarchy. Their wealth also permitted them to purchase the princely thrones of the Wallachian and Moldavian principalities after the Turks' desperation for cash became so acute in the eighteenth century that the Ottoman government was forced to sell those positions to the highest bidders. Their knowledge of the world outside the empire made the Greek merchant families invaluable to the Turks as a source of intelligence regarding Western European and Russian developments, and they predominated in the Ottoman "ministry" of foreign affairs as diplomats and interpreters. The Turks' head of foreign affairs was nearly always a Greek.

By virtue of their commercial and political position, the Phanariote and Thessaloniki Greeks maintained direct and near-continuous relations with Western Europe and Russia. Greek trading colonies were established throughout Central-Eastern and Western Europe by the beginning of the eighteenth century, and by the end of that period Ottoman-Russian treaties had opened the Black Sea to them as well. In establishing a permanent Greek presence outside the borders of the Ottoman state, the Greek trading colonies served as channels through which Western and Russian ideas flowed into the empire and spread among the powerful Greek merchant class. By the turn of the eighteenth century, such foreign ideas were permeated increasingly by Western nationalist concepts. Fertilized by an eighteenth-century revival of neoclassical interest in the West, which idealized the ancient Greek past and sparked widespread activity in publishing Greek-language texts, and abetted by Napoleon's attempted continental blockade against England, which further opened the door to Greek commerce in Europe and extended the Greeks' shipping volume and income, the Greek merchant colonists evolved into the nationalist vanguard for their brothers within the Ottoman Empire.[4]

The Greek nationalist movement began among the colonists and expatriates in the cultural sphere, with Adamantios Koraïs's creation and standardization of a modern Greek literary language and Evgenos Voulgaris's efforts to retrieve the Greek classical past. But under the heady influence of Napoleonic France and the efforts of the rest of Europe and Russia to suppress it, the Greek nationalists in the trading colonies turned to political revolutionary activity. Beginning with the founding of the Society of Friends *(Philike hetairia)* in the Ukrainian Black Sea port of Odessa by Greek traders in 1814, secret revolutionary societies soon sprang up in numerous Greek merchant colonies throughout Europe. With the defeat of Napoleon, the Greek revolutionaries turned to Orthodox Russia for support of their plans, especially since one of their number from Corfu, Ioannes Capodistrias, had been appointed Russia's foreign minister by Tsar Alexander I (1801–25).[5]

Though nationalist ideas filtered among the Phanariotes within the Ottoman Empire from the Greek merchant colonies abroad, the cultural aspects found far greater acceptance among them than did the revolutionary. After all, those Greeks had a vested interest in preserving Ottoman society as it stood. They controlled the Orthodox *millet* and dominated the empire's economic and foreign affairs. Their position of power and influence was such that they stood head and shoulders above all other non-Muslim subjects in the empire. All important *millet* administrative positions were in their hands. Their language reigned supreme throughout the Balkan Orthodox world, to the point that Greek threatened the more native Church Slavonic literary languages of the Orthodox Bulgarians and Serbs. Rejecting the revolutionary aspects of nationalism, the Ottoman Phanariote Greeks embraced the cultural-linguistic ones, which reinforced among them an already existing discriminatory sense of Greek cultural-ethnic superiority over all other non-Greek—mostly Slav—Orthodox members of the *millet* under their control. This, in turn, led to a deeply rooted anti-Greek ethnic reaction among many non-Greek Orthodox believers in the empire that later evolved into outright national hostility once they, too, espoused the concepts of nationalism themselves.

In 1821 a Greek nationalist revolution against Ottoman rule erupted when the agitation of the Greek Black Sea merchants for action against the Turks coincided with Russian imperialist aims at dominating the Balkans and opening the Mediterranean to Russian naval activity. A Russian invasion force, led by a Greek general, Alexander Ypsilantis, and including a Greek *hetairia* contingent, unsuccessfully attempted to take control of the Romanian Principalities, which the Greek nationalists mistakenly considered Hellenized by a century of Phanariote rule. However, they had failed to realize that, to the Romanians, who had suffered greatly at the hands of those Phanariote rulers, the Greeks were a greater enemy than were the Turks. Though a failure, news of the Ypsilantis episode sparked a rebellion among the oppressed Greeks in the Morea, who conducted an initially successful guerilla war against the divided and weak Ottoman forces in the region.[6]

The Turks' first reaction to these developments was to hang the Greek patriarch from the gate to his cathedral in the Phanar. They then set about finding the military wherewithal to crush the Greek rebellion. In 1824 the Turks called in Egyptian troops, the only effective military forces left in the empire, to quell the uprising on the mainland. In the midst of the fighting, the Greek rebels fell into squabbling among themselves. As Egyptian successes against the Greeks mounted, Western Europeans, imbued with philhellenic sympathies and by then in the throes of the Romantic Movement, grew fed up with the slaughter of fellow Christians in Greece by "infidel" Muslims. Western volunteers (including the poet Byron, who died in Greece) streamed into the region to fight on the side of the rebels, whom they mistakenly considered the direct descendants of the classical ancients. Public opinion in England, France, and Russia eventually overcame the then-current concept of nonintervention in revolutionary wars implicit in the Concert of Europe policy established in 1815 at Vienna. Those three states dispatched fleets to the eastern Mediterranean, and in 1827 their combined intervention brought the destruction of the Egyptian-Ottoman fleet in Navarino Bay, effectively resulting in the Greeks' complete independence from the Turks in 1829.[7]

The new Greek nation-state was in size a far cry from that envisioned by most Greek nationalists. The British, in an effort to obstruct any pan-Orthodox support the Greeks might lend to Russia's imperialist goals in the Balkans, limited the state to little more than the Morea and the region of Athens. With thousands of ethnic Greeks remaining outside the borders in areas ardent nationalists considered historically Greek, there arose a powerful irredentist movement among them known as the Great Idea *(Megale idaia)*. In its more tempered form, the Great Idea called for the incorporation of all the Greek-inhabited Aegean and Ionian islands, as well as the territories lying north of the 1831 border on the mainland. In its more extreme and demagogic form, the Great Idea called for the restoration of the Byzantine Empire as the natural Greek nation-state, whose borders could be defined by territories in which the Greek language dominated within the Ottoman Orthodox *millet*. In its least imperialist form, the Great Idea encompassed the regions of Epiros and Thessaly, which were predominantly inhabited by Greeks. It also demanded the region of Macedonia, which possessed an ethnically mixed population, of which Greeks, Bulgarians, and Serbs predominated.[8]

Unlike the Greeks, the Serbs and Bulgarians did not enjoy advantageous sociopolitical positions within the Ottoman Empire. Both had possessed independent medieval states and Orthodox church organizations of their own that had been destroyed by the Turks' advance into Southeastern Europe over the fourteenth and fifteenth centuries. After 1454 both eventually were placed by their Turkish conquerors under Greek ecclesiastical-administrative control within the Orthodox *millet*. By the close of the sixteenth century, the native Orthodox Serb and Bulgarian aristocracies had been eliminated, by their assimilation into the Ottoman provincial warrior class, which resulted in their conversion to Islam and, thus, removal from the Orthodox *millet,* by death, or by emigration outside the borders of the empire. With the disappearance of their native leadership classes, the subject Serbs and Bulgarians were reduced to the lowest rungs of the Ottoman social ladder—to that of non-Muslim *reaya* ("the flock," in the context of human "sheep" who were protected and fattened so that they could be shorn for the benefit of their Turkish "herders"). Their sole purpose within Ottoman society was to produce the taxes, goods, and services necessary for sustaining the Islamic military-administrative structure of the empire with the least direct involvement of their Muslim Turkish masters, who thus were free to devote their own time to military, administrative, and pleasurable activities. Because lucrative Ottoman commercial endeavors were conducted mostly by the empire's Greeks, Jews, and Armenians, supplemented by a few outsiders such as Croats from the city-republic of Dubrovnik, Serbs and Bulgarians existed almost exclusively as peasants, craftsmen, and local merchants. Fortunately for both peoples, the complex web of the Ottoman socioeconomic system imposed on them offered opportunities for developing new social elements that ultimately would play leading roles in throwing off Islamic Ottoman domination once they were exposed to and indoctrinated by Western European concepts of modern nationalism.

Although the rank of non-Muslim *reaya* was the humblest in the Ottoman social system, not all of its members were equally inconsequential in status. In return for providing a variety of services that the Turks were unable or unwilling to perform themselves, groups of *reaya* were given corporate recognition by the Ottoman government and granted certain privileges not enjoyed by the rest of the non-Muslim *reaya* class—freedom from assorted special taxes, levies, or personal prohibitions that applied to the others. Services in the countryside that carried such privileged recognition included breeding and supplying livestock (for either food or transportation) for the Ottoman military and the capital at Istanbul, ore and precious metal mining, road and bridge maintenance and protection, and serving as local militia guarding mountain passes against bandits on important lines of military and commercial communications. Groups of Serb and Bulgarian peasants who served in such capacities grew wealthier and more locally independent over time than did the mass of their conationals, who remained outside the privileged ranks. In towns and cities Serb and Bulgarian artisans and local merchants were integrated into the Ottoman guild system, which extended to them all of the socioeconomic benefits enjoyed by that economically important sector of society, while the *millet* institution permitted them to retain their native Orthodox self-identities. By the late eighteenth century, the Serb and Bulgarian rural corporate service groups and urban artisans and local merchants had begun to coalesce into new middle-class sectors for their respective populations. It was they who were first exposed to nationalist ideas emanating from the West and who provided the leadership in the Serb and Bulgarian nationalist movements of the nineteenth century.[9]

While the sociopolitical lot and the socioeconomic development of both Serbs and Bulgarians were similar in most respects, there were some important differences. The root of that distinction lay in the geographical locations of the two peoples within the Ottoman Empire. Because of their position along the northern Balkan borders of the empire, the Serbs enjoyed weak but continuous contact with the West through Dalmatia, the Croatian military border, and across the Danube frontier. Despite the frailty of such direct contact with the outside world, the proximity of the border guaranteed its continuity. Outside influence on the Serbs increased over time as Ottoman power peaked in the sixteenth century and began sliding into noticeable decline. Beginning in the late seventeenth century and building thereafter, Western and Russian influences from across the Danubian border grew among the nascent Serb middle class of privileged rural service groups and urban guildsmen. The Bulgarians, situated deep within the borders of the empire, lacked such close contact with the world outside, so their nationalist development was retarded chronologically, and the original Western intellectual inspiration for it reached them primarily through Greek and Serb filters.

⋊ ⋉

The rise of modern Western-style nationalist sentiment among the Serbs was linked to events that occurred in the Ottoman Orthodox *millet* during the mid-sixteenth century and to the Habsburg-Ottoman wars of the late seventeenth. When the Orthodox *millet* was established in 1454, the medieval Serbian Orthodox church, with its independent Patriarchate of Peć (Ipek), was subordinated by the Turks to the Greek Patriarchate of Constantinople and reduced to the status of an archbishopric. In 1557 Mehmed Sokollu (Sokolović), a Serb who had been "collected" as a youth in the Ottoman child levy *(devşirme)* and had risen to the position of grand vezir, the second-highest office in the empire after that of sultan, successfully had the Serbian church recognized as an autonomous organization within the Orthodox *millet* (hence the title archbishop-patriarch for its head, seated in Peć). As such, the church was staffed primarily by Serbian clergy and was insulated against direct Greek cultural and ethnic control. As the decline of the empire became more apparent and oppressive during the seventeenth century, the Peć Serbian church grew increasingly sympathetic to Habsburg military efforts against the Turks in the Balkans. In the 1680s Habsburg forces penetrated deep into

Serb-inhabited regions of the empire and the Serbian church overtly expressed its pro-Habsburg sentiments. But the Westerners proved unable to make their inroads into the empire permanent. When they withdrew north of the Danube, the Serbian church was left exposed to harsh Turkish reprisals for its support of the Western enemy. In 1690 Peć archbishop-patriarch Arsenije Černojević fled the empire for the Habsburg Empire's Vojvodina region just north of the Danube. He was followed by some 180,000 of his Serbian flock.[10]

Habsburg emperor Leopold I (1657–1705) extended the Habsburg military border system into Vojvodina in 1699, and he granted the Serb immigrants, whom he relished as new border guardians, numerous privileges, the most significant of which was autonomy for their Orthodox church. (In 1713 an independent Serbian archbishopric was established in the Vojvodina town of Sremski Karlovci.) As members of the military border organization who possessed a recognized autonomous church, the Vojvodina Serbs were free to develop their native Orthodox East European culture within the Habsburg Western European world, while they also enjoyed unhindered exposure to the intellectual movements current in the West and, through their Orthodox church connections, Russia. Despite occasional frictions with their Western European Austrian and Hungarian hosts, the Serbs inside the Habsburg Empire developed an East-West European intellectual alloy that eventually would constitute modern Serbian nationalism.

That merging of the two cultural streams took place primarily within the ranks of the Orthodox church, from which it was spread to the Serbian lay believers, first in Vojvodina and then southward across the Danube among those in the Ottoman Empire. In the Orthodox world monasteries traditionally played the leading role in cultural, intellectual, and educational life. The Muslim Ottoman conquest of Orthodoxy's Balkan heartland only served to strengthen that situation. In the Serb monasteries founded after the immigration in Vojvodina's Fruška Gora Mountains, the Serbs' pre-Ottoman history was rediscovered by the monks in original studies written by Western and Russian authors. They passed their reawakened sense of the Serbian past on to the Vojvodina Serb community and subsequently disseminated it to the Ottoman Serbs, either directly across the Danube or through the multiethnic monastic communities of Mount Athos in the southern Balkans, with which all Orthodox communities maintained close and continuous contact because of its prestigious tradition of Orthodox cultural leadership dating back to the ninth century. Even after the influence of the Vojvodina Serbs' religious leadership was diminished by the increasingly powerful attraction among them of Western secular ideas and learning, and after the autonomy of the Peć Serbian church within the Ottoman Empire was abolished in 1766 and Greeks placed in charge, Serbian Orthodox monks continued to play an important role in wedding Western nationalist concepts to Eastern cultural realities.[11]

Dimitrije (Dositej) Obradović, a Fruška Gora monk who had grown discontented with the artificial Church Slavonic literary language used by the church and the limited number and intellectual scope of books available to the Serbs through that written medium, sparked the Serbian national revival at the end of the eighteenth century. His outspoken public dismay with the Serbs' church-led cultural position resulted in his being defrocked and in his subsequent extensive travels throughout Western Europe, where he imbibed the latest ideas of the Enlightenment and rationalism. Upset with the paucity of secular works written in a vernacular understandable by most Serbs, Obradović proceeded to create an exclusively Serbian literary language (which, unfortunately, was artificial, despite all of his best but emotionally charged efforts) and to produce both original works and translations expounding his anticlerical, rational, and Enlightened concepts for the education of his fellow Serbs.[12]

At the turn of the eighteenth century, Obradović's work of Serbian national revival was taken up inside the Ottoman Empire itself by Vuk Karadžić, a Serb goatherd who had received a monastic education. By that time the Vojvodina Serbs' century of exposure to Western and Russian ideas, culminating in Obradović's Westernizing efforts, had sparked in them a growing sense of modern national self-identity. In 1804 an uprising of Serbs inside the empire erupted in reaction against the arbitrary and anarchistic rule of the local Turkish governor of Belgrade and his Janissary garrison. The rebels were aided by the Ottoman central government, which armed them to assist in bringing the Belgrade anarchists back under government control. The Serb rebels were led by Djordje Petrović, a prosperous pig dealer whose large size and swarthy complexion earned him the nickname of Karadjordje (Black Djordje), and whose profession and former experience as a sometime bandit won him support among the Serbian middle and renegade classes. Karadžić joined one of the rebel bands as a secretary to its commander.

The Serb rebellion attracted much support among the Vojvodina Serbs, who sent significant volunteers and supplies to Karadjordje. The emigré Serbs also attempted to establish a military alliance between the Serbian rebels and Russia, which went to war against the Turks in 1806. Karadjordje's rebels captured Belgrade in the same year. Soon the influence of the Westernized Serbs north of the Danube had transformed the Serbian rebellion from an armed attempt to reestablish legitimate Ottoman rule over the Serb-inhabited territories of the Ottoman Empire into a revolutionary struggle for Serb independence. When the Russians signed an armistice with the Turks in 1807, however, the Serbs were left facing the full brunt of available Turkish forces.

Reprieved by renewal of the Russo-Turkish war in 1809, the Serb rebels found themselves abandoned when their Russian allies were compelled to sign the Treaty of Bucharest in 1812 so that they could face Napoleon's impending invasion. Once again left to the mercies of the Ottomans, the Serbs fell into internal disarray and the Turks reoccupied their rebellious territories in 1813. Both Karadjordje and Karadžić fled the empire for safety in the Habsburg Empire, and the Serbian uprising was temporarily stifled.[13]

Vuk Karadžić made his way to Vienna, the Habsburg capital, where he fell in with Jernej Kopitar, a young Slovene scholar working to awaken ethnic-national sentiments among his fellow conationals in the Habsburg Empire. Both men were heavily influenced by the early Romantic ideas that were then emerging in the West. Karadžić swiftly collected and, in 1814, published a collection of Serbian folk songs and stories that proved an immediately popular success. So impressed was he by the simplicity and directness of the common language used by the Serb peasants that he turned his full attention to Serbian philology. By the time he produced an expanded, four-volume edition of his original folk collection in 1824, Karadžić had devised a refined and accurate Serbian Cyrillic literary language that reflected the vernacular realities of his fellow Serbs. And because he used as his linguistic foundation the Hercegovinian dialect, which essentially represented a transitional bridge between spoken Serb and Croat, Karadžić's reforms ultimately became the basis for the modern conception that there existed a common Serbo-Croatian language, with all of the nationalist connotations that this entailed. Despite the violent opposition of the Serbian Orthodox church, which defended the linguistic priority of Church Slavonic, Karadžić's reformed literary language eventually won acceptance among all the Serbs by the time of his death in 1864.[14]

While Karadžić was setting off on the road to creating the literary foundation for modern Serb national self-identity, events among the Serbs in the Ottoman Empire proceeded apace. In 1815 they rose again against the Turks. This time the Serbs were committed to establishing their complete independence from direct Ottoman control. Karadjordje was still in Western exile, so his place as rebel leader was taken over by Miloš Obrenović, a middle-class individual with an abiding personal hatred of Karadjordje, whom he accused of poisoning his half brother in the past. Through dogged military leadership, astute diplomacy, and highly refined bribery of Turkish officials, Obrenović won recognition from the Turkish government as prince of an Ottoman province of Serbia in 1817. When Karadjordje returned and voiced opposition to Miloš's seemingly pro-Turkish approach, he was assassinated by Obrenović's supporters, sparking a deadly blood feud between the two future Serbian royal families that would plague Serbian politics into the mid-twentieth century. By the terms of the Treaty of Adrianople (Edirne) in 1829, which ended yet another Russo-Turkish war (1828–29), the Serb province of Belgrade was recognized as an autonomous state within the Ottoman Empire, governed by a hereditary princely family, the Obrenovićes. The Ottoman sultan formally recognized the autonomous Principality of Serbia the following year.[15]

Over the course of the forty-eight years that separated the initial nationalist victory of 1830 and the recognition of a completely independent Serbian nation-state in 1878, the Serbs consistently agitated to expand the Balkan territories of their principality at the expense of the Turks and of other Orthodox Slavs as well. Among them there emerged a powerful nationalist program borrowed from that originally formed by the Croats in the Habsburg Empire—that of a large South Slav (Yugoslav) federation—with themselves, by right of primacy in first gaining independence from their foreign rulers, as the leading element. Within the parameters of such a federation, the Serb nationalists espoused the goal of re-creating a Greater Serbia that would encompass all of the Balkan territories once held subject to the medieval Serbian state at its height under Stefan Dušan in the mid-fourteenth century. For the most part, the Serbs and their nationalist program were supported on the European international scene by Russia, which considered them a useful tool in its own diplomatic efforts to further its own imperialist ambitions in the Balkans at English, Habsburg, and French expense.[16]

The outbreak of an anti-Ottoman revolt in Bosnia-Hercegovina in 1875 provided the Serb nationalists with their first real opportunity to throw off Ottoman suzerainty entirely and to commence expansion of the Serbian nation-state. It also opened the lid on extremely terse European Great Power rivalries. In 1876 Serbia, in conjunction with the Serb-inhabited autonomous state of Montenegro (which remained outside of Serbia proper under its own prince and which had its own pretensions to leadership in a future, united Greater Serbia), declared war on the Turks in aid of the rebels and in hopes of acquiring the two rebellious Ottoman provinces. Russia publicly and materially expressed its support for the Serb move, which resulted in England intensifying its efforts to preserve intact what was left of the declining Ottoman Empire in Europe, so as to foil any increased Russian presence in the strategically crucial Balkans that might be gained by a Serbian victory. The Habsburgs, removed from German affairs in Europe by the Prussians in 1866, now sought to validate their Great Power status by dominating the Serbs and by expanding their empire into rebellious Bosnia-Hercegovina. They too could not afford to permit the Russians a strong foothold in the Balkans.[17]

The international crisis sparked in 1876 by the Balkan rebellion and war seemed calmed when the Serbs were crushed. England was able to call an international conference in Istanbul to force reforms and a new, Western-style liberal constitution on its Turkish allies. Events, however, that earlier in the year had occurred in the Ottoman Bulgarian provinces, and the Turks' subsequent inability to abide by the new constitution, led to the outbreak of a new Russo-Turkish war in 1877–78, in which the Russians were spectacularly victorious. In efforts to head off a major Anglo-Russian European war that the Russian victory appeared to promise, Bismarck invited all the European Great Powers to Berlin in 1878 for a congress to mediate the crisis. At that meeting, Russia's Balkan allies in the war—Serbia, Montenegro, and Romania—were given their complete independence from the Turks. The Serbs, additionally, were permitted to retain some of the territories in southeastern Serbia that they had won after renewing their war effort in 1877, and the Habsburgs were permitted to occupy Bosnia-Hercegovina. The most fateful decision taken at Berlin, however, was the dismantling of the large, independent Bulgarian state that the Russians had forced the Turks to recognize in the 1878 Treaty of San Stefano, which had ended the original hostilities. This was done at England's insistence to prevent Russia from gaining a permanent Balkan presence through a Bulgarian puppet state that could dominate the Bosphorus and Dardanelles straits. Such a presence would, in turn, provide Russia's Black Sea fleet with the ability to threaten England's most direct line of sea communications with India by way of the eastern Mediterranean.[18]

Although rewarded at Berlin with full independence and additional territory, the Serbs left the congress bitter and frustrated. The Habsburg occupation of Bosnia-Hercegovina made the future incorporation of those provinces into a Greater Serbian nation-state highly problematic. After 1878 the Serbs were forced to concentrate on expanding to their south, into a region that their traditional ally, Russia, had handed to the upstart Bulgarians at San Stefano but that had been returned to Turkish control at Berlin. As far as the Serb nationalists were concerned, it was unthinkable that the region could be held by any nation-state other than their own, since it had formed the central core of the great medieval Serbian state of Dušan. The region in question was Macedonia.

✄ ✄

Lying at the center of the Balkan crisis of 1876–78 were the Bulgarians, whose late-blooming nationalist movement furnished the pretext for the Russo-Turkish War of 1877–78, its fateful Berlin settlement in 1878, and the consequent explosion of the Macedonian Question.

The Bulgarians had been among the first of the Southeastern Europeans to fall under Ottoman control in the late fourteenth century, and they were among the last to acquire independence from the Turks in the late nineteenth. During most of that five hundred-year period, they essentially remained cut off from the world outside the borders of the Ottoman Empire, except for mostly circuitous religious cultural contacts with fellow Orthodox Russians, primarily by way of the multiethnic monastic community on Mount Athos and of wandering monks, who traditionally visited Russia in search of alms for their brother houses inside the empire. Located in the very heart of the Ottoman Balkans, far from the empire's borders and in close geographical proximity to the Ottoman capital at Istanbul, astride all the vital overland military, administrative, and commercial lines of communications between the capital and its outlying European provinces, the Bulgarians were perhaps the most completely subjugated non-Muslim European population in the empire.

The Bulgarians shared the sociopolitical and socioeconomic fate of the Serbs—membership in an Orthodox *millet* that was controlled by ethnically foreign Greeks; the loss of their traditional native aristocratic leadership class; incorporation into the Ottoman *reaya* peasant and urban guildsmen classes; and the gradual emergence of a middle class from the ranks of the "privileged" elements created by the general Ottoman social system—but they faced additional challenges to their ethnic self-identity. Because of their strategic geographical situation, the Bulgarians were forced to accept into their midst large numbers of Muslim Turkish colonists, who were settled by the Ottoman central authorities both to guarantee the dependability of traffic along the overland communications lines through the Bulgarian provinces and to repopulate Bulgarian territories that had suffered demographic devastation during the continuous warfare that characterized the fourteenth century in the southeastern regions of the Balkans.

The continuous presence of numerous Muslim Turks among the Bulgarians created certain pressures for their assimilation into the Islamic community that other non-Muslim populations of the empire did not experience. Having far fewer Turks settled among them (and most of those almost exclusively were relegated to urban centers), these other groups did not have to deal firsthand with Muslims on a daily basis in both the countryside and in the towns. Mundane familiarity with Turks provided the Bulgarians with a continuous comparative yardstick by which they could measure their own sociopolitical and socioeconomic situations against those of their Muslim neighbors. Over the course of the five centuries of Ottoman rule over them, hundreds of Bulgarians found the comparison unacceptable and took to local anti-Ottoman banditry and rebellion. On the other hand, thousands of Bulgarians weighed the differences and opted for the advantages offered by conversion to Islam, despite the fact that such an act removed them from the Orthodox *millet,* with which

Bulgarian ethnic self-identity, like that of all other non-Muslims, was linked. Conversion to Islam transformed the Bulgarian converts into "Turks" within the *millet* context. The conversion process was aided by the widespread popularity among the Muslim colonists of syncretic, mystical *derviş* orders, whose Islamic beliefs and rituals often appeared to resemble the corrupted forms of folk Orthodox Christianity practiced by the mostly illiterate, uneducated Bulgarian peasant masses. Lacking direct contacts with the world outside the Ottoman Empire, the Bulgarians were forced to depend on their Orthodox faith almost exclusively for the strength to resist the continuous threat-in-being to their ethnic self-identity.

In 1394 the Turkish conquerors abolished the independent Orthodox church of the second medieval Bulgarian state, with its Tŭrnovo Patriarchate, and handed it over to the Greek patriarchate. The oldest Bulgarian church in the Balkans, the Archbishopric-Patriarchate of Ohrid, established in the late ninth century under the first medieval Bulgarian state, suffered a less drastic fate than that of Tŭrnovo. Although Ohrid retained its autocephalous status after the Ottoman conquest of the region, and the title "Bulgarian" remained attached to the office of archbishop-patriarch until 1767, when its autonomy was finally abolished and it was placed under the direct control of the Greek patriarch in Istanbul, nearly all of the clergy staffing its hierarchy were Greeks during most of the Ottoman period. Unlike the Serbs, who through circumstance managed to retain control of their church's hierarchy into the eighteenth century, the Bulgarians found themselves relegated to the lowest clerical-administrative positions in the religious institution that represented their interests to the Ottoman government through the Orthodox *millet*. By the seventeenth century, a noticeable ethnic animosity had developed between Orthodox Bulgarians and Greeks, which soon began to spill over into the cultural realm.

Suffering under Turkish social and Greek religious domination, any cultural reinforcement of Bulgarian ethnic self-awareness rested in the grassroots efforts of Bulgarian monks and priests to preserve a sense of Slavic identity among their conationals through Orthodox literary and educational endeavors. Within the field of church literature, the Bulgarian clergy succeeded in shaping a new Bulgarian literary language that reflected the vernacular more closely than did the fossilized Church Slavonic, in which an increasing number of secularly tinged but still religious works were produced. Beginning in the seventeenth century and increasing thereafter, church schools were opened in Bulgarian towns and villages that taught literacy in the new language to a growing number of artisans, local merchants, miners, and livestock traders who were evolving into a true Bulgarian middle class. When the Bulgarian monk Paisii, at Hilendar Monastery on Mount Athos in 1762, produced the first highly fictionalized modern history of the Bulgarians, the earlier cultural efforts of the Bulgarian lower clergy had prepared the way for that work's sparking the national awakening of the middle-class Bulgarians in the early years of the nineteenth century.[19]

Paisii Hilendarski produced his Bulgarian history in the new Bulgarian literary language to combat the intense cultural threat to Bulgarian identity that he perceived posed by the combination of Greek domination of the Orthodox *millet* with increasing Greek pretensions to ethnic cultural superiority. In his fervent effort to provide his fellow Bulgarians with a glorious history of their own, Paisii turned to Byzantine and Russian source materials available in the monastic libraries on Mount Athos. Not satisfied with what he found, Paisii traveled to the Vojvodina Serb monasteries of Fruška Gora, where he consulted Croat sources and Croat translations of Western histories, as well as further Russian works, before returning to Athos and completing his important task. Afterward, he wandered throughout the central Balkans discussing his manuscript with fellow Bulgarian monks and having copies of it made for further dissemination. Thus began the Bulgarian national revival.

It was a quiet beginning to say the least. Paisii, a humble individual, did not mind if his name did not appear on the many copies made of his work. (It was not until the late nineteenth century that the Bulgarians generally recognized him as the father of their national movement.) By the opening of the nineteenth century, Paisii's history had made an impact on the Bulgarian middle-class artisans and merchants, many of whom had by then associated themselves with Greek commercial enterprises both inside the Ottoman Empire and in the Greeks' Black Sea merchant colonies. They began investing some of their newfound profits into secular education for the Bulgarians (the first modern Bulgarian secular school was founded in 1835) and supporting book printing in the new Bulgarian literary language that would disseminate Western Enlightened, liberal, and nationalist concepts among their population. (All of the presses were located outside the Bulgarian provinces of the Ottoman Empire because the Turks rightly feared the nationalist import they would have on the Bulgarians; the most prolific Bulgarian printing and publishing center was Istanbul.) By the middle of the nineteenth century, a large sector of the Bulgarian middle class was committed to pursuing a nationalist agenda aimed at both religious independence from the Greeks and political independence from the Turks.[20]

Two approaches to a Bulgarian nationalist program emerged as a result of the dual nature of the Bulgarians' subordinate situation. One was evolutionary, in that the first goal was to win official religious separation from the Greeks within the context of the empire's Orthodox *millet,* after which that success

could be parlayed into political autonomy, ultimately leading to fully independent nation-state status. The other took a revolutionary road that used the
successful Serbian and Greek uprisings as models to be followed and that looked
to Orthodox Russia (and, secondarily, Orthodox Serbia) as the source of outside support. Of the two, the evolutionary approach enjoyed the earliest and
strongest support among the early Bulgarian nationalists.

The Bulgarians felt the cultural ramifications of the rise of Greek nation-
alism in the late eighteenth century in the increasing efforts made by the
Greek patriarchate to entrench Greek cultural superiority within the Orthodox
millet. After the successful Serbian and Greek national revolutions, Greek-
language schools were established in association with all the seats of high
Orthodox prelates throughout those regions still lying within the borders of the
Ottoman Empire, and the upper church clergy exerted pressure on the
Orthodox members of the *millet* to attend. Non-Greeks in the church hierarchy were forced to become Hellenized if they hoped to advance inside the religious administration. The Bulgarians constituted the single largest non-Greek
ethnic component in the Orthodox *millet* by the middle of the nineteenth century, and the growing Hellenization process had its affect on the increasingly
influential Bulgarian middle class. So associated with the Ottoman ruling
establishment had the Orthodox *millet* become that Hellenization came to signify acceptance into the ranks of those who counted in Ottoman society,
politically, culturally, and economically. Ironically, some of the leading early
nineteenth-century Bulgarian middle-class nationalists often spoke and wrote
Greek in their personal lives while, at the same time, they called for the
expansion and elevation of Bulgarian language and education in public.
Hellenization was so pervasive in nineteenth-century Bulgarian society that
less Grecophone Bulgarians readily believed rumors of Greek prelates' willful destruction of Bulgarian works of literature and art, whether the tales had
any basis in fact or not.[21]

As secular education expanded among the Bulgarians, the Greeks' pretense
of cultural superiority served to consolidate a nationalist effort to throw off Greek
millet authority completely. Bulgarian religious nationalism received a boost
from an unexpected quarter when, in 1856, the Turks issued a reform edict—
the *Hatti Hümayun*—that included an article for the reorganization of the *millets*.
An Orthodox church council met in 1860–62 to discuss the reorganization, but
the Bulgarians were underrepresented and failed to win the right to elect their
own native bishops. Wealthy Bulgarian merchants in Istanbul, realizing early
on that the council would not provide for a Bulgarian church free of Greek control, announced in 1860 that the Bulgarians would no longer recognize the
authority of the Greek patriarch or of his fellow Greek subordinate prelates.

With this notice, the Bulgarian Church Question, the opening phase of the mature Bulgarian national movement, was launched.

A bitter decade-long conflict between Bulgarians and Greeks began within the Orthodox *millet*. It was from the start a nationalistic dispute. No doctrinal positions were involved. The Bulgarians demanded a church of their own— in essence, a separate Bulgarian *millet*—that would define, in Ottoman terms, the geographic extent of a Bulgarian national territory, while the Greeks viewed the Bulgarian demands as a threat to Hellenism and the future inclusion of Hellenized territories in an enlarged Greece based on the Great Idea and centered on a re-Christianized Constantinople. Over the course of the church struggle, the Bulgarians toyed with French Catholic and American Protestant missionaries, who had entered the Ottoman Empire in hopes of gaining Bulgarian converts. But despite the national-cultural assistance lent by the American Protestants in developing a reformed form of a modern Bulgarian literary language, the Bulgarian nationalists viewed all of the missionaries as pawns in forcing Russia to influence the Ottoman sultan in their favor by playing to Russia's Orthodox and imperialist fears. The ploy worked. Concerned that the Bulgarians might renounce Orthodoxy in favor of those foreign faiths, and thus remove themselves from Russian influence, in 1870 Nikolai Ignatiev, the Russian ambassador to Istanbul, forged a compromise solution to the church issue. When that effort failed because of the Greek patriarch's intransigence over a minor technicality, Sultan Abdul Aziz (1861–76) issued an imperial decree recognizing an independent Bulgarian church—the Bulgarian Exarchate—with jurisdiction over large tracts of three regions within the empire—Bulgaria, Thrace, and Macedonia—and the ability to acquire further territories should two-thirds of their inhabitants vote to join. Official Ottoman recognition, confirming the sultan's earlier decree, came two years later, in 1872.[22]

The effects of the Exarchate were far-reaching. The Bulgarians were handed a concrete territorial definition for a Bulgarian national heartland, which the Russians later would use in shaping the ill-fated Bulgarian nation-state borders at San Stefano. Moreover, Bulgarian nationalists saw the officially recognized ability to extend territorially the jurisdiction of the Exarchate as an Ottoman-sanctioned opportunity for future nation-state expansion in the Balkans. From the Greek point of view, the Exarchate was both a blow to Greek nationalism, because it removed from Greek cultural influences regions claimed, according to the Great Idea, by right of the Orthodox *millet,* and an asset, since it eliminated the perceived threat of Slavic mongrelization to Greek culture and ethnicity in territories marginal to the Great Idea (such as those north and northwest of the Balkan Mountains, which were undoubtedly

Bulgarian). The Exarchate virtually guaranteed that future nationalist conflicts could not be avoided in regions where the two sides' claims coincided. Furthermore, as events related to the Bulgarian national movement continued to play themselves out after the founding of the Exarchate, the Serbs were forced to deal with the Exarchate's implications as well.

Once the struggle for the establishment of an independent Bulgarian church had been won, the nationalist momentum swung to the revolutionary approach. This was not a natural development of victory in the evolutionary sphere but a shift forced on the Bulgarian nationalists by the revolutionaries themselves. They had been a minority voice in the Bulgarian national movement from the outset. Most Bulgarians were not anxious to overthrow the Turks by force. The mass of Bulgarian peasants were politically inactive but sympathetic to the idea of possessing an Orthodox church of their own. Most of the new middle-class supporters of nationalist ideas were comfortable with their newfound relative prosperity, for the Greek and Serbian revolutions had resulted in their being handed the economic activities within the empire that those peoples had once controlled. They favored the evolutionary religious approach to national satisfaction because it entailed the least amount of economic and social disruption for their lives. Their stance was reinforced by various nineteenth-century Ottoman reform efforts, collectively known by the title of *Tanzimat,* which aimed to modernize the empire more along Western lines. This was especially beneficial to the Bulgarians in the 1860s, when they found themselves governed by Midhat Pasha, a vigorous and enlightened provincial administrator who transformed the region under his authority into a model province. (He even established a Bulgarian-language printing press.)[23]

Yet despite general middle-class resistance, a small band of Bulgarian revolutionaries rose from their ranks and persisted in efforts to create by force a Bulgarian nation-state from the 1830s on. A series of ill-fated uprisings broke out in the 1840s and 1850s, but they received little moral, and no material, support from the outside, so they were crushed. The emerging class of revolutionaries was forced either outside the empire or underground. They were led by a group of highly literate poets and writers who eventually were supported by a community of wealthy Bulgarian merchants residing in the Romanian capital of Bucharest, just a few miles north of the Bulgarian heartlands across the Danube. Their original leader was Georgi Rakovski, who burned out his short life incessantly agitating for a national uprising through writing, publishing, and constant revolutionary organizing. His place soon was taken over by other Bucharest-based revolutionaries-writers, such as Lyuben Karavelov and Hristo Botev, or by ex-Orthodox clerics, such as Vasil Levski, who devoted and often gave their lives to the revolutionary cause.

The first Bulgarian revolutionary committee founded in Bucharest was composed essentially of conservative middle-class merchants who dreamed up "safe" revolutionary schemes that depended on outside—either, Russian, Serbian, or even Turkish (!)—support or intervention for their success, so that actual Bulgarian participation would be minimal and any failure could be attributed to miscarriages by non-Bulgarians. The fiery authentic revolutionaries—Karavelov, Levski, and Botev—bore little truck with the lackluster schemes of the Bucharest merchants. The Russian-educated Karavelov and the monastically trained Levski founded their own revolutionary organization in 1871 and set to constructing a secret network of revolutionary cells among the Bulgarian population south of the Danube. Their plans for an uprising were stifled when the Turks got wind of the affair; then Levski was captured and executed in 1872. His roles as revolutionary organizer and agitator were taken up by two young radical nationalists, Stefan Stambulov and Hristo Botev.[24]

The 1875 revolt in Bosnia-Hercegovina spurred the radical Bulgarian revolutionaries in Bucharest into action. A Bulgarian uprising was hastily prepared to take advantage of the Turks' preoccupation with the rebellion to the northwest, but it fizzled out before it got started. In the spring of the following year, 1876, a Bulgarian uprising did break out in the Sredna Gora and Rhodope mountain regions of the Ottoman Empire. That sad affair had been planned even more haphazardly by a young revolutionary firebrand, Georgi Benkovski. The ill-armed and highly disorganized rebels managed to do little more than publicly rally, sing patriotic songs (whose lyrics had been penned by the Bucharest revolutionary leadership), and butcher their mostly pacific Muslim neighbors in the villages. Because few elementary security precautions were taken, such as sealing off the regions in rebellion so that word could not reach the Ottoman central authorities rapidly and guarding strategic bridges and passes, the Turks were able to organize swift retaliation against the Bulgarian rebels. Within a month the Turks had crushed the uprising and reestablished control over the rebellious Bulgarian territories. True to his Romantic personal proclivities, the poet-revolutionary Botev, on hearing of the uprising's defeat, then led a small band of Bucharest-based revolutionaries across the Danube in support of a cause already lost—as were the lives of he and his followers soon thereafter.[25]

Had the Turks merely quashed the affair, the 1876 Bulgarian uprising would have gone virtually unnoticed by a European world preoccupied with the looming international crisis resulting from events surrounding the highly profiled revolt in Bosnia-Hercegovina. These pitted the foreign imperialist policies of England and Russia against one another. Unfortunately for all concerned, the Turks, lacking adequate numbers of regular troops because of the war with Serbia far to the northwest, were compelled to use irregular *başıbazuks* to quell the Bulgarians. Those irregulars were drawn from local Muslim inhabitants in the Bulgarian regions, many of whom had suffered at the hands of the Bulgarian rebels or had heard horror stories of how the rebels had maltreated Muslims who fell into their clutches. Their blood running hot with revenge, the Turkish irregulars laid into the Bulgarian population in the regions that had risen, making little distinction between rebels and passive peasants. There followed an orgy of destruction, pillage, rape, and enslavement. The number of Bulgarians who perished in the "massacres," whether innocent of rebellion or not, before the irregulars' wrath burned itself out was at least 15,000. (Bulgarian nationalist claims reached as high as 100,000.)

Word of the atrocities perpetrated on the Bulgarians by the *başıbazuks* began filtering to the world outside the Bulgarian lands in June 1876 by way of American-run Robert College outside Istanbul. The majority of the student body was Bulgarian at the time, and many began receiving tidings of the grisly events from their families back home. Soon the Western diplomatic community in the Ottoman capital was abuzz with rumors, which eventually found their way into the news media in the West. Rumor-mongering news stories about Turkish atrocities against Christians in the Ottoman Empire were particularly unwelcome in England, where the government of Benjamin Disraeli was firmly committed to supporting the Turks as a buffer against Russian expansion into the eastern Mediterranean, a situation already tense because of the ongoing crisis over the uprising in Bosnia-Hercegovina. A renowned American journalist from Ohio, Januarius A. MacGahan, who happened to be in London at the time, was hired by the *Daily News,* a newspaper that opposed the Disraeli government, to report on the massacre stories firsthand.

Accompanied unofficially by a member of the American legation in Istanbul, Eugene Schuyler, a seasoned diplomat and Russian scholar, as well as by Walter Baring of the English legation, who officially was sent along for the express purpose of whitewashing any unpleasantness that might be uncovered, MacGahan toured the stricken territories of the Bulgarian uprising. While the reports of both Americans confirmed the savagery of the Turks' retribution on the Bulgarians, MacGahan's purple prose describing the massacres, splashed across the front pages of the *Daily News,* galvanized public opinion in England against Disraeli's pro-Turkish policy. Most public political support for the Turks melted when William Gladstone, the opposition's leader, published his pamphlet, *The Bulgarian Horrors,* which was based more on Schuyler's objective report on the situation than on MacGahan's emotionally charged journalistic polemics. With hands tied by public pressure (even Queen Victoria [1837–1901] questioned why her government was supporting Muslim infidels against Christians in this matter), Disraeli was forced to stand aside when Russia (where MacGahan's reports in translation had been circulated to St. Petersburg newspapers) declared war on the Ottoman Empire in 1877 with the publicly proclaimed goal of winning for the Bulgarians a free nation-state of their own.[26]

Although the war began somewhat inauspiciously because of fumbling leadership in the Russian supreme command and unexpectedly stiff Turkish resistance, especially at the siege of Pleven, by the end of the year the Russians had crushed all Turkish military formations in the field. By the end of February 1878 Russian forces, accompanied by a smattering of Bulgarian volunteer contingents, were in sight of Istanbul itself, and it seemed that Russia would finally realize its imperialist dream of acquiring the "Second Rome" (Constantinople) and validating its claim to imperial leadership of all the Orthodox East European world. By that time, the English government had come to realize that liberating Christian Bulgarians was one thing, but Russia in direct possession of the most strategically crucial location in the eastern Mediterranean was another entirely. An English fleet had been dispatched to the region earlier with orders to intervene should the Russians attempt a coup and snatch Istanbul. With the Russians at the doorstep of the Ottoman capital, the English fleet demonstrated in the straits, and the Russians, taking the less-than-subtle hint, forced the Turks to sign the Treaty of San Stefano in early March.

By the terms of the treaty, Serbia, Montenegro, and Romania were to be granted complete independence from the Turks. Russia was to receive certain territories in eastern Anatolia. But the most important part of the treaty involved the establishment of an autonomous Bulgarian Principality and the setting of its borders. According to the terms imposed by the Russians, the new Bulgarian state was to include virtually all of the central Balkans lying between the Danube in the north, the Albanian Alps to the west, the Aegean Sea to the south, and the Black Sea to the east. Only small regions around Istanbul, Edirne, and Thessaloniki were excluded from the new state. At the stroke of a pen, the Russians placed into Bulgarian hands the provinces of Bulgaria Proper (less Dobrudzha in the northeast, which was given to Romania in compensation for Russian annexation of Bessarabia), Thrace (less the three cities already mentioned), and all of Macedonia. It was to be the single largest state in the Balkans. This was intentionally so. By rewarding the Bulgarians' aspirations with borders exceeding even those defined by the Exarchate, Russia expected a rich reward in return. Unable themselves to control directly the strategic straits, Bulgarian gratitude would accomplish that for them. Greater Bulgaria was intended to be little more than a Russian puppet.[27]

The Russians probably expected that there would be strident international opposition to San Stefano Bulgaria but assumed that, though they might be forced to amend the new state's territorial extent in the future, they would still retain Bulgarian loyalty no matter where the country's borders ultimately might lie. Events proved them right on the former count and somewhat mistaken on the latter.

All of the European Great Powers and all of the Balkan states raised a howl when the terms of San Stefano became public. It was obvious that the treaty would need modification if the peace of Europe was to be maintained. Bismarck, eager to demonstrate the international weight of the newly created Germany, invited all concerned to a June congress in Berlin to work out a final acceptable treaty. As it turned out, only the concerns of the Great Powers were addressed at Berlin. Those of the Balkan states were listened to politely but had little, if any, weight in the deliberations. The Turks were reduced to spectators at their own funeral, ignored and insulted by all sides. By mid-July 1878, after intense negotiations among the participating powers, the Turks received the dictate of the final treaty. So too did the small Balkan states, whose own future fates were involved as much as that of the Turks.

Most of the non-Bulgarian provisions of San Stefano were upheld at Berlin. All of the states that had received their independence in the former were recognized as such in the latter (though Serbia and Montenegro actually lost territorial additions in the final treaty); Russia retained its acquisitions in Anatolia, as well as Bessarabia; Romania received its slice of Dobrudzha. Greece, which was not included under San Stefano, received nothing at Berlin. (In fact, it lost territory since it was forced to watch the Turks hand over control of Cyprus to England.) In a completely new development unrelated in any way directly to San Stefano, and to the utter dismay of the Serbs, Habsburg Austria-Hungary was permitted to occupy rebellion-torn Bosnia-Hercegovina as well as the Sandjak of Novi Pazar, which separated Serbia from Montenegro, thus preventing their unification into a single Great Serbian state.

It was the Bulgarian provisions of San Stefano, those which had necessitated the Berlin congress in the first place, that underwent drastic modification. The large principality created by the Russians in their original treaty with the Turks was divided at Berlin essentially into four parts. Bulgaria Proper, lying north and northwest of the Balkan Mountains, emerged as the autonomous Bulgarian Principality with an elected prince who governed under technical Turkish suzerainty. The region south and southeast of Bulgaria and northwest of Turkish Thrace was designated the Ottoman province of Eastern Rumelia, whose capital would be located in Plovdiv. Its governor was to be a Christian appointed by the sultan and approved by the Great Powers. Western Thrace, which lay along the shores of the Aegean south of Eastern Rumelia, was returned to direct Ottoman control, thus cutting off

any possible Bulgarian access to that sea. Also returned to direct Turkish administration was the region of Macedonia.

While the Berlin settlement may have headed off the immediate war crisis
by satisfying the imperialist concerns of the Western Great Powers over
Russia's successes in the Balkans, it created heated and deep-seated dissatisfaction among the small Balkan states. The dismemberment of San Stefano's
Greater Bulgaria struck the Bulgarians' short-lived national jubilation like a
hammer blow. Euphoria swiftly changed to disillusionment and then to stubborn resolution to win back that which had been lost at Berlin. Their faith in
their brother Orthodox Russians was shaken, even though the new liberal-
democratic Bulgarian government was shaped with Russian encouragement,
Russians held most of the prominent positions in the principality's ministries,
and the infant Bulgarian military was trained and officered by Russians. The
strong Russian presence attempted to dampen the growing Bulgarian national
resentment of the Berlin settlement but, in the end, proved incapable of stifling
its dangerous momentum. The Serbs, forced to accept Habsburg occupation
of territories they considered their national preserve, felt deeply betrayed by
their longtime Russian allies, who had shown themselves willing to give
away to Bulgarians other regions just as important to their national aspirations.
They found it expedient to make an accommodation with the Habsburgs to free
their hands for dealing with their new Bulgarian national rivals in the south.
The Greeks, their national territorial ambitions having been bruised at Berlin,
were resolved to bend every effort to win what they considered their rightful
borders in the north. The nationalist ambitions of all three of those Balkan peoples would collide violently in the region of Macedonia.

The national struggle among the three states of Bulgaria, Greece, and Serbia
for the acquisition of all or part of Macedonia began following the unification
of Eastern Rumelia with the Bulgarian Principality in 1885. This was accomplished over the vehement protests of Russia, which, not wishing to upset the
international apple cart at that time, withdrew all its advisors, ministers, and
military officers from Bulgaria. Russia's actions prompted Serbia, out of a growing fear that Bulgarian nationalist momentum from the unification would
carry them into Macedonia, to take the opportunity to chasten the Bulgarians
further. Serbia declared war on Bulgaria in late 1885, expecting an easy victory and further territorial acquisitions. Instead, the Bulgarians turned back the
Serb invasion forces and Serbia itself was invaded. Only Habsburg threats to
intervene on behalf of the Serbs stopped the victorious Bulgarians, and a

peace treaty was signed by the two sides in March 1886, on the eighth anniversary of San Stefano. The unification of 1885 was secured.[28]

Following the two rapid national victories in the face of seemingly overwhelming odds, the Bulgarians' nationalist fervor burned hot. Bulgaria's first prince, Aleksandŭr I of Battenberg (1879–86) had paid the price for defying the Russians and leading the successful unification movement by subsequently being kidnapped by Russian agents and, after returning briefly to the throne, abdicating in 1886. His successor, Ferdinand I of Saxe-Coburg (1887–1918), seized upon Bulgarian nationalist aspirations as a useful tool for satisfying his personal ambitions. His gaze soon became fixed on Macedonia. He believed that if he succeeded in incorporating the region into his principality, that dramatic national coup would bring him acclaim among his adopted people and respect within the European international community.[29]

From 1878 on, the history of inter-Balkan state relations was largely focused on who would possess the region of Macedonia or, at the very least, how it would be divided among the various contenders for its possession. In size, Macedonia in the late nineteenth century was roughly that of West Virginia. It encompassed the Ottoman administrative regions of Thessaloniki, Bitola (Monastir), and Kosovo, and its Vardar and Morava river valleys, which formed a veritable corridor for a communications line linking East-Central Europe with the Aegean Sea, had been important militarily and economically since classical times. Its port city of Thessaloniki had been a thriving and important commercial center for the Byzantine Empire and remained so for the Turks, while its plains were extensive and fertile.

Macedonia was an ethnic meeting ground, where disparate peoples—primarily Albanians, Bulgarians, Greeks, Serbs, and Turks—lived in close proximity to one another, often intermingling. In its northwestern and western border regions were large numbers of Albanians. Serbs were found in the north, with a few mixed in with the Albanians in the northwest. In the south, especially in and around Thessaloniki, were Greeks, who could also be found mixed among the Albanians in the extreme southwest of the region. Turks inhabited most of the region's towns, and their villages were scattered throughout the central and south-central areas, particularly around Bitola. Also present were seminomadic Vlahs and Gypsies, who migrated among seasonal residences spread over the entire region. A populous Jewish merchant community resided in Thessaloniki, and some Jews could be found in most Macedonian towns of any note. They were frequently joined by Armenian merchants. Bulgarians populated the eastern frontier territories of Macedonia, and they extended southward to the Aegean shores, where they mixed with the Greeks in the area of Thessaloniki and to its east. That much of the ethnodemographic picture of

Macedonia was relatively certain. What was uncertain was the ethnic composition of the region's extensive core territories, whose majority population blended into the more ethnically distinguishable inhabitants living in peripheral zones just described.[30]

The ethnicity of the majority population of Macedonia was the main bone of contention in the Macedonian Question as it emerged in the nationalistically charged late nineteenth century. That fact requires some explanation.

Since the coming of the Turks in the fourteenth and fifteenth centuries, Macedonia had remained perhaps the most isolated and backward region of the Ottoman Empire. Its population at the time of the Ottoman conquest was predominantly Slavic, as can be inferred from the consistently important cultural role the region played in the medieval states of Bulgaria and Serbia. It might be conjectured that, for that very reason, the inhabitants were left ignorant and illiterate—as lowly Slav peasants, they were of little account within the Greek-dominated Orthodox *millet* and so experienced a fate similar to that imposed on the Bulgarians. After the two titular Slavic churches of Ohrid and Peć were abolished in the eighteenth century, the population of Macedonia was left completely under the jurisdiction of the Greek patriarch precisely at a time when Greek cultural chauvinism was emerging within the *millet,* resulting in a strong process of Hellenization throughout the region. But, ironically, the population's essential illiteracy insulated all but a few against the full brunt of Greek cultural assimilation. They remained Slavs.

Until the 1870s, when nationalists from the surrounding Bulgarians, Greeks, and Serbs began agitating among them, the inhabitants of Macedonia persisted in holding to their *millet* religious self-identities. Specific ethnicity, defined primarily by spoken language, meant little to them. Most spoke Slavic and that was enough, just as it had sufficed for centuries. Their loyalties were to their local villages and to their Orthodox faith, which differentiated them from their mostly Muslim neighbors. All that changed rapidly for them once the issue of the Bulgarian Exarchate exploded in their midst after 1872.

No better example of the innate linkage of religion with nationalism in the Balkans can be found than the Bulgarian Exarchate. The Bulgarians won an independent church of their own before they acquired a state, and the boundaries of their church stretched far beyond those of their state once it was established at Berlin in 1878 and augmented by the incorporation of Eastern Rumelia in 1885. From the outset, the state's consistent foreign policy in the Balkans was to transform the boundaries of the Bulgarian church, which closely paralleled those of San Stefano, into the borders of the Bulgarian nation-state. That the Bulgarians had a good chance at succeeding in their national goal raised a frightening specter before Greek and Serb eyes.

What disconcerted the Greek and Serb nationalists was the Turks' recognition of the Exarchate's right to assume religious jurisdiction over any territory in the Ottoman Empire in which two-thirds of its Orthodox population voted for membership in the Bulgarian church. While few, if any, consciously ethnic Greeks or Serbs would vote to join the Exarchate, the majority of the Orthodox population in Ottoman-controlled Macedonia lacked any such concrete ethnic self-identity. The Greeks especially were aware that it was extremely likely that the Macedonian Slav majority would naturally place themselves under the authority of an Orthodox church that was culturally Slavic and whose literary-liturgical language possessed great affinity to their own native vernacular. The Serbs, slower to discern the Bulgarian threat in Macedonia to their overall nationalist plans because of their preoccupation with Bosnia-Hercegovina throughout the 1870s, initially paid little notice to the Exarchate's potential dangers to future Serbian expansion.[31]

The Bulgarians lost little time in propagandizing for the Exarchate in Macedonia. As had the Serbs since the 1830s, Bulgarian evolutionary nationalists had actively fertilized the Macedonian field through connections forged with the typically Ottoman-spawned Slav middle-class elements in Macedonia that had emerged by the early nineteenth century. Although the Bulgarians' national revival had been late-blooming, that of the Macedonian Slavs had lagged even farther behind. During the decades preceding the founding of the Exarchate, Bulgarian books and teachers circulated among the Slav communities of Macedonia, where they found a mostly warm welcome, partly because the Macedonian Slavs were "starving" for education and literature that they could understand, and partly because of the recognized close linguistic affinity between their native tongue and that of the Bulgarians. So well received were the early Bulgarian cultural efforts in Macedonia that a number of leading figures in the pre-1870s Bulgarian national revival itself—such as the Miladinov brothers, Dimitŭr and Konstantin—were, in fact, Macedonian Slavs.[32]

With the establishment of the Bulgarian Exarchate, representatives from all of the Macedonian Orthodox bishoprics expressed their wish to join. The Greek patriarch responded by declaring the Exarchate schismatic and by anathematizing the exarch, Antim. Although the success of the Exarchate seemed assured, it soon became plain that the Macedonians' wishes had to be legally validated by actual vote counts. Pro-Exarchate Bulgarians began traversing the Macedonian countryside exhorting and soliciting the Slav population in the villages. Pro-Patriarchate Greeks, unwilling to lose the *millet* monopoly in the region that they had enjoyed for well over a century, attempted to counter the Bulgarian proselytizing with similar efforts of their own. The two sides' heated religious-national campaigning soon degenerated into terrorism and bloodshed. Organized rival gangs of Macedonian exarchatists and patriarchatists resorted to intimidating the Slav villagers and frequently came to blows. Deaths mounted. The Macedonian villagers' very act of voting often was carried out under the threat of mortal danger from one or both sides. By the time an independent Bulgarian state was created in 1878, most of the Orthodox Macedonian Slavs had joined the Exarchate, but the price had been heavy.

After their military defeat by the Bulgarians in 1886, the Serbs came to realize the full national implications of the Exarchate's victory in Macedonia. Now that Bulgaria had united Eastern Rumelia to itself, prevented the Serbs from tearing away any of its northwestern territories, and acquired a new prince who made no secret of his ambition to incorporate Macedonia under his rule, the Serbs were forced to act in Macedonia if they hoped to keep alive their own national expansionist aspirations. They found encouragement from Austria-Hungary, which sought to mollify Serb frustrations over being denied Bosnia-Hercegovina by turning their attention southward to Macedonia. During the second half of the 1880s, the Serbs stepped up their propagandizing efforts among the Macedonian Slavs. Serb teachers, priests, and eventually gangs joined in the Macedonian religious "campaigning" on behalf of the Serbian Orthodox church but scored few outright victories against the more popular Bulgarian effort. They did, however, manage to intensify the terror experienced by the Macedonian Slav villagers, large numbers of whom fled eastward across the border into Bulgaria seeking asylum and expecting aid. Once there, they quickly developed into a separate and powerful force in Bulgarian politics, demanding state intervention in Macedonia.[33]

All the while the Christian contenders for the minds and hearts of the Macedonian population were enmeshed in the church question, Macedonia lay under direct Ottoman control. This reality was a key factor in the 1880s, when the outwardly religious facet of the struggle for Macedonia perceptibly gave way to blatant nationalism with the concerted entry of the Serbs. The Bulgarian Exarchate may have won out over the Greek and Serbian patriarchates, but the Turkish administration and garrisons remained, as did the armed Christian bands. Sporadic fighting among the Christian contenders continued, but, as the church question stabilized in the Exarchate's favor, its Macedonian supporters increasingly turned their attention to guerilla attacks against the Turks. They were supported as far as possible with arms and volunteers from the Macedonian immigrants inside Bulgaria.[34]

The official position of the Bulgarian government regarding the troubles in Macedonia was touchy. Although nationalist sympathies lay with the exarchatist guerillas, the principality technically remained an autonomous state within the Ottoman Empire under the supreme authority of the sultan. While Prince Ferdinand may have dreamed of gloriously annexing Macedonia to his realm, his powerful prime minister, the former revolutionary organizer Stefan Stambulov, realized that Bulgaria needed time to develop economic and diplomatic strength and support before setting out on expansionist policies, and that time could be bought only at the expense of keeping on the good side of the Turks and their English patrons. Overt Bulgarian support for anti-Turk activities in Macedonia did not square with the evolutionary policy espoused by the former revolutionary turned prime minister. Instead, Stambulov conducted a policy of peaceful intervention in Macedonia, often cooperating with the Turks against the guerillas by tightening Bulgaria's borders with the troublesome province. In return, the Turks rewarded his moderate approach and peaceful stance with concessions to Bulgaria in Macedonia, among which were the appointments of three Bulgarian bishops to Macedonian exarchatist dioceses in 1890.

Although Stambulov's moderate policy was proving effective, it seemed far too timid and slow for the thousands of Macedonians who had immigrated into Bulgaria. They cried out for vigorous government action against the Turks in support of the mostly exarchatist Christians in Macedonia. The immigrants brought the tactics of intimidation that they had learned in their homeland during the church "campaigns" to the streets of Sofia, Bulgaria's capital. Placing himself at the head of the nationalist movement, while at the same time signaling a policy shift away from England and the Ottomans and toward Russia, Ferdinand dismissed Stambulov from his post in 1894. The next year the former minister was assassinated brutally by Macedonian revolutionaries. It was rumored that Ferdinand had a hand in arranging the deed.[35]

The year before Stambulov was sacked by Ferdinand and Bulgarian policy concerning Macedonia began to change (1893), a small band of anti-Turk revolutionaries secretly met in the little Macedonian town of Resna. They proclaimed themselves the Internal Macedonian Revolutionary Organization (IMRO) and later produced a revolutionary program aimed at creating an autonomous state of Macedonia, completely independent from the Ottoman Empire, Bulgaria, Greece, and Serbia. They viewed Macedonia as an organic territorial whole that could not be divided, and they considered all of its inhabitants "Macedonians," no matter their religion or ethnicity. Such were the humble beginnings and original program of Europe's first consciously organized political terrorist group. From the date of its founding until 1934, IMRO never ceased conducting its activities. Within a few years, IMRO had spread throughout Macedonia, training men and gathering arms in preparation for a great mass uprising against the Turks.[36]

(In an interesting sidenote to the story of IMRO, the first non-Balkan Great Power victimized by the first European political terrorist organization was the United States. In 1901 a local IMRO leader, Jane Sandanski, kidnapped and held to ransom Ellen Stone, an American Protestant missionary working in eastern Macedonia, for the express purpose of extorting a large sum of money from the American government to be used for purchasing weapons for fellow IMRO revolutionaries. Stone's political abduction—the first time ever an American was so treated abroad—proved a successful publicity stunt for IMRO. Newspaper correspondents hounded the trail of the American hostage negotiators, making her kidnapping front-page news. The $66,000 ransom that was eventually paid Sandanski was raised through a highly publicized subscription campaign in America. By the time she was finally released and returned to the United States, Stone had been converted to the cause of her IMRO captors. She devoted herself to public lecturing and writing popular articles in *McClure's Magazine* on Macedonia and the righteousness of the revolutionaries' struggle. Her pregnant companion in the abduction, Ekaterina Tsilka, had given birth during her captivity, and she too stumped America after her release, offering even more popularly attended lecture appearances, in which baby Elena played a starring role. Thus the Americans came to accept their earliest concession to terrorist intimidation!)[37]

IMRO's "Macedonia for the Macedonians" revolutionary program was a logical result of two decades of turmoil and bloodshed, in which the native population of the region was cynically, often brutally, manipulated and abused solely for the national interests of outsiders. The people had been reduced to little more than statistics used to support the various contenders' nationalist claims—so many churches, so many schools, and so forth, of this or that side. (In any event, all the statistics were massaged by the various contenders' nationalist biases.) Although Bulgarian affinities still remained among the Macedonian Slav majority, they had been worn thin because of the domineering approach the Bulgarian-born exarchatist clergy often took relative to their Macedonian-born flocks, and because of the self-superior airs assumed by many Bulgarian educators and intellectuals who appeared in Macedonia after 1872. These disturbing tendencies had intensified after Bulgaria's independence in 1878 and again following the 1885 unification. As for the Greeks, only a small fraction of the Slav Macedonians had been Hellenized in the first place; for most Macedonians, the Greeks were foreigners who seriously, often thuggishly, threatened their native Slavic culture. Finally, though the Serbs were Slavs, their language was noticeably different from the Macedonians' and they had proven themselves just as brutish and violent as the Greeks in treating with the native Macedonian inhabitants. No Serbs or Greeks were enrolled in IMRO.

Originally, IMRO was a decentralized affair, composed of loosely connected independent regional groups. In 1894 Goce Delčev, a young, Sofia-trained Macedonian revolutionary, transformed it into a highly effective underground rebel network controlled by a central revolutionary committee. He also extended IMRO's field of operations outside of Macedonia to include Turkish-controlled Thrace, which stretched eastward from Macedonia along the Aegean coast to Edirne and beyond. IMRO headquarters were established in Thessaloniki, and representatives were sent to Sofia, Athens, and Istanbul. Along with the network of revolutionary regions, districts, and communes into which IMRO was divided, the organization established its own internal civil administration, with administrators at all levels, postal and courier services, internal police forces, courts, and newspapers. Each district maintained one or more armed units that conducted guerilla operations in the countryside. In towns IMRO maintained terrorist cells for use if and when needed.

Soon after Delčev and his supporters reorganized IMRO, it split into two factions over the issue of future Macedonian autonomy. Delčev, supported by Sandanski and others, held to the original goal of an autonomous Macedonia, independent from all surrounding states. He adamantly opposed Macedonia's incorporation into Bulgaria, which a number of his fellow revolutionaries advocated. Viewing the liberation struggle against the Turks as the first necessary step leading to Macedonia's eventual unification with Bulgaria, Delčev's opponents moved to Sofia in 1895 and, with the assistance of Ferdinand and his now subservient government, founded their own organization in competition with IMRO—the External Macedonian Revolutionary Organization (EMRO). Blessed with the direct support of the Bulgarian state and backed by the influential Macedonian immigrants, EMRO members soon were able to gain majority representation in IMRO's governing central committee, and in 1901 an EMRO representative from Thessaloniki, Ivan Garvanov, became its president. Thus the pro-Bulgarian faction of the Macedonian revolutionary movement emerged dominant.[38]

The two organizations not only held opposing views concerning the ultimate future of Macedonia, but they also espoused differing tactical approaches in the revolutionary struggle. IMRO focused on organizing the general population for a mass uprising and tried to avoid armed activities as much as possible. In 1897 it was forced to retaliate when the Turks discovered a part of its underground network, but preparation and training for the great revolutionary event remained uppermost in IMRO priorities. EMRO, on the other hand, embraced armed activities from the start. It carried out political assassinations of its opponents and organized raiding parties into Macedonia from its Bulgarian home base—the first such raid occurred in 1895.

The EMRO Macedonian raiders frequently were joined by former or inactive Bulgarian army officers.

All the while Macedonian and Bulgaro-Macedonian revolutionary activity was fomenting, the Serbs and Greeks were not idle. In Serbia the Society of Saint Sava had been founded in 1886 with the express purpose of whipping up Serbian nationalism in Serb-claimed regions, and especially in Macedonia. By 1889 the society's activities came under the direct authority of the Serbian foreign ministry. The Turkish administration in Macedonia welcomed the Serbs' activities, hoping to use them to counterbalance the rising Bulgarian efforts in the 1890s. As for the Greeks, a secret National Society was founded in Athens in 1894 with the goal of liberating all Greeks still under Turkish control. Its primary aim was to combat the Bulgarian national push into Macedonia. With most of its leadership staffed by Greek army officers, and supported by the wealthy Greek merchant communities as well as the Greek consuls in various Macedonian towns, the society propagandized heavily and sponsored bands of raiders into Macedonia to fight both Turks and Bulgarians.[39]

A fourth, seemingly unlikely, outside contestant in the Macedonian entanglement had also emerged by the end of the 1870s. Romania, far to the northeast of the region, began supporting educational efforts for the many seminomadic Vlahs who roamed the Macedonian countryside in their seasonal migrations among settlements. Claiming the Latin-speaking Vlahs as kindred nationals, the Romanians staked out a minor voice in the Macedonian fracas. Because Macedonia lay too far from the Danubian borders of Romania, no pro-Romanian rebel bands joined the nationalist fray. It was obvious that the Romanians kept their hand in the Macedonian till merely as an investment to own leverage in possible future nationalist dealings with the main contenders.

The heated nationalist animosities among the Bulgarians, Serbs, and Greeks over possession of Macedonia tended to obscure the obvious fundamental factor in solving the Macedonian Question—before any nationalist decision could be reached, the Turks first had to be expelled from the region. As early as 1867, Serbian Prince Mihail Obrenović (1860–68) had reached that conclusion regarding all of the Balkans. He began attempts to form a confederation of Balkan Orthodox Christians to drive the Turks out, but his efforts were cut short by his assassination the following year at the hands of his family's Karadjordjević enemies. In the emotionally charged nationalist atmosphere surrounding Macedonia in the late 1880s and early 1890s, both Serbia and Greece tried to bring Bulgaria into anti-Ottoman alliances, the terms of which would delineate peaceably all their respective claims on Macedonia, but to no avail. Both Stambulov and Prince Ferdinand rejected the proposals, though for different political reasons, and when the Serbs and Greeks attempted to continue without the Bulgarians, they soon discovered that their own claims in Macedonia were for the most part mutually exclusive as well.

Although the contending Balkan states failed to address the problem of evicting the Turks from Macedonia, the Macedonian revolutionaries did not. In early 1903 the Bulgarian-dominated IMRO leadership decided to raise a concerted anti-Turk guerilla-type uprising later in the year, despite the fact that many of the organization's district units were materially unprepared. Delčev, Sandanski, and others of the original IMRO leadership were opposed to the decision, but after Delčev was cornered and killed by the Turks in the spring, the opposition was forced into line behind the plan. In August 1903 the Ilinden uprising (named after the saint's day on the Orthodox calendar—2 August— dedicated to St. Elijah [Iliya]) was proclaimed. The rebels managed to consolidate their hold on the region of Bitola briefly, and a short-lived "republic" was established around Kruševo by a group of ideologically socialist revolutionaries within IMRO. Bulgaria, uninformed of IMRO's plans and unprepared for war with the Turks, was caught off guard by the uprising and did little more than keep its border with Macedonia open to appease the numerous Macedonian immigrants and to assuage the nationalist sympathies of the Bulgarian population. It took the Turks nearly three months to put down the rebellion, which was accomplished with the usual indiscriminate devastation and violence perpetrated on the general population, whether actively involved in the uprising or not. Hundreds of villages and thousands of homes were destroyed, and a new flood of immigrants poured across the border into neighboring Bulgaria.[40]

The Ilinden debacle stirred the European Great Powers into action over Macedonia. Austria-Hungary and Russia, the two most directly interested in Balkan matters, hammered out the so-called Mürzsteg reform program for the stricken Ottoman province and had it approved by the others. Inspectors from Austria-Hungary and from Russia were to be attached to the Ottoman inspector-general in Macedonia, and a foreign general and staff were to command a reformed Turkish Macedonian *gendarmerie*. The reform also called for Ottoman judicial reorganization and Turkish financial assistance for returning refugees and rebuilding programs. The Turks had no choice but to accept the provisions of the reform if they wished to retain any support among the European Great Powers, especially that of England. Yet far from dampening the unrest within Macedonia, the Mürzsteg program probably stoked it, since one of the provisions in the reforms called for a future administrative reorganization of the province along ethnic lines. This resulted in each of the Balkan states contending for Macedonia intensifying its propaganda efforts in the province to improve its position once that future reorganization was undertaken.

Given the nature of nationalist "campaigning" in Macedonia, their increased efforts were accompanied by heightened violence. In the heat of the nationalist struggle over Macedonia, the contending Balkan states—Bulgaria, Serbia, and Greece—were locked into a confrontational situation that precluded any result other than deadlock.

⟨⟨ ⟩⟩

Deadlock grew out of the three states' resort to history as validation for their respective nationalist claims on Macedonia. In true Romantic fashion, each party presented an argument justifying Macedonia's incorporation into its own nation-state based on considerations of proprietary cultural-ethnic continuity in the region traceable back at least to medieval times and, in the case of Greece, to antiquity.

By the late nineteenth century, the Greeks were intoxicated by the classical Hellenic heritage that Western Romantic philhellenes had brought to them in the heady days of the Greek revolution. The knowledge that ancient Greece and its culture lay at the very root of European Hellenic tradition provided Greek nationalists with a claim to national preeminence that none of the other Balkan nationalities could match. They proudly could point to such illustrious and widely recognizable ancestors as Leonides, Pericles, Plato, and Aristotle, who had been models of Greek bravery, political acumen, and intellectual genius centuries before any of their neighbors (other than the Albanians, who were then just beginning to develop a sense of national consciousness but were still discounted by the others) had even arrived in the Balkan Peninsula and begun to taste the fruits of civilized society. Through Alexander the Great, the Greeks could claim to have attained the height of superiority in all the known classical world, defeating their centuries-old Persian adversaries, reaching the very gates of India, and, in the process, spreading their culture throughout. And when those latecoming, originally barbarian, neighbors whom they had to contend with in the Balkans had been exposed to civilization, it had been in the form of a Greek-shaped Byzantine Orthodox variety that lay at the very core of Eastern European civilization itself. Even when the Greek world had been inundated by the Muslim Ottoman Turks, the Greeks had demonstrated their intrinsic superiority over the infidel Islamic oppressors by maintaining the cultural reality of defeated Byzantium through the Greek Orthodox church and its place of preeminence in the Orthodox *millet*.[41]

In the late nineteenth century the intensity of feeling surrounding this Greek national mythology was heightened by the fact that the Greeks could point to outside forces that consistently appeared to place obstacles in the path toward forging a large nation-state to which they believed their past entitled them. Following independence from the Turks in 1831, England and the Ottomans had kept their national territory restricted on the mainland to the barest limits possible, encompassing only the Peloponnese and Attica. In 1863 England had handed them the Ionian Islands, but during the Russo-Turkish War of 1877–78, when the Greeks of Thessaly had revolted against the Turks, although Greece declared war in support of them, the Great Powers constrained the country from actually taking action. Then at Berlin in 1878, England gained Cyprus, to which the Greeks laid claim, while they were put off with promises of future acquisitions in Thessaly and Epiros. The former was ceded to them by the Turks in 1881, along with part of the latter. When in 1886 the Greeks attempted to take advantage of the pro-Bulgarian uprising in Eastern Rumelia by threatening war with the Turks in an effort to force them to concede further territories, the Great Powers issued an ultimatum ordering the Greek forces to stand down. Greek refusal resulted in a Great Power blockade of the country until the Greeks finally were forced to comply. An anti-Turk insurrection in 1896–97 in Crete, which also was claimed by the Greek nationalists, was followed in 1897 by a quick and decisively unsuccessful war conducted by Greece against the Ottomans, during which both the Serbs and Bulgarians stood idly by. Great Power intervention spared the defeated Greeks the full measure of Turkish retribution for their foolish action, but, at the same time, they forbade any unification of the island with the mainland nation-state.[42]

Perceiving that they were constantly being forced to play the underdog by the European powers, the Greeks found recourse in intensifying their nationalist mythology—developing an extreme version of the Great Idea program, reinforced by allusions to classical antiquity. The nationalist struggle for Macedonia was a particularly apt target for that approach. There was no doubting that the Greek-led Orthodox Ottoman *millet* had exerted uncontested domination over the region for more than a century prior to the founding of the Bulgarian Exarchate, and that Macedonia had played an important role in the Byzantine Empire, providing a name for one of that state's strongest and longest-lasting imperial dynasties (867–1057). Moreover, classical Hellenic Greek power and culture was personified in Greek and Western minds by Alexander the Great (337–23 B.C.), king of ancient Macedon and briefly ruler of the known Hellenic world. Through Alexander, the Greeks laid claim to Macedonia as direct heirs of the region's earliest inhabitants. They proclaimed him and his people Greeks, and they alleged that the descendants of the ancient Macedonians had survived in the region through successive waves of Roman, Gothic, Turkic, and Slavic invasions that had swept over the Balkan world during the twenty-one centuries since Alexander's day. As proof for this contention, the Greeks stressed the continuous use of the name "Macedonia" for identifying the region throughout that long period, no matter the dominant ethnicity of the state that happened to control it at any given point in time, be it Greek, Slavic, or Turkic. For Greek nationalist purposes, Macedonia was ancient Macedon, and ancient Macedon was Greek.[43]

Such was the nature of the Greeks' nationalist claim on Macedonia during the heyday of the Macedonian Question (and such it remains today). Although it possessed intrinsic appeal for Westerners, because their consciousness of European civilization's Hellenic roots generally predisposed them to take a philhellenic perspective in the matter, the Greek nationalist mythology was mostly that—myth masquerading as history. Any objective historical analysis of the Greek argument has a difficult time accepting Alexander as having been ethnically Greek. Not even the Greeks of his own time considered him one of themselves. They viewed him and his people as militant barbarians who mimicked Greek culture to compensate for their lack of native civilized development. It was their military predominance, and not their "Greekness," that brought the Macedonians suzerainty over a fragmented and weak Greek world in the fourth century B.C. The ethnic Greeks were dragged into Alexander's grand imperialist schemes by force of arms, and they never willingly relinquished their conscious distinction between themselves and the Macedonians.

Even more historically untenable was the Greek claim that any sort of ethnic continuity was maintained in the region in the face of centuries of foreign invasions of the Balkans. This was particularly the case concerning the Slavic inundations of the sixth through seventh centuries; by that time ancient Macedonian ethnicity was probably already declining because of previous inroads by Romans, Goths, and Hunno-Turks. During the Slavic invasions most of the indigenous inhabitants of the Balkan interior, including those in the region of Macedonia, were forced either to flee to the coastal areas, where the Byzantine military could offer some protection, or to hole up in the interior's fortress towns, where they were surrounded by the Slavs who settled the countryside, isolated, and eventually assimilated into the interlopers' ranks. It did not require the existence of an ethnically Greek population to preserve the name "Macedonia" in such a situation, since it was just as likely that the Slavic newcomers merely retained the name that traditionally was used for identifying the region among the few natives who remained, as well as among the Slavs' constant Byzantine protagonists. The name persisted as a regional rather than as an ethnic label throughout the successive periods of initial Bulgarian control (ninth through early eleventh centuries), Byzantine recovery (eleventh and twelfth centuries), Bulgarian reconquest (thirteenth through early fourteenth centuries), Serbian control (mid-fourteenth century), and finally Ottoman conquest (late fourteenth century). Those ethnic Greeks who could be found in the region by the late nineteenth century were located in its south, in and around Thessaloniki and southward, in areas where former Byzantine reconquest efforts had proved successful and where continuous Greek coastal maritime commercial activities were concentrated. What little pro-Greek ethnic sympathies that did exist among the Slavs in the interior of Macedonia were the result of the Orthodox *millet*'s heavy-handed Hellenization efforts of the late eighteenth and early nineteenth centuries.[44]

Of the Greeks' two Slavic contenders for Macedonia, the national case of the Bulgarians held the most historical water. The Turkic Bulgars had swept out of the steppes of west-central Asia, southward across the Danube into the Balkans, in the seventh century. At first merely interested in plundering the Slavic settlements and in extorting cash tribute from the area's nominal Byzantine rulers, by 679 a group of Bulgars, led by their tribal chief Asparuh, settled just south of the Danube in the northeast Balkan region of Dobrudzha. Byzantine efforts to evict them failed, and in 681 a military treaty recognizing their existence south of the Danube was signed. From their Dobrudzhan foothold, the successors of Asparuh relentlessly expanded the territories under their control, either as opponents or as allies of Byzantium, until, by the mid-ninth century, the Bulgar state controlled most of the north and central Balkan regions, all of what is today Romania, and its northwestern frontier abutted that of the Holy Roman Empire in the regions of Pannonia and Moravia. The conversion to Orthodox Christianity of its ruler, Prince Boris I (852–89), served to bring cultural unity to that vast, multicultural agglomeration and opened the gates to the final ethnic assimilation of the Turkic Bulgars into the mass of their Slavic Balkan subjects.

Under Boris's son, Simeon I (893–927), Bulgaria achieved its historical apex, encompassing virtually all of the Balkan Peninsula except Croatia, Thessaloniki and Greece to its south, and eastern Thrace. Simeon posed such a threat to Byzantium's continued existence that the Byzantines, having barely escaped his claim to the imperial throne in 924, were forced to recognize the Bulgarians officially as second only to themselves in international power politics. Simeon's state forged the mechanism for preserving Byzantium's Eastern European civilization among the non-Byzantine Orthodox Slavs by creating the Cyrillic literary alphabet, which afforded them the ability to both entrench and further develop Orthodox culture in their own terms. Thanks to the late ninth- and early tenth-century Bulgarians, the Orthodox Slavic world (including the Russians) was given the wherewithal to preserve its various cultural self-identities and to play a continuously important role on the historical world stage.

Bulgaria's leadership in the Slavic world was short-lived. It fell swiftly into political decline following Simeon's death. By the close of the tenth century the state was reeling from Russian and Byzantine invasion, and in 1018 it was finally crushed by the Byzantines and wholly incorporated into their empire for the next 167 years. Although a resurrected Bulgaria appeared in 1185 and briefly regained control of much of the territory once held under Simeon, the changed political situation in the Balkans and the inability of the Asen ruling dynasty to maintain centralized control over its increasingly independent feudal subordinates precluded its development into a stable, dominant political force. By the opening of the fourteenth century, Bulgaria was internally divided and pressured by Byzantine, Serbian, and Hungarian neighbors. Defeated by the Serbs in 1330, Bulgaria lost its role as leader in the Balkan Slavic world, and involvement in the civil wars of Byzantium brought further weakness and internal division. The state was in no effective position to resist the growing Ottoman threat in the Balkans that intensified after 1354. Forced into vassalage to the Turks in the 1370s, Bulgaria was finally overcome by them in 1393 and directly incorporated into their Islamic state three years later.[45]

Bulgarian nationalists claimed the region of Macedonia on the basis of two historical arguments related to the overall course of medieval Bulgarian history.

The first posited that the Macedonian Slavs had been brought under Bulgar control in the late seventh century by a group of Bulgars who had broken off from Asparuh's band prior to their crossing of the Danube. Led by their tribal chief Kuber, those Bulgars had first settled in Pannonia, from which they allied themselves with the Avars and accompanied them on their raids into the Balkans. When the Avars moved back into Pannonia, Kuber's Bulgars established themselves in Macedonia during the 680s and gained control over the local Slavic population, after which there developed a situation similar to that in Bulgaria proper to the northeast—a small Bulgar ruling class exerting control over a large Slavic subject population. In the mid-ninth century the Macedonian Bulgars and their territories were incorporated into the expanding Bulgar state. Thereafter, Macedonia was indistinguishable from the Bulgar-controlled regions of the southern Danubian heartlands—the Danubian Plain (Bulgaria proper) and Dobrudzha. The same cultural and ethnic assimilation process, especially following Boris's conversion to Orthodoxy, affected them all. When the eastern portions of Bulgaria fell to Byzantium in the late tenth century, the western half, centered on Macedonia, continued to defy the Byzantines under its ruler, Tsar Samuil (976–1014), and even to expand into the empire's Greek heartlands until Samuil's crushing defeat at the hands of Emperor Basil II *Boulgaroktonos* (976–1025), known as the "Bulgar-killer." Bulgarian nationalists pointed to the similarity in language that existed between the Macedonians and Bulgarians in the late nineteenth century to verify their claims that the Macedonian Slavs were, in fact, Bulgarians who spoke a western dialect of the primary Bulgarian language, retaining most of the linguistic characteristics that made Bulgarian unique among fellow South Slavs—especially the definite article ending commonly attached to nouns. (Interestingly, nineteenth- and early twentieth-century American Protestant missionaries working among both Bulgarians and Macedonians in the Ottoman Empire concurred in this conclusion.)[46]

The second Bulgarian nationalist claim was associated with the first. The single seminal achievement of the Bulgarians was the creation of the Cyrillic alphabet in the early tenth century. This had been undertaken with the patronage and support of Tsar Simeon, who had welcomed into Bulgaria the refugee disciples of Cyril and Methodius from Moravia. Two of them, Kliment and Naum (whom the nationalists claimed were Slavs from Macedonia), were settled in or near the Macedonian town of Ohrid, where Simeon appointed Kliment as the first bishop of an independent Bulgarian Orthodox church. While at first the new church functioned using the Glagolitic Slavic alphabet originally designed by Cyril, its complex and cumbersome characters soon demonstrated the need for a more simplified Slavic writing system to increase the numbers of trained native Slavs in the church ranks to replace the then-dominant Greek control. According to the Bulgarian nationalists, Kliment and Naum led the move to design and propagate a new Slavic alphabet, based on modified Greek letters and named Cyrillic, in honor of their mentor. (Both Serb and Macedonian nationalists dispute this claim, saying that both Kliment and Naum persisted working in Glagolitic in opposition to the Greek-influenced Cyrillic, which they contend was developed at Simeon's palace school at his capital of Preslav. The thrust of their contention is to demonstrate the cultural-ethnic separateness of the Macedonian Slavs from the Bulgarians.) From Macedonia, the new alphabet was spread throughout the extensive territories under Simeon's control, thus providing him with the basis for displacing the Greek clergy then in Bulgaria and creating an officially independent Slavic state church organization that lay at the center of Orthodox political culture.[47]

Both nationalist claims still are alive in Bulgaria today.[48]

The Greeks' other Slavic contender for Macedonia—Serbia—also advanced historical claims to the region. Slavic Serb tribes had been settled in the Byzantine Empire's northwestern Balkan territories in the early seventh century by Byzantine emperor Heraclius (610–41) to serve as border guards against the growing incursions of the Avars. They remained tribally divided and under Byzantine suzerainty until the early ninth century, at which time the Serbs of the Raška region (roughly today's Kosovo province of Serbia) managed to create a small state of their own that was still under Byzantine overall control. The Serb nationalists claimed that Raška was then converted to Orthodox Christianity by Cyril and Methodius, but there is no documentation for this contention—every Balkan Slav nationalist program felt constrained to forge linkages with the two Byzantine missionary brothers. More likely influences from the powerful Bulgarian state effected the Raškan Serbs' conversion to Orthodoxy. In any event, they were incorporated into Bulgaria by Simeon in the early tenth century, and they remained under Bulgarian authority until the early eleventh-century collapse of Samuil's state.[49]

In the mid-eleventh century the Serbs of the Zeta (Montenegrin) region of the Byzantine Empire managed to establish a modicum of independence from Byzantium, and in 1077 their ruler Mihail (1051–81) was granted a royal crown by the pope in an effort to gain a permanent foothold in the Orthodox East following the Great Schism of 1054, which divided the Christian world into western Roman Catholic and eastern Orthodox halves that have persisted into the present. But the Zeta Serb tribal kingdom, isolated in its mountainous environment, was of little consequence in the Byzantine Balkans. A truly influential Serbian state emerged with the reign of Stefan Nemanja (1159–96) in Raška, who after 1180 managed to throw off direct Byzantine control (1190) and unite Zeta, northern Albania, and much of present-day eastern Serbia under his authority. A devout adherent of Orthodoxy, Nemanja definitively planted his Serb state firmly in the East European Orthodox East. After abdicating in favor of his son Stefan (1196–1227), the true founder of the Nemanja dynasty, the former ruler first retired to a Serbian monastery and then to Mount Athos, where he joined another son, Rastko (known as St. Sava), in founding the large and influential Slav monastery of Hilendar (Hilandar, in Serbian).[50]

Nemanja's son Stefan had received a royal crown from the pope in 1217, but his brother St. Sava had managed to gain recognition of an independent Serbian Orthodox archbishopric from the Greek patriarch, with himself as first incumbent, and had then crowned Stefan in 1219 as an Orthodox ruler, spelling the end of Catholic attempts to dominate the Serbs. Stefan the First Crowned and his successors succeeded in preserving and expanding the new Serbian kingdom against Byzantine, Bulgarian, and Hungarian threats throughout the thirteenth century. In the fourteenth, under Stefan Uroš II Milutin (1282–1321), Serbia conquered the northern areas of Macedonia. With the decisive victory in battle over the Bulgarians outside of Velbuzhd (Kyustendil) in 1330 and the disintegration of Byzantium in civil war, Serbia under Stefan Uroš III Dečanski (1321–31) emerged as the dominant power in the Balkans. His son Stefan IV Dušan (1331–55) brought Serbia to the pinnacle of its historical power and glory.

Dušan ruled over a Serbian state that included Raška, Zeta, Macedonia, Albania, Epiros, and Thessaly down to the Gulf of Corinth. He pushed the Hungarians, who had steadily encroached into the Balkans during the century prior to his reign, north of the Danube and incorporated Belgrade and its environs into his large Balkan Serb state. Attempts to conquer Bosnia and Hercegovina proved unsuccessful, but Dušan cemented an alliance with the Bulgarians that spread Serbian influence into the eastern Balkans. At his Macedonian capital of Skopje in 1346, Dušan had himself proclaimed emperor of the Serbs, Greeks (Byzantines), Bulgarians, and Albanians, and was crowned as such by the archbishop of Peć (Ipek), whom he then raised to the position of independent Serbian patriarch. A legal code for his Serbian "empire" was promulgated, and Dušan's court at Skopje took on all the outward appearances of Byzantine splendor. Before he could execute a planned advance on Byzantium's capital, Constantinople, and make good on his imperial pretensions, Dušan died.

His death in 1355 was a catastrophe for the Orthodox Balkans, since it removed the last force capable of withstanding the advance into Southeastern Europe of the militantly Islamic and expansionary Ottoman Turks. Soon after his death, Serbia fell into internal disarray, with local rulers throwing off the central authority of the weakened successors to the Serbian throne. Bulgaria had already been reduced to virtual impotence by both the Serbs and by internal political division, while the Byzantine Empire, wracked by civil war and stripped of all its territories outside those in close proximity to Constantinople, was militarily helpless. In 1389 the Serbs of the north, under their Prince Lazar (1371–89), were crushed decisively by the Turks in the Battle of Kosovo Polje, and, although Serbia managed to survive for the next seventy years as a client state of either the Ottomans or the Hungarians, it never again exerted any independent power. In 1459 the Turks eliminated the last Serbian stronghold at Smederevo. Serbia ceased to exist.

Macedonia had disappeared under Turkish rule long before the final extinction of Serbia. For a time after Dušan's death, Macedonia had maintained an independent existence of sorts under its local ruler Vukašin, who styled himself king. In 1371 Vukašin assembled a military alliance of local Balkan warlords to oppose the Turks and looked to Bulgaria for assistance. Lacking support from the more powerful Bulgarians, who had been intimidated by Turkish threats of reprisals from aiding the alliance, Vukašin pushed ahead with his plans and met the Turks at Chernomen, near the Maritsa River in Thrace. His forces were utterly defeated and he perished in the combat. The battle opened the gates into Macedonia to the Turks, who soon thereafter incorporated the region directly into their expanding state.

It is doubtful that Serbian control of Macedonia, which lasted less than a century, made a lasting impact on the ethnic composition of the Macedonian Slavs, even though Dušan's powerful state was centered on it and its capital at Skopje. Bulgarian control over the region prior to Dušan had been of long duration, and Bulgarian cultural influences had been at play even longer. Perhaps more important, the linguistic evidence appeared to indicate that, from the area of Skopje northward, there existed a transitional zone between the Serbian and Bulgarian languages spoken as the vernacular by the Slavic population. While the Serb nationalists claimed all of Macedonia down to the environs of Thessaloniki in the south on the basis of Dušan's state, both the historical and ethnical evidence used to support their assertions were tenuous.[51]

➤◄ ➤◄

The volatile atmosphere surrounding the struggle over Macedonia among Greeks, Bulgarians, and Serbs spawned two previously nonexistent national movements. The most obvious was the rise of an independent Macedonian consciousness among the Slavs who inhabited the region. Under near-constant pressure and harassment to choose between the forceful claims of either the Bulgarians or the Serbs, and growing increasingly resentful over the airs of superiority assumed by those fellow Slav contenders in dealings with them, many Macedonian Slavs decided to forsake the choice and opt for independent ethnic self-identity. That had been the program of the original founders of IMRO, such as Delčev. Submerged by the successful takeover of the Macedonian revolutionary movement by pro-Bulgarian agents in 1901, the Macedonia for the Macedonians concept gradually reemerged over the years following the unsuccessful, pro-Bulgarian IMRO Ilinden uprising of 1903. Given the fact that, of the three major contenders, only Bulgarians had been represented in IMRO, which most Macedonian Slavs believed represented their interests, the independent Macedonian national movement was actually anti-Bulgarian in its thrust—the other two sides, Serbs and Greeks, were considered of no valid account from the start.[52]

An interesting historical argument arose in support of an independent Macedonian nationality that ultimately reached its maturity only after World War II and Tito's construction of a federated Communist Yugoslavia composed of six independent "historic" republics, of which one was Macedonia. The Macedonian nationalists quite simply stole all of the Bulgarian historical argument concerning Macedonia, substituting "Macedonian" for "Bulgarian" ethnic tags in the story. Thus Kuber formed a "Macedonian" tribal alliance in the late seventh century; Kliment and Naum were "Macedonians" and not

"Bulgarians"; the medieval archbishopric-patriarchate of Ohrid, which Kliment led, was a "Macedonian," not a "Bulgarian" independent church, as shown by the persistence of Glagolitic letters in the region in the face of the Cyrillic that were spawned in Bulgaria; and the renowned Samuil led a great "Macedonian," rather than a "western Bulgarian," state against Byzantium (giving Slav Macedonia its apex in the historical sun). Under control of the revived Bulgarian state, and later under the Serb Dušan, the Macedonians had maintained their ethnic differences from their "foreign" masters, as demonstrated by their "king" Vukašin, who had died attempting to keep an independent Macedonia free from the Ottoman Turks. When ethnic-national consciousness reawakened among the Macedonian Slavs in the nineteenth century, the cultural revivalists, such as the Miladinov brothers, were consciously "Macedonian," and not "Bulgarian," in their efforts.[53]

The obviously plagiarized historical argument of the Macedonian nationalists for a separate Macedonian ethnicity could be supported only by linguistic reality, and that worked against them until the 1940s. Until a modern Macedonian literary language was mandated by the socialist-led partisan movement from Macedonia in 1944, most outside observers and linguists agreed with the Bulgarians in considering the vernacular spoken by the Macedonian Slavs as a western dialect of Bulgarian. In the interwar period (1918–39) the official language of Macedonia had been Serbian by compulsion, with the use of Bulgarian forbidden. The World War II socialist partisans in Macedonia proceeded to establish a commission to create the new "official" Macedonian literary language, which was presented to the world the following year (1945). From then on, it became the legal first language of the Macedonian Slavs, with Serbo-Croatian a recognized second language and Bulgarian officially proscribed.

The new Macedonian literary language was based intentionally on a dialect spoken in the central Vardar area of the region, so as to be removed as far as geographically possible from both Bulgarian and Serbian linguistic contaminations. Moreover, a separate Macedonian Cyrillic alphabet was devised to make the new language as unnecessarily different from Bulgarian as possible, with the inclusion of wholly new letters found nowhere else and a few Serbian characters thrown in for good measure. Since the Macedonian vernacular was primarily primitive in its native development, most of the words used were better related to folktales and songs than to the modern age. "Bulgarianisms" were replaced by folk substitutes, and modern Bulgarian, Serbian, or Russian terminology for technical and other twentieth-century expressions were intentionally avoided in favor of Western, including American, terms. The result not only made literary Macedonian as different as humanly possible from its brother Slav languages, but it created a veritable linguistic hodgepodge, which approached the French meaning of *macedoine* when referring to a mixed salad. Led by the Skopje socialist linguist Blaže Koneski, and given international recognition in 1952 by Yale-produced Harvard Slavic professor Horace Lunt, the artificially created and structured Macedonian literary language ultimately provided the socialist-mandated ethnic validity for an independent Macedonian nationality. Over four decades of state socialization and education of Macedonian Slav children in that concept may have succeeded in creating such a creature in actual fact.[54]

The second completely new nationalist development that was born in the chaos and contention surrounding Macedonia was, ironically, a modern Turkish movement that eventually succeeded in creating the current nation-state of Turkey following World War I. It began in the 1860s when Westernized Turks within the Ottoman ruling establishment, who were critical of continued traditional Islamic means of governing and opposed to the cynical policy of superficial reform espoused by the sultans, were forced to flee abroad. Establishing themselves in Paris, by 1902, when a congress of political emigrés from the Ottoman Empire was called to organize action against Sultan Abdül Hamid II (1876-1909), the Westernized Turkish radical reformers had acquired the name of Young Turks. They soon discovered that they shared only a dislike of the sultan; on most other points they disagreed among themselves. Some stood for centralization of the existing Ottoman state under Turkish predominance, while others called for decentralization and full ethnic autonomy for all of the empire's subjects.[55]

While the Young Turks argued in Paris, officers of the Turkish units stationed in Macedonia acted. The military movement involved Mustafa Kemal, founder of a Turkish nationalist revolutionary organization while in Damascus in 1905 that had been absorbed into the empire-wide secret military officers' organization, the Society of Liberty, headquartered in Thessaloniki. The society essentially espoused the Turkish ultranationalist, centralization program of the extremists among the Young Turk emigrés. Well organized and having nourished strong support among the rank and file of the units they commanded, the Macedonian military officers, led by one Enver Pasha, revolted in 1908 in response to a planned Western Great Power intervention into Macedonia to halt the continued unrest that had followed the suppression of the Ilinden uprising. Afraid that such action would result in a partition of the Ottoman Empire, the military leaders in Macedonia put a well-considered plan into operation. An ultimatum to implement a reform constitution that originally had been imposed on the Turks in 1876 by the Great Powers but never put into force was telegraphed to the sultan in Istanbul. The Third Army Corps in

Macedonia demonstrated its support for the ultimatum, and the government was constrained to comply.

The jubilation of Westerners outside the empire and of non-Muslims within soon turned to anger and fear as it became apparent that the new military holders of power in the empire were intent on preserving it as a Turkish nation-state. The Young Turk military revolutionaries, under the name of the Committee for Union and Progress, subordinated the sultanate office to their will. They initiated a policy of centralization and Turkish hegemony formerly unknown in the Ottoman Empire and counter to the spirit of the constitution that they had ostensibly risen to instate. With the new policy's stress on Turkish national identity, virtually every non-Turkish subject population in the empire was forced to react against the new regime, whether they were Muslim or not. It was the reaction against the rise of Turkish nationalism and the increasingly brutal attempts at its repression by the Young Turk Ottoman authorities that spawned the nationalist awakenings of the Albanians, Arabs, and Armenians. The pseudo-Western ultranationalist program of the Young Turks would ultimately lead to atrocious massacres of the Turks' subject populations (such as of the Armenians) and to the swift disintegration of the Ottoman Empire during and after World War I. Out of that debacle, Mustafa Kemal, one of the leading figures in the 1908 Macedonian military revolt, would manage to win broad support for his Western-style Turkish nationalist ideals from among the Turks of Anatolia and succeed in militarily establishing the modern secular state of Turkey in the 1920s, winning as a result the title Atatürk (Father of the Turks).[56]

Besides the Young Turk uprising in Macedonia, the year 1908 also witnessed the outright annexation of Bosnia-Hercegovina by Habsburg Austria-Hungary. The resulting overthrow of the balance of power in the Balkans and the threat of a possible Habsburg-Russian conflict over the issue of hegemony in the region caused an uproar in the international community. Ferdinand of Bulgaria took the opportunity of the Great Powers' preoccupation to declare his country completely independent of Ottoman suzerainty, thus freeing him to pursue his ambitions in Macedonia unfettered by any trace of Turkish restraint. A bloody military coup in Belgrade during 1903 had overthrown the pro-Habsburg Serbian Obrenović dynasty and installed the Russian-looking Karadjordjevićes, but Russia's preoccupation in the Far East with Japan forced the new Serbian ruler Petr I (1903–21) to attempt an accommodation with Bulgaria to resist mounting Habsburg hostility. The consequent rapprochement between the two Slavic Balkan states was short-lived, floundering over the issue of Macedonia, and seemed doomed once Ferdinand made his move for independence in 1908.[57]

The ongoing repressive Turkish nationalist policies of the Young Turks played into the hands of the Balkan nationalists, eventually permitting them to overcome their mutual animosities briefly and to form an anti-Turkish military alliance in 1912. That development was heavily encouraged by Russia, which was by then freed from its commitments in the Far East and eager once again to stymie Habsburg ambitions in the Balkans by forging an anti-Austrian Balkan coalition. Secure in the knowledge that Russia was supportive of a Serb-Bulgarian alliance, and taking advantage of the Turks' involvement in a war with Italy over Tripoli that erupted in 1911, the two Balkan Slavic states hammered out a military treaty of mutual assistance in early 1912 that was aimed at both Austria-Hungary and the Ottoman Empire. A secret annex dealt with the future fate of Balkan regions still lying under Turkish control. The Sandjak of Novi Pazar, Kosovo, and a large strip of northern Macedonia ("Old Serbia") were to go to Serbia. Western Thrace, with its Aegean coastline, was ceded to Bulgaria. The bulk of Macedonia was to be formed into an autonomous province, which the Bulgarians had long sought through their control of IMRO and which would actually serve as a Bulgarian puppet state until such a time as it could be incorporated directly into Bulgaria. Should the autonomous province prove an unworkable idea, the secret provision provided for its further division, with Bulgaria and Serbia each receiving additional strips of territory and the remaining areas subject to Russian arbitration as to their final allotment.

Later in the year a Greek-Bulgarian anti-Turk military alliance was signed, in which no territorial issues were defined since both states desired the important Macedonian port of Thessaloniki. In the fall, by which time all the Balkan states were intent on attacking the Ottoman Empire, Montenegro signed alliances with both Serbia and Bulgaria that committed it to initiating hostilities against the Turks by the end of September, to be followed soon thereafter by Bulgaria and Serbia. Thus the Balkan League attained its final composition. All of its members were heavily armed and united in their determination to pursue unrelenting offensive warfare against their common Islamic enemy. Meanwhile, the Ottoman state was harried by Italian attacks and in internal disarray. In May 1912 the Albanians had risen in rebellion against the Young Turk policies and succeeded briefly in forcing them from office. The Ottoman military's morale and strength were collapsing under pressure from external and internal defeats. Furthermore, the Bismarckian system of alliances that had succeeded in dividing all of Europe into two opposing camps made it difficult for the Great Powers to take any effective moves toward defusing local crises without their first consulting both allies and enemies as to the extent of action acceptable by all concerned. By October 1912, conditions could not have been better for the Balkan allies to commence their common war on the Ottoman Empire.[58]

Ignoring Russian pleas to wait, or at least to realize that the Great Powers would never consent to the Balkan states' annexing any Turkish territory conquered by force, Montenegro declared war on the Turks on 7 October. Ten days later all the other Balkan allies followed suit. There was little doubt that the war was fought primarily to decide the ultimate fate of Macedonia. When viewed in such a light, it is obvious that the formation of the Balkan League and its military nature constituted a deft piece of nationalist strategy on the part of the underdogs in the Macedonian struggle—the Serbs and the Greeks—to nullify the advantages held by the natural front-runner, Bulgaria. Simple military geography forced the Bulgarians, the easternmost of the allies, to focus the overwhelming thrust of their military efforts in the wrong direction, against the main Turkish forces in Thrace, while their three allies faced mostly demoralized and understrength enemy units in the west, in and around Macedonia itself. Serb forces easily overran and occupied close to two-thirds of Macedonia and then went on to invade Albania. Greek troops pushed into northern Epiros and into the southern areas of Macedonia, occupying Thessaloniki over loud Bulgarian protests. Meanwhile, the Bulgarians found themselves in a bloody contest over possession of Edirne and received a gruesome foretaste of trench warfare in their assaults on the successive Turkish fortified defensive positions of Lüle Burgas and Çatalca, the latter almost within sight of the Ottoman capital of Istanbul. By the time Edirne fell to a Bulgarian siege in March 1913, only Istanbul itself and Shkodër, in Albania, remained of Turkey-in-Europe. In April an armistice was signed. In May the Treaty of London ended hostilities.

The ink had barely dried on the treaty before dissention arose among the victorious Balkan allies over the disposition of the conquered territories. The European Great Powers had decided that an autonomous Albania had to be created in the western Adriatic region of the Balkans. Their planned Albanian state included areas ceded to Serbia in the original Serb-Bulgarian alliance treaty. In compensation for that loss, the Serbs demanded a larger share of Macedonia, to which the Bulgarians adamantly objected. Both the Bulgarians and the Greeks were soon at loggerheads over possession of Thessaloniki. Smelling nationalist blood, the Romanians, who had remained neutral during the war, then placed a bid for part of Dobrudzha, south of the Danube, which had been in Bulgarian hands since the Berlin Treaty of 1878. Russia attempted to smooth the frictions among the allies, but relations between Bulgaria, on the one hand, and Serbia and Greece, on the other, grew steadily worse. In June 1913 the latter two states concluded an anti-Bulgarian alliance to defend their zones of occupation in Macedonia against possible Bulgarian encroachment, and then they proceeded to win Montenegrin support. Both Romania and the Turks also were approached, but they gave no concrete assurances that they would support any future action against the Bulgarians. As tensions mounted, Russia urged all three of the main protagonists to send representatives to St. Petersburg for talks leading to a peaceful settlement, but the Russian initiative was ignored.

While the diplomats argued and schemed, all three of the contentious allies were transferring troops to the lines established in and around Macedonia. Border clashes between Bulgarians and their increasingly belligerent allies multiplied. Nationalist emotion within Bulgaria rapidly built to fever pitch. The army grew restless, demanding either action or demobilization. Bulgarian public opinion, whipped up by the hysterical agitation of various Macedonian immigrant groups who threatened to assassinate Ferdinand and important members of his government if they did not act, clamored for war against both the Greeks and the Serbs. The military high command, which had hurriedly redeployed the bulk of the army from the eastern front facing the Turks to the western front facing Macedonia, assured Ferdinand that all was ready for decisive action. In late June the command was given to attack the Serbian and Greek positions in Macedonia. It proved a naive and foolish move.

Serbia and Greece immediately declared war on Bulgaria. Montenegro followed suit, and in July both Romania and the Ottomans did likewise. The Bulgarians found themselves in an untenable military position, assaulted on two fronts, and could offer only meager resistance to the concerted attacks of their enemies. They were easily defeated by the Serbs and Greeks in Macedonia, while the Turks managed to regain all of Thrace up to and including Edirne, and the Romanians captured Dobrudzha, eventually occupying the Bulgarian capital of Sofia itself. In a little over a month the Second Balkan War was over, disastrously, for Bulgaria. Again, deft diplomatic efforts on the part of the anti-Bulgarian allies had succeeded in maneuvering the Bulgarians into a disadvantageous position, in this case forcing them to play the role of aggressors and thus forfeiting any sympathetic support from among the international diplomatic community. The defeated state was stripped of most gains won in the first war, including Western Thrace and its Aegean port of Kavalla (which was placed into Greek hands), Edirne and most of Eastern Thrace (which reverted to the Turks), and most new acquisitions in Macedonia, except for a slice in the Pirin Mountain-Struma River areas. Romania retained much of Dobrudzha, while Greece and Serbia divided the rest of Macedonia between themselves—the Greeks retaining Thessaloniki and the southern portions of the region; the Serbs acquiring the lion's share of the central and northern portions, including Bitola.[59] For all intents and purposes, the borders established for Bulgaria and Greece in 1913 proved relatively permanent into the present day. Those of Serbian Macedonia did as well, though they came to denote an independent socialist republic following World War II and an independent state of Macedonia after 1991.

◄ ►

The net results of the Balkan wars were a national humiliation for the Bulgarians of the first magnitude. From 1870, with the founding of the Exarchate, until 1912, and the outbreak of the First Balkan War, there had been little doubt in their collective mind that Macedonia would eventually be joined to the Bulgarian nation-state. History and culture had appeared to validate that certainty. Objective Western observers, such as the Americans, had concurred. So too had Russia, their powerful fellow Slavic and Orthodox ally— the Russians had even given the region to them at San Stefano in early 1878. As the Ottoman Empire had slipped deeper into internal chaos, making its dismemberment seemingly imminent, impatience over actually acquiring Macedonia had lit an increasingly fervent nationalist fire among the Bulgarians that, by 1913, reached fever pitch. But in little over a month in that year, all of their nationalist hopes and dreams had been dashed. A nationalist depression, followed by frustration and then deep rumblings of revenge, descended on the Bulgarians.

When the Serbs' overconfident sense of nationalism, stoked by success against the Bulgarians in Macedonia, led them to venture boldly into intensifying dangerous revolutionary activities in Bosnia-Hercegovina, the cataclysmic result was World War I. Bulgaria, still smarting from the recent defeat by former allies, at first remained neutral, savoring the harsh price charged Serbia by the Central Powers in the war for its nationalist pretensions. Both they and their Entente enemies made efforts to woo Bulgaria to their causes, since the country's location—between the Ottoman Empire to its south and Serbia and Romania to its north—was strategically significant in the grand plans of both sides. If Bulgaria could be brought into the Entente, it would completely cut off the Turks from their German Central Power allies and establish a strong front in support of the Serbs against Austria-Hungary in the Balkans. Thus the Central Powers would be divided and their weakest link—the Turks—isolated and rendered ineffectual. On the other hand, should Bulgaria be brought into the Central Powers' ranks, it would establish a solid and well-connected military bloc, able to outflank Serbia and to contain the Greeks in the south of the Balkans, should they decide to enter the war on the side of the Entente.

Tsar Ferdinand of Bulgaria, having learned the lesson of haste in 1913, played Bulgarian neutrality to the hilt. Both sides proffered territorial concessions to the Bulgarians in 1915 to win their allegiance. The Entente offered the eastern half of Serbian Macedonia and a chunk of Turkish Eastern Thrace. Ferdinand countered with demands for all of Macedonia, part of Eastern Thrace, and virtually all of Western Thrace, including the port of Kavalla, which was then in Greek hands, and the section of Dobrudzha lost to Romania in 1913. The Entente's negotiating position was restricted severely by the fact that Serbia was an ally over whom they ostensibly had gone to war, Greece was almost an ally, and Romania, also neutral, was being wooed along with Bulgaria. Meeting the Bulgarian demands entailed forcing concessions from allies and friends alike. The Central Powers had no such concerns. They freely granted Ferdinand all that he desired, since they cost them virtually nothing—the Turks were persuaded to turn over to Bulgaria a strip of land along the Maritsa River.[60]

In October 1915 Bulgaria entered the war on the side of the Central Powers, intent on winning all that had been lost in 1913, and more—complete control of all Macedonia. The Bulgarian forces inflicted a telling blow on the Serbs, driving them into the sea through Albania, and then bottled up French and English forces in Thessaloniki and southern Macedonia until the closing months of the war in 1918. By that time the Bulgarians' heavy-handed administrative measures and self-superior cultural policies had managed to alienate the Macedonian Slavs under their occupation. The general war exhaustion and internal chaos of Austria-Hungary, Bulgaria's closest military ally, led to the rapid collapse of the Bulgarian forces facing the Entente allies in the Balkans in September 1918. In a matter of fifteen days the front disintegrated, and Bulgaria signed an armistice ending the fighting. Ferdinand abdicated. Much of Bulgaria was occupied by the victorious allies, and the Serbs retook their former portion of Macedonia. The Versailles Treaty of Neuilly, signed in 1919, stripped Bulgaria of nearly all its wartime territorial gains, including Macedonia and Western Thrace, and required its recognition of the new state of Yugoslavia, to which Macedonia was attached. For good measure, the country was forced to pay hefty war reparations, and its army was severely restricted in size and materiel.[61]

After suffering two successive national humiliations, the post–World War I Bulgarian government of Boris III (1918–43), headed by Prime Minister Aleksandŭr Stamboliiski, attempted to dampen ultranationalist ferment over Macedonia by developing friendly relations with the new Serb-dominated Yugoslav government and by clamping down on IMRO activities in Bulgaria. Stamboliiski's conciliatory efforts only resulted in stirring up the intense hatred of IMRO leaders and nationalistic army officers, who staged a concerted coup against him in 1923, in the course of which Stamboliiski was brutally murdered. IMRO then stepped up its terrorist raids from Bulgaria into Yugoslav Macedonia.[62]

The IMRO terrorists found much popular support among the Macedonian Slavs. Following the end of the war, the Serb Yugoslav government initiated a policy of Serbianization in Macedonia in an effort to remove permanently any possibility of future pro-Bulgarian sentiment among its population. The Macedonians received no official recognition as a separate nationality. They were forced to use Serbian as their official and as their educational language, and they were rarely placed into high government or church offices. The Serb government called them "Serbs" and their region "South Serbia." In the face of such cultural-ethnic discrimination, the Macedonian Slavs not only clandestinely supported the IMRO terrorists who entered their land from Bulgaria, but formed similar secret organizations of their own to combat the overweening Serbs. They established contacts with the Croatian *Ustaše* terrorists and frequently conducted joint actions with them—the assassination of Serb-Yugoslav king Aleksandr I (1921–34) in Marseilles being a case in point.[63]

In the 1920s IMRO was entrenched in the Pirin region of southwestern Bulgaria, over which it exercised veritable total governing control. It even collected taxes from the local population to finance its terrorist efforts. For all practical purposes, the region became a small Macedonian state within Bulgaria. The governing IMRO grew increasingly terroristic in its activities and forceful in its demands for Macedonia's annexation by Bulgaria. The Serb authorities of Yugoslavia erected a heavily fortified border with Bulgaria, which constituted a 400-mile stretch of barbed wire, ditches, pillboxes, and watchtowers, in an effort to prevent IMRO raiders from penetrating into the country. But though IMRO appeared just as formidable as earlier, it was wracked by internal dissention over policy and objectives.

The old division between annexationists and autonomists that had persisted since the early days of the organization's founding was multiplied with the appearance within its ranks of Communists seeking the creation of an autonomous socialist republic of Macedonia. A short-lived coalition of all three views in the early 1920s gave way to internal civil war. Between 1924 and 1934, when IMRO was finally outlawed by the Bulgarian government, some 400 individuals were killed in the intraterrorist fighting that degenerated into gangsterism. The streets of Sofia took on the aspect of those in Chicago during the Capone years. The pro-Bulgarian annexationists, led by a young Ivan Mihailov, briefly enjoyed the protection of the government and the king. Their non-Communist opponents, who called for an autonomous Macedonia within a Bulgarian-Yugoslav federation, did not and suffered accordingly. But

calmer heads within Bulgaria soon tired of the violence. Realizing that a nor-
malization of relations with Yugoslavia was necessary for any future chance
of peace in the Balkans, a group of reserve officers and progressive intellectuals carried out a government coup in 1934 that established a one-year dictatorship. As one of their first acts, IMRO was banned. Mihailov was forced
to flee the country, and IMRO was effectively suppressed.

By the time of its demise, IMRO had fallen from being a true revolutionary organization to a racketeering-gangster operation that extorted money
from the thousands of Macedonian immigrants living in southwestern
Bulgaria. It was heavily involved in illegal drug manufacturing and smuggling,
and operated numerous opium refineries in its southwestern heartland.
Blackmail, extortion, "protection," forced "contributions," and "taxes" became
its primary game, providing it with property assets valued in the millions of
dollars. Ultimately, IMRO came to espouse no concrete nationalist political
or revolutionary program other than the retention of its wealth and power
through the use of empty slogans and naked violence.[64]

All the while IMRO was terrorizing both Bulgaria and Serb-held Macedonia
during the 1920s and early 1930s, Boris's successive governments were
forced to deal with the ballooning problems caused by huge reparations
imposed by Versailles, an agrarian economy that placed the country in further
debt and greatly dependent on the whims of the world market, a flood of
increased Macedonian and Thracian refugees, and continuing border incidents
with both Greece and Yugoslavia. Communist activity rose, culminating in an
uprising in 1923 following the coup against Stamboliiski. The military dictatorship established in 1934 gave way to one controlled by the king himself in
1936, which proved unpopular within the country.

By 1938 Boris managed to conclude formal agreements with both
Yugoslavia and Greece that lessened the tensions in the Balkans. Bulgaria
was permitted to rearm, which it had already started to do with German support even before its two contentious neighbors had tendered their permis-
sions. German influence in Bulgaria increased as Hitler proffered Boris, a
German by ethnicity and personal inclination, the usual economic treaty that
he used to tie potentially useful allies to his purposes. Hitler needed Bulgaria
as a friend and ally in the Balkans to ensure tranquility on his southern flank
while he first dealt with the West and then, later, with the Soviet Union. A
friendly Bulgaria would keep the rest of the Balkans in line out of fear that
Germany would permit the Bulgarians to take by force all those territories

they claimed on nationalist grounds but had been prevented from acquiring in the past.

The price Hitler paid for Bulgarian friendship was, first, southern Dobrudzha, which he forced his Romanian friends to cede to Bulgaria by the Treaty of Craiova in 1940. Within six months, Bulgaria joined the Axis agreements and was in position to cash in on its German alliance when Hitler was forced to deal militarily with Yugoslavia and Greece so that he could conduct his planned invasion of the Soviet Union with a secure Balkans on his right flank. The price for Bulgaria's participation in the 1941 Balkan Campaign was Macedonia.[65]

In April Bulgaria occupied most of the region, with pro-Italian Albanian forces permitted to do the same in the extreme west. This second Bulgarian foray into Macedonia in as many world wars proved even less happy than the first. The Bulgarians comported themselves as occupiers and earned very little gratitude from the natives for releasing them from Serb control. The occupying forces soon found themselves faced with growing partisan efforts controlled by the Communist parties of both Bulgaria and Yugoslavia. Almost immediately, a dispute over administrative authority erupted between Tito's Yugoslav movement and the Bulgarian party organization headed in Macedonia by Sharlo Shatorov. Tito demanded armed action, while Shatorov urged caution. The Soviet-controlled Comintern, blistering from the German invasion of the Soviet Union, backed Tito, but the Macedonian Communists were uncomfortable with the idea of continued Yugoslav affiliation, given past experience. By 1943 Tito's organization began to win over the Macedonian Communists' reluctance to ally themselves with Yugoslavia through Tito's public rejection of the old Greater Serbian approach formerly taken by the Yugoslav Communist party before his rise to overall control. By late summer 1944 his strictly "Yugoslav" movement was finally triumphant within the Macedonian partisan ranks. At the Monastery of St. Prohor Počinjski in August 1944, the Macedonian Communist partisans proclaimed the creation of a Macedonian People's Republic that would take its equal place among the other five republics in Tito's planned federated socialist state of Yugoslavia.

Only in the last year of the war (1944) did the Macedonian Communists conduct effective, organized partisan military operations in Macedonia. By that time, Axis defeat was all but certain. In mid-November the Bulgarians and their supporting German troops were ejected from Macedonia, and in early September the Soviet Red Army knocked Bulgaria out of the war for good. Immediately following the cessation of hostilities in the region, Tito broached a plan for a socialist South Slav federation composed of Yugoslavia and Bulgaria with the Bulgarian Communist party leader, Georgi Dimitrov.

Negotiations between the two concerning the proposed project continued until Tito's 1948 split with Stalin, at which time Dimitrov, a close associate of the Soviet leader (if that was ever actually possible!), broke off the talks permanently. Soon thereafter, the Macedonians inhabiting the southwestern region of Bulgaria lost the official cultural and ethnic recognition as a separate nationality that they had enjoyed there since the late nineteenth century. Even had the Tito-Stalin split never occurred, it seems highly unlikely that the two sides could have satisfactorily agreed on a compromise regarding the nature of Macedonia's position in the planned federation.[66]

While Tito was playing up socialist Slavic unity with his Bulgarian neighbors, he was involved in nurturing the socialist movement in Greece. In mid-1944 his Macedonian partisans were in contact with fellow Slav Communists in Greek Macedonia. The Greek Communist party held to the traditional Greek nationalist line when it came to Macedonia. Just as the Greek governments during the interwar years had imposed a heavy program of Hellenization on those Slavs living in the Macedonian territories they had won—calling them "Slavophone Greeks" and forbidding them to use their native Slavic language under penalty of jail, banishment, or outright violence—the Greek Communists refused to cede control over the Macedonian Slavs in Greece to the Macedonian Communists of Yugoslavia. They were intent on keeping all Greek territory under Greek control.

At the end of 1946 the Greek Communists instigated a guerilla war against the Allied-supported Greek government that escalated into the Greek Civil War (1946-49). They sought support from Tito's Yugoslav party, and they readily accepted military and political assistance from socialist Slav Macedonia. The Tito-Stalin break in 1948 strained relations between the Yugoslav and Greek Communists, and it caused a split within the Greek Communist leadership over continuing relations with Tito and the potentially separatist Macedonian Slav Communists, who had taken a leading role in the war. Early in 1949 the Greek Communists decided against continued reliance on the Yugoslav Macedonians in their struggle. In July Tito closed the Macedonian border with Greece to any further assistance to the Greek Communists, and the Greek Civil War rapidly ended in their defeat.[67]

◄► ►◄

Post–World War II socialist Macedonia enjoyed official recognition as a separate Slav republic in Tito's Yugoslav federation. Its official language was the artificially constructed Macedonian of Koneski and Lunt. The recognized "nation" of that so-called nation-state was the Macedonians and, most specifically, the Macedonian Slavs. Yet Slavs did not constitute the only element in the small socialist republic's population. There also existed various "nationalities," officially recognized under Yugoslav law but subject to unofficial discrimination on the part of the "nation" in reality. Least numerous of those minority groups in Macedonia were Jews, Vlahs, Tsintsars (related to the Vlahs, only urbanized rather than rural pastoralists), Gypsies, Turks, and Albanians. Few Macedonian Jews survived the upheavals of World War II and, of those who did, most emigrated to Israel after the war. The seminomadic lifestyles of the Vlahs and Gypsies were heavily affected by the socialist government's attempts to bring "productive" economic order to their existence during the 1960s, but they achieved only limited success. The Turkish presence in Macedonia had been far larger before the end of World War II, after which there occurred a mass emigration to Turkey. Among those who remained were numbered a few *Torbeses,* Muslims whose Christian Slav ancestors had converted to Islam during the Ottoman period.

Until the post-1945 era, few of the Slav majority in the Macedonian population, and rarely any of the three nationalist contenders for the region, took seriously the single largest non-Slavic ethnic element in Macedonia—the Albanians. Perhaps the primary reason for their being ignored in the national fervor was their late-blossoming sense of nationality. Until 1878 the Albanians' Muslim self-identity had sufficed, given the theocratic, *millet*-based nature of Ottoman sociopolitical and sociocultural existence. The Muslim Albanians had played an important and continuing role in Ottoman Muslim circles from the time of their incorporation into the Turkish empire and the conversion of most to Islam in the fifteenth century. Only when the issue of continued Ottoman existence was raised to a serious level of international consideration by the Congress of Berlin in 1878 did the Albanians begin to look to a future not tied directly to the Turks.[68]

The Albanian Roman Catholic minority possessed close contacts with fellow conational emigrés in Italy, through whom they were exposed to Western nationalist concepts. This they passed on to the Muslim Albanian majority, who began to feel threatened by the Young Turks' rising ultra-nationalist Turkish policies after 1908. The Muslim-led but unsuccessful Albanian nationalist uprising of 1912, aimed at winning an autonomous nation-state of their own, gained Western, especially Italian, sympathy and support. In 1913 the Albanians gained their independent state in the Treaty of London, which ended the First Balkan War. Although the Great Powers did not establish definite borders for the new state at that time, they forbade Greek, Serb, and Montenegrin encroachment into regions considered to be mostly Albanian in ethnic composition, causing much resentment among those victorious and land-hungry

Balkan states. With borders ill-defined and governing institutions in flux, Albania was caught up in World War I. The Italians landed in the country in the first months of the war and gradually came to occupy most of its southern territories, while the Serbs and Montenegrins did likewise in the north. In 1916 all of them were evicted by Austria-Hungary, and the Albanian government of Essad Pasha fled to Italy. At war's end, a new government, led by Turhan Pasha, faced Serb-Yugoslav and Italian incursions, and succeeded in evicting the latter in 1920.

Problems then arose with the new Yugoslav state. The Serb-dominated government encouraged the Albanians of Yugoslav Kosovo to proclaim a pro-Yugoslav Albanian state in 1921, thus giving the Serbs an excuse to intervene inside independent Albania. They were successful in having their creature, Ahmed Bey Zogu, installed as Albanian premier in 1922, but a revolution against the Serb puppet, supported by Italy and led by Fan Noli, forced Zogu out. In retaliation, a Serb-organized counterrevolution in 1924 succeeded in overthrowing Noli and returning Zogu, who in 1925 was proclaimed president and given almost dictatorial powers. Ties with Italy thereafter grew, while Yugoslav influence waned. With Italian support, Zogu was proclaimed King Zog I (1928–39), after which, his head turned by his new royal title, Zog steadily broke his ties to his Italian benefactors. In 1934 the Italians intimidated Zog into reversing his anti-Italian policies with a strong naval demonstration along the Adriatic coast. This was followed by intensive Italian trading and financial investments in Albania. Still not content with Zog, who continuously resisted Italian attempts to control his government's policies, the Italians invaded Albania in the middle of the international confusion caused by Hitler's complete takeover of Czechoslovakia in 1939, pushed out Zog, and forced the Albanians to recognize the Italian king Victor Emmanuel as their ruler.[69]

During World War II, Albania became the battlefield between Greeks and Italians (later also Germans) in 1940-41. Left under Mussolini's fascist control after the defeat of Greece in 1941, the Albanians found their liberator in Enver Hoxha, a Communist partisan leader operating under the wing of Tito's powerful Yugoslav organization, who succeeded in expelling the fascists in 1944. The Tito-Stalin split of 1948 erected an ideological wall between socialist Albania and socialist Yugoslavia that precluded any possible common development among the Albanians living on opposite sides of the border separating the two states. The Albanians of Serbian Kosovo and of Macedonia were left to fend for themselves as ethnic-national minorities in Slav Yugoslav republics. For most of the post-World War II era, the Yugoslav Albanians were aware that they enjoyed a standard of living significantly higher than that of their conationals in Maoist, isolated Albania.

That knowledge permitted them to tolerate somewhat their minority status in Yugoslavia.

✄   ✄

All the threads of Balkan history, as well as of the various Balkan nationalisms, pass through and intersect in Macedonia. The explosive potential of that simple fact, which was amply demonstrated from the initiation of the Macedonian Question in the 1870s, was suppressed following 1945 by the iron will of Tito through the Yugoslav federation that he created and oversaw. The gradual unraveling of the socialist federation of Yugoslavia that set in following Tito's death in 1980, coupled with the collapse of faith in any future benefits continued adherence to socialism might bring following the onset of Gorbachev's perestroika policies, and the subsequent reemergence of old-fashioned nationalism among the various "nations" and "nationalities" within the dying state, opened the door for a renewed outbreak of the Macedonian Question.

Following the example set by Slovenia and Croatia earlier in 1991, Macedonia, led by a coalition of nationalist parties, declared its independence from the Serb-dominated rump of Yugoslavia (Serbia and Montenegro) by the close of the year. Initial Albanian street demonstrations in the capital of Skopje were dampened by the admission of Albanians to the ruling government cabinet by the end of 1992. To mollify the Turks in the country, a Turk was admitted as well, all of which made the Macedonian the only such multiethnic governing body in post-Communist Eastern Europe. If the Macedonians were expecting smooth international recognition of their independence, they were sorely mistaken. Only Bulgaria, followed swiftly by Turkey, proffered the expected response. Both, of course, possessed various historical-national reasons for doing so. General international recognition was stymied by Greece, which played on its NATO and European Union (EU) memberships in an attempt to head off what it considered a real threat to its nation-state territory in the north. The Greeks too had historic-national reasons for their stubbornness.

Not only had Greece pursued a near-fanatical nationalist program throughout the entire course of the original Macedonian Question, between 1870 and 1912, but once it had secured control over those Macedonian territories won in the Balkan wars, it had undertaken a radical campaign of forced Hellenization on the population in those regions with the intent of eliminating forever any trace of Slavic existence. Yet despite the legal suppression of the Slavic vernacular, the police intimidation of so-called Slavophone Greeks, the officially sanctioned terrorist destruction of Slav villages, the forced emigrations of recalcitrant Slavs, the resettlement of large numbers of Anatolian

Greeks who had been forced out of Turkey by Atatürk's successful revolution, and other assorted acts of anti-Slav violence perpetrated by the Greeks in their Macedonian possessions, they proved unable (or unwilling) to overcome their fear of the Slavs north of their borders and their doubts as to the effectiveness of their policies on the Slavs inside them. The fact that the Greek Communists who fought in the civil war mostly had hailed from Greek Macedonia, and that their Slav Macedonian Communist allies had openly broadcast their notions that the Greek Macedonians should be united with socialist Slav Macedonia, further fed the Greeks' paranoia over the national situation in their northern territories.

The Greek civil war, the dictatorial *junta* of the colonels, and the ongoing confrontation with Turkey over Cyprus since the Turkish invasion and partition of the island in 1974 kept Greek nationalism burning at fever pitch like few others in Eastern Europe following the close of World War II. Using as a pretext the probably innocent, but unfortunate, adoption by the new Skopje Macedonian government of the Sunburst of Vergina, a royal symbol of ancient Macedon, as the state's official insignia, the Greek government dragged out its old historical arguments concerning Alexander the Great and ancient Macedon. It promptly and hysterically canvassed its NATO and EU partners in efforts to squash any possible swift recognition of the new Macedonian state. The Greeks' ultranationalist hysteria involved in their argument's forced objectivity was transparent: The name "Macedonia" was Greek and not Slavic; the name was geographic and not ethnic; the mixed-ethnic inhabitants of the Republic of Skopje (as the Greeks insisted on calling former Yugoslav Macedonia) had no right to claim symbolic affinity with ancient Macedon; and so forth. Little of such argument made sense if considered objectively. It mattered not that the name "Macedonia" was Greek originally or that it was regional rather than ethnic. Over the course of centuries, every administration that had held sway in the region—Roman, Byzantine, Bulgarian, Serbian, Ottoman—used the name as a traditional means of regional identity. That the ethnically mixed inhabitants of the region could acquire a common regional identity historically was not an uncommon phenomenon for such a situation. Belgians were ethnically Walloon (French) and Flemish (Dutch); the Swiss were French, German, and Italian; Canadians were English, French, and Native American; and the Americans were a hodgepodge of any number of ethnic groups. Only the Greeks' objection to the use of the ancient sunburst of Macedon as the new state's official symbol held some water, since it had nothing to do with the native traditions of any ethnic group living there. But whether the leaders of the new state were attempting to plagiarize "Greek" traditions and hinting at future territorial expansion at Greek expense or merely found the symbol graphically powerful was the unanswered question. The nationalistically emotional Greeks assumed the worst.

The Greeks truly feared the possibility that the Skopje government's use of the name "Macedonia" and the ancient sunburst symbol meant that it harbored future territorial claims on Macedonian Greece, including the port of Thessaloniki, and that a residual pro-Slav national affinity still existed among some elements of the Greek Macedonian population despite the radical Greek nationalist pogroms of the past. Their frenzied campaign on the international stage against recognition of independent, post-Yugoslav Macedonia succeeded in delaying such action until 1993, largely because of their NATO and EU membership and partly because, as the Greeks fully realized, most Westerners held an innate philhellenic sympathy that was not easily overcome. In the end, the Greeks' prolonged nationalist hysteria over the matter, their periodic embargoes on much-needed supplies intended for Macedonia landing in Thessaloniki, and their forging of closer ties with the ultranationalist Serb Milošević government (and the anti-Albanian/anti-Macedonian overtones those ties implied) wore thin the philhellene sentiments of their Western allies. In 1993 the new state of Macedonia won recognition in the United Nations, which was soon followed by individual states of the international community, including the United States.

Still, the Greeks persisted in ratcheting up their anti-Macedonian nationalist campaign. Mass demonstrations fanned by ultranationalist rhetoric in Thessaloniki were televised to the world. In April 1994 that city's port was closed to all traffic destined for Macedonia. In the old terrorist tradition, the Greeks infiltrated bands into southern Albania, sparking not only strong Albanian protests against Greece but also, because of the nationalist danger posed by such actions, requests for Albanian political autonomy within Macedonia. As a result, the Greeks' Western allies imposed an embargo on Greece and issued strong warnings against continued Greek aggressiveness. Meanwhile, Turkey, Greece's NATO partner but perennial national enemy, moved closer to Bulgaria, despite that country's atrocious anti-Turk policies during the final decade of Communist rule.

Taking the "long view," by mid-1994 Macedonia had reemerged as the tinderbox of the Balkans. With ultranationalist Serbia and Greece aligned against Albania, Bulgaria, and Turkey, all that was missing for igniting a general Balkan war was the match. That could be supplied either by the warfare raging in Bosnia-Hercegovina spreading through Sandjak to Kosovo and then spilling over into Macedonia, or by an outright Serbian victory in Bosnia-Hercegovina despite all of the West's protests over their barbarous actions, which the Serbs could then interpret as a green light to deal with their Kosovo Albanian Muslims in a similar fashion without worrying about effective Western intervention. In such a situation, it would be difficult to restrain the Albanians in Albania and Macedonia from acting in support of their conationals in Kosovo. Once that occurred, Macedonia would explode and all of the parties would be drawn into the struggle. A third scenario for detonating a general Balkan war would find the Greeks so nationalistically aroused that they would precipitate hostilities while the West was still focused on the conflict in Bosnia-Hercegovina but disunited in its responses, most probably by escalating the sort of actions already taken against Macedonia and Albania in the hope of forcing one or both to overreact aggressively.

In any event, no matter how the flame might be lit, once it was (should it be), little could be done to put out the fire before the inevitable explosion. Bulgaria, Turkey, and Albania would be forced to intervene in Macedonia to protect their national interests (and ambitions). This would be especially imperative for Bulgaria, given its past involvements with Macedonia and the post-1991 development within its southwestern Pirin region of a separatist Macedonian party intent on breaking away from the country and joining the new Macedonian state. So too would Greece and Serbia feel constrained to enter the Macedonian fray, but on the opposing side. Not only would war in the Balkans become general, but it would spell the end of NATO in its present sense.

As bad as that development would be, things could grow a lot worse very quickly should such a war commence. With US troops on the ground in Macedonia caught in a military situation in which forces would be approaching from all sides, America could not help but become involved. Since the purpose of their presence is essentially anti-Serb, pro-Albanian, and, after recognition of Macedonia, pro-Macedonian, America most likely would be forced to stand with the Macedonians, Bulgarians, Turks, and Albanians against the Serbs and the Greeks. Given past performances in the Gulf War and in the various ineffectual efforts regarding Bosnia-Hercegovina, America would not participate as the lone Western state involved. That reality would lead to the inevitable expansion of hostilities with EU and NATO involvement in some form or another. Neither would have a chance of surviving such a situation intact as it is currently constituted. And finally, given Russia's historical involvement in the Balkans, it would be unrealistic to assume that it would not become involved in such a general conflict. The question would be: On which side? Would Russia support its Serbian or its Bulgarian traditional allies? The answer to those questions could well make the difference between localizing the nationalist conflicts to the Balkans or initiating World War III.

Of course, none of the speculation need happen at all. Cool heads and calm diplomacy based on a deep understanding of the explosive nationalist dangers posed by Macedonia can prevail. What is needed is honest objectivity, especially on the part of the Western powers that must provide the clear-headed leadership, direction, and example for the highly agitated Balkan states. What cannot be afforded is a Western approach predicated on ignorance of the deep-seated, complex, and long-lived nationalist atmosphere surrounding Macedonia. In the conditions existing in the Balkans during 1994, Macedonia is far from being "safe," even if it is two hundred miles from Sarajevo.

THE BORDERS OF POLAND

- – – – – – Current International Border
- ▬ ▬ ▬ ▬ Current Border of Poland (Established 1945)
- • • • • • • • Interwar Border of Poland (Established 1921)
- ▬▬▬▬ Border of Poland-Lithuania at its Greatest Extent (1634-1635)

0   100   200   300
MILES

BETWEEN WARSAW AND MOSCOW

● ○ ●

Perhaps no other region of Eastern Europe better demonstrates the critical relationship between geography and human development than does the Great Polish Plain of Northeastern Europe. Bounded on the north by the Baltic Sea and on the south by the highlands of the Carpathian and Sudet mountains, the region is merely a cross-section of the vast transcontinental plain that spans the Eurasian landmass from Flanders in the west to the Siberian Verhoyansk and Cherskiy mountains in the east. Nature has placed few natural obstacles across the course of the Great Eurasian Plain, and those that do impede its passage in some way—the Ural Mountains and the Central Siberian Uplands—lie deep inside Central Asia.

For the human societies that came to inhabit the northeast European region of the open Great Plain—Poles, Lithuanians, Ukrainians, Belorussians—the sealike, rolling environment, lacking both natural north-south barriers affording protection or separation from neighbors and abundant natural resources, exerted a continuous and decisive influence on their cultures and histories. It shaped them into microcultures that cherished highly such human qualities as rugged, independent individualism, cunning, and volatility. To their north, inhabiting areas of the plain that were even less naturally fruitful and mostly covered by forests, bogs, and marshes, were the Prussian Germans and the Great Russians. Their inhospitable environments molded them into societies whose cultures reflected such human social characteristics as authoritarianism, discipline, stubbornness, and organization.

While the two variations in the Great Plain's habitat—open and wooded—bred differences in the human microcultures developed by the inhabitants of each, the overriding lack of physical barriers and the paucity of natural resources were factors common to both. Thus their societies shared many characteristics. In both areas they tended to exhibit aggressiveness, which often bordered on foolhardiness. All of them leaned toward imperialism because of a commonly perceived need to control as much of the available but limited natural resources as possible. Those societies living on the open plain grew quick to respond to outside threats against what lands they possessed and just as swift to threaten the holdings of their neighbors in attempts to gain more. The forest societies honed their traits of discipline and social organization to do likewise. Yet despite the expansionary drives environmentally spawned by the Great Plain, only those societies—the Prussian Germans and the Great Russians—that succeeded in establishing firm roots in regions outside the plain proper, which could provide more readily natural defenses and increased resources, managed to create for themselves strong, stable states able to withstand the uncertainties and scarcities of the plain environment alone. Although the open plain-dwelling Ukrainians, Lithuanians, and Poles all succeeded in winning territorially large states of their own at times in the past, their inability to push much beyond the confines of the Great Plain doomed them to eventual collapse. What states they salvaged from the ruins of their expansionary efforts thereafter lay at the mercies of their more successful Russian and German neighbors.

The sweeping human conflicts in Northeastern Europe that accompanied the microcultural development of the societies of the Great Plain since the ninth century could not help but become merged with the macrocultural discords between the Eastern and Western European civilizations, once the Ukrainians, Great Russians, and Belorussians opted for the Orthodox Christianity of Byzantium but the Poles, Lithuanians, and Prussian Germans aligned themselves with Rome and Catholicism—a civilizational process that reached its maturity by the close of the fifteenth century. From that time into the present, the Great Polish Plain of Northeastern Europe served as one of the tumultuous battlegrounds between the two European civilizations. And of all the human societies inhabiting that region, that of the Poles has been located at its most tempestuous epicenter.

⚔ ▷

The Poles emerged abruptly into history in 963. In that year Saxon Germans, who were pushing eastward, stumbled on an existing, well-organized Slavic state that until then had been unknown to anyone in the Germanic European world. That state was ruled by a tribal chieftain named Mieszko I (ca. 960–92), who bore the title of *piast* (an office that originally meant second-in-command, but which Mieszko's family used so successfully to establish its rule over the various tribes within the state that it became the family's dynastic name). A shrewd individual, Mieszko quickly realized that the Poles' paganism made them vulnerable to increasing pressures from the Christian Germans, who could use the cause of converting the Poles as an excuse to win political domination over them and control of their territories. Mieszko pulled the rug out from under the German pressure by forging contacts with the Roman papacy through the already Christianized Slavic Czechs of Bohemia. In 965-66 the Poles officially converted to Roman Catholicism and placed themselves directly under papal protection, thus assuring the continued independence of the Polish state from the Germans of the Holy Roman Empire.[1]

The papacy welcomed the allegiance of the Poles since it needed allies on the Holy Roman Empire's eastern flank against the growing competition of the German emperors for recognition of ultimate temporal authority in medieval Western Europe. (For similar reasons, the papacy encouraged the conversion of the pagan Magyars in Pannonia and bestowed on them a hereditary royal crown in 1000.) To help ensure Polish independence from the Germans and to further solidify their loyalty to Rome, around the year 1000 the papacy granted the Poles their own Catholic archbishop under the direct authority of Rome, thus removing them from any German ecclesiastical-political control. The Polish archbishop's seat in the town of Gniezno also soon became the capital of the Piast rulers, demonstrating the close linkage of the independent Polish state with that of the Polish Roman Catholic church organization.

From its establishment as a Christian European state until the early fifteenth century, Poland was firmly ensconced in the political and cultural affairs of Catholic Western Europe. Mieszko's son and successor, Bolesław I the Brave (992–1025), brought stable administration to Poland. He attempted to create a large West Slavic state under his direct authority, briefly acquiring the Czech Bohemian throne (1003–4) and moving against Kievan Russia in Ukraine. At his death, a six-year dynastic struggle ensued, in which Czech Přemysls briefly occupied the Polish throne in their turn. Under the Piast Bolesław II the Bold (1058–79), Poland was immersed in the investiture conflicts between Rome and the Holy Roman Empire on the side of the papacy, and, during the reign of Bolesław III Wrymouth (1102–38), the near-constant wars between Poland and the German Holy Roman Empire resulted in the recognition of Polish independence from any claim of control by the German emperor. Wrymouth pushed the borders of his state northward to the shores of the Baltic Sea, Christianized the pagan Pomeranians, and incorporated their territories. For the first time in its history, Poland had broken the land lock of the Great Polish Plain.[2]

At Wrymouth's death, however, Poland was plunged into internal chaos over the royal succession. Part of the problem lay in the nature of the Polish royal crown itself. Unlike the hereditary crown granted the Magyars in 1000, the papacy bestowed on its Polish royal allies only personal crowns recognizing the authority of its individual wearer alone. Each new ruler had to apply to Rome for renewed recognition of his authority. The implied uncertainties regarding royal legitimacy had repercussions in the matter of succession to the throne.

In Poland the system of succession to such an essentially personal crown had not been stabilized by Wrymouth's death. The Poles were still an essentially tribal people, though almost two centuries of full participation in the affairs of Catholic Western Europe had instigated political and social developments that were moving Polish society beyond the strictly tribal level—developments such as recognized royal leadership and the emergence of social stratification, with the rise of a warrior-knight aristocratic class collectively termed the *szlachta* (derived from the German word for "estate": *geschlecht).* The close contacts with Rome and the Germans slowly brought to Poland the influence of their concepts of primogeniture regarding royal succession. Western notions of primogenitor percolated among the Piasts in competition with the Poles' more traditional ideas of family seniority for determining the heir to the throne, in which the eldest surviving brother of the leader succeeded at the latter's death. The seniority approach to leadership prevailed in most tribal societies but proved, more often than not, highly disruptive because of the sibling rivalries that almost always ensued, while primogeniture, in which the eldest surviving son succeeded his father as ruler, represented a step ahead in political development since it succinctly defined the recognized heir to the throne.

The seniority principle held in Poland. Wrymouth, through his contacts with the Kievan Russian state in western Ukraine, attempted to standardize it by adapting the Kievan rotary system of succession. In Kiev the tribal Russians had created a somewhat functioning legitimation of seniority among the members of their Rurik ruling house by ranking regions within the state in order of political precedence. The leader of the Kievan state—the grand prince—held the town and region of Kiev itself. His brothers were each given regional principalities ranked successively lower than that of Kiev. At the death of the grand prince, the brother holding the next highest ranked principality moved to Kiev and became the new grand prince, while the other surviving brothers each moved up one slot in the provincial ranking.[3] Wrymouth had five sons and, using the Kievan model, divided his Polish kingdom into five regions. He retained the town and region of Cracow (Kraków) as the royal capital and principality. At his death, it was expected that his eldest son would inherit Cracow and, along with it, recognized leadership in the state based on seniority. His other sons would each then rotate their holdings according to their ages to reflect the new ranking.

Just as the rotary seniority system eventually broke down in Kiev, representing an innate weakness of an essentially tribal state that made it vulnerable to more highly centralized foreign enemies (in the Kievan case, the Mongol-Tatars), its Polish manifestation failed almost immediately. Instead of the rotary system stabilizing the tradition of seniority, at Wrymouth's death the state was plunged into anarchy. His sons had a difficult time accepting the political realities of the rotary regions, while their own sons set out to subdivide their fathers' regions further. The conflicts the system instigated among the various family members wracked the Polish state with internal disunity. For the following 150 years, although certain individuals of the Piast family laid claim to the personal royal crown, it was difficult to tell who actually ruled in Poland. In the midst of the internal political discord, Poland was devastated by two Mongol invasions, in 1241 and 1259, which led to the invited colonization of Hanse Germans and the Teutonic Knights in the northern regions of the state to help rebuild, redevelop, and protect territories hard hit by the eastern intruders. Near the end of that long period of internal anarchy, the foreign Bohemian Czech Přemysls claimed the Polish royal throne for themselves. Only the papacy's recognition of the Piast Władisław IV Łokietek (1305–33) as hereditary, rather than personal, king of Poland finally put an end to the long struggle for the Polish throne and lent the royal office a sense of solidity that it had never before possessed.[4]

With the country once again stabilized internally, the Poles resumed a leading role in the affairs of the West. Close contacts with Bohemia continued. Bohemian king Charles I of Luxemburg (1346–78), who also reigned as Holy Roman Emperor Charles IV from 1347, established Prague as both his royal and imperial capital and transformed the city into the leading political and cultural center in Eastern Europe. He represented a powerful role model for Polish king Casimir III the Great (1333–70). When Charles founded in Prague the first university east of the Rhine River in 1348 in an effort to centralize higher education in Bohemia and to institutionalize Czech cultural development, Casimir followed suit by establishing a similar institution, the second founded in Eastern Europe, in his capital at Cracow in 1364. From that time on, Cracow represented not only Poland's political capital but its cultural fountainhead as well.[5]

Although political stability and cultural flowering characterized Poland during the fourteenth century, the Poles' problems with the Teutonic Knights and a growing settler population from the German Hanse towns in the Baltic shore regions of the north caused continuing difficulties for the Polish state. The German presence threatened Poland's continued hold on Pomerania and, through it, access to the Baltic Sea. The Poles proved unable to handle effectively the increasingly independent Teutonic Knights, and violent clashes between Poles and Knights intensified throughout the fourteenth century.

All the while the struggle with the Germans in the north escalated, the Piast ruling family weakened. At Casimir the Great's death, the throne passed to the foreigner Louis of Anjou (1370–82), whose reign, in turn, was followed by a period of civil strife until, in 1384, the last remaining member of the Piast dynasty, the princess Jadwiga, succeeded to the throne as the "Maiden-King" (1384–86). Partly out of desperation in facing the dangers posed by the Teutonic Knights along the shores of the Baltic, in 1386 Jadwiga married Władisław V Jagiełło (Jogailo, in Lithuanian), prince of Lithuania, who, like the Poles, found his mostly pagan state threatened by the Knights' militant presence. Jagiełło converted to Catholicism a year before the marriage and assumed the Polish throne (1386–1434), thus uniting the two states of Poland and Lithuania through his person as common ruler. In 1410 his combined Polish-Lithuanian forces decisively defeated the Knights in the Battle of Grünwald (Tannenberg) and brought Poland brief domination of the Baltic shore of Northeastern Europe.[6]

Events from the death of Casimir the Great through the union of Poland with Lithuania had a lasting impact on the future fate of Poland. Throughout that period, the real power and authority of the ruler dwindled while that of the Polish nobility grew. Lacking male heirs, Casimir forged an agreement with his nephew, Hungarian king Louis of Anjou, authorizing Louis's succession to the Polish throne in return for his guaranteeing the privileges of the Polish nobility. Casimir's action instituted the elective principle in Poland that gave the nobility the right to chose their kings rather than merely to accept them out of simple heredity. The nobles took advantage of the exhaustion of Piast male progeny to exact further concessions from Louis, who had no male heirs of his own. To ensure their elections as rulers, Louis's daughter Jadwiga, and then her husband Jagiełło, had to relinquish additional royal privileges to the increasingly dominant nobility of the country. By the fifteenth century, the position of the Polish king was greatly limited in its actual power and extremely restricted in its authority relative to the Polish aristocratic class, which had gained the sole right to elect the ruler of the state, exacted legal recognition of its status as a closed, well-defined political entity, won numerous tax exemptions, and removed the ruler's central control of the noble-led Polish military.[7]

Jagiełło's situation in Poland lay in stark contrast to his position as grand prince in Lithuania. There the ruler was hereditary and the nobles, though powerful, were mostly bound to his central authority. Only the fact that Jagiełło came to the Polish throne as an already widely acknowledged strong ruler who could handle the Teutonic Knights and would take an interest in furthering the position of Poland in the Baltic and western Ukrainian regions led the independent-minded Polish nobility to link their interests with his. They saw a strong Poland under Jagiełło as a boon for their dominant position within the state. In uniting Poland with Lithuania, which at the time was three times the size of Poland and controlled vast territories in Ukraine fronting the Mongol-Tatar Golden Horde on the steppes, Jagiełło opened to the Polish nobility the prospects of playing a leading role in the single largest state in Europe, one that stretched from the Baltic Sea in the north to the Black Sea in the south.[8]

Fifteenth-century Jagiełłonian Poland-Lithuania emerged as a Western European Great Power that rivaled the rising fortunes of the Austrian Habsburgs. It was, in fact, the first European state that consciously attempted to attain such an exalted international position. In 1440 Polish king Władisław VI Jagiełło (1434–44), Jagiełło's son and successor, won election to the Hungarian throne as László I, but after his death in the Battle of Varna against the Ottoman Turks, the Jagiełłonians lost the Hungarian crown until 1490. Władisław, the son of Casimir IV Jagiełło (1447–92), the eventual successor of Władisław VI on the Polish throne, acquired the royal crown of Bohemia in 1471 as Vladislav II (1471–1516) and then that of Hungary (1490–1516). His son Louis II (1516–26) then succeeded him on both thrones. The acquisition of the Bohemian and Hungarian thrones by the Jagiełłonian family of Poland-Lithuania was part of a conscious expansionary process—sometimes termed the "Jagiełłonian System" by modern historians—aimed at countering the growing power of the Habsburgs in Central-Eastern Europe. The dynasty's "system" of Great Power politics reached its height around the year 1500. By that time it was coordinated through congresses of Jagiełłonian rulers from the various lands under the family's control meeting in Warsaw on a periodic basis.[9]

The death in 1526 of Louis II Jagiełło, king of Hungary and Bohemia, in the Battle of Mohács against the Ottoman Turks, and the subsequent acquisition of those vacant thrones by Ferdinand I of Habsburg (1526–64), effectively brought the Jagiełłonian Great Power bid in Western Europe to an end. Various factors contributed to the Jagiełłonians' failure to concentrate their resources to successfully face outside pressures or to consolidate their holdings into a unified empire that might have survived Mohács. Internally, their system failed to become integrated. From first to last, Jagiełłonian Eastern Europe remained a composite of separate states, each of which was uniquely different from the others. All were essentially dominated by native aristocratic classes whose interests were strictly parochial and proprietary. Their Jagiełłonian rulers, therefore, could not forge a common direction for action, since each had to be concerned with his own regional affairs. Taken as a whole, the disparate problems combined to preclude any true political consolidation of the separate lands under Jagiełłonian control.[10]

Failure to consolidate internally resulted in a similar failure in foreign policy. The Habsburgs, who represented the principal rivals of the Jagiełłonians in Central-Eastern Europe, exerted constant political pressure on the Jagiełłonians holding the Bohemian and Hungarian thrones during the fifteenth century, which resulted in their eventual success in acquiring them following Mohács in 1526. Habsburg success against the Jagiełłonians was aided by the intense challenge to the Jagiełłos' system posed by increasing Ottoman Turkish pressures on Hungary throughout the same period. Their Czech Bohemian subjects, more concerned with the dangers of a possible German Habsburg royal takeover, had little interest in actively contributing to the defense of Hungary's southern border against the Turks along the distant Danube frontier in the Balkans, while the Poles and the Lithuanians, lying even farther removed to the north than did the Czechs and constituting the system's core populations, were even more preoccupied with immediate problems to their east than with those of far-off Hungary. By the time they realized that the Ottoman presence in the Balkans would eventually pose a threat to their holdings in Ukraine and affect their dealings with Russia in the east, it proved too late. In the final analysis, the Jagiełłonians were forced to choose among securing and maintaining a relatively fragile imperial policy in the west, defeating and subjugating the Germans in the north, or retaining and defending their native homelands in the east against the Russians. Mohács settled the question as far as a Western empire was concerned. But both the northern German and the eastern Russian problems faced by the Jagiełłos were never satisfactorily solved.

Much has been made of the Poles' historical problems with the Germans, and rightly so. There can be no denying that Poles and Germans have engaged each other in determined, often deadly, clashes since the thirteenth century, when the Teutonic Knights (who by then had been expelled from Hungarian Transylvania) were invited into Poland to assist a local Piast duke in overcoming the pagan Baltic Prussians. But, after accomplishing the task, the Knights decided to carve out a territory for themselves at Polish expense rather than to continue as mercenary troops of the Poles. Until their crushing military defeat by Jagiełło's combined Polish-Lithuanian forces at Grünwald, the expanding Prussian state of the Teutonic Knights posed a constant threat to the medieval Polish state, blocking it from access to the Baltic Sea and, thus, from the lucrative Hanseatic commercial contacts with the markets of Western Europe. Although the German threat to Poland lessened after Grünwald, which resulted in Prussia's submission to Polish suzerainty, Teutonic Prussia remained in existence as an autonomous ducal principality. Eventually the Prussian religious state underwent secularization during the Protestant Reformation in the sixteenth century and won complete independence from Poland in the mid-seventeenth, when the Holy Roman imperial Hohenzollern Elector of Brandenburg laid definitive hands on the Prussian ducal throne.

The loss of Prussia to the Brandenburg Hohenzollerns had fateful consequences for Poland. It was they, in the guise of Brandenburg-Prussian king Frederick II the Great (1740–86), who in 1772 initiated the policy of partitioning Poland with Russian empress Catherine II the Great (1762–96) and Habsburg empress Maria Theresa (1740–80) that eventually led to the total disappearance of the Polish state in 1795. For the 123 years following the third and final partition, what had once been Poland lay divided among the Prussian, Russian, and Habsburg empires, and that part which lay inside Prussia tended to be governed with a heavy, but civil and legal, German hand. When World War I brought the rebirth of an independent Polish state as part of the victorious Entente allies' goal of national self-determination of peoples in Eastern Europe, the Poles were left holding a good deal of East Prussian and Silesian territory and facing a beaten and nationally humiliated western neighbor that believed the Poles had been unfairly granted too much of what was rightfully, and historically, German.

It was only with the rise of Adolf Hitler and the Nazis in Germany during the 1930s that the long-standing historical conflicts between Germans and Poles descended to the level of barbaric hatred. In pursuing his aim of definitively entrenching the dominant presence of the Germanic "Aryan race" in the heart of Europe, Hitler instituted a campaign of German demographic expansion by officially stimulating the German birthrate. To make room for the planned burgeoning of the German "master race," increased territory was needed. Hitler looked to the east and considered the vastness of the Great Polish Plain as offering a perfect solution for his demographic ambitions. He overcame the fact that the region was already inhabited by Slavic Poles first by using the existence of the Polish Corridor, a strip of Polish-held land that cut off German East Prussia from Germany proper created by the Versailles Treaty to give Poland direct access to the Baltic, as a pretext for initiating a military invasion of Poland in 1939 (and thus sparking World War II). The Nazis then set about following an ideological propaganda campaign inside Germany that portrayed the Slavic Poles as somewhat subhuman, which lent perverted credence to the genocidal policies they followed inside conquered Poland during the four years they occupied the defeated state. At least 3 million Poles were exterminated during World War II, and those who escaped that fate were subjected to the most degrading conditions. The Nazis transformed Poland into the chief killing ground in their concerted efforts to rid their future Europe of all those they considered undesirable, human "vermin"—Jews, Eastern Slavs, Gypsies, political opponents, among others—through organized, methodical extermination.[11]

When in the last years of World War II the Soviet Red Army provided the Poles with an opportunity to avenge themselves on their barbaric and defeated German oppressors, they did not hesitate. Polish anti-German reprisals for the enormities committed by the Nazis in Poland continued after the end of the war. The terms of the Potsdam Treaty in 1945 moved Poland's western border—the so-called Oder-Neisse river line—some 100 to 150 miles deeper into former German territories than it had ever been in history (to compensate the Poles for huge territorial loses to the Soviet Union in the east that pushed Poland's post-World War II eastern border westward between 170 to 350 miles). In 1945 the Communist-led Polish government instigated a policy aimed at deporting or otherwise ridding the country of the millions of Germans left living within the new borders to make room for some 3.5 million Poles who moved from their homes in the territories newly acquired by the Soviet Union. An estimated 5.5 million Germans succeeded in fleeing Poland after the war; as many as 1.7 million were killed without having the chance to do so. Some 60,000 Germans remained, primarily in the southwestern Silesian region of the country.[12]

After the Berlin Wall fell in late 1989 and the impetus for the reunification of the two post-World War II Germanys grew, the Poles successfully interjected themselves into the so-called Two-Plus-Four talks (so-called because representatives of both East and West Germany met with negotiators from the four postwar allied occupation countries—the United States, the Soviet Union, the United Kingdom, and France) in Ottawa, Canada. The talks were aimed at hammering out the tricky details of a newly united Germany regarding its membership in NATO and other such cold war-created situations as, for example, differences between the two Germanys' electoral laws, interior administrations, and currencies, as well as the issue of Soviet troop withdrawals. The Poles were permitted to join the general discussions regarding the matter of the common German-Polish border. They succeeded in having all the participants agree to recognize as definitive their existing western border with the new Germany, despite the small amount of separatist activity that had emerged among German nationalists inside Poland soon after the Wall came down. A Polish-German treaty to that effect was signed in late 1990, and it was followed by a mutual friendship agreement in mid-1991, which included a provision by which the Poles pledged to respect the cultural and national rights of the Germans residing in Poland.[13]

When American president Bill Clinton visited Prague in January 1994 seeking to win over the newly independent Northeastern and Central-Eastern

European countries to a NATO-related Partnership for Peace rather than full membership in that military alliance, he was met with strong and publicly announced reluctance on the part of President Lech Wałęsa and his Polish government. The Poles desired full membership in NATO to protect themselves against any possible future threat to the borders of their state, because NATO membership would represent a guaranteed, concrete military alliance with the West. The historical memory of Poland's Western allies leaving the country in the lurch in 1939 still burned in the nation's collective mind. But while that past failure of Western friendship chiefly involved the German threat posed by Hitler, such was not the case at the Prague meetings with Clinton. In 1994 the Poles were far more concerned with a longer-lived and more deep-seated fear for their future security. It was a fear born of centuries of warfare, oppression, and domination related to the civilizational conflict between Western and Eastern Europe, in which they had played the traditional role of lightning rod. It was, quite simply, a fear of Poland's historical primary enemy—Russia.

The union of Poland and Lithuania brought about by the marriage of Jadwiga to Jagiełło in 1386 might be considered the most significant single event in the history of Poland. Viewed with historical hindsight, the union proved a disaster, although the Poles at the time (and later Polish nationalists) did not see it that way. Despite victory over the Teutonic Knights at Grünwald, the acquisition of a strong, expansionist ruling dynasty to replace the failed native Piasts, and vast western Eurasian territories that provided the illusion of greatness (all of which tended to give the Poles, especially the aristocracy, an inflated image of themselves), the union with Lithuania decisively shifted Poland's orientation from the West to the East. It thrust Poland into Russia. By doing so, the Jadwiga-Jagiełło marriage determined that Lithuania would cease to serve as a buffer between the Poles and the Russians and that Poland ultimately would become the battleground between Western and Eastern Europe in Europe's northeast.

By the same token, the marriage union ultimately proved disastrous for Lithuania as well. Since the twelfth century, Lithuanian tribes had been the principal competitors of the Kievan Russians for control of the western Eurasian steppe lands, such as of Volhynia (western Ukraine) and Polotsk (Belorussia). By the time Kiev was crushed by the Mongols in the thirteenth century, the various Lithuanian tribes were undergoing consolidation into a state ruled by the Ryngoldas family, which emerged as the Mongols' primary enemy in Western Eurasia. The Lithuanians' control of Volhynia and Polotsk during the

thirteenth and fourteenth centuries led to the spread of Orthodox Christianity
and of Russian language and culture among them to such an extent that
Lithuania grew more Russianized and less pagan Lithuanian culturally. By the
mid-fourteenth century, Lithuania controlled all of Belorussia and nearly all
of Ukraine, including the old Russian capital of Kiev. By the end of the century, with the decline of the Mongol-Tatar Golden Horde in Western Eurasia,
it faced only one other major competitor for control of the former Kievan
Russian state—the Grand Principality of Moscow to its east.[14]

Lithuania at the time of Jagiełło's marriage to Jadwiga was thus a vast, highly
Russianized state whose primary interests lay in confronting Muscovy in the
east for the mantle of successor to Kiev. Most of its subjects were ethnically
and culturally Orthodox Russians of one sort or another (Ukrainians or
Belorussians), who were permitted to retain those identities by their Lithuanian
aristocratic lords, many of whom themselves had forsaken their native paganism and converted to Orthodoxy. The only thing that Lithuania held in common with Catholic Poland was the threat of the German Teutonic Knights cutting
them off from access to the Baltic Sea and its commercial potential. Jagiełło
was willing enough to sacrifice his official paganism in 1385 for conversion
to Catholicism and the Polish marriage to help him open the Baltic. In fact,
some of his royal Lithuanian predecessors had done likewise. But his marriage
entailed the eventual incorporation of Lithuania into Poland. Most remaining
pagan Lithuanians turned Catholic, and the Lithuanian aristocrats who did so
received privileges similar to those held by the native Poles.

The Russified Orthodox elements within Lithuania resisted the Polonization,
especially the dominance of Roman Catholicism, that accompanied the marriage. Jagiełło was forced to grant his native land full autonomy under a modified union with Poland in 1413, permitting the Lithuanian nobility to elect a
separate grand prince subject only to Polish approval. From that date until 1447,
Lithuania as an autonomous state pursued an expansionist foreign policy in the
east separate from that of Poland. But in the latter year, Casimir IV, Jagiełło's
son and grand prince of Lithuania since 1442, was elected king of Poland and
the union was definitively renewed. Throughout the rest of the fifteenth century, power inside Lithuania shifted from the grand prince to the aristocracy
in a process that resembled that formerly experienced in Poland. Polish aristocratic culture gradually but determinedly took root among the Lithuanian
nobility until, with the official treaty of union signed in Lublin in 1565, the
Lithuanians accepted direct Polish control over all their affairs and Catholic,
Westernized Poland emerged as the culturally dominant partner in the union
initiated by the fateful marriage alliance 179 years earlier. But the successful
dominance of the Poles over the Lithuanians exacted a heavy price—the

Poles were forced to concentrate on the inherited problems posed by the centuries-old Lithuanian rivalry with Muscovite Russia in the east to the detriment of their own essential interests, which historically lay in the west.[15]

Having reoriented Poland in the "wrong" direction and reduced Lithuania to Polish domination, the Jagiełłonian dynasty died out in 1572. Despite all of the outward international notoriety won during their stint on the throne of the united state, the family presided over an internal fragmentation of political authority that left Poland-Lithuania one of the most decentralized and fragile states in all of Europe. Unlike Hungary and Bohemia, whose native Árpád and Přemsyl dynasties had managed to fashion a sense of internal political centralization under their two royal "crowns" of St. István and St. Vaclav, respectively, the Jagiełłonians failed utterly to stem the tide of rising aristocratic political privilege at the expense of the royal throne in Poland-Lithuania that they had inherited.

That the Jagiełłonians managed to retain as much power as they did while ruling over the Poles resulted from a division within the aristocratic class itself. The large landholding magnates *(pany)* and the lesser gentry *(szlachta)* were almost constantly at odds with each other. Jagiełłonian rulers tended to favor the latter to limit the power of the former, who frequently ruled their vast estates on the plain as independent ministates. Already enjoying extensive privileges won in the fourteenth century, the gentry received even more favorable rights under Casimir IV in the fifteenth. No laws could be passed and no wars could be declared by the king without the consent of the general assembly of the gentry, known as the *sejm*. By the close of the fifteenth century, the Statute of Piotrkow (1496)—often termed the Magna Carta of Poland—solidified the position of the gentry in Polish society by restricting middle-class city dwellers' rights to own land and peasants' rights to move freely. In 1505 the national *sejm* at Radom won royal recognition as the supreme decision-making organ in the state, the members of which were elected by the nobles at their provincial assemblies. Six years later, in 1511, the *sejm* established serfdom in Poland-Lithuania, at a time when that disreputable institution was dying out in most of Western Europe. When the last Jagiełłonian ruler, Zygmunt (Sigismund) II August (1548–72), died, the crown of Poland-Lithuania, elective in theory since the late fourteenth century, became so in fact.[16]

Polish nationalists have hailed the emasculation of the royal throne and the political dominance of the native nobility through their national assembly during the fifteenth and sixteenth centuries as a great victory for representative government—as a noble republic unique to Eastern Europe at the time. It was, in fact, an internal catastrophe that rewarded the selfish particularism of the local nobles at the expense of state unity, removed virtually all central political authority, polarized Polish society between the aristocratic "haves" and the common rural and urban "have-nots," stifled progressive governmental reform, fossilized an essentially feudal military system, and, perhaps most important of all, made Poland's continued existence contingent on the interests and rivalries of foreign, often neighboring and antagonistic, states.

The internal political situation of Poland during the sixteenth century was complicated further by the entrance and entrenchment of the Protestant Reformation during the reign of Zygmunt I Jagiełło (1506–48). Protestantism had taken root in 1518 and had thereafter gained ground in the Baltic lands and in many urban centers of the country, despite various royal attempts to stem its spread. Lutheranism gained such widespread support among the Prussian Germans that the duchy of the Teutonic Knights was secularized in 1525 and placed under the rule of the former grand master of the order, Albrecht of Hohenzollern, opening the door to its future alliance with the Brandenburg branch of the Hohenzollern family in 1618 and repudiation of its status as Polish vassal state. Under Zygmunt II, the last Jagiełłonian Polish king, Protestantism became widespread inside Poland, with the appearance of Calvinism and Antitrinitarianism among the powerful Polish aristocracy, who viewed their conversion as another means of reinforcing their independence from the authority of the Catholic king.

Although Zygmunt II eventually was able to check the spread of Protestantism by instituting methods of Catholic Counter-Reformation, which had sprung from the Council of Trent (1545–64), and supporting the work of the recently founded (1565) Polish-Lithuanian chapter of the Jesuits, Protestant activity remained very much alive and lent a noticeable quality of religious toleration to Polish society in general during a period in European history that was characterized by religious intolerance. Poland became a haven for various religious refugees who fled the intense persecutions that swept the states of Europe farther west. Included among those welcomed into Poland during the sixteenth century were large numbers of Ashkenazi Jews, who flocked into Poland from the various German territories.[17]

The last Jagiełłonian was immediately succeeded on the Polish throne by Henri Valois (1573–74), who was elected by the nobility because his power base in France was far removed and only after he had agreed to sign the *Pacta Conventa,* a document formally recognizing the right of the Polish aristocracy to elect their kings and strictly limiting royal authority over them. Henri, however, paid the price for the Polish throne only because he viewed his election as merely a stepping stone for his true personal ambition—acquisition of the French crown. He willingly gave away Polish royal authority because he had no real interest in governing Poland in the first place. When his brother French king Charles IX (1560–74) died, Henri forsook Poland for

France, leaving the country without a leader and in political disarray, and with the power of royal central authority weaker than it had ever been in the past. Despite concerted efforts by the Catholic Habsburgs to secure the Polish crown following Henri's departure and the internal political confusion that ensued, the Polish nobility ultimately elected as king the Magyar prince of Transylvania, István Báthory (1575–86). Báthory was the husband of the last remaining Jagiełło, Anna, daughter of Zygmunt I. Significantly, although Báthory was a staunch Catholic himself, his Transylvanian domains were also famous for the religious toleration they enjoyed. Moreover, Báthory was renowned as a forceful military leader, a fact that won him high regard among the Polish nobility, who were at that time enmeshed in a long-standing and violent war with Muscovite Russia over control of the Livonian Baltic coastal region.[18]

◄◄⋈   ⋈►►

The Livonian War (1558–82) was merely the latest round in a series of conflicts between Poland-Lithuania and Muscovite Russia that began soon after the fateful marriage of Jadwiga and Jagiełło. As early as 1399, only a crushing military defeat by the Mongols prevented the Lithuanians from capturing Moscow and acquiring all of the territories of west Russia. In the fifteenth century Lithuania played a continuing role as either friend or foe of the Great Russians, depending on circumstances, in shaping the rise of Moscow to political dominance among the various Russian principalities and in assisting Moscow in throwing off Mongol control. Muscovite grand prince Ivan III the Great (1462–1505), who definitively broke the power of the Mongol-Tatar Golden Horde over Great Russia, considered Lithuania his principal enemy. In a process of continuous but undeclared border warfare during the 1480s and 1490s, Ivan progressively stripped Poland-Lithuania of many frontier regions in Ukraine and won over the allegiance of numerous Russian local nobles from Lithuanian authority by playing to their sense of Russian ethnic and Orthodox religious self-identities. In 1500 his Muscovite Russian-Crimean Tatar forces defeated the Lithuanians in a major battle in Ukraine but could not force the defeated to relinquish their hold on the region.[19]

Sporadic border warfare between Moscow and Lithuania continued throughout the first half of the sixteenth century, which further served to enhance the power of the Muscovite rulers within Great Russia and to enlarge the territories lying under their control. Although Lithuania lost additional territories to Russia, most notably Smolensk in 1514, Lithuanian influence remained strong in Russian internal politics. When Ivan IV the Dread ascended the Muscovite grand princely throne at the age of three (1533–84), the regency established was first in the hands of his mother Elena Glinskii, a scion of a powerful Lithuanian aristocratic family.[20]

Ivan IV can be credited with forging the Muscovite Great Russian state into a power to be reckoned with in European affairs. His often violent internal centralizing policies, which he pursued once he attained personal control of the Muscovite throne in 1547, stemmed from the numerous abuses he suffered at the hands of the regency following his mother's death in 1538, at which time state power passed to the heads of influential aristocratic *boyar* families, among whom were numbered the Glinskiis and a few other Lithuanian houses. More important, Ivan was determined to carry out the imperialistic policies implied by the rise among Russian ruling circles of the Third Rome Theory, which had attained fruition during the reign of his father, Vasili III (1505–33), and which proclaimed Muscovite Russia the God-ordained successor of defunct Byzantium as the one and only Orthodox Christian empire on earth. While that political ideology potentially had broad ramifications relative to Russia's role within Europe in general, at the very least it called for the reunification under Muscovite aegis of all territories once held by the former Kievan Russian state. Many of those lands were in Polish-Lithuanian hands at the time Ivan ascended the throne of Moscow in his own right.[21]

Poland-Lithuania was spared Ivan's imperialist pressures for nine years following his attainment of undisputed control over Muscovy. Ivan chose first to expand to the south, at the expense of the shattered Mongol-Tatar Golden Horde. Between 1552 and 1556, he systematically waged successful war on the Tatar states of Kazan and Astrakhan along the Volga River in the southern Central Asian steppes. Ivan's victories gave Moscow control of the entire course of the Volga, the defeated Tatar states became Russia's first non-Slavic acquisitions, and the conquests pioneered the way toward further expansion to the east and southeast by breaching the Ural Mountains barrier and opening the Caspian Sea to Russian trade. Ivan himself was transformed into the successor of the Tatar *hans* of the old Golden Horde, and many steppe-dwelling Tatar peoples voluntarily submitted to his authority.[22]

In the midst of the Kazan and Astrakhan wars, trading relations were established between Muscovy and England by way of the White Sea through Moscow's primary port of Archangel and through a few Baltic ports in Russian hands. The newly made commercial contacts with England led Ivan into what would prove to be his most important foreign involvement. Both Poland-Lithuania and the German state of Livonia were fearful of growing Muscovite power under Ivan. They attempted to cut Muscovy off from direct relations with the West, which could provide the Russians with much-needed technical and economic aid in further developing their expansive capabilities, by instituting a blockade of Baltic ports against Ivan. The result was the Livonian War, which involved Muscovite Russia, Poland-Lithuania, and Sweden, and which had important ramifications for the futures of all three participants. Having defeated the Tatars in the south, Ivan decided to invade Livonia in 1558 to guarantee Moscow a Baltic outlet for expected commercial expansion with Western Europe that could be used year-round, unlike the White Sea port of Archangel, which was closed for months by ice during the winter.

Livonia was a small German state situated along the shore of the Baltic north of Poland-Lithuania and possessing an important port at Riga. It was a direct descendant of the large territories once held in the region by the Teutonic Knights. There had evolved over time two branches of Knights—those in the south, who had given the Poles so much trouble in the past and who had secularized their state as Prussia in 1525, and those lying farther north on the Baltic, who had posed problems primarily for the Lithuanians and the Muscovite Russians and who remained a religious-military order until their secularization in the early 1560s. The secularization of the southern, Prussian branch of Knights had weakened the position of the northern ones, who were under growing pressure from the Great Russians and Ivan. When Ivan's forces invaded their territories, capturing the ports of Narva and Dorpat and threatening Riga, the German Livonians turned to Poland-Lithuania for support, in return for which they were willing to acknowledge some sort of Polish-Lithuanian suzerainty. An agreement was reached and the German Livonian military order was secularized. The southern half of their former lands—Courland—was placed under direct Polish-Lithuanian authority, while the northern half—Livonia—was governed by Gothard Kettler, the last grand master, and afforded Polish-Lithuanian protection.

Soon Ivan was faced with both Polish-Lithuanian and Swedish enemies in his bid to control the Livonian-Estonian Baltic regions. The Swedes, desirous of solidifying their growing pretensions to European Great Power status by expansion in the Baltic, had entered the war in the late 1560s. Ivan stubbornly refused to cut his loses as reverses followed reverses throughout that decade. Muscovy's resources were strained to the limit when, in 1571, the Crimean Tatars, whom Ivan had failed to conqueror in his earlier wars in the steppes, opened a southern front against it and then managed to attack and to sack Moscow itself. Numerous Russian *boyars* defected to the Lithuanian forces during the war, including Andrei Kurbskii, one of Ivan's oldest and most trusted advisors. Although the war took a heavy toll on the Russians, their enemies proved unable to deliver a swift and decisive knockout blow despite their frequent victories on the battlefield.[23]

It was during the course of the Livonian War that the Union of Lublin (1569), which definitively joined Poland and Lithuania under overall Polish control, was effected. Ivan was thus forced to deal with a large and powerful united

Polish state, whose militant leaders, once Báthory was elected king in 1572, were beginning to express desires of converting Muscovite Russia to Catholicism. Despite the innate political divisions within Poland stemming from the power of the aristocracy relative to that of the king, Báthory's forceful personality and demonstrated military skills permitted him to reorganize the Polish army effectively and to expand the cavalry to the point that the long-standing but bloody stalemate that had characterized the Livonian War for some years was turned in Poland's favor. After repeated successes, Báthory invaded Russian territory in 1581 and advanced victoriously as far as Pskov.

Ivan was forced to ask the pope to mediate an end to the war that had come to wrack his initially promising personal reign. Pope Gregory XIII sent as a mediator the Jesuit Antonio Possevino, who worked out a settlement of the long conflict in the Baltic. Poland-Lithuania received Livonia and Polotsk, while Sweden attained Narva and most of the Baltic coastline north of Livonia.[24] Russia's ambitions in the Baltic were shattered for the moment and the Muscovite state was virtually impoverished. By killing his only competent son and heir in a fit of rage in 1581, Ivan the Dread virtually assured the collapse of strong central authority in Russia for some three decades following his death in 1584. He was succeeded by his personally devout but feeble-minded son Fedor I (1584–98), the last of the Rurik dynasty, who was dominated by powerful Russian *boyar* families, led by Boris Godunov. Godunov, in turn, rose to the throne as Fedor's successor (1598–1605), sparking widespread dissatisfaction among his fellow Muscovite aristocrats by the aura of superiority that he swiftly assumed. Forced to resort to official terrorism to maintain control of the Russian throne, and unable to rectify growing social tensions building within Muscovy as a result of rising aristocratic dominance, Godunov plunged the state into internal anarchy. The legacy of Godunov's brief reign came to be known within Russia as the "Time of Troubles."

Russia's Time of Troubles was the period of Poland's apex. During that brief time, Poland achieved its outlet on the Baltic, controlled vast territories stretching from the Baltic to the Black Sea, occupied Moscow itself, and laid direct claim to the Muscovite throne.

When Báthory died in 1586, the royal chancellor Jan Zamoyski, one of the chief architects of both the Lublin Union and the *Pacta Conventa,* advanced a plan for securing Poland's position in Eastern Europe. He considered Muscovite Russia the primary enemy, so the election of a new king to succeed Báthory required a candidate who could assure that Russia was locked in the north from any further expansion at Poland's expense. The Livonian War had demonstrated that Sweden was able to play such a role. There was, however, a problem involved with Sweden: Its Vasa ruling house was Protestant. Fortunately for Zamoyski, one member—Zygmunt, the son of Swedish king Jan III Vasa (1568–92)—had been educated by Jesuits and remained staunchly Catholic. Although Zamoyski dreamed ultimately of creating a Polish-Lithuanian-Swedish union through the election of Zygmunt III Vasa as Polish king (1587–1632), Zygmunt's Catholic proclivities worked against its materialization and, in the long run, actually helped bring on Poland's decline.

Báthory had proven himself a stout supporter of the Catholic Counter-Reformation in both Transylvania and Poland, and in both states the power and influence of the Jesuits had increased under his rule. Yet he personally tempered his support of Catholicism with clear-headed political objectivity so that religious radicalism was never permitted to upset legally recognized internal political relationships between ruler and aristocracy. With the election of Zygmunt III, the Jesuits found a royal patron who shared their determined fervor to advance the cause of Catholicism at the expense of all other competing religious beliefs. Under Zygmunt, the Jesuit-led Counter-Reformation made rapid headway within Poland. Protestantism was first checked and then rolled back, as increasing numbers of Protestant nobles were enticed or forced to renounce their apostasy and to return to the Roman faith. As Poland grew more Catholic, the level of anti-Semitism rose. Since the level of anti-Semitism historically always was directly related to the number of Jews present within a given Christian, especially Roman Catholic, society, and since Poland's former period of religious toleration had attracted a large number of Jews fleeing pogroms in the German states, by the opening of the seventeenth century Poland became one of the most notoriously anti-Semitic states in all of Europe.

Zygmunt and his Jesuit minions found a particularly attractive field for Catholic religious imperialism in the vast Polish-controlled Belorussian and Ukrainian lands. In these, most of the population held to Orthodox Christianity. A concerted effort was made to win those Orthodox believers over to an official church union with Rome. The highly educated Jesuits were well aware of the first serious attempt at uniting the Orthodox East with the Roman Catholic West made at the Council of Florence in 1439, when the emperor of a dying Byzantine Empire had been forced to agree to a union of the two churches on terms dictated by the papacy in return for what proved to be futile promises of aid against the encroaching Ottoman Turks. By those terms, the Orthodox faithful had only to compromise four of their dogmatic beliefs (acceptance of the pope as head of the united church instead of leadership by ecumenical councils alone; acceptance of the *filioque* clause in the Nicæan Creed that defined the Third Person of the Holy Trinity [procession of the Holy Spirit from both the Father *and from the Son* instead of from the Father only]; the use of unleavened instead of leavened bread in the sacrament of Holy Communion; and acceptance of the Catholic belief in a purgatory), while they were free to continue believing in all the rest of their traditional dogma and to retain their traditional organization and rituals.

To Zygmunt Vasa's mind, forcing such a church union on his Orthodox subjects would attain two important goals. First, it would win huge numbers of converts for the Catholic faith and vast new territories for a papacy whose authority was sorely beleaguered by the Protestant movements in the West. This, in turn, would open the way toward converting the now-weakened Muscovite Russian state, thus eliminating the last remaining serious Orthodox challenger to papal claims of supremacy in the overall Christian world. Second, a successful union of the Orthodox subjects in Poland with Rome would cement the power of the Catholic Polish king and nobility in the two-thirds of Polish-Lithuanian territories whose inhabitants were native Russians and Orthodox. The union would ensure that Muscovite influence among the formerly Orthodox subject population would be removed and that the Polonized territories of Ukraine and Belorussia might then serve as a secure springboard for further Polish advances against Moscow, perhaps leading to the conquest of Muscovy itself. All told, the unionist plans of the Polish Jesuits espoused by Zygmunt possessed the potential for making Poland the greatest single power in papal Christendom.

Beginning in 1595, Zygmunt and the Jesuits initiated a campaign of persuasion, pressure, and oftentimes violence against the Orthodox clergy of Ukraine and Belorussia in an effort to win their acceptance of an official union with the Roman Catholic church. By the following year, 1596, nearly all of the high Orthodox clergy in the two regions were successfully persuaded to support the unionist plan. An official proclamation announcing the union of the two churches was signed in the town of Brest. The Union of Brest created a new form of Catholic Christianity in Poland-Lithuania known as the Uniate church (sometimes also called the Byzantine Catholic church). Its terms required the acceptance by the Orthodox unionists of the four dogmatic issues originally enunciated in the Union of Florence over 150 years earlier, while the new Uniate membership was permitted to retain the rest of their old religious beliefs and traditions. So successful were the Jesuit efforts, and so widespread was the acceptance of the union on the part of the Orthodox high clergy within Poland-Lithuania, that in the early decades of the seventeenth century Orthodoxy was on the verge of becoming extinct in Ukraine because there were no Orthodox bishops left to ordain priests or other members of the clergy and thus preserve Orthodox institutional continuity.[25]

Within seven years of the Brest Union, Zygmunt was handed an opportunity to attempt to achieve the ultimate fulfillment of the second goal involved in the Uniate plan—the conquest of Orthodox Russia by Catholic Poland. In 1603 there surfaced inside Poland a pretender to the Muscovite throne that was then occupied by the unpopular *boyar* Tsar Godunov. Claiming to be Dimitri, a young son of Ivan IV thought to have died in infancy, the pretender won support for a bid for the Russian throne from a number of influential Polish aristocrats, who saw him as a useful tool for their future aggrandizement in Muscovy. Zygmunt and the Jesuits were sympathetic to the pretender's cause, especially since his secret conversion to Catholicism proffered future possibilities for the religious conversion of the Russians and, through it, for Poland's ultimate takeover of Muscovy itself should the pretender's cause succeed.

In 1604 Dimitri the Pretender invaded Muscovy supported by substantial numbers of Poles and Ukrainians. His forces soon were swelled by masses of Russians disaffected by the rule of Godunov, the majority of whom came from the ranks of rebellious Cossack border populations. Despite initial military setbacks suffered by Dimitri, dissatisfaction with Godunov's harsh rule among the general Russian population led to the defection of most organized Muscovite troops to the pretender's ranks. Godunov died in 1605 and his young son Fedor was unable to rally any strong support from the *boyars* and their military followers. By the summer of that year, Dimitri sat on the throne of Russia as its new and popular tsar (1605–6).

The honeymoon enjoyed by Dimitri and his subjects proved all too brief. He surrounded himself with Polish aristocrats, upon whom he conspicuously showered favors of all kinds, and who treated the native Russians in a domineering and offhand fashion, no matter their social station or political position. He showed no respect for the traditional customs and institutions of the Muscovite court over which he presided. He openly reviled the Orthodox church and its teachings, encumbering it with heavy fiscal demands and, in 1606, going so far as to marry the daughter of his original, greedy Polish aristocratic supporter in a blatantly elaborate Catholic wedding ceremony attended by thousands of Poles but abhorred by his shocked Russian subjects. It took little effort on the part of the quickly discontented Russian *boyars* to whip up violent general opposition to that creature of their traditional Polish enemies—landgreedy aristocrats and the hated Catholic Jesuits. Soon after Dimitri's wedding, a *boyar*-instigated popular uprising in Moscow resulted in the butchering of hundreds of Poles and Lithuanians and in Dimitri's murder. Those Poles who escaped with their lives fled the city.[26]

Rather than solve the dynastic question caused by the extinction of the Rurik house in Russia, or the additional problem of Polish intervention in Muscovite internal affairs, the massacre of Dimitri and his minions merely brought on a new phase of warfare and anarchy. The *boyars* elected as Dimitri's successor one of their own, Vasili IV Shuiskii (1606–10), but the act only demonstrated to the rest of the Russian population their determination to preserve a social structure based on aristocratic supremacy upheld by the heavy hand of serfdom. Those Russians who originally had supported Dimitri—mostly Cossacks and peasants, with some few relatively more progressive-minded noble families—refused to accept the results of the Moscow uprising. When the border Cossacks rose in rebellion against Vasili, the revolt quickly was transformed into a general peasant uprising against the imposition of serfdom. Civil war became social war, with all of the horrendous atrocities that commonly attend such a conflict.[27]

In the midst of the turmoil afflicting Russia, a new pretender "Dimitri" surfaced among the Poles, who used him as an excuse to attack Muscovy once more. They were officially supported by King Zygmunt, and in 1608 the new pretender invaded Russian territory with a large contingent of Polish-Lithuanian troops in tow. Two years of warfare ensued, during which the Poles managed to penetrate deep into the Muscovite interior but proved unable to capture Moscow. While the new Dimitri lay just outside the Russian capital futilely holding court among his few *boyar* followers, Zygmunt himself took the opportunity to invade Muscovite lands for the sole purpose of capturing as much Russian territory for Poland as possible. Outside Smolensk in 1610, he was approached by a delegation of rebel Russian nobles, who offered the tsar's crown to his young son Władysław on condition that the boy convert to Orthodoxy. But before final agreement could be reached, a Swedish mercenary force, hired by the besieged Vasili at the price of Russia's renunciation of its claims to Livonia and Karelia on the Baltic, drove Dimitri and his allies from in front of Moscow. Zygmunt then ordered a Polish general advance on the Russian capital. Vasili's forces were soon defeated by the Poles and his government dissolved. Polish forces then occupied Moscow. In 1610, with Moscow in Polish hands, the pretender murdered, and King Zygmunt negotiating for the Russian crown, the rising tide of Polish fortune in the east of Europe reached its high water mark.

⊯ ⊱

Poland's imperialist fortunes rose, crested, and slipped into decline within the span of some forty years. It is not coincidental that the four-decade apex of the Polish state fell during the reign of its Vasa Swedish monarch, Zygmunt III. He, more than any other single individual, must be credited with most of both the credit and the blame. Unfortunately for the Poles, blame far overshadowed credit.

As it turned out, Zygmunt was an imperialist of the first magnitude, but he also was a ruler of limited ability and little political foresight. Although his staunch espousal of the Catholic cause paid short-term dividends through the Uniate successes in Ukraine and Belorussia, it eventually sowed the seeds of anti-Polish dissent in those same territories following the failure of the Polish intervention inside Russia during the first two decades of the seventeenth century. By that time, his narrow-minded Catholicism had already spoiled any chances for a Polish-Lithuanian-Swedish union dreamed of by Zamoyski when, in 1599, Zygmunt was deposed as king of Sweden (1592–99) by rebellious subjects who rejected his absolutist policies and his attempts to restore Catholicism in their lands. During 1609 and 1610, the Swedes were more than happy to intervene in Russia on behalf of the doomed Vasili against their despised former sovereign. And with Polish fortunes at their height with the capture of Moscow in 1610, Zygmunt spoiled the triumph by reneging on the negotiations that would have placed the tsar's crown on the head of his son Władisław by demanding it for himself instead.

That such a staunchly Catholic ruler as Zygmunt claimed the crown of Orthodox Russia was more than even the pro-pretender Russians could accept. Unlike Władisław, who had agreed to convert to Orthodoxy to gain the throne, it was obvious that Zygmunt harbored no such intention. The anti-Shuiskii Russian opposition considered it unthinkable that a Catholic monarch would rule over Orthodox Russia. Unwilling to countenance a Catholic tsar, the Russians permitted the throne to remain vacant. For three years Russia lay without a ruler, a power vacuum at its center and anarchy and foreign invaders reigning in its provinces.

By 1611 a powerful reaction against continued Polish dominance in Russian affairs swept through Muscovy, as both aristocratic and common followers of the murdered second pretender organized a strong militia and commenced new hostilities against the Poles. Ukrainian Cossacks provided the bulk of the Polish forces mobilized to face the new Russian militia, which possessed as its core Volga Cossacks who had been the loyal supporters of the late pretender. Zygmunt countered the Russian reaction by capturing Smolensk, while the Swedes took advantage of the continued turmoil in Russia by seizing Novgorod in the north. It was the darkest moment in the Time of Troubles.

Light began to return to Russia in 1612, when the Russian militia stormed Moscow and Zygmunt's efforts to retake the city were thwarted. Early in the following year, with roving bands of Poles, Swedes, and Cossacks continuing to devastate the countryside, an assembly of notables from all levels of Russian society (except the enserfed peasantry)—the *zemskii sabor*—elected a new, native, Orthodox tsar, Mihail I Romanov (1613–45), the young son of Filaret Romanov,

one of the aristocratic supporters of the two pretenders who had attempted to negotiate Władisław's succession with Zygmunt and who was then sitting in a Polish
prison because of those efforts. Few realized at the time that Mihail would be
the first of the second and last ruling dynasty of Russia. He was young—barely
sixteen years of age—sickly, and, most important of all in the eyes of the jealous *boyar* aristocracy, weak. While he was beloved by the natives of Moscow
and by the Volga Cossacks, he was acceptable to the aristocratic elite only for
those very qualities, and also because he was related to the old Rurik dynasty
through his great-aunt, who had been the first wife of Ivan IV the Dread.[28]

The new young tsar was able to take advantage of the growing sense of
Russian patriotism that had emerged among the populace as a result of the devastating Polish and Swedish interventions in the affairs of their state and of the
militia activities organized to counter them. With the Volga Cossacks, the
Muscovite middle class, and most of the gentry behind him, Mihail, though a
weak individual possessed of little political ability, was able to gain the grudg-
ing support of the powerful *boyars,* and two decades of political chaos came
to an end in Russia. In 1617 a peace treaty was signed with Sweden. Russia
abandoned all of its claims on Livonia and gave to Sweden its few remaining
Baltic ports in Karelia, but the Swedes returned Novgorod to Russia. The Poles,
pushed back from Moscow but still holding much Russian territory along the
old border, including Smolensk, were permitted to retain their border conquests
by a truce signed in 1618. The truce provided the Russians with a welcome
breathing spell to reorganize their shattered military and to build up much-
depleted resources for the resumption of the conflict, which both sides knew
was inevitable.[29]

Soon after the truce was signed with Russia, Zygmunt's continued machinations to win back his Swedish throne from Gustavus II Adolphus (1611–32)
embroiled Poland in a new war with Sweden. It dragged on unsuccessfully until
1629, when a truce was signed that recognized the Swedes' conquest of Polish
Livonia. Three years later, in 1632, the truce with Russia expired and the
Russians immediately reopened hostilities by unsuccessfully attacking
Smolensk. With its army surrounded and its commander executed, the Russians
were forced to sign an "eternal peace" with the Poles in 1634. By the terms of
that accord, Władisław VII Vasa, Zygmunt's son who was by then king of Poland
(1632–48), renounced his long-standing claim to the Russian throne.

With the Time of Troubles in Russia at an end, with stable native government restored under the Romanov tsars, and with Polish intervention in
Russian internal affairs definitively put to rest by the "eternal peace," the focus
of Polish-Russian confrontation shifted from Moscow to the Ukrainian border regions of the Great Plain and their volatile Cossack populations. For Poland

in the mid-seventeenth century, the consequences of that conflict came to be known as the "Deluge," which was brought on by the emergence of the so-called Ukrainian Question.

⧫   ⧫

The question as to the ethnicity of the Ukrainians was vague and relatively unimportant until the middle of the seventeenth century. There was no doubting that historical and cultural ties existed between the inhabitants of Ukraine and of Muscovite Russia. Ukraine, with its capital at Kiev, had been the original heartland of the first medieval Russian state. The thirteenth-century Mongol-Tatar conquest of Kiev and most of its lands had sown chaos and disruption among all of the East Slavic Russians. While the open steppelands lay at the mercy of the Asiatic invaders, some East Slavs (later known as the Great Russians) managed to establish new population centers in the northern forest regions of Western Eurasia, over which Moscow eventually gained dominant control, threw off Mongol-Tatar suzerainty, and commenced to build a second imperial Russian state.

    Although it first was rumored that the Mongol-Tatar inundations had annihilated the original Kievan Slavs, it became obvious over the course of the fifteenth and sixteenth centuries that the Ukrainian lands ravaged by the invaders were heavily populated by groups of East Slavs, many of whom were known as Cossacks. The Muscovites persistently believed them to be fellow Russians (they called the Slavs of Ukraine "Little Russians") who were forced to live outside the borders of the rising "Third Rome." As such, the Great Russian Muscovites felt compelled to bring them back within the Russian fold by reincorporating them into a God-ordained Russian imperial state that, at the very least, would encompass all the territories of the old Kievan state within its borders. With the end of the Time of Troubles, Romanov Russia was prepared to begin that near-sacred mission. During the second half of the seventeenth and throughout the eighteenth centuries, Moscow bent its efforts toward the conquest of all lands on the Great Eurasian Plain that it considered ethnically and historically Russian.

    In the nineteenth century Ukrainian nationalists came to contest heatedly Great Russian pretensions of controlling Ukraine based on an assumed common "Russian" ethnic tie. They refuted blood-brotherhood with the Great Russians by claiming that the ancient East Slavs were divided into two related but different groups—Russians and Ukrainians. Such being the case, according to Ukrainian historians, medieval Kiev was actually a Ukrainian and not a Russian state. While Ukrainian Kiev thrived, the Russians existed in their northern forests as primitive tribal people, who began to emerge from their backward condition only after Kiev fell into decline. It was, in fact (again according to the Ukrainian nationalist interpretation of Russian history), northward-fleeing escapees from dying Kiev who had set Moscow off on its road toward Russian reunification and expansion. Much of the Ukrainian perspective on "Russian" history appeared in the work of one of the most renowned early twentieth-century Russian historians, Vasili Klyuchevsky.

For the sake of objectivity, it should be noted that the origins of ethnic Ukrainians remain uncertain to the present day. The very word "Ukraine" was derived from the Slavic for "borderland." Prior to the coming of the Mongols in the thirteenth century, Kiev and its territorial possessions constituted the very heartland of the medieval Russian (technically, Rus') state, so we cannot imagine that they were ever conceived of as border regions by any of their inhabitants, including those who lived in the forested north. Until the late twelfth century at the earliest, when Kiev slipped into definite decline, there probably was no discernable ethnic difference between the Slavs of the southern steppes and those of the northern forests. All were merely East Slavs adhering to the loose identity of "Russians" (the people of Rus'). During the five centuries that separated the decline of Kiev from the Polish-Russian conflicts over Ukraine following the Time of Troubles, the region experienced a great deal of demographic turmoil. By the mid-seventeenth century, there definitely did exist a difference in ethnic awareness between the inhabitants of the two "Russian" regions. In Romanov Muscovite Russia the population possessed a Russian self-identity that had been overtly manifested in their anti-Polish reaction during the Time of Troubles. In Ukraine there were the Cossacks, who held tenaciously to a sense of separateness from the Muscovite population, even though many of them, if not most, probably were descendants of Great Russian ancestors.[30]

The formation of a Cossack ethnicity in Ukraine was an interesting human development. In many respects, the process resembled that which created a distinct Australian ethnicity out of a conglomeration of English political, social, and criminal outcasts who found themselves living together in a new, vast, and sparsely populated land. The Mongol-Tatars' invasion, and the continuing threat of their presence, left the open steppe region of Ukraine greatly depopulated by the close of the thirteenth century. That situation persisted until the fifteenth century, when internal conditions within both the Muscovite and Polish-Lithuanian states spawned demographic movements back into the mostly abandoned steppes to their south. The rising power of large landlords in those states increasingly led peasants to flee the land for freedom in the vast but dangerous open spaces, where they could live beyond the authority of their aristocratic oppressors.

Throughout the sixteenth century, the flight of Polish-Lithuanian and Russian fugitives to the Ukrainian steppes intensified, as landlordism in both states became increasingly entrenched and onerous for the resident peasant populations. This was especially the case in Muscovite Russia after the legal institution of "restricted years"—years in which no peasant movement off the land was permitted. In Muscovy under Ivan IV the Dread, the old nobility was virtually destroyed and a new royal aristocracy created, which was even more exacting toward the peasantry than before. That development in Muscovite Russia led to a flood of peasants escaping to the sanctuary from aristocratic control offered by the open steppes to the south, even during "restricted" years. By the close of the sixteenth century, the Ukrainian steppes were teeming with fugitives, most of whom were originally from Muscovite Russia and the rest from Poland-Lithuania.

As a measure for self-defense, the fugitives on the steppes acquired the name of Cossacks and organized themselves into a number of populous military organizations (which could, at times, include as many as 80,000 men) that operated in the wide no-man's land separating the southern borders of Muscovy and Poland-Lithuania from the Black Sea coastal territories controlled by the Crimean Tatars. Each group of Cossacks carved out a particular area of the steppe for itself, and the area under its control came to identify the group. For example, individual groups of Cossacks took up positions along the Don, Volga, and Dnieper rivers. The westernmost group of Cossacks—the Zaporozhe (so named because they were centered "beyond the cataracts" of the lower Dnieper River)—were the most prominent of all the Cossack groups in the seventeenth century. Although the territory that they controlled technically lay within Polish Ukraine, the Zaporozhe Cossacks functioned, for all practical purposes, outside of Polish authority. Because of the effective military potential proffered by the Zaporozhe Cossacks, the Poles were content to accept essentially nominal suzerainty over them until the seventeenth century.[31]

All of the Cossack groups held certain general characteristics in common. Each was organized as a rudimentary democratic society into which anyone could be accepted, so long as the newcomer agreed to abide by the group's established laws. The group's leader—*hetman* (sometimes *ataman*)—was selected by direct and open election, in which every Cossack male had a vote. During times of warfare, the *hetman*'s orders bore supreme authority. To keep the hated institution of landlordism out of their territories, Cossacks were not permitted to engage in agriculture. They thus supported themselves by fishing, hunting, trading, and plundering. The latter vocation was extremely popular and frequent among them. When unable to carry out fruitful warfare with their more settled neighbors—the Poles, Russians, Tatars, and Ottoman Turks (once the Turks had incorporated the Crimean Tatars into their empire during the sixteenth century)—Cossack groups would conduct wars among themselves to acquire the means for continued existence.

Life on the open steppes shaped the Cossack fugitives into extremely freedom-loving and mobile societies that militantly cherished their independence from the restrictive control of the more settled states to their north. Constantly forced to deal with the seminomadic Tatar peoples who shared the Great Plain with them, the Cossacks acquired many of the traits exhibited by their perennial Asiatic neighbors and enemies. They adapted Tatar dress, personal appearance, customs, and, perhaps most important, mounted military tactics to their strong native Slavic Orthodox culture. Their semi-Tatarization served to reinforce their separateness from the settled Poles and Russians, whose society they rejected, and created among them the nascent roots for a sense of unique ethnicity. The Muscovites considered them fellow Russians; the Poles viewed them as valuable but heretical (Orthodox) allies; and the Turks held them to be either Poles or Russians, depending on which state they were at war with at the time.[32]

By the opening of the seventeenth century, the independence of the Cossack organizations, though they were still numerous and militarily powerful, was showing signs of being doomed. The open steppe, on which the Cossacks' continued freedom and lifestyle depended, was under increasing pressure from the powerful states that flanked it—Poland and Russia from the north; the Ottoman Turkish Empire from the south. The pressing question became when, how, and into which state the Cossacks were going to be integrated rather than if integration would happen at all. Their militant adherence to Christianity precluded any realistic possibility that they would seek their future within the Islamic Ottoman Empire, so the issue was reduced to the rivalry between Poland and Muscovite Russia. Whichever of the two states that succeeded in winning over the Cossacks would acquire increased military resources and extensive territorial gains, which would translate into political and cultural dominance in Eastern Europe and Western Eurasia. As it turned out, Poland (and the Western European civilization it represented) lost the seventeenth-century contest for the Cossacks and Ukraine to Russia (and Eastern European civilization). The struggle proved long, bloody, and decisive for all concerned.

⋈ ⋊

A religious controversy within Poland at the end of the sixteenth century lit the match that eventually led to the explosion of the "Deluge" and to the subsequent precipitate demise of Polish fortunes in the East by the end of the seventeenth century. The creation of the Polish-controlled Uniate church at Brest, in 1596, and the resulting Polish policy of anti-Orthodox persecutions in Ukraine provided the spark. As noted earlier, the Poles had religious and political reasons for their unionist actions—with two-thirds of their territories populated by Orthodox inhabitants, they could not afford the risk of cultural-political influences on them emanating from Orthodox Russia. Although the official unionist pressure succeeded in nearly eliminating the upper hierarchy of the Orthodox church in the Ukraine by the early decades of the seventeenth century, the lower clergy and the majority of the common Orthodox faithful held to their traditional beliefs. The champions of Orthodoxy and the spokespersons for opposition to the official Polish Catholic unionist policy were the Zaporozhe Cossacks.

Within Poland, the Cossacks were beginning to feel the constraints of Polish suzerainty by the time the Poles instituted their anti-Orthodox unionist policy. Already a number of the Cossacks were "registered" by the Polish government in an attempt to exert a modicum of authority over those unruly, oftentimes unreliable, subject-allies. In return for having themselves and their lands listed in official Polish military muster rolls, the registered Cossacks were provided with equipment and supplies by the Polish government. But such registration often proved as dangerous for the government as it was beneficial, since the Cossacks often used their registration benefits to carry out local revolts instead of to conduct Polish military operations. By the early seventeenth century, instead of helping bring the Zaporozhe Cossacks under closer government authority, the policy of registration had become a means for those formidable freebooters to extort large quantities of arms and equipment from the Poles. Polish attempts to curtail Zaporozhe independence through military means, registrations without gifts of arms, the settlement of Catholic Polish aristocrats on steppelands, the reduction of unregistered Cossacks to the status of serfs for the new landlords, and, finally, confiscations of registered Cossacks' lands caused growing anti-Polish aggravation among them. When in the 1630s the hard-pressed Orthodox church in Ukraine turned to them for help in fending off the Poles' unionist pressures, the Zaporozhe Cossacks were more than eager to comply.

The initial Cossack uprisings of the 1630s were generally unsuccessful. The Poles' policy of registering only a portion of the Cossack population actually led to a growing social differentiation within Ukrainian society between registered Cossacks, who considered themselves a privileged elite, and ordinary Cossacks, who, along with a growing numbers of non-Cossack peasants, developed an antagonistic relationship with their registered compatriots. In 1648

Cossack resentment of Catholic Polish policy and the internal social tensions within Cossack society were taken advantage of by Bogdan Khmelnitsky, a former Ruthenian nobleman who had been mistreated by some powerful local Lithuanian lords. He had then fled to the Zaporozhe Cossacks, who elected him *hetman*. The revolt he led against the Poles in the years 1648–53 aimed at winning increased Cossack autonomy within Poland and expansion in the numbers of registered Cossacks subsidized by the Polish government. Although militarily successful at first, Khmelnitsky's forces proved unable to sustain their advantage and were ultimately forced to sign a peace treaty with Poland that reduced Cossack territory in Ukraine and lowered the number of registered Cossacks in Polish military employ.[33]

In 1654 Khmelnitsky turned to Moscow for help. His move was strongly supported by Ukrainian ordinary Cossacks and peasants, and it signaled the tilting of the uneasy power balance that had been established between Poland and Russia in the "eternal peace" of 1634. At Pereiaslavl in 1654, Khmelnitsky and the Muscovites signed a pact that placed the eastern regions of Ukraine under Russian protection, confirmed Zaporozhe Cossack autonomy, and elicited the sworn allegiance of the Ukrainian Cossacks and peasants to the Russian tsar. The legal realities of the Ukrainians' oath to the tsar at Pereiaslavl were matters of differing interpretations at the time (and continue to be so today). The Cossacks considered Pereiaslavl as an alliance between two separate states; the Russians viewed it as a surrender of Cossack independence to Russian authority and as a reunion of ancient Russian lands with the rest of Russia. The actual relationship between the two was not spelled out clearly. One thing was certain—Khmelnitsky had requested Russian aid, and that fact placed the Cossacks in a somewhat subordinate position once the Russians agreed.[34]

The Pereiaslavl Pact initiated a prolonged and bloody conflict between Russia and Poland for possession of Ukraine that blazed until 1667. During that period, known in Polish history as the "Deluge," Poland was devastated almost to the point of extinction, not only by Muscovite and Cossack invasions but also by Swedish, Tatar, and Ottoman Turkish incursions, as those latter states sought to take advantage of the Poles' preoccupation with the Russians to expand their own territorial ambitions. In 1655 Swedish king Karl X Gustavus (1654–60) opened the First Northern War with Poland, using the refusal of Polish king Jan II Casimir (1648–68), a Vasa, to recognize his royal legitimacy as a pretext for further Swedish expansion in the Baltic. The following year (1656), Swedish forces invaded Poland and won a major victory over the Poles outside Warsaw. Polish resistance virtually collapsed and the Swedes overran nearly all of the Polish interior. Poland seemed on the verge of utter extinc-

tion until the state was saved by a miracle (at least according to Polish nationalist mythology). With Polish hopes reduced to the survival of a final fortified
stronghold—Częstochowa Monastery—under siege by Swedish troops in
1657, the outnumbered Polish garrison was inspired by a vision of the Virgin
Mary and inflicted an incredible defeat on the invaders. Soon thereafter Polish
forces rallied and drove the Swedes out of Poland. Poland had survived.
When hostilities with Sweden ended in 1660 at the Treaty of Oliva, Jan II was
forced to renounce any claim the Vasa's had on the Swedish throne and to cede
Livonia to King Karl XI (1660–97), who had succeeded Karl X.[35]

While Swedish forces devastated the interior of Poland, Russian and
Cossack troops hammered the Ukrainian possessions in the east. Smolensk and
much of both Ukraine and Belorussia were captured by the Russians, and as
Muscovite pretensions to East Slav hegemony grew with the victories, Tsar
Alexis (1645–76), Mihail Romanov's successor, took to proclaiming himself
ruler of all the Russians ("Great [Muscovites], Little [Ukrainians], and White
[Belorussians]"). But two developments dampened the apparent victory of
Moscow over the Poles. First, Khmelnitsky died in 1657, and his death shattered the fragile unity of both anti-Polish Cossack and Russian interests and
of the privileged Cossack leadership with the Ukrainian lower classes. Most
of the Cossack leadership gravitated to Ivan Vygovsky, who repudiated the
Pereiaslavl Pact with Moscow and sought accommodations with Poland and
the Crimean Tatars. In 1658 Vygovsky signed an agreement with Poland in
which the Poles granted extensive autonomy to Ukraine under Zaporozhe hegemony. The new pact almost created a Polish-Lithuanian-Ukrainian union,
with the Poles retaining their overall position of dominance. A year later
(1659), Vygovsky's Cossack forces defeated the Muscovites in battle on
behalf of Polish interests. Unfortunately for the Poles, internal chaos at home
resulting from the Deluge and Vygovsky's overthrow by a rebellion of ordinary Cossacks and Ukrainian peasants prevented them from gaining full
advantage of the newly transformed situation in Ukraine.[36]

Second, beginning in 1658 and continuing into 1662, Ukraine was invaded
by Ottoman Turkish and Crimean Tatar forces that posed serious problems for
all of the protagonists in the struggle for the region. With the Poles fighting the
Russians, Swedes, and even the Habsburgs, they once again faced complete catastrophe with the addition of Turkic and Tatar enemies in the south. Russia was
hard-pressed to maintain its successful momentum in the war against Poland
because of the Cossack defections and was gravely concerned about losing
"Russian" territories to the Muslim interlopers. Moreover, Moscow came to view
Swedish successes in the First Northern War as a threat to further Russian expansion in the Baltic. The Ukrainian Cossacks, wracked by civil war and rebellion

surrounding the Vygovsky succession, were divided and lay exposed to the immediate threats of the Turks and Tatars. For all sides, the prolonged Russo-Polish war was proving costly and exceedingly devastating.

In 1667 the Poles and Russians brokered an armistice at Andrusovo, which essentially ended the long war between them at the Cossacks' expense. Ukraine was partitioned: Russia gained Smolensk and eastern regions of Ukraine on the left bank of the Dnieper River, including Kiev; Poland retained western Ukraine and territories on the right bank of the Dnieper, and regained control over Belorussia. Desultory fighting broke out again between the two states soon after the armistice was signed and dragged on for another nineteen years. The conflict finally ended when another "eternal peace" was concluded between Poland and Russia in 1686, in which the terms of Andrusovo were confirmed.

The Andrusovo Armistice was a culmination of intense and successful Polish diplomatic efforts to remove the presence of all foreign forces from within the state, thus effectively terminating the Deluge. Poland managed to survive the debacle, but at the high cost of forfeiting vast tracts of formerly Polish territory in Ukraine and on the Baltic. Andrusovo can be construed as the first partition of Poland, for it served as an example of what the Poles might be forced to accept out of desperation for the land-hungry rulers of Russia, Prussia, and Austria a century later.

⋈ ⋊

The Deluge and Andrusovo together represented a turning point in Polish history. Poland survived as a state reduced in size and decaying internally. A rapid decline set in following 1667, until the Polish state disappeared completely from the map of Europe in 1795.

Perhaps the single most critical factor in the fall of Poland from greatness was the state's lack of a viable sociopolitical system able to hold together the country under the strains exerted on its vast and vulnerable borders by the Deluge. By the mid-seventeenth century, Poland was disintegrating from within. So powerful had the Polish nobility grown vis-à-vis royal central authority that no real unity of purpose could be forged among them to defend effectively the interests of the state as a whole. Government through the *sejm* was paralyzed by the use of the infamous *liberum veto,* which granted each individual member of that aristocratic assembly the right to defeat any resolution placed before it by voicing his lone protest. No governing assembly could function under such a condition. The *liberum veto* was first used in the 1650s during the Deluge, and it was applied increasingly thereafter. Although the vetoes of lesser nobles could be overcome effectively, those of the powerful princes, as well as those with strong foreign backing, could not. Such a powerful political tool as the *liberum veto* could be abused easily—and it was.[37]

Frustrated by the inability of the throne to conduct concerted policy and disgusted with the selfish antics of the Polish aristocrats in the *sejm*, Jan II abdicated in 1668. An intense succession struggle resulted in the Poles finally electing as king a native, Michał I Wiśniowiecki (1669–73), against whom the "Right Bank" Cossacks in Polish Ukraine rebelled. The Cossack rebels successfully won Ottoman Turkish military aid in 1672, and the Turks swiftly managed to tear Podolia (extreme southwestern Ukraine) away from Poland and to force Michał to grant western Ukraine independence under Turkish protection. The *sejm* refused to ratify the treaty concluded between their king and the Turks, so the war was resumed and Polish forces placed under the military leadership of Jan Sobieski, a powerful and influential prince. Sobieski gradually drove back the Turks, and, when Michał died in 1673, he was elected King Jan III (1674–96). Although Sobieski rightly won fame as an able military commander—he definitively ended Ottoman military expansion in Europe at Żurawno in 1676 and played a decisive role in crushing the Ottoman threat to Vienna and the heart of Western Europe in 1683—he proved unable to overcome the increasingly anarchistic stranglehold on government exerted by his fellow aristocrats at home.[38]

As for the Polish nobility, Sobieski's military prowess raised a potential native threat to their continued independence from royal authority. For Sobieski's successor in 1697, they once again turned to outside royalty in an effort to prevent one of their own from acquiring too much power over them. The Elector of Saxony, Augustus II the Strong, was elected Polish king (1697–1733). Motivated by the possibility of strengthening the Saxon position within the Holy Roman Empire through kingship in Poland, Augustus accepted the throne. He allied himself with Russian tsar Peter I the Great (1689–1725) for the purposes of despoiling Swedish king Karl XII (1697–1718) of his Baltic possessions in hopes of increasing royal authority in Poland by leading a military reconquest of Livonia. The resulting Great Northern War (1700–21) was fought mostly on Polish territory. An early Polish invasion of Livonia (1700) was followed swiftly by a Swedish counterinvasion of Poland (1701–2). Karl captured both Warsaw and Cracow, and the shaken Polish magnates dethroned Augustus and elected in his stead Stanisław Leszczyński (1704–9), a pliant creature of the Swedes. In 1706 peace with Sweden was attained and Poland was forced to renounce any claims on Livonia. With Karl's decisive defeat by the Russians at Poltava in 1709, however, Augustus was able to return to Poland and drive out Leszczyński. All that had been gained by his venture against Sweden in the Baltic had been additional devastation of Polish territory and further deterioration in the internal political situation. Although few realized it at the time, the prolonged death agony of Poland had begun.[39]

Following his reinstatement as king, Augustus's efforts to increase royal power at the expense of the Polish aristocracy served to stir up new internal disorders and an uprising of nobles. As Poland continued its decline into domestic political chaos, Russia came to view the situation as a golden opportunity for finally acquiring all of the long-sought "Russian" lands—Ukraine and Belorussia—and for possible political domination of its traditional Polish nemesis. Over the remaining decades of the eighteenth century, the Polish nobility unwittingly did their best to ensure that a Russian takeover of their state proved relatively easy.

The internal problem in Poland rested with the constitutional development of the state. This process in Poland had been vastly different from that experienced in Russia, the Poles' large, traditional enemy. The contrast in political culture between the two major Slavic powers in the European East was stark, and it reflected the civilizational chasm that separated them. East European, Orthodox Russia had evolved a centralized, autocratic political culture with roots sunk deep in Byzantine tradition. In Russia the Orthodox Christian political culture of Byzantium—which considered the imperial ruler God's direct representative on earth, who was chosen to rule over a divinely sanctioned Christian world-state—had been given a heavy dose of Asiatic despotism during the long period of medieval Mongol-Tatar domination the Russians experienced. There emerged in Russia a political culture that was expressed as Orthodox Christian absolutism. Although Peter the Great imposed numerous Western European-like reforms on his conservative, often reactionary, ruling aristocracy, these measures essentially were changes in the forms (such as beard-cutting, mode of dress, institutional and social titles, and the like) rather than in the substance of Russia's Byzantine-Mongol cultural traditions. For all of the outward display of Russian Westernization, Peter and his successors on the Russian throne continued to view themselves in the traditional role of supreme autocrat-despot until the extinction of the tsardom in 1918. And in political reality, since the position of the Russian aristocracy relative to their divinely ordained, all-powerful tsar was consistently insecure, there never existed in Russian history any effective legal—only practical—limitation on the authority of the ruler. As a consequence, eighteenth-century Russia was one of the most highly centralized and powerful states on the European scene.[40]

In Catholic Poland, on the other hand, a strong tradition of elected kingship had arisen over the centuries, grounded in medieval Germano-Slavic traditions of government through assemblies of notables and reinforced by the secularizing political effects of the Renaissance and Reformation. While in the past certain dynasties had managed to gain near-hereditary right to the throne, such as did the Jagiełłonians, by the time the Vasa house renounced it in the mid-seventeenth century, Polish kingship was strictly elective and subject to the whim of the *liberum veto*. Every royal succession thereafter found numerous contenders competing for election. Political power rested in the hands of a wealthy, self-interested aristocracy who, if they shared any political preoccupation in common, it was to ensure that royal authority over them remained as weak as possible. As a result, by the eighteenth century Poland perhaps was the most highly decentralized state in Europe. The Polish royal office had been so reduced in effective power that the king was a mere political figurehead. That situation, of itself, did not constitute a fatal political flaw, since limited monarchies could (and still do today in Europe) function effectively. The fatal defect in Poland was the utter absence of any politically united, powerful governing class that could fill the vacuum created in central authority by the emasculation of the royal office. Instead of forging an effective parliamentary class, the Polish nobility had evolved as a class of selfish, individualistic oligarchs, who displayed little and sporadic responsibility toward the Polish state as a whole.

Prior to the end of Augustus's reign in 1733, only one political tradition in the *sejm* served to provide a sense of general political responsibility for the Polish aristocracy—the *Rákosz*. The term was of Hungarian origin: It was the name for a piece of flatland lying outside Budapest where in medieval times Magyar nobles held their political meetings that eventually evolved into the Hungarian National Diet. Under the Jagiełłonians, the term had entered Poland and came to signify a gathering of the Polish nobility. Until the second half of the seventeenth century, the two major power groupings within the aristocracy—the large magnates *(pany)* and the lesser gentry *(szlachta)*—tended to exert their common authority in the *sejm* through compromise. As Poland's fortunes in the east deteriorated during the late seventeenth and early eighteenth centuries, and as foreign invaders increasingly ravaged the heart of their state, the two factions grew less amenable to such agreement. When compromise measures could not be molded, one or the other of the two would declare "a *Rákosz*"— a legal rebellion for the purpose of carrying out the faction's political agenda.

So long as such action remained strictly an internal Polish affair conducted for some general benefit of the state (or at least of the major aristocratic faction) as a whole, the *Rákosz* worked as the only effective means for overcoming the innate divisiveness that characterized the political role of the native aristocracy. By the early eighteenth century, with the cementing of the *liberum veto,* it ceased to work. Outside powers—especially Russia, Sweden, and Prussia—were able to buy the votes and vetoes of members of the *sejm* to further their own ends.

When *Rákoszes* were declared, the foreigners instigated opposing factions to form "confederations"—groups of nobles united in pronouncing those actions rebellions against the legitimate authority of the state and not merely legalistic means to political ends within the confines of the law. By multiplying the use of the *liberum veto* and through manipulating a series of *Rákoszes* and confederations, Poland's foreign enemies succeeded in keeping the state politically weak and in preventing any successful efforts at internal reform. The situation led to the disintegration of Poland.[41]

Once Russia victoriously ended the Great Northern War with Sweden in 1721, it was free to meddle seriously in Polish internal affairs, and by doing so led the field of foreign powers that considered tampering with the flawed constitutional order of Poland advantageous to their interests. The matter of electing a successor to Augustus II in 1733 virtually opened the door to wholesale foreign machinations inside Poland. The Poles reelected Leszczyński and found support for their choice from France, since the candidate was the father-in-law of French king Louis XV (1715–74). At the time of the election, European Great Power politics consisted of two primary and opposing camps: One was led by Habsburg Austria and included England, the Low Countries, Piedmont, and the Holy Roman Empire, with Russia apparently in ambiguous sympathy; the other was led by France in uneasy partnership with Spain and Sardinia, and with Prussia playing an uncertain role similar to Russia in the opposite camp. Russia considered Leszczyński's reelection unacceptable because of his pro-Swedish sympathies and garnered support from the Habsburgs. They, in turn, insisted on the election of Augustus's son and namesake as the legitimate successor to the Polish throne. The Russians then invaded Poland in overwhelming force and drove Leszczyński to Gdańsk (Danzig), thus sparking the War of the Polish Succession (1733–35). In retaliation, France declared war on the Habsburgs. The main theater of military operations then shifted from the Gdańsk region to Italy and the Rhine River frontier separating France and the Holy Roman Empire. Leszczyński was forced to flee Poland for Prussia, and the war ended in 1735 with Italy profoundly changed and Russian-Habsburg policy in Poland victorious.

King Augustus III of Saxony (1734–63), the successful Russian-Habsburg royal candidate, expended little interest or time on his kingdom. During the two decades of his disinterested reign, Russia blatantly increased its encroachment on Polish internal affairs, causing a growing amount of anti-Russian sentiment to arise among a segment of the nobility led by the Potocki family. The Potocki noble faction longed for the reestablishment of an aristocratic constitution and sought support from France. They were opposed by another aristocratic faction led by the Czartoryski family, who proposed strengthening royal authority, abolishing the *liberum veto,* and other more centralizing political reforms. The Czartoryski group looked to Russia for backing.[42]

In 1764 the Czartoryskis managed to elect one of their own family to the throne—Stanisław II Poniatowski (1764–95)—aided by intense pressure exerted on the Polish nobility by Russian empress Catherine II the Great, who considered Poniatowski a malleable puppet because of a prior intimate relationship. In the process, Russia and Prussia formulated a cooperative policy regarding Poland aimed at keeping the state weak and docile to their increasingly common imperial interests. Once king, however, Poniatowski attempted to act independently from his powerful Russian patroness and to institute the much-needed Czartoryski reform program for strengthening the Polish state. Both rulers soon realized their mistakes. Catherine had no intention of creating a truly independent and effective Polish monarchy, and Poniatowski came to regret his attempts to buck Catherine's wishes. When Russia and Prussia insisted on the Poles' granting their Orthodox, Uniate, and Protestant subjects rights equal to those enjoyed by Roman Catholics under law, the storm of protest that swept through the Polish aristocracy led to the formation of the Confederation of Bar in 1768. The confederates soon received the active support of France, and civil war erupted inside Poland between the pro- and anti-Russian aristocratic factions. Russia invaded Poland once again and the French instigated the Ottoman Turks to declare war on Russia in support of the confederates. So inglorious was the Turkish military effort in southern Ukraine that the Habsburgs were brought to the brink of war with Russia to preserve the balance of power in Europe.[43]

As Europe tottered on the edge of a general war among all the Great Powers so soon after the Seven Years War (1756–63) had crystallized a new balance among them, Prussian king Frederick II the Great, fearful of renewed military involvement in a conflict that could prove immensely expensive, struck upon the idea of partitioning segments of hapless Poland among the powers with primary interests in Polish affairs in an effort to defuse the tense international situation. In the deal forged among Russia, Prussia, and Habsburg Austria in 1772, Russia was granted Belorussia and slices of Polish Ukraine; the Habsburgs received Galicia, Bukovina, and part of Podolia; and Prussia stole Polish Prussia, a corridor of territory that had separated East Prussia from Brandenburg Prussia, less the cities of Gdańsk and Toruń. The First Polish Partition stripped Poland of a third of its territory and almost half of its inhabitants.[44]

Poniatowski and the *sejm* were left no choice but to accept the partition. Too late, the Poles began instituting political reforms that, had they been effected earlier, might have spared the state the humiliation of foreign partition. A new constitution was passed in 1791 that transformed the elective kingship into a hereditary one, vested executive power in the royal office and a newly created council of state, placed legislative power in the hands of a two-chambered *sejm,* and abolished the *liberum veto.* The constitution, in effect, was a Polish declaration against the encroaching empires that surrounded Poland. Had not the Poles' internal political structure been so undermined by centuries of aristocratic selfishness, it might have placed them in position to establish a modern, effective Polish state.[45]

Although Prussia and the Habsburgs accepted the revamped Polish political system, Russia opposed it, and organized a confederation of Polish aristocrats in support of the old order. The pro-Russian confederates were backed by a Russian military invasion of Poland, which sparked a similar act on the part of the Prussians, who feared to be left out of any possible territorial aggrandizement that might result. To avoid further bloodshed, another bargain was struck between the two invading powers at Poland's expense. In early 1793 the Second Polish Partition was implemented. Russia took most of both historic Lithuania and Polish Ukraine, including Podolia. Prussia pilfered Gdańsk, Toruń, and Great Poland (the section of the Great Polish Plain lying between Silesia in the south, Polish Prussia in the north, and Mazovia in the east). Moreover, the Poles were forced to accept a treaty of alliance with Russia, granting that empire the right of free entry for its military forces into that part of the Polish state left intact, as well as control of rump Poland's foreign relations.[46]

Already by the time of the first two partitions, the newly maturing Western European concept of nationalism had sunk firm roots among the Polish nobility. Within a year of the second spoliation of Poland, a truly national uprising erupted against the larceny of the partitions. Vastly outnumbered by the forces of both Russia and Prussia, the rebels, led by Tadeusz Kościuszko, put up a brief heroic but futile fight before their inevitable defeat. Kościuszko was captured and Warsaw was taken by the Russians. In 1795 the third and final partition of Poland was implemented. By its terms, Russia grabbed what remained of Lithuania and Ukraine, as well as Courland on the Baltic; Prussia took Mazovia, with its capital of Warsaw; and Habsburg Austria, not to be left out of the final division of Polish spoils as it had been in 1793, obtained that portion of the Cracow region that it had not taken in the first partition. As a result of one of the last great acts of monarchical, pre-national European power politics, Poland ceased to exist. But the Poles as a "nation" remained alive.[47]

When the final two partitions of the Polish state were implemented, the French Revolutionary Wars, which started a process that forever changed the core political culture of Western Europe, had already begun. Along with "Liberty, Equality, and Brotherhood," the armies of the revolution spread the notion that the borders of a liberal-democratic "nation" were somehow sacred. As the Poles dropped into "national" oblivion with the total elimination of their state and its borders, the idea of an innate "enlightened" sacredness about nations and their borders was commencing its successful rise to prominence in Western European political consciousness.

The humiliated and discontented Polish nobility constituted a highly receptive audience for the nationalist revolutionary message communicated by France to the rest of Europe. After French emperor Napoleon I Bonaparte (1804–15) transformed the radical republican ideology of the revolution into one stressing nationalist-imperial interests, the Poles were brought into direct contact with the French through Napoleon's 1806–7 Jena-Auerstädt, Eylau, and Friedland campaigns against both Prussia and Russia. Playing to the Poles' agitated national awareness, Napoleon first issued calls for uprisings in the Polish territories held by his two enemies. Following Prussia's military demise at Jena-Auerstädt, Napoleon advanced against the Russians and whatever remained of the Prussian army into former Polish lands and established his primary headquarters at Warsaw. The Polish nobility grew nationalistically ecstatic. Napoleon's appearance removed the presence of Russian and Prussian administration from much of former Polish territory, and Napoleon himself seemed to hold out the promise of imposing a resurrected Greater Polish state on the defeated partitioning powers.

With Napoleon's defeat of the Russians at Friedland in 1807, the last major military obstacles to French dominance in Central-Eastern and Northeastern Europe were shattered, and both Russia and Prussia were forced to sign the Treaty of Tilsit. As part of the terms the French emperor imposed on the defeated states, Prussia was to cede to Napoleon all of its lands taken from Poland since the First Partition in 1772, including Gdańsk, for the purpose of creating the Grand Duchy of Warsaw (the name "Poland" was not used, at the insistence of Russian tsar Alexander I [1801–25]). In turn, Russia was constrained to officially recognize the independence of the new "Warsaw" state. Far from satisfying the national ambitions of the Polish nobility for a truly independent Poland, the Grand Duchy was placed under direct French suzerainty. Napoleon looked on it as a useful tool for furthering French imperial interests—the vengeful and nationalistic Poles would serve as a Damocles sword for keeping the defeated states in line with French dictates. He gave only ambiguous support to the Poles' nationalist aspirations—just enough to keep them expectantly loyal but not enough to give them real freedom of action. His tactics worked.

Because of the illusion created by Napoleon's tact that Polish national resurrection lay just after the next successful military campaign, Poles fought
loyally and bravely as France's dependent and dependable allies until the bitter end arrived for Napoleon at Waterloo in 1815. An army-size Polish military force accompanied Napoleon in his ill-fated 1812 invasion of Russia, the
Poles' most intransigent enemy, and additional Polish troops were among the
most trustworthy units in his desperate attempts to stave off total military defeat
by the combined, overwhelming forces of all the European Great Powers
during 1813 and 1814. Poles formed part of Napoleon's private personal
guard during his exile on Elba, and Poles died in the carnage at Waterloo
attempting to bring their idol, and potential national benefactor, once again to
imperial power in Europe.

At the Congress of Vienna in 1815, the victorious anti-Napoleon allies
attempted to redraw the map of Europe for their own benefit and to suppress
any future threat to the old monarchical order posed by liberal-democracy and
nationalism through imposing a police-state regime in all territories under their
control. As a part of their grand remapping scheme, most of the Grand Duchy
of Warsaw, composed of partition spoils originally held by Prussia and partly
by Austria, was handed over to Russia outright. Tsar Alexander insisted on
Russia being compensated for its efforts in defeating Napoleon. Since Russia
had played the leading Continental role in the success and possessed the single
largest military force in Europe at the time, the rest of the allies at Vienna were
obliged to appease him with the Polish spoils he sought, especially as they
desired similar compensation for themselves in other areas. With the territorial reward attained at Vienna, Russia came to hold the largest and most populous segment of former Poland of all the partitioning powers.[48]

Alexander organized his new Polish acquisitions into an autonomous
Kingdom of Poland in permanent union with Russia, with the Russian tsar serving as hereditary ruler. The Poles were granted an administrative system separate from that of Russia, a national *sejm,* and their own military forces. They
were permitted to continue using their native language in all official capacities. A viceroy represented the tsar inside the kingdom and Russian generals
were placed in overall command of the Poles' military. On the whole, the position of the Catholic Poles within the Orthodox Russian imperial state was not
overly negative. A fiction of Polish national existence was maintained by the
Russian-imposed royal constitution, and the Polish aristocracy were confirmed in their dominance within the autonomous kingdom. Adam
Czartoryski, a Polish prince, was a longtime friend of Tsar Alexander who had
served as an important Russian minister during the wars and had helped influence the tsar in his creation of the kingdom.[49]

For a brief early period of time after the establishment of the kingdom, Czartoryski and many of his fellow Polish nobles mistakenly entertained the idea that Alexander would even further the Poles' nationalist cause by turning over control of vast Ukrainian territories to them. But civilizational differences and long-standing historical enmities between the Poles and the Russians were not overcome so easily, despite the tsar's seemingly more "enlightened" perspective. After 1820 Alexander gradually succumbed to a personal inclination toward Orthodox religious mysticism, and, as he grew more mystical, he acted more in line with the traditional Byzantine-Mongol autocratic political culture of Russia than with that of the West. Alexander became adamantly unwilling to abide by the terms of the kingdom's constitution, and he found "Third Rome" Russian claims to Ukraine and Belorussia far more compelling than the friendship of his few Polish confidants. In the end, instead of attempting to build upon the leniency toward them extended by Russia to gradually expand and solidify their independence, the Polish nationalist aristocracy wasted the opportunity by increasing their agitation for more immediate satisfaction of their extreme Greater Poland nationalist dreams.[50]

Following Alexander's death in 1825 and the refusal of his brother Konstantin, a popular viceroy in the Polish kingdom, to succeed him, pressure for the Russification of the Poles was exerted by the dead tsar's younger brother Tsar Nicholas I (1825–55), a far less intelligent and open-minded individual than either of his two elder siblings. Nicholas attempted to bring the Polish kingdom more closely under Russian control by imposing strict discipline in Polish military and civil matters, and he sought to weaken the position of the Polish nobility by placing restrictions on their relations with their enserfed peasantry. Spurred on by growing nationalist pretensions and fear for their continued class privileges, and abetted by their autonomous situation within the Russian Empire, members of the Polish aristocracy set about preparing an armed nationalist uprising against continued Russian domination. The outbreak of liberal-democratic revolutions in Paris and Belgium in 1830, and Nicholas's proposal to send the Polish army to suppress them, provoked the Poles into action. Refusing to assault their former French benefactors, they expelled the Russian garrison from Warsaw, established a revolutionary government, declared the Romanovs deposed as hereditary rulers, and proclaimed the reunion of Poland with Lithuania.

The Polish Revolution of 1830–31 was doomed to failure from the start. Nationalism among the Poles was restricted almost exclusively to the ranks of the nobility. The peasantry, who were predominantly serfs lorded over by the aristocrats, were ignorant of such sentiment and were far more concerned with the oppression placed on them by their fellow Polish landlords than with notions of national independence. In their minds, one overbearing aristocrat was as bad as another, no matter the nationality. The Polish nobles made no attempt to win the support of their peasants; rather they placed their hopes in Western—primarily French—help that ultimately failed to materialize. Moreover, the nationalist aristocracy itself was divided between moderate and radical wings that proved unable to overcome their internal dissensions. When Russian forces invaded the kingdom, the rebels were left facing them unsupported and divided. They swiftly were defeated in battle and Warsaw fell into Russian hands. Soon after, the revolution collapsed. The victorious Russians abrogated the former constitution and replaced it with an organic statute that abolished the Poles' political rights, removed most of their administrative autonomy, and initiated a period of intensive Russification in the kingdom.[51]

On the demise of the 1830 revolution, there followed a massive emigration of Polish intellectuals, scholars, military leaders, and nationalists to the West. Most wound up in Paris, where the Hôtel Lambert became the unofficial capital of a Polish nationalist government-in-exile, led by Czartoryski, who was often referred to as the uncrowned king of Poland. The exiles were of all political persuasions, running the gamut from moderate liberals (Whites) to extreme radicals (Reds). Counted among their numbers were great writers, such as Adam Mickiewicz, and composers, such as Fryderyk Chopin—men who transformed the national debacle of 1830 and its subsequent diaspora into the apex of modern Polish cultural attainment. Out of their political and cultural efforts in exile rose the definitive symbolism of Polish nationalism: Poland became the "Christ of Europe," crucified for the sins of others.

So active were the Polish exiles and so adamant were they in their nationalist goals that they quickly won a reputation as Europe's most dedicated and professional group of revolutionaries. From the 1830s through the 1860s, Poles were prominently involved in every European revolutionary movement as both combatants and as ideologues. They constantly sought out revolutionary situations, and they injected their own nationalist agenda into every effort that they joined. Numerous Poles fought in the ranks of the various German and East-Central European revolutionary forces during the Revolution of 1848, and Polish General Józef Bem commanded the last stand of all Hungarian troops in Transylvania against an overwhelming Russian invasion in 1849. Although the relentless, high-profile efforts of the Polish emigrés won them renown, sometimes glory, and widespread sympathy among political leaders in the West, those achievements failed to gain them their nationalist goal. No nineteenth-century Western state was willing to risk its own political interests in the international European arena by aiding the exiles in reestablishing an independent Poland.[52]

While the exiles were carving their names in nineteenth-century European revolutionary history, the Kingdom of Poland languished under the organic statutes. Yet despite the curtailment of Polish autonomy, the kingdom still enjoyed an exceptional position within the Russian Empire. It retained its status separate from the rest of Russia, and its nobility managed to enjoy a less restricted sociopolitical existence than did their Russian counterparts. Three decades of Russification efforts following 1830 succeeded in creating a strong pro-Russian faction among conservative elements in the aristocracy and had won a certain amount of sympathy for Russia among the Polish peasantry. This situation was aptly demonstrated in events surrounding the abolition of serfdom in Russia by Tsar Alexander II (1855–81) and the 1863–64 Polish Revolution.

When Alexander II discovered that his initial attempts at strengthening his empire by means of social reform—emancipating the vast serf population—could make little headway against the vested interests of the native Russian aristocracy, he flanked the opposition by arranging for an assembly of Lithuanian nobles to petition him publicly for such reform in 1857. Moderate (White) Polish nobles threw their support on the side of the reform effort, and Alexander was given the green light to initiate the needed reforms of 1861. While the bulk of the reform program, as finally adopted, dealt with the (inadequate, as it turned out) emancipation of all serfs in the empire, including those in the Polish kingdom, it also made important positive changes in legal, administrative, and military matters. In 1864, for the first time in its history, local government in Russia, including that in Poland, was made elective and freed of class restrictions. In that same year the empire-wide judicial system was removed from the control of local aristocrats and reorganized along French lines under a system of justices of the peace and trial by jury, supported by a newly created bar association.

The antiaristocratic and socially equitable thrusts of the reforms proved threatening to the more radical Polish nationalists (Reds), who realized that liberalization of sociopolitical conditions within the kingdom would create increased acceptance of Russian suzerainty and thus erode their position for winning independence for Poland. Alexander had hoped to earn Polish support for his reforms in 1862 by restoring much of the pre-1830 original organization to the kingdom. Most of the Whites supported Alexander's attempts, but the Reds, fearful that their dreams of an independent, radical Polish republic would be fatally undermined by pro-Russian sentiment, instigated local disturbances aimed at sabotaging the liberalizing efforts. Many of the radicals, including their leaders, were aristocratic university students, so, when in 1863 the Russian authorities attempted to squelch Red activities by drafting students into the army, most fled to the countryside, where they established a revolutionary council and organized resistance forces. Thus began the second anti-Russian revolution among the Poles since the creation of the Polish kingdom.

The Polish Revolution of 1863–64 had even less chance of success than did the one in 1830. Since there no longer existed a separate Polish military, the rebels were forced to make do with guerilla tactics against the powerful regular Russian army. Yet the radical Poles' revolutionary fervor proved infectious. Soon rebellions were raised in Lithuania and in Belorussia. The outside Great Powers of Europe, preoccupied with problems surrounding the unification of Italy, did little to support the rebels beyond ineffectual diplomatic protests, which ultimately served only to foment strong reactionary nationalist sentiment among the Russians. An army was dispatched to crush the rebellion, which made gradual but steady progress, partly because the Russians were able to deliver on promises of peasant emancipation made to a peasantry that was suspicious of its native landlords' motives in that matter. In fact, the Polish rebel leadership was growing increasingly divided over that very issue: Some desired real emancipation while most sought only to proclaim empty decrees. Left unsupported from abroad, lacking sympathy from among the masses at home, and with their leadership factionalized, the Polish rebels finally were suppressed by the Russians with great severity in 1864. The autonomous Kingdom of Poland was abolished and its territories incorporated directly into the Russian Empire. Russian provincial administration was established, the Russian language was made obligatory in Polish schools, the University of Warsaw was closed, and, in a move demonstrating that the protagonists were consciously aware of the cultural roots of their enmity, the Roman Catholic clergy was exposed to judicial discrimination by the Orthodox Russian ruling establishment.[53]

Russia's thorough defeat of the 1863–64 revolution dampened nationalist activity among the Polish nobility for the following three decades. Realizing that Russian rule would not be ended quickly, many foreswore nationalist activity and turned to economic endeavors in the hope of building a strong base for some distant, future nationalist effort. Members of the nobility entered businesses in droves. Witnessing such an unexpected development, the Russian authorities assumed that Polish nationalist spirit was broken and so did all they could to encourage the situation, thinking that Polish economic development would bury Polish nationalism forever. By the close of the nineteenth century, much of the industry operating in the imperial province of Poland was supported by heavy Russian investment.[54] It seemed an ironic situation for the Poles, who possessed a reputation as the most radically nationalistic people in all of Europe.

Polish nationalism reemerged inside the imperial province of Poland during the 1890s as part of the widespread revolutionary development that had arisen in Russia as a whole. By that time, the Russian revolutionary movement had changed from the populist, romantic bent that had characterized its early programs in the 1860s to one emphasizing scientific socialist, Marxist tenets. During the post-1863 decades, nationalist activity among the Poles in the imperial province languished, but across the border with Austria-Hungary, in the Polish Galician territories acquired by the Habsburgs in the partitions, the Poles were given a free hand to develop national political parties. The Habsburgs used their Galician Polish aristocracy as a counterweight to the growing national aspirations of the Czechs, Croats, and Germans in their multinational empire, so they permitted the Poles in their territories a relatively large measure of political autonomy. As a result, Austrian Galicia, with its historical capital of Cracow, became the heartland of modern Polish nationalism. (Such was not the case with the Poles living in Prussian partition territories, where the 1870 unification of a German nation-state led to steady and efficient Germanization efforts.)[55]

The Habsburgs' hands-off policy regarding their Polish subjects resulted in the formation of actual Polish political parties espousing nationalist agendas, which were eventually transplanted into the Russian imperial province of Poland after the 1905 Russian Revolution led Tsar Nicholas II (1894–1917) to grant extremely limited liberal-democratic political participation in government. There they formulated nationalist political platforms under the heavy influence of the current general Russian revolutionary movements, while maintaining close ties with the nationalist Galician wellspring. Three major parties emerged out of the political contacts with the Austrian Poles. One was the National Democratic Party, led by Roman Dmowski, who operated out of Galicia. As a mainstream Western European-like liberal-democratic party, it sought wider autonomy, approaching near independence, for the Poles in Russia, and it assumed that the solution to the Polish national dilemma could only be a Russian one. The National Democrats thus generally expressed a pro-Russian, progressive liberal-democratic reform platform. A second Polish nationalist party was the Polish Socialist. Led by Józef Piłsudski and centered in Russian Poland, the Polish Socialists differed very little from the National Democrats in their goals, except for an additional stress on certain socialist objectives and for a less pro-Russian stance on the issue of a successful solution to the Poles' national problem. Therefore, the Polish Socialists were more adamant in their calls for complete Polish independence than were the National Democrats. The third was the Social Democratic Party of the Kingdom of Poland and Lithuania, which was led by Róża Luxemburg, who would die in the unsuccessful Spartacus Uprising in Berlin in 1918. The Social Democrats found support for their radical socialist agenda in all of the partitioned territories of former Poland, and, like the Polish Socialists, they sought nothing less than the reestablishment of a completely independent Polish state.[56]

In 1914, at the outbreak of World War I, which found Russia, an Entente ally, pitted against the other two partitioning Central Powers, Germany and Austria-Hungary, the Polish nationalists were provided with the opportunity to win an independent Poland. Both sides in the conflict courted the support of the Polish political parties, and the Poles found themselves placed in the enviable position of playing them off against one another for the maximum benefit to their nationalist cause. Dmowski, who had fled to Paris in 1917, and his National Democrats remained fairly consistent in their pro-Russian stance until the Bolshevik Revolution of 1917 took Russia out of the war, after which their hopes were pinned on a Western Entente victory. Piłsudski, on the other hand, maintained a pro-German posture early in the war, even going so far as to organize a Polish legion military force to combat the Russians. Changing political conditions inside the Central Powers as the war progressed, Piłsudski's subsequent imprisonment as a potentially dangerous non-German nationalist, and Russia's removal from the war led him to throw his political weight and military force to the Entente following his release shortly before the war ended in 1918. While Dmowski concentrated on diplomatic activity among the anti-German allies, Piłsudski fought in the field, winning prestige and respect among the ranks of the Polish nationalists.

America's entry into the war on the side of the Entente in 1917 ensured that one of the consequences of an Entente victory would be the resurrection of an independent Polish nation-state. That goal was expressly stated as one of the Fourteen Points proclaimed by President Woodrow Wilson upon the United States' entrance into the conflict. The idealistic aims of the Fourteen Points, which sought the universal adoption of the "national self-determination of peoples" principle, espoused by the Americans sparked such widespread sympathy among the war-weary populations in Europe that the other Entente allies—France and England, especially—were forced to adopt them publicly as their own. It was a matter of course that the Poles, who constituted Europe's most noted "nation" without a state of its own, were to receive one at the hands of the victorious allies. Once the reestablishment of a Polish nation-state became a definite war aim of the Entente, the Polish national movement was transformed from one seeking the best political deal possible from the various partitioning powers into one demanding the re-creation of the Greater Poland of old, despite the fact that such a state would repudiate the principle of national self-determination of peoples since it would, perforce, include significant numbers of non-Poles—particularly, Lithuanians, Ukrainians, Belorussians, and Germans. A set of fortuitous circumstances at the end of the war conspired to provide the new radical nationalist program with the possibility of success.[57]

By the end of 1918, all three of the partitioning powers had fallen. Germany was exhausted by the war and was forced to accept an armistice to end the fighting. Austria-Hungary disintegrated as its various national groups began carving out of the dead empire as much territory as possible for their future independent national states. Russia, knocked out of the war in 1917 and plagued first by liberal-democratic and then Communist revolutions, dissolved in a vicious civil war between Lenin's Bolshevik government, on one hand, and an assortment of anti-Communist and pro-tsarist forces, on the other. As these situations evolved, Piłsudski managed to hammer together a political arrangement with Dmowski that aimed at taking maximum advantage of the conditions prevailing to found the new Greater Polish nation-state.

In October 1918 the Ukrainians, attempting to establish a state of their own independent of Moscow and Lenin's Bolshevik government, invaded Galicia. The German-founded and supported Polish Regency Council then declared war on Ukraine the following month, and, within three days of that declaration, proceeded to proclaim an independent Polish Republic. Piłsudski, recently released from prison, was given full military power by the regency, which then promptly resigned. Under his now-supreme authority, the Poles cleared Galicia of Ukrainians and made additional westward advances, capturing Poznań and Great Poland from the Germans by year's end. At the same time, Piłsudski forged agreements with Dmowski and other nationalist leaders that permitted the founding of a coalition government for the new Poland early in 1919, with himself installed as provisional president.[58]

Poland may have had a government and control over much of its Mazovian and Great Polish regions in early 1919, but it utterly lacked any truly definite and internationally recognized borders. The government immediately set about conducting a policy of national military expansion to win definitive control of all prepartition Polish territory before the victorious Entente Powers could meet in Versailles and determine the official map of postwar Europe. It was hoped that, by presenting the Versailles Peace Conference with a fait accompli so far as the new Poland's borders were concerned, there would be no other recourse than to officially recognize them. Polish troops invaded Lithuania and captured Vilnius; Belorussia was also entered; skirmishes were started with the Czechs over disputed areas of Silesia; and Ukraine was entered. Yet despite the Poles' efforts at territorial aggrandizement in the east, the Versailles mapmakers issued a dictate near the end of 1919 that drew Poland's

new eastern border—the so-called Curzon Line—farther west than the Poles
had hoped. Piłsudski, already elevated to marshal and invested as chief of state,
and his militant nationalist supporters refused to accept the Versailles settlement, since the Curzon frontier did not include Vilnius or most of western
Ukraine and Belorussia.[59]

Early the following year (1920), the Poles demanded that Lenin grant Poland
the 1772 boundary with Russia, which would thus satisfy most of the nationalist's territorial claims. Lenin did not accept the Poles' demands but made serious efforts to work out a compromise border settlement with them. The
inevitable breakdown of the negotiation efforts unleashed a bitter, wide-ranging
military conflict among Poles, Russians, and Ukrainians on the open Eurasian
steppes not seen since the seventeenth century. Polish forces swept deep into
Ukraine, taking advantage of a downturn in Bolshevik fortunes as the White
opposition in the civil war made its last concerted effort to crush the Reds, over-
running nearly all of the region and capturing Kiev. Unfortunately for the
Poles, Bolshevik military commander-in-chief Lev Trotsky was able to repulse
the White threat decisively, which freed the Bolsheviks to turn their concentrated attention on the Polish forces in Ukraine. The Poles were swept out nearly
as swiftly as they had entered, and, as resistance against the Red military operations collapsed, the Poles were pushed out of Lithuania. Within four months
of the start of the war, Russian Bolshevik forces lay at the doorstep of Warsaw
and the grand imperialist dreams of the Polish nationalists were shattered.

Only Piłsudski's infectious personal leadership and vigorous French military assistance enabled the Poles to rally against the Russians and to make a
desperate and successful stand on the outskirts of their capital. The "Miracle
of Warsaw" turned the tables once again in the war. Bolshevik forces were driven from before the city, and their setback soon turned into a general retreat.
Russian forces were swept from Poland back into Lithuania and Ukraine, and
peace negotiations were opened in Riga during October. The definitive Treaty
of Riga was not signed until the following year (1921), in which the Poles
secured a substantial part of their territorial claims in the east. By defying the
border dictate of their Entente allies at Versailles, and by their willingness to
risk all on the chance for greater nationalist gain, the Poles at Riga succeeded
in winning a Poland larger than any had imagined possible just four years previous. Post-Riga Poland not only included the western territories delineated
at Versailles (part of Polish Prussia [the "Polish Corridor"], Great Poland, Galicia
[with Cracow], part of Silesia, and Mazovia), but it now also encompassed a
large slice of western Ukraine and smaller slices of Lithuania and Belorussia.
In 1922 Vilnius and its surrounding district were incorporated into Poland
by plebiscite.[60]

Although Riga went a long way toward satisfying Polish nationalist goals for resurrected Poland, it created more problems for the Poles than it solved. Once again Riga demonstrated the difficulty of establishing firm national borders on paper when there existed no defensible geographic features to secure them. A bitter feud erupted over the Vilnius issue between the Poles, who viewed the Lithuanians as historical but second-class national partners, and the Lithuanians, who in true nationalist fashion cherished their newly won independence from both Poland and Russia. Despite the verdict of an international conference in 1923 that confirmed Poland's continued possession of the city, the Lithuanians refused to accept the decision as final. A technical state of war between the two disputing states continued to exist, though there was no actual combat. As for the long steppe border with Russia (the Soviet Union after the end of the civil war in 1921), only the political disruption and economic exhaustion of the Soviets caused by revolution, civil war, and international intervention had brought the Russians to the table at Riga. They accepted the border settlement in much the same fashion as the Romanovs had accepted the "eternal peace" treaties with Poland in the seventeenth century—it was necessary so that the state could stabilize and consolidate its resources for a future effort to regain "Russian" territories under Polish control. Coupled with the fact that, in the west, the Germans were dissatisfied over their border with Poland, and particularly upset over the existence of the "Polish Corridor," which separated their East Prussian territories from the main trunk of Germany, Riga merely succeeded in determining that the new Polish nationalist state had to fear continuously for virtually all of its lengthy and disputed borders.[61]

Post-World War I Poland was in poor shape for maintaining such an arduous task. To do so, the state needed to be strongly unified so as to concentrate all of its human and material resources in the effort. But Poland was reconstructed out of territorial pieces that for the previous 123 years had experienced three different developmental processes because of the varying cultures of the three partitioning powers. On the economic level, the new borders disrupted the economic arrangements that had been forged between the various partition lands and their respective partitioning owners. New economic relationships had to be forged among the three disparately developed portions of the state, and that process required time. Until economic integration could be achieved, Poland was unable to benefit fully from its material resources. On the political level, the Poles who had some experience in such matters had acquired it from three different sources. The former Russian Poles had experienced aristocratic oligarchy, then autocracy, and, finally, limited party politics after 1905. The Poles of Habsburg Austria had been exposed to limited autocracy, then limited oligarchy-parliamentarianism, and, finally, universal male suffrage after 1907. Prussian-German Poles endured autocracy, constitutional monarchy, and a certain amount of progressive parliamentarianism. Again, time was required to construct the sort of political training that could integrate the various political experiences and produce leaders capable of formulating and governing a viable statewide political agenda. The fact that Poland's borders with its traditionally belligerent neighbors could be defended only on paper and not on the ground itself meant that little of the time necessary for pulling the country together economically and politically could be expected. Finally, on the ethnic level, Poland was multinational because of the misguided dreams of the ultranationalists who desired the territorial resurrection of the Poland-Lithuania of old. Besides Poles, Lithuanians, Ukrainians, Belorussians, and Germans were included in the population delineated by the new borders. Most, if not all, of those minorities held little or no stake in a Polish national state and, therefore, could not be counted on to defend the borders against future encroachments by their conationals from outside Poland. A significant Jewish population was viewed by the Catholic-nationalist Poles with distrust and scorn, and thus were increasingly isolated from mainstream Polish society. Given the ultranationalist bent that characterized Polish leadership after World War I, it is doubtful that the disparate minorities in the post-Riga state could have been welded into trustworthy Polish citizens in any reasonable amount of time.[62]

Concern over protecting Poland's far-flung, naked borders dominated the Poles' foreign policy in the period between the two world wars (1921–39). Because the state was sandwiched between two traditional national enemies—Germany on the west and Russia (Soviet Union) on the east—both of which were disgruntled over their situations following World War I and, therefore, potentially dangerous for the Poles should either desire to solve its woes at Poland's expense, two schools of thought emerged among the Polish leadership. It seemed only logical that Poland's future lay in a general alliance with either Germany or Russia. Piłsudski, who either directly or from behind the scenes dominated Polish politics until his death in 1935, originally favored the pro-German tact until 1918, while Ignacy Paderewski, the noted pianist and Poland's first premier, and Dmowski's National Democrats looked to Russia early on, but their position was discredited somewhat by the Russo-Polish War of 1920–21. When Piłsudski came to undisputed, dictatorial power in the 1920s, he bent his efforts at suppressing Communist political activity in the state and at strengthening the Polish economy. Relying on promised French backing for securing Poland's borders and making use of continuing hostilities with Lithuania over Vilnius and Czechoslovakia over Teschen Silesia, he invested heavily in expanding the Poles' own military forces. The victory over the Bolsheviks in 1921, the Soviet

Union's continued internal exhaustion, and the Polish military buildup created a false sense of strength in the mind of Piłsudski and his fellow nationalists, who mistakenly came to believe that Poland was becoming one of the post–World War I European Great Powers.[63] That was a grave mistake.

Great Power status had to rest on more than mere nationalist fervor and outward military display. Power required the availability of strong, dependable human and material resources and the political leadership able to use them adroitly. These interwar Poland lacked. The population of the state was, for the most part, poor and backward compared to the rest of Western Europe. Moreover, it was divided along ethnic-nationalist lines and, therefore, unreliable as a human resource for Great Power nationalist policy. Poverty was widespread because, as primarily an agricultural state, Poland was one of the most backward regions in Europe. Neither Prussia-Germany nor Habsburg Austria had fostered industrial development in the Polish territories they had acquired in the partitions, preferring to emphasize agrarian activity for both economic and sociopolitical reasons. Only Russia had sponsored industrial endeavors in its Polish territories in a bid to replace Polish nationalism with material contentment. But the state of Russian industrial development had lagged behind that of Western Europe in terms of technology and know-how, so the industries that Poland possessed after its resurrection could not compete with those in the West.

Both the flawed human and industrial realities meant that the military strength of the state, on which Polish nationalist pretensions were grounded, was actually a hollow shell. Its value was even further undermined by the romantic, backward-looking perceptions of the national leadership, who committed the most common mistake that any government could make—that is, preparing for the next war as if it would be fought like the last. (In this case, the "last" for the Poles had been in the eighteenth century!) During the interwar period, the Poles could boast of possessing one of the most outwardly colorful and numerically large military forces in Europe, for a state its size. Unfortunately, it contained too many outdated cavalry units on horseback (the Poles' traditional military forte, born of the steppe environment) and too few modern armored units (the less glamorous but more effective mechanized "cavalry" of industrialized society).

Poland depended on a 1921 alliance with France to provide the necessary international support for the security of its borders with Germany and Russia (the Soviet Union). At first the Poles were far more concerned with their western borders with Germany than with those facing Russia, since the Soviet Union was undergoing near-continuous internal upheavals, which had commenced with the fall of the tsars and continued through the Communist revolution, the civil war, and into the Stalinist period with the five-year plans, the collectivization of agriculture, and forced heavy industrialization. To all appearances, the Soviet threat looked weak. And though Germany had been intentionally crippled by the terms of the Versailles Treaty, the presence of France on its western, Rhine border seemed to provide added assurance that the Germans would not be so foolish as to cause trouble for the Poles to their east. With such international circumstances prevailing, the Poles easily succumbed to an illusive self–image of their Great Power status.[64]

The sand foundation of that illusion began to surface following the onset of the Great Depression of 1929. The global character of industrial capitalism was dramatically and tragically demonstrated for the first time when the economy of the United States faltered in October of that year. Falling stocks in America dragged with them the economies of the Americans' European trading partners, who were less self-sufficient and increasingly dependent on American goods and markets. Though the United States was badly shaken by the Great Depression, its European partners were devastated by runaway inflation and massive unemployment. Hardest hit were the agricultural states. By 1930 Poland was in the throes of severe economic depression and general want.

Just as heavily affected by the Great Depression was Germany. The misery that attended economic decline there served to undermine what little credibility the faltering and flawed Weimar Republic possessed. In 1933 the Germans turned for succor to a man and his party who promised to cure all of the economic, political, and social ills inflicted on Germany as a result of the putative nature of the Versailles Treaty and of the supposed machinations of Jewish industrialists. Playing on the Germans' feelings of unfair and undeserved national humiliation and vulnerability, Adolf Hitler and his Nazis promised them not only a radical solution to their current woes but a future in which they would dominate all of the European world. By constantly harping on the topic of a threatened German nationalism—from Communists, Jews, the victorious Entente allies of the previous war, and from the rise in power of "inferior" European peoples, such as the various Slavic nations— and by emphasizing an assumed innate German national strength through exaggerated militarism, Hitler swiftly gained the near-total, blind faith of the Germans. Their faith in Hitler was more firmly cemented as the Nazis artificially stimulated the German economy through expanded military spending, vast civic building projects, and barterlike trade agreements with the smaller, economically hard-hit states of Eastern Europe. The inherent dangers of fascist ultranationalism—dictatorship, censorship, police-state law and order, the abrogation of constitutional law and individual rights—went nearly unnoticed and unopposed in the superficial national euphoria generated by the Nazis.

The military mentality of the Polish national leadership was piqued by the successful German Nazi approach. Displaying their traditional Western European cultural perspective, the Poles developed a closer affinity for Hitler's militarized Nazi Germany than for Stalin's more chaotic socialist Soviet Union. Having signed a nonaggression pact with Stalin in 1932, the Poles hastened to forge a similar agreement in 1934 with Hitler once he attained unchallenged power. While it was hoped that the two pacts would counterbalance one another, thus securing Poland's borders for at least a decade, the Poles thereafter moved noticeably in the direction of Germany as the key for unlocking their national future. The Poles' pro-German affinities were manifested in increasingly exaggerated displays of militarism, rising rabid anti-Semitism, heightened anticommunism, and blatant authoritarianism in government, all of which had existed prior to the 1934 German agreement but not nearly in so overt and widespread a fashion. France, Germany's most persistent European enemy since the 1870s, seemed to approve tacitly of the Poles' new pro-German affinities by stressing the anti-Communist nature of its support for Poland.[65]

Secure in the belief that the alliance with France gave them a powerful international friend and that written agreements with both of their neighbors and historical enemies protected their borders, the Poles were lulled deeper into the illusion that their nation-state was safe.

Had the Poles been less blinded by their militant nationalism and more practical in their approach toward foreign affairs, they would have realized that all the premises on which they based their sense of national security were flawed. France, their most crucial military and economic ally, lay far to the west, separated from Poland by Germany, one of the primary threats to their borders. While there were seeming advantages to that situation—any German threat to Poland would face a French counterthreat to its rear—it presupposed, at the very least, that France was dedicated enough to its Polish alliance to risk a general war in the Poles' behalf. But in the 1930s France was undergoing severe internal political and economic instability, and thus was far more concerned over problems at home than over creating additional ones by defending faraway allies. The Soviet Union certainly experienced massive domestic upheavals connected with collectivization and industrialization, but its Communist ruler, Josef Stalin, commanded a powerful, highly centralized party organization that ensured strong centralized government, which was backed by the single largest military force on the European continent. Despite the disruption caused by Stalin's radical socioeconomic policies, the Soviet Union was swiftly creating the human and material resource bases for true Great Power status in Europe. Once those processes reached maturity, Stalin, a man of vast political ambition and rock-hard character, was likely to take the first available opportunity to test his state's position on the international stage by dealing with the problem closest at hand—the disputed Ukrainian-Belorussian border with Poland. As for Hitler's Germany, had any Polish leader taken the time to read *Mein kampf,* he would have realized that Hitler was dedicated, from the time of formulating his earliest Nazi political agenda, to the total destruction of the Polish state so that its territories could be used as "living space" for a rapidly expanding German Aryan race. In his book, Hitler laid out—step by step—how he would achieve that goal: (1) reoccupying the heavily industrialized Ruhr-Rhineland; (2) annexing Austria to Germany; (3) intimidating the Central-Eastern European states by dismembering Czechoslovakia, the region's only functioning democracy, and annexing the industrialized, German-inhabited Sudetenland; (4) neutralizing any immediate Soviet threat to German expansion through diplomacy; and (5) invading Poland.[66]

By 1938 Hitler was noticeably on schedule. Two years earlier (1936) he had called the bluff of the old Entente allies and successfully pulled off the German reoccupation of the Ruhr-Rhineland. In March 1938 Hitler successfully manipulated the annexation of Austria, which raised a great deal of international diplomatic hubbub but little real deterrence to Hitler's agenda. The Poles took advantage of Europe's preoccupation with the annexation crisis to force Lithuania to accept a Polish-imposed end to their squabble over Vilnius. Before the year was out, Hitler moved against Czechoslovakia, and when that state was dismembered at a conference of European Powers held in Munich, the Poles once again seized the opportunity opened by Hitler to satisfy their nationalist ambitions against neighbors—they annexed a slice of Czech-held Silesia centered on the city of Teschen. Up to that point, the Poles could feel at ease with their pro-German policy since Hitler's fundamental agenda had brought them two swift, bloodless national successes. They failed to realize that his next two steps would involve them directly, and that Hitler, having succeeded at every step to date, had no intention of deviating from the proscribed program.

Having reestablished Germany's Great Power status in Europe by successfully redrawing the Versailles map through his annexation of Austria and his dismantling of Czechoslovakia, Hitler turned to preparing for his destruction of Poland. It was obvious that to invade Poland successfully and then stave off any expected French or English retaliation, Hitler had to come to terms with Stalin and the Soviet Union. That proved easier than expected, given the rabid anti-Communist rhetoric and political show trials that the Nazis employed in their bid to attain and then retain power in Germany. All the while Hitler railed against the Soviet Union in public, behind the scenes he established relations with the Soviet leadership that resulted in secret German military training on Russian soil (in violation of the Versailles Treaty) and in increased trade in goods and raw materials between the two states.[67]

It seems that the two totalitarian leaders shared some important things in common: rule over states that were considered somewhat outcast by the other European Great Powers, and a suspicion that Western liberal-democracy posed a fatal threat to their continued enjoyment of power. For his part, Hitler believed that a neutral but friendly Soviet Union would serve as a useful tool in future dealings with Poland and the West. After he had dealt successfully with both, his hands would then be free to turn on Stalin and continue his agenda beyond Poland—crushing Russia and transforming Ukraine into the breadbasket and the Caucasus into the oil field for the planned German-Nazi world-state. Stalin, on the other hand, viewed the emerging division of the European powers into pro- and anti-German camps as a boon for the Soviets. He hoped that the two, both considered anathema in his eyes, mutually would exhaust themselves by war, thus removing any possible threat to the Soviet Union from the West.

As 1939 opened, both Hitler and the Western liberal democracies vied with each other for an agreement with Stalin. Stalin's primary concern in the matter was to secure an alliance that would both prevent any invasion of Soviet territory and give the Soviets the best price for their cooperation. The "best price," as far as Stalin was concerned, involved turning over to the Soviet Union the three Baltic states and Finland, which had been created at the end of World War I out of former Russian lands, as well as the rest of Ukraine and Belorussia, which had been militantly torn from Russia by the Poles with Western assistance in 1921. In essence, Stalin sought to attain once again old Russia's "Third Rome" territorial claims. Since the Western powers were ideologically committed to upholding the Versailles map of Europe, they held out little in the way of adequate territorial compensation for Stalin's friendship. A national imperialist and pragmatist, Hitler had no such qualms over violating Versailles-created borders, as he had so publicly demonstrated in the recent past. In late August 1939 German foreign minister Joachim von Ribbentrop and Soviet foreign minister Vyacheslav M. Molotov hammered out a nonaggression agreement between the two states that had far-reaching consequences for Poland and, indeed, for all of Europe.

On the surface, the Ribbentrop-Molotov Pact was a standard agreement between Germany and the Soviet Union that pledged mutual nonaggression, nonparticipation in alliances against one another, and the maintenance of neutrality should either of them become involved in a war with others. The pact's true significance was contained in a secret protocol attached to the agreement, which divided Eastern Europe into mutual spheres of influence. The Soviets were to receive the Versailles-created independent states of Finland, Latvia, Estonia, and Lithuania, as well as the region of Bessarabia (Moldova) from Romania. Most important as far as the Poles were concerned, the pact gave Stalin the right to annex those portions of Belorussia and western Ukraine to the east of Versailles' Curzon Line that Poland had attained at Riga in 1921. Germany was given a free hand in the rest of Poland and Central-Eastern Europe. With the signing of the pact, Hitler accomplished the step necessary for his next agenda item—the invasion and conquest of Poland.[68]

The Poles became aware of the approaching danger from Hitler soon after the dismembering of Czechoslovakia. Hitler managed to squelch all of their efforts to gain increased security through forging alliances with other East European states—with the pro-German states of Hungary and Romania particularly. Growing suspicious of Hitler's intentions, the Poles attempted to revive their relations with the Soviet Union and the Baltic states, and by early 1939 there were increasing anti-German demonstrations in major Polish cities. When Hitler coerced Lithuania into ceding the Baltic port of Memel to Germany in March of that year, the Poles came to realize that their pro-German foreign affinity had been misplaced. Hitler then submitted direct demands to Warsaw for transferring the city of Gdańsk to Germany and for the right to build a German highway and railroad line across the "Corridor" to link East Prussia with Germany proper. He proffered Poland a nonaggression pact and a guarantee of its borders in return.

The Poles rejected Hitler's demands and England, finally jettisoning its appeasement policy toward Germany, hastened to proclaim an Anglo-French guarantee of Polish independence and immediate aid should the country be attacked. It was, however, an empty gesture since no agreement for joint action existed between England and France at that moment. By the time such a coordinated common policy was established, the Ribbentrop-Molotov Pact had been signed and the armies of both Germany and the Soviet Union were poised to enter Poland.

After a number of border incidents between German and Polish troops, Hitler's well-trained, highly mechanized forces swept across the western border of Poland on 1 September 1939. The Poles put up stubborn resistance but were forced to fall back before the invaders' technological superiority. Within three days of the invasion, France and England declared war on Germany and World War II officially began. The practical ineffectiveness of the Poles' alliances with the two Western powers was readily apparent—they were too far removed and too unprepared to lend any sort of real military assistance. The Poles were left alone to face the fate Hitler and Stalin held in store for them. On 17 September the German invasion was transformed into national catastrophe when Soviet troops began streaming across Poland's eastern borders. Two days later German and Russian troops met near Brest-Litovsk, and Poland's doom was sealed. At the end of the month, the defeated state was officially divided between the two aggressors. Germany received Gdańsk and the "Corridor," as well as a large area of western Poland. The Soviets acquired all of the disputed western Ukrainian and Belorussian territories as far west as the Bug River. What might be termed the "fifth" partition of Poland (if one counts the 1667 Andrusovo partition of Ukraine as the first) had been implemented.

The partition lasted less than two years. Having thrashed Scandinavia, Holland, Belgium, and France, and having reduced England temporarily to a besieged island fortress, in 1941 Hitler unleashed Operation Barbarossa against the Soviet Union. The struggle on the Eastern Front between the two continental powerhouses was perhaps the single most crucial field of operations in World War II. In terms of sheer human and material resources, deaths, devastation, and decisive combat, no other theater of the war matched the awesome conflict between Germany and the Soviet Union on the Eurasian steppes. Early in the operations, the Soviets were pushed out of their Polish acquisitions and forced back as far as Moscow itself, where they finally were able to stabilize their lines of defense and hold the Germans. Not until late 1942 did the Soviets manage to build up enough men and material resources to decisively swing the military initiative in their favor at Stalingrad, where an entire German army was annihilated in early 1943. For the rest of that year, German defeats at the hands of the Soviets multiplied into a military debacle of major proportions, and they were driven relentlessly westward. In 1944 the Soviets swept the Germans out of Ukraine, and by midyear they were pouring into Poland with the German forces reeling before them. Hitler's eastern imperialist agenda had bled Germany white, and his anemic state was on the verge of total collapse.

Soviet operations in Poland during 1944 demonstrated the peculiarly malevolent nature of the historical Russo-Polish relationship. As Soviet troops closed on Warsaw, the Polish underground—anti-German partisans known as the Polish Home Army who, unlike most such organized movements during the war, were nationalists rather than Communists—declared an uprising in the capital on 1 August. They counted on assistance from the Soviet forces that had reached the Praga outskirts of Warsaw, just across the Vistula River from the center of the city. Their hopes were gravely disappointed. Seeing an opportunity for eliminating the heart of the Polish nationalist element by having the

Germans do the dirty work, Stalin refused to order an advance across the river to relieve Warsaw or to provide the Poles with any assistance whatsoever. In fact, he even forbade the Western allies to overfly the city for purposes of dropping supplies to the outgunned and outmanned Polish Home Army or to land in Soviet-held territory. In a month of intense, brutal fighting, in which close to 80 percent of Warsaw was destroyed, German SS units crushed the Poles while masses of Soviet troops sat on their hands just across the Vistula River from the bloody scene. Only after the Poles surrendered and their historic capital was reduced to rubble did the Soviets advance and easily clear the city and surroundings of German forces.[69] By crucifying Warsaw, Moscow guaranteed that no organized, effective native Polish national resistance existed to foil its plans for a future, Sovietized puppet Poland.

⊁⊲   ⊳⊁

As the war entered its final year in 1945, the leaders of the anti-German alliance—British prime minister Winston Churchill, Soviet premier Stalin, and American president Franklin D. Roosevelt—met at Yalta, in the Crimea, to thrash out the postwar political settlement in Europe. The fate of Poland was high on their working agenda. The two Westerners were growing wary of their Communist ally and were particularly concerned with the threat of a Soviet-led Communist takeover of Eastern Europe. But they were then facing the possibility that Greece might explode into civil war between royalist and Communist factions. Churchill was especially concerned because of traditional English interests in keeping the eastern Mediterranean free of any threats to its imperial sea-lanes of communications with India. He feared Communist control of Greece could pose such a threat in the future. Earlier in Moscow, in an act of almost incredible flippancy for a tested diplomat, Churchill offhandedly assured Stalin of predominant "influence" in future Polish affairs in exchange for similar British "influence" in Greece. Stalin readily agreed, as did Roosevelt, at Yalta: The fate of Poland was decided.

Having agreed that postwar Poland would exist as a veritable satellite of the Soviet Union, the Yalta peacemakers then set about fixing the future borders of the state. The Curzon eastern border created by an older set of similar peacemakers at Versailles, but ignored by the nationalistic Poles, once again was confirmed by the new. Thus Stalin's infamous stab in Poland's back of 1939 was officially validated by the same Westerners who had condemned the action at the time it occurred. With the Yalta agreements, "Russia" finally owned a recognized western border that encompassed all of its historically claimed "Russian" lands. But the Poles, whose violated national borders were, after all, the cause that brought the West into battle against Nazi Germany in the first place, were left to pay the price for the ensuing war by, ironically, having their prewar borders violated again by their victorious allies. The tragic irony of the situation forced a new border rectification for Poland at the Potsdam Conference held shortly after Germany surrendered. There was no question concerning the renewed state's eastern border with the Soviet Union. The Soviets were to receive the Yalta-established line, and no amount of Polish nationalist objection could overcome the stark military and political reality of the situation. The Allied powers agreed to provide Poland with compensation for the loss of its eastern territories to the Soviet Union by the acquisition of formerly German lands extending as far west as the Oder and Neisse rivers. Taken in tandem, the Yalta-Potsdam border decisions literally moved the state of Poland some 100 to 150 miles farther west than it had ever been in the past. Only a state without any naturally definable borders could have been treated in such a fashion.[70]

It was Yalta-Potsdam Poland that fell to the Communists and, through them, to Soviet control in 1947. It was Yalta-Potsdam Poland that began anti-Soviet disturbances in 1956 that spread more volatilely to Hungary. It was Yalta-Potsdam Poland that experienced a constant and massive Soviet military presence throughout the period of the cold war, serving as the East Bloc's main line of defense against any possible NATO assault from Germany. It was Yalta-Potsdam Poland that witnessed the rise of the anti-Communist Solidarity trade union movement in 1980. And it was Yalta-Potsdam Poland that threw off Communist rule and Soviet control in 1989.

Now that a Polish national government is once again in control of Poland, and Russian troops are being forced out of its territories, the question as to the location and security of the current state's borders must be considered. If the more radical, ultranationalist elements in Russia gain any measure of concrete power in Moscow, will they accept continued expulsion from Poland and Lithuania? On the other hand, will radical Polish nationalists make demands on neighboring Lithuania, Ukraine, and Belarus, or attempt to Polonize those few Germans, Lithuanians, and Ukrainians still residing within the state's borders? Should presently unforeseen circumstance bring about a conflict between Poland and any of the Russian states, would NATO guarantee Poland's Yalta-Potsdam borders, and how? While such questions might appear highly speculative in Western eyes, the dramatic and devastating consequences of Poland's historical border problems has taught the Poles by hard experience never to take their territorial security for granted.

BOSNIA-HERCEGOVINA

AUSTRIA

HUNGARY

Danube R.

SLOVENIA
Varaždin

Ljubljana

Zagreb

Drava R.

Osijek

VOJVODINA

Rijeka

CROATIA

SLAVONIA
Sava R.

Vukovar

Novi Sad

Banja
Luka

Bihać

BOSNIA

Bosna R.

Tuzla

Belgrade

Zadar

Jajce

Srebrenica

Drina R.

DALMATIA

Sarajevo

SERBIA

Split

Višegrad

Šibenik

Goražde

Neretva R.

Mostar

HERCE-
GOVINA

Drina R.

Novi Pazar

MONTENEGRO

Dubrovnik

Kotor

Cetinje

KOSOVO

0 10 20 30 40
Miles

—·—·—· International border

············· Regional border

—— Border of Bosnia-Hercegovina

COX 07 94

ALBANIA

BOSNIA: SHOTS HEARD
'ROUND THE WORLD

● ○ ●

uring the past 122 years certain acts of violence in Bosnia-Hercegovina, a small, obscure region in the northwestern corner of the Balkan Peninsula, have had a profound affect on European and world events. In 1875 an uprising against declining Ottoman Turkish rule in the area and its attendant maladministration sparked an international crisis that brought Europe to the brink of war between the Western European Great Powers, led by England, and Russia. In 1914 gunshots by a young pro-Serb Bosnian nationalist felled the archduke of Austria-Hungary in the streets of Sarajevo and precipitated World War I. And in 1992 there erupted among three distinct segments of the Bosnian-Hercegovinian population, following the 1991 collapse of Yugoslavia, outright civil war, which brought into question the nature and shape of international political relationships in the post-cold war world. Yet despite the detonator-like quality of disturbances in Bosnia-Hercegovina for world events over the past century, the people who inhabit the area have remained puzzling and their history murky to a large proportion of Westerners.

A stumbling block to Western understanding of the 1992 conflict in the Balkans was the Western nationalistic cultural perception that countries, perforce, represented "nations." The name "Bosnia" (which we will use to designate the combined but distinct regions of Bosnia and Hercegovina, unless otherwise noted) itself had disappeared from common usage on the international stage following World War I because the area had been incorporated into the new Yugoslavia created by the Versailles Treaty. Yugoslavia—originally called the Kingdom of Serbs, Croats, and Slovenes in an unsuccessful attempt to mollify the national feelings of the dominant Serbs' other two subsidiary partners prior to the adoption of the more common name in 1929—did not come close to approaching the criteria of a Western-style nation-state. It supposedly was the common political manifestation of three different ethnonational groups—Serbs, Croats, and Slovenes—but the total population of the state included some sixteen other such groups of varying size—Macedonians, Montenegrins, ethnically Slavic Muslims, Albanians, Hungarians, Turks, Slovaks, Bulgarians, Romanians, Ukrainians, Gypsies, Vlahs, Italians, Czechs, Germans, and Russians, in statistically descending order—who could be considered minorities only in the nation-state context. The dominant Serbs made an effort to solidify their position relative to their two subordinate partners and the smaller minority groups by organizing the new state as a centralized monarchy under their native Karadjordjević dynasty and dividing its historic provinces into purely geographical regions, called *banovinas,* in an attempt to deemphasize territorial claims by the numerous non-Serb ethnic groups within the state's borders and to "denationalize" some groups entirely. For example, Macedonia was designated "Vardar (or South) Serbia" to emphasize the Serbs' historic claims on the region, and, to squelch any native Macedonian or Bulgarian national claims, its inhabitants were officially classified as Serbs. To obstruct the nationalist claims of the Croats, the Serbs' most troublesome partner in the new state, the area of historical Croatia—Croatia proper, Slavonia, and Dalmatia—was divided among three *banovinas,* and the two provinces of Bosnia and Hercegovina were split among four.[1]

Following World War II and the establishment of a socialist state under Marshal Josip (Broz) Tito, Yugoslavia was reorganized as a federation of six autonomous republics that reflected more historical identities—Serbia, Montenegro, "Triune" Croatia, Slovenia, Macedonia, and Bosnia-Hercegovina. When Yugoslav socialism collapsed in 1991 under the heavy blows of rampant inflation, economic muddle, and reawakened nationalism, the artificial nation-state created at Versailles and given life support by Tito dissolved into its socialist-era federal component parts. Three of the six former autonomous republics—Slovenia, Croatia, and Macedonia—declared themselves fully independent nation-states by the end of the year. Two—Serbia and Montenegro (both essentially Serbian in ethnonational consciousness)—maintained their federal association as "Yugoslavia" while emphasizing their continued separate ethnonational identities. And one former republic—Bosnia-Hercegovina, which possessed no "nation" in the accepted Western nationalist sense—initially attempted (unsuccessfully to date) to shape itself into a viable multicultural-multiethnic state.

Once Westerners were able to come to terms with their initial shock over the rapid dissolution of Yugoslavia, a state that they had long taken for granted as stable and viable, they had little trouble accepting the cultural reality of most of the successor states. After all, the successors were readily seen as common, mainstream Western-like nation-states. Croatia was the state of the Croats; Slovenia that of the Slovenes; Serbia, Montenegro, and Macedonia were likewise.

Of course, the lone exception was Bosnia-Hercegovina, where no single dominant ethnonational group existed. There was a sort of common territorial identity that could be applied to the inhabitants of the region, but that was all. Little wonder, then, that, when fighting erupted among the disparate elements composing the Bosnian population in 1992, onlookers in the West initially had difficulty in grasping the situation. As the Westerners farthest removed from the scene, Americans in particular were confused by the conflict. Instead of "Bosnians" killing each other in a straightforward civil war, reports of the conflict spoke of Serbs, Croats, and Muslims assaulting one another in a seemingly baffling welter of bloodletting. It appeared only logical that, because a republic of "Bosnia-Hercegovina" had existed in former socialist Yugoslavia and that republic had proclaimed itself an independent state in 1992, there had to be "Bosnians" whom the new state represented. Eventually, the ethnic mantle of "Bosnians" was bestowed on the Muslim combatants by the West, since both the Serb and Croat belligerents could be identified with existing ethnonational nation-states lying outside the borders of Bosnia. Although that development served to simplify the situation in Western minds, it did little to further the West's understanding of the actual nature of the Bosnian conflict, and it contributed to the continued haplessness of the West's efforts to bring the fighting to a workable, viable conclusion.

᚛ ᚜

While on the surface the warfare in Bosnia since 1992 appears to Western eyes motivated by intense nationalist rivalries among three very different ethnonational groups, such a conclusion is both superficial and flawed. This is so because the West projects on the situation its own cultural perceptions. But Western cultural projections on Bosnia do not fit fully the human realities involved in the conflict, a fact that has resulted in the utter failure of all the West's efforts to broker a lasting peace among the belligerents over the first two years of the war. By proceeding as if the three warring parties in Bosnia all represent distinct ethnonational groups, Westerners commit the mistake of lumping together the proverbial human apples and oranges.

Two of the three parties—the Croats and the Serbs—fit the Western ethnonational perception rather well. They identify themselves as distinct Slavic ethnic entities, each with its own language, alphabet, customs, dress, and religious belief. They have joined in combat for the express purpose of carving out for themselves national territories within Bosnia that they both claim by historical right. The third warring group—the Muslims (sometimes called "Bosniaks" in the past)—have no ethnic self-identity to speak of in Western terms. They are Slavs who speak the same language as both the Serbs and the Croats, and they use both of the two Slavic alphabets when writing, depending on whether the form written is Serbian or Croatian. Many of their customs and much of their dress are similar to those of their enemies. The fundamental trait that separates them from the others is not ethnicity but religion, which alone definitively sets them apart from their Christian Serb and Croat neighbors.

Indeed, religion, far more so than simple ethnicity, outwardly expresses the essential human divide among the three belligerent parties in Bosnia. The simple Christian-Muslim separation is obvious: Christian Serbs and Croats are opposed to Muslim Serbs and Croats for control of the state. But the religious partition is more insidious than such a simple scenario. Ethnically, very little outwardly distinguishes Serb from Croat other than their respective form of Christian religious belief. Their spoken languages are so similar that, since the early nineteenth century philological efforts of the Serb Vuk Karadžić, they have been considered merely the two major branches of a common Serbo-Croatian tongue. Only the fact that the Serbs predominantly hold to the Orthodox, while the Croats embrace the Roman Catholic, form of Christianity conclusively sets them apart as separate ethnicities.[2] Thus the Christian-Muslim confrontation among the Bosnian population is complicated by an Orthodox Christian-Roman Catholic Christian antagonism, which often has found the outnumbered Roman Catholic Croats forging loose alliances with the more numerous Muslims to combat the numerically large Orthodox Serbs.

Religion considered simply as a system of dogmatic belief, however, does little to explain the intense animosities that the three contenders hold toward each other. True, Western Europe possesses firsthand experience of the devastation that can be wrought by contending religious beliefs and the centuries-long legacy that such confrontations can generate, in the 150 years of religious warfare spawned in the early sixteenth century by the Protestant Reformation. But closer examination of such religious conflicts usually demonstrates that the fundamental issues involved run much deeper than explicit matters of dogma. Europe's Religious Wars actually were fought to decide the question regarding the nature of political authority in the West, as to whether it rested ultimately in the hands of the spiritual leadership (the papacy) or in those of the temporal rulers (regional monarchs or assemblies). The century and a half of religious conflict in Europe determined the issue in the latter's favor. It is precisely the matter of ultimate worldly authority that has maintained Catholic-Protestant animosities over the centuries since the Religious Wars (as, for example, the Protestant attacks on Catholic candidate John F. Kennedy during his 1960 presidential campaign in the United States, or the "antipapist" sentiment alive among English Anglicans vividly illustrates). At its very core, religion is a society's attempt to institutionalize, as closely as possible, the most basic perceptions of its common reality. And since a society's shared perceptions of reality constitute its culture, religion, no matter the particular dogma involved, is one of the most fundamental conduits of cultural expression.

Culture operates within human societies on two levels. The lowest is that of microculture—what Westerners today call nationality (or, at least, ethnicity). This form of culture is basic to all human groups that are distinguishable from all others because of certain unique, common traits (or norms) that they express as their own, as, for example, language, dress, customs, mannerisms, cuisine, and particular form of religious belief, among many such factors. The highest level of human culture can be called macroculture, but is more commonly (and comfortably) termed "civilization." Civilization is a highly sophisticated, heavily institutionalized form of culture that binds together a number of individual societies and their microcultures into a larger, unified human society by providing them with an ultimate shared sense of common reality. A civilization's culture shapes the accepted framework within which its member societies express their various microcultures, acting much like a mold for a molten alloy in heavy industry. Given the crucially transcendent nature of civilization for its member societies, only a unique, fundamental, and universal form of religion or philosophy (or a combination of both) serves as its most basic vehicle of expression.[3]

The three contending Bosnian populations all manifest microcultural differences to some extent, but, except for the religious factors, these are relatively so slight that it is hard to imagine that they could be the source for so much intense mutual animosity among them. But as we already have noted, each differs from the others in its elemental form of religion. The religious differences among Catholic Croats, Orthodox Serbs, and Muslims in Bosnia run much deeper than mere matters of dogma or the name of the single God in whom they all believe. The differences go to the root of all the belligerents' innate sense of universal human reality and their own unique place within it. Each sees the others as posing a threat to its belief in the "way things are" and "must be." While Westerners may discuss political, economic, social, national, territorial, and other such factors involved in the conflict (and the spokespersons for the contenders do likewise for the benefit of the West), the war in Bosnia, from its beginning and into the present, primarily is a cultural struggle on the level of civilization. It will come to some sort of conclusive end only when this fact is taken into serious account by all concerned so that the differences can be accommodated. That will be no easy task.

⋈   ⋈

History has determined that the frontiers of three separate and distinct civilizations—Western European, Eastern European, and Islamic—meet in Bosnia-Hercegovina. That meeting ground is a small, extremely rugged region less than half the size of the state of Pennsylvania, lying in the Balkans' Dinaric Alps and housing a pre-1992 population of over 3.6 million people. It has been said that, if one could take a huge iron and flatten its terrain, Bosnia-Hercegovina then would stretch larger than all the rest of Europe. Close to 50 percent of the region's land is covered by forest, and the combination of mountains and forest have created an environment that has forced its inhabitants to cluster mostly in small, scattered villages located in the various sporadic highland plateaus, the only places where agriculture can be pursued realistically. What cultivation that is undertaken is subject to poor soil and water problems, which tend to determine that crops are relatively spotty in productivity and poor in quality. The chief rural activity is sheep rearing on the natural mountain pastures that dot the region's landscape, making wool, hides, mutton, and tallow the most important agricultural products.

The region is rich in natural resources. Forest products, such as lumber, wood furniture, and paper, constitute important industries. Brown coal and lignite are plentiful, if not particularly high quality and environmentally clean, sources of energy. The Drina, Bosna, and Neretva rivers provide excellent hydroelectric power. Iron ore mining is an old and important industry in the environs of Sarajevo and in the eastern stretches of Bosnia, while bauxite is extracted in Hercegovina. Precious metals were once an important industry in Bosnia, and the town of Srebrenica, the name of which is derived from the Slavic word for silver, was a thriving silver mining center in the past. The Sarajevo-Zenica area of central Bosnia serves as the primary manufacturing center for most of the industries fed by the region's natural resources, especially in the fields of metallurgy and timber processing. Because of the plenitude of its material resources, Bosnia-Hercegovina has been a prize sought by an assortment of its neighbors since the Middle Ages.[4]

The early history of the region remains somewhat cloudy and imprecise. We know that it was hard hit by the Turkic Avar invasions of the Balkans in the late sixth and early seventh centuries, and that in the seventh century its indigenous Illyrian inhabitants eventually were either displaced by Slavic settlers, who followed in the train of the rapacious invaders, or assimilated into their ranks. At the time of the Avar-Slavic invasions, Bosnia-Hercegovina was considered an inland portion of the Byzantine province of Dalmatia by its rulers. The settlement of the Slavs and the consolidation of their hold over the region led to its separation from the Byzantine-held Adriatic coastal area, during which time it acquired the name "Bosnia"—the land centered on the Bosna River. Between the seventh and tenth centuries two relatively stable Slavic states emerged on either side of Bosnia. To its west and northwest was Croatia, and to its east was Serbia. On its southeastern frontier lay Hum, a separate region that came mostly under Serbian control, which later would evolve into the province of Hercegovina. The territory of Bosnia became a bone of contention between the Croats and Serbs, with control passing back and forth between them, until an independent Bosnian state emerged in the late twelfth century under the rule of a certain Kulin (ca. 1180–1204).[5]

In 1102 the Slavic Kingdom of Croatia was joined to the Magyar Kingdom of Hungary through a personal royal union—the Hungarian king Kálmán (1095–1119) became ruler of both. By the terms of the union, the Croat nobility preserved most of their domestic political autonomy at the cost of handing control of overall foreign relations and military leadership to the Hungarian king. The union opened a new field for Hungarian foreign policy, and over the following four centuries Hungary played a continuing and important role in the political affairs of the northwestern Balkans. On the Adriatic, Hungary-Croatia vied with Venice for control of the Dalmatian coast, while, in the interior, it sparred with the Serbs over Bosnia and regions of northern Serbia to the south of the Danube around Belgrade. In the 1120s Hungary-Croatia briefly held the region of Bosnia but lost it in the 1160s to Byzantine emperor Manuel I Komnenos (1143–80). It was only after Manuel's death that Kulin, the dominant local Bosnian lord, came to power. He did so by acknowledging nominal Hungarian suzerainty, for which he received the title of *ban* (provincial ruler, usually denoting official/nominal subordination to the Hungarian crown), while clandestinely working to attain full independence for his holdings.[6]

Kulin managed to succeed in his quest by commercially developing Bosnia's silver mining industry, by establishing lucrative trade arrangements with Dubrovnik, and by parrying the powerful cultural-political influences in Bosnia of Roman Catholicism, rooted in Hungary-Croatia, and Orthodoxy, emanating out of Serbia, through Bogomilism, a dualistic Christian heresy condemned by both of the mainstream branches of Christianity. Its roots sunk deep in early medieval eastern Manichæism and Paulicianism that had been transplanted from their Asian homelands to the Balkans as a result of earlier Byzantine population transfers, Bogomilism emerged in Bulgaria in the tenth century. The name of the heresy was derived from its semimythical Bulgarian founder, Bogomil

(Beloved of God). While it is certain that the Bogomils believed in some sort of dualistic spiritual reality that pitted a metaphysical "good" against a material "evil," rejected the established Christian church institutions and all of their material manifestations, preached the value of poverty, simplicity, and asceticism, and espoused antiestablishment concepts that condemned most of the then-existing political and social institutions, virtually no historically objective data regarding the particulars of their beliefs have survived. So ardent were the efforts of both the Catholic and the Orthodox churches to eradicate such a dangerous and, not surprisingly, popular heresy that none of the Bogomils' actual writings survived the centuries-long, determined, and destructive persecutions to which they were exposed. All known information about them stems from the documented writings and actions of the Bogomils' most adamant enemies, as well as from extrapolations based on the beliefs of Western European Cathar, Albigensian, Patarine, and Waldensian sects, all of which appear to have been western extensions of the original Bogomil movement.[7]

Despite the persecutions, Bogomilism spread from Bulgaria into nearby Macedonia, and from there to the northwest Balkans and on into Western Europe through Bosnia. Kulin and his family were accused of being devoted to the Bogomil belief by Catholic Hungarian and Orthodox Serbian rulers eager to gain Bosnia for themselves. It was asserted to the pope that Kulin was attempting to make Bogomilism the state religion of the Bosnian lands under his authority, which by then were considered Roman Catholic because of their past Hungarian-Croatian connection. But when Pope Innocent III preached a crusade against Kulin and the heretics, the Bosnian ruler wisely felt constrained to announce his adherence to Catholicism and to permit a Catholic synod in Bosnia (which possessed its own Roman Catholic bishop under the general authority of the Dubrovnik archbishop) to condemn Bogomilism (1203) before the German crusaders recruited by the pope arrived. (Five years later, Innocent organized a crusade in France that exterminated the heretical Cathars there with unparalleled brutality.) Despite Kulin's supposed recantation and the decision of the Catholic synod, the heresy continued to spread among the general Bosnian populace. Under Ban Ninoslav (ca. 1232–50), most inhabitants of Bosnia were considered Bogomil by Catholic outsiders. Two crusades, led by the Hungarians wishing to reexert their direct control over the region, unsuccessfully attempted to exterminate the perceived heresy and to subordinate the banate of Bosnia more closely to Hungary. Aided by the Mongol invasion of the northern Balkans in 1241, which temporarily shattered the Hungarian kingdom, and uniting the Bosnian population behind him by openly supporting the so-called heretical Bosnian faith, Ninoslav managed to stave off continued Hungarian efforts to conquer

Bosnia until his death in 1250. To the end, he maintained to the papacy that he was a good Catholic ruler who had supported the heretics merely to defend his realm from foreign invaders.[8]

Following Ninoslav's death, the pope, at Hungarian insistence, removed the bishop of Bosnia from the authority of the Dubrovnik archbishop and placed the Bosnian Catholics under that of Kalocsa. It was a crucial mistake for both the Catholic church and the Hungarians as far as Bosnia was concerned. The Bosnians rejected the new ecclesiastical administration and refused to permit any Hungarian-appointed bishop into their lands. The Hungarians and the papacy thus became enemies in Bosnian eyes, and the Bosnians were branded even more fervently as heretics by their antagonists. The inhabitants of the banate, in turn, solidified an autonomous church of their own, which both the papacy and the Hungarians stigmatized as Bogomil. Perhaps it was, given Bogomilism's widespread earlier popularity and seeming native political support. But a bit of historical uncertainty regarding this issue exists, since nearly all of the extant sources mentioning Bogomilism (in the guise of "heresy" or "heretics," under the assumption that Bogomilism was the source) were products of the Bosnians' papal and Hungarian antagonists, while existing documents from Bosnia itself tend to indicate that a nascent Bosnian church, though intentionally schismatic from papal control, had emerged and remained nativistically Roman Catholic in its dogma. Thus Bosnia retained its independence, both politically from Hungary and spiritually from Rome, under the authority of its native *bans* and local bishops into the fifteenth century.[9]

Under Ban Stjepan Kotromanić (ca. 1318–53) Bosnia evolved into an important player in the political affairs of the northwestern Balkans involving Hungary-Croatia and Serbia. Kotromanić, originally Orthodox through his Serbian mother, converted to Catholicism and gained recognition of Bosnia's continued autonomy under a very loose nominal Hungarian suzerainty. Kotromanić himself solidified good relations with the Hungarians by marrying his daughter to Hungarian king Louis I of Anjou (1342–82). He successfully resisted a Serbian invasion led by Tsar Stefan IV Dušan (1331–55) in 1350 and expanded the territory under his authority to include parts of Croatia (now called Krajina) in Bosnia's northwest and most of Hum (Hercegovina), gaining control of the Neretva River Valley to the Adriatic. Thus, for the first time, the region that would become known as Hercegovina was tied to that of Bosnia.

Hum—far more so than Bosnia—was mountainous, rocky, and arid. Pastoral sheep raising played a dominant role in its economy. The region's population was composed of Slavs and Vlahs, though most of the latter eventually were assimilated into the dominant Slavic element. From the mid-twelfth to the first quarter of the fourteenth century, when Kotromanić acquired most of its lands,

Hum was ruled by Serbian princes and the majority of the population held to the Orthodox faith. Catholics in Hum lived mostly in the coastal areas that abutted Catholic Dalmatia, but the existence of numerous Orthodox in their midst caused constant tensions between the two segments of the coastal population, as well as between Hum and Catholic Dalmatia. In the early thirteenth century most of Hum was occupied by the Serbs of Raška, and an Orthodox bishopric was established for the region at Ston, Hum's traditional capital. A small area west of the Neretva River maintained a tenuous independence from the Serbs into the early fourteenth century and the rise of Kotromanić.[10]

It was under Kotromanić's rule that a full-fledged autonomous Bosnian church emerged as an important factor within the state. Headed by a bishop with the native title of *Djed* (grandfather) and staffed by clergy drawn exclusively from monasteries of Catholic origin, the Bosnian church enjoyed close ties with the *ban* and his rule. Outside Bosnia, the papal claim that the Bosnians were "heretics" (that is, Bogomils) persisted. Franciscan missionaries were sent by Rome to win back the Bosnian population to papal Catholicism. They established themselves in the region by 1342 and steadily proceeded to expand their operations. Kotromanić, Orthodox and not Bogomil in faith, converted, and from that moment until the Ottoman Turkish conquest of Bosnia in the fifteenth century, all Bosnian rulers were Roman Catholic. Yet despite the success of the missionaries at the top of the Bosnian state, most of the region's local nobility and population continued to cling either to their autonomous Bosnian (or Bogomil, as the case might have been) faith or to that of Orthodoxy.

Meanwhile, Kotromanić continued to develop Bosnia's mining industries, especially silver and lead, by opening new mines and by increasing trading contacts with Dubrovnik, which lay close by on the Dalmatian coast. Saxon German miners were brought in from Hungary to provide the necessary technical expertise, and Dubrovnik colonists handled the mines' administrative and financial operations. Since by the middle of the fourteenth century most mines in Europe were declining, Bosnia began to prosper as a primary supplier of silver and lead. Bosnian towns flourished, craft industries mushroomed, and commerce thrived. As Dubrovnik merchant and Saxon mining colonists formed the predominant element in the rapidly expanding and increasingly wealthy Bosnian urban population, and as both were Catholic, the Franciscan missionaries found ready support in the thriving towns. The native Bosnian church was thus restricted to the rural regions that were left mostly unaffected by the ore mining boom initiated by Kotromanić.[11]

Medieval Bosnia reached its apex under Ban Tvrtko I (1353–91), Kotromanić's successor. The beginning of his reign was inauspicious. Kotromanić had created a territorially large state but one governed through a weak central admin-

istration. At his death, Bosnia began to dissolve into a number of local principalities that freely chose when and if they would obey the young successor. King
Louis of Hungary stripped Tvrtko of western Hum and a number of Croatian
lands and then confirmed the helpless young man as his vassal *ban* of Bosnia.
Moreover, Tvrtko's loyalty to Hungary was thought guaranteed by Rome's continuing calls for action against the "heretical" Bosnian church, though Tvrtko
himself was a confirmed Catholic. Any attempt by the new *ban* to shirk his duties
to the Hungarians thus could be countered by a Hungarian "religious" crusade
against the Bosnian church with papal blessings. Contrary to Hungarian expec-
tations, however, Tvrtko managed to consolidate his authority within Bosnia,
after a brief period in 1367 when he lost his throne to a noble uprising. With
renewed Hungarian backing he regained power in Bosnia, and by the early 1370s
he was in firm control of most of the region's territories.

    With his Bosnian lands united under his authority, Tvrtko set out to med-
dle in the affairs of the Serbs lying to his east. He gained hold from the Serbs
of nearly all Hum and of the entire Adriatic coastline between the Gulf of Kotor
and Dubrovnik. Having expanded Bosnia by acquiring a good deal of Serbian
territory, and playing on his maternal Serbian ancestry (his grandmother was
of the Serbian royal Nemanja family, which had died out as Serb rulers in 1371),
Tvrtko aimed at being crowned king of Serbia and Bosnia. He was so in
1377, but no Serb nobles outside the borders of his enlarged Bosnian state recognized him as their ruler. From that year until the Ottoman conquest of
Bosnia in 1463, all Bosnian rulers used the royal title rather than that of *ban*.
Following the death of Hungarian king Louis in 1382, Tvrtko took advantage
of the subsequent regency to extend his control over much of Croatia and
Dalmatia, adding the names of both to his assumed royal title.

    To expand Bosnia's commercial presence on the Adriatic, in 1382 Tvrtko
built a new port town at the mouth of the Gulf of Kotor, Novi (today called
Herceg-Novi), but this brought him into conflict with Dubrovnik, which
enjoyed commercial trade monopolies in Bosnia dating to the early days of
Kotromanić's reign. A blockade of Novi soon forced Tvrtko to recognize
Dubrovnik's continued economic position in his state. In fact, Dubrovnik
merchants came to play important roles in Tvrtko's government, and they
expanded their trading and mining colonies in Bosnia during his reign. Each
new expansion of Dubrovnik activities brought with it an increased Franciscan
missionary presence.[12]

    On Tvrtko's death in 1391, his Bosnian kingdom-banate remained intact,
though the central power of his successors was weak relative to the strong
regional authority of the various local nobles. These powerful aristocrats
seem to have maintained the Bosnian state because it was deemed in their best

interests to do so, rather than to fragment it into small local principalities that would have been easy prey for the neighboring Hungarians and Serbs. The king-ban exerted effective authority only over the central territories of Bosnia, while the local nobility reigned in the areas conquered by Kotromanić and Tvrtko, a few of whom ruled virtually as independent monarchs with their own subordinate vassals and military forces. Such regional particularism was aided by the existence within the state of three separate Christian religions—Catholicism, Orthodoxy, and the Bosnian church. Each tended to dominate in given areas of the kingdom-banate to the relative exclusion of the others, thus preventing any one of them from serving as a vehicle for overall state integration.

In the early fifteenth century the Bosnian rulers and local nobles became involved in the Hungarian succession struggle between Sigismund (Zsigmond) of Luxemburg (technically king, 1387–1437) and Ladislas (Ulászló) of Angevin Naples. Though their loyalties were divided, the king-bans and most of the Bosnian nobles from the non-Croatian lands backed the loser, Ladislas. When the reigning Bosnian king-ban turned to Sigismund in 1403, a major-ity of the nobles threw their loyalties behind Tvrtko's illegitimate son Tvrtko II Tvrtković (1404–9; 1421–43), who became a puppet for the pro-Ladislas faction. This permitted the Hungarians to initiate annual military campaigns against Bosnia until the end of 1408, when Sigismund inflicted on the Bosnians a sound military defeat. Tvrtko II was deposed early in the follow-ing year and a Hungarian vassal installed as king-ban, who enjoyed the loy-alty of nearly all the powerful Bosnian nobles. Sigismund then parceled out sections of Bosnia to his most loyal Balkan vassals, one of whom was Stefan Lazarović, prince-despot of Serbia (1389–1427), who was granted Srebrenica for his support, the richest silver-mining town in Bosnia. Until the Ottoman conquest at the end of the fifteenth century, Srebrenica and its environs remained in Serbian hands, despite a number of Bosnian military efforts to recap-ture them.

By the time Sigismund solidified Hungarian control over Bosnia through his puppet ruler, the Ottoman Turks had penetrated deep into the heart of the Balkans. In 1389 they crushed Serbia at the Battle of Kosovo Polje, and soon thereafter they conquered Macedonia. By 1396 Bulgaria was completely assimilated into their rising empire. Lazarević's Serbian state was reduced to Ottoman vassalage fol-lowing Kosovo, and the Turks began looking toward the northwest as an area for continued Balkan expansion. In 1414 and 1415 Bosnia became the battleground between the Turks and Hungary, and in the latter year the Hungarians were defeated, opening Bosnia to the influences of the victors and exposing Croatia to Ottoman raids. Bosnia then degenerated into endemic civil war among its regional aristocrats, during which Tvrtko II managed to regain his lost throne.

Although Bosnia's ore-mining economy attained its greatest productivity under Tvrtko's restored rule in the 1420s, the state was exposed to perennial threats from the rapacious Ottoman Turks. In seeking help from the Hungarians, the only logical ally in such a situation, Tvrtko II both irked the Turks and frightened his powerful local nobility, who saw Hungary as a menace to their continued regional autonomy. Civil discord within Bosnia drew into its vortex not only the Turks and the Hungarians but also the Turks' Serb vassals, who took advantage of the unsettled conditions to annex further Bosnian territory. Tvrtko lost the eastern regions of Bosnia and Hum to those Orthodox neighbors, and Turkish forces held footholds within the borders of Bosnia itself. The king-ban was forced to drop his Hungarian alliance and become a Turkish tributary vassal ruler to maintain his hold on the Bosnian throne.

Sigismund's death in 1437 proved unfortunate for Bosnia and for the Balkans in general. When Albrecht, his successor, died just two years later (1439), Hungary was thrown into civil war and thus unable to lend support to its nominal Balkan allies against the continuing Ottoman threat. Serbia was brought under even tighter Turkish control in 1439. Turkish raids into Bosnia increased in frequency and intensity thereafter, since Bosnia thus came to border directly on the Ottoman state. Tvrtko's authority over his nobility grew progressively weaker as they came to realize that the Turks, and not their native ruler, were the source of real political power in the region. They increasingly turned to the Turks for aid in their constant conflicts among themselves and with their king-ban. Yet Tvrtko's death in 1443 did nothing to stop the internecine squabbles among the powerful local Bosnian lords. When a Hungarian-led crusade to liberate the Balkans from the Turks was crushed in the next year (1444) near the Bulgarian Black Sea port of Varna, the Turks were free to turn their unobstructed attention back onto Bosnia. The Bosnians made efforts to find allies in the West—Hungary and Venice, primarily—and their attempts were accompanied by an increase in the presence of Roman Catholicism within Bosnia as the price that the Westerners exacted for their promised but tenuous aid.[13]

In 1448 Stefan Vukčić, lord of Hum (1435–66) and a strong political opponent of the Bosnian king-ban Stefan Tomaš (1443–61), declared his independence from Bosnian authority and assumed the title of *herceg* (duke, based on the similar Hungarian-German title *herzog*), ruling over Hum, which consequently acquired the name Hercegovina (Land of the Herceg) in common parlance. Vukčić intentionally linked his title and state to Saint Sava, the native patron saint of Serbia, in an effort to gain the support of powerful Serbian despot Djordje Branković, a puppet ruler of the Turks (1427–56), and through him the friendship of the Ottoman conquerors. During the continuing warfare between Bosnia and the Serbs over possession of Srebrenica and its silver mines, Vukčić aided the latter. In return for Ottoman backing, he was forced to pay the Turks tribute.[14]

Ottoman encroachment on Bosnian territory quickened during the 1450s. In 1451 the Turks captured the village of Vrhbosna, which then was renamed Sarajevo and developed by the Ottoman conquerors into Bosnia's major city. The tribute the Turks charged the rulers of Bosnia and Hercegovina was steadily increased, causing the Bosnian king-ban unsuccessfully to intensify his efforts at winning back the rich Srebrenica area from the Serbs and the *herceg* to redevelop the old port of Novi at the mouth of the Bay of Kotor as an Adriatic commercial hub (at which time the city acquired its permanent name, Herceg-Novi). To complicate matters further, both states suffered from the political instability caused by civil wars among their respective nobilities.

Following their capture of Constantinople in 1453 and the extermination of the Byzantine Empire, the last vestige of the ancient Roman world in Europe, the Ottoman Turks ratcheted up their pressures on Bosnia and Hercegovina. The remnants of Branković's briefly rejuvenated autonomous Serbia disappeared under Turkish blows in 1459 with the fall of the Serbs' last fortress, Smederevo. Unfortunately for Bosnia, the commander of the futile Serbian defense of the fortress was a Bosnian, whom the rattled Hungarians falsely accused of treachery in the affair. The resulting rift with Hungary came at a crucial time for Bosnia, since, with the complete incorporation of Serbia into the Ottoman Empire, its Turkish enemies stood squarely along the state's entire eastern frontier. King-Ban Tomaš was forced to seek aid from the papacy, which, in turn, demanded that the ruler squelch the autonomous Bosnian church as the price of its assistance. Tomaš, a Catholic, agreed, and for the first time a native ruler of the state undertook the long-sought persecution of the native Bosnian church. The church, restricted mostly to monasteries, lacking a secular clergy, and not particularly widespread at that time, essentially collapsed as a functioning institution within Bosnia. Most of its monastic adherents converted to official Catholicism, and those who did not sought exile in Hercegovina and elsewhere. Its lay believers, who were not all that numerous, were left leaderless. Yet despite granting the Catholic Westerners what they had long desired by quashing the Bosnian church, no effective papal help against the Turks materialized.

King-Ban Stefan Tomašević succeeded his father as ruler of Bosnia in 1461. The pope bestowed on him a papal royal crown, but that did little to assist him in facing the inevitable doom that loomed over Bosnia. In 1463 the Ottomans swiftly overran both Bosnia and Hercegovina. Thereafter, they gradually incorporated Bosnia directly into their empire, but Hercegovina, with

Hungarian military assistance that transformed both it and Bosnia into a perennial battlefield, managed to stave off a similar fate for another eighteen years, until finally falling entirely in 1481. For the next 400 years, Bosnia and Hercegovina lay immersed in the Islamic world of the Ottoman Empire.[15]

⊲ ⊳

Throughout its entire medieval existence, Bosnia served as a cultural battleground between Catholic Western European civilization, in the guise of Croatia-Dalmatia, Hungary, and the papacy, and Orthodox Eastern European civilization, represented by Serbia. As we have seen, for most of the period between the mid-twelfth and the late fifteenth centuries, the balance between the two was tipped slightly in favor of the West, with Hungarian-Croatian and papal influences playing a more active and continuing role within Bosnia than those exerted by Serbia. Orthodox Eastern Europe's presence in Bosnia expanded only during the final century of Bosnian independent existence with the acquisition of Orthodox Hum and Serbia's expansion into the Srebrenica eastern frontier areas. During that final century, various of the powerful Bosnian regional nobles and their vassals used religious affiliation—Catholic or Orthodox—as one of their political weapons in the constant civil warfare that they conducted among themselves and with the reigning king-bans, a factor that cut across simple geographic east-west lines and thus tended to intermix expression of the two separate cultures throughout the territories of the Bosnian state.[16]

The essentially weak Bosnian rulers, who usually directly controlled only the central, interior areas of the state with any certainty, generally attempted to maintain Bosnia as an autonomous middle ground between West and East by tacitly supporting a native Bosnian church, which leaned more toward Catholicism than to Orthodoxy. That middle-of-the-road experiment ultimately proved unsuccessful since, no matter the church's actual dogma, it was easily branded as Bogomil heretical by both of the contending cultural sides because that heresy had passed through Bosnia on its spread into Western Europe. Moreover, although the Bosnian church may have had its early roots in the popular Bogomil movement of the tenth through twelfth centuries, by the time it matured in the fourteenth, it apparently was restricted mostly to monasteries and, without a secular clergy to cement and expand loyalty among the general population, it thus lacked a broad popular base within the state. Culturally isolated and limited in influence, the Bosnian church easily became a pawn and a victim in the foreign policy game played among the Bosnian rulers, the local Bosnian nobility, and the Western powers in the Balkans.

We have emphasized the issue of the Bosnian church because most past historians of the Balkans have considered it as having played a major role in the entrance of the third cultural protagonist into the civilizational frictions in Bosnia—Islamic civilization—shortly after the region fell into Ottoman hands.

According to the traditional interpretation, the Bosnian church was unquestionably Bogomil and widespread among the Bosnian population from the start and remained heretical and popular through the Ottoman conquest. Because over that period they were subjected to continuous discrimination and persecution by both Catholic and Orthodox alike, the numerous Bosnian Bogomils, who included among their ranks a large number of the local regional lords, converted to Islam when given the opportunity to do so by the Turks. The Bogomil factor thus accounted for the fact that, of all the former Balkan Christian states conquered by the Turkish invaders and then incorporated directly into their empire, only Bosnia witnessed conversions to Islam on such a mass scale that Muslims came to constitute the largest single element in the population. Conversion ended the persecutions and ensured that their sociopolitical status was maintained, despite the change in overall cultural-political authority.

Research on the Bosnian church issue conducted over the past few decades has advanced a different interpretation regarding the nature of the church. It focuses primarily on sources from within Bosnia itself, and it finds no concrete evidence for the existence of Bogomilism among the Bosnians for most of the medieval period. On the contrary, it paints the picture of an originally Catholic-spawned church that was centered almost exclusively on monasteries, possessing no secular clergy working closely with the general Bosnian population, thus enjoying no mass popular base (not even from the Bosnian local aristocracy), and exerting only a sporadic political influence on internal Bosnian affairs. Its greatest political role came during the late thirteenth and part of the fourteenth century, when it rejected direct papal authority by spurning administrative control of a Rome-appointed Hungarian bishop and then created its own independent, schismatic internal organization. For all intents and purposes, the Bosnian church ceased to exist in the final years before the Ottoman conquest.[17]

In our brief survey of medieval Bosnian history, we have generally adopted the more recent interpretation regarding the nature of the Bosnian church, although there are enough gaps in the sources on which the interpretation is based to speculate that Bogomilism possibly may have been present and played some minor role in shaping the church's organization and dogma. But if the newer interpretation is more accurate than the traditional one, then the simple explanation of Bogomilism for the mass conversions to Islam among the Bosnians within the Ottoman Empire must be significantly modified as well.

◥ ▷·

The so-called Ottoman System of state organization was unique among all those existing in Europe during the fifteenth through seventeenth centuries. Western European states during that period underwent a slow and painful process of development from fragmented feudal decentralization to loosely centralized regional monarchies, which for the most part remained subject to certain limitations placed on their overall authority by assemblies of still-powerful aristocracies. The Habsburg Empire, which emerged as the primary Western antagonist of the Turks in the early sixteenth century, never managed to consolidate strong centralized leadership to the extent that its aristocracy was effectively subordinated to the imperial throne. Neither did the Holy Roman Empire of Germany, which the Habsburgs also ruled. In France and England, effective centralization of their respective monarchs' authority was only beginning to be evidenced by the seventeenth century. The same might be said for Prussia and Sweden. Moreover, the road to political centralization in Western Europe was marked by a long and bloody series of religious conflicts sparked by the rise of the Protestant Reformation in the early sixteenth century and settled by the end of the Thirty Years War in the middle of the seventeenth, when the victory of the secular over the spiritual authorities in the struggle for ultimate political power in Europe was recognized by the Treaties of Westphalia in 1648. Strong, centralized states did not mature fully in Western Europe until the end of that century.

As for the Ottoman Turks, theirs was an authoritarian centralized state from its beginnings as a militant Islamic principality bordering on the remnants of the Byzantine Empire in Asia Minor in the thirteenth century, and it remained so until it slipped into irretrievable decline in the late sixteenth. The Ottoman Empire was ruled by a sultan, who served as the supreme military commander charged with expanding the borders of his Islamic theocratic state at the expense of the "unbelievers" of Europe, and who was the supreme source of civil authority responsible for furthering and enforcing correct Islamic law within the territories under his control. Theoretically, the sultan was considered the ultimate owner of those territories, which he was expected to use so as to further the state's military and civil capabilities in the general interests of Islam. To ensure the sultan's ability to exert the authority necessary to carry out his responsibilities throughout the state, sometime during the early fourteenth century the Ottomans developed a unique system of central administration based on institutionalized slavery, the bulk of which was filled by non-Muslim war captives and by youths gathered in periodic child levies conducted among certain of the Ottomans' European Christian subjects. All members of the government bureaucracy and holders of all important provincial military-civil administrative posts, as well as the rank and file of entire elite guard standing military units, were household slaves of the sultans, who held over them the power of life and death. Given that fact, and the additional one that all posts within the central and provincial administration were filled strictly on the basis of individual merit and ability, the Ottoman sultans long reigned over the most effective and efficient centralized administrative system existing in Europe. No other European power during the period of the Ottomans' ascendancy could rival them in terms of the straightforward, unambiguous authoritarian simplicity of their political culture, and their centralized administration was the envy of their Christian European rivals.

The Ottoman Empire itself was organized along the lines of a statewide military compound in keeping with its militant Islamic origins. As supreme military commander, the sultan's capital served as chief headquarters and supply depot for the Turkish forces. The provincial administration under the sultan's central control was also the military organization, with both military and civil authority combined in each office within the overall administrative hierarchy. Every provincial administrative unit—from the largest to the smallest—was responsible for fielding a set number of cavalrymen that reflected its territorial size. The provincial cavalry constituted the bulk of the Ottoman military forces, while the elite standing slave guard units, especially the Janissary infantry and the four guard cavalry regiments, served as the effective shock troops in battle or siege.

A pseudofeudal system of land use, administered and regulated by the central authorities in the capital, supported the large number of Ottoman provincial cavalry. The system was "pseudo" because, unlike the classic feudal system of Western Europe, the recipient of an Ottoman "fief" did not receive ownership rights to the land involved, or to the peasants or townspeople who inhabited it. The system was strictly financial in nature. A provincial military-civil official or warrior was granted the right to collect all or a share of taxes due from the inhabitants of a certain parcel of land on condition that the recipient fulfill military service duties demanded by the state. That conditional arrangement was spelled out in a deed of investiture issued to the officer or warrior by the Ottoman central authorities, in which was specified the extent of the parcel involved, the amount of revenues attached to the parcel for the recipient's personal use (scaled relative to his military-civil rank), and the military expenses that the recipient was expected to meet out of the grant's revenues (such as his personal weapons, armor, and mounts, as well as the size and equipment of his personal retinue, all of which he had to provide on being called to muster). Failure to fulfill the military conditions or the abuse of rights attached to the grant usually resulted in the central government's revoking the "fief" and redistributing it to another candidate.

Since both the central and provincial administrations of the Ottoman Empire were predicated on the continuous support provided by the military revenue-fief system, the productive, taxpaying nonmilitary subject population of the state played a crucial role in Ottoman domestic affairs. The economic well-being and productivity of the rural and urban civilian inhabitants had to be nurtured, protected, and, if at all possible, regulated by the sultan's government to ensure a stable and constant source of requisite tax revenues. One of the most important duties of the state was to protect its common, nonmilitary subjects against both abuse from the provincial military-civil class and outside threats that might tear territories, along with their inhabitants, away from the empire, both of which could have dire consequences on the tax base supporting the fundamental sociopolitical system. The nature of the relationship that existed between the Ottoman ruling establishment and its subjects was aptly expressed in the official term used by the state authorities to identify the nonmilitary subject population—*reaya,* which meant "a flock of sheep," bearing the connotation that they needed careful shepherding so that they could be fleeced beneficially in the interests of the state.

Out of the need to protect and husband the interests of the taxpaying subject population of the empire, there emerged officially created special conditions for conquered non-Muslim populations. As an Islamic state, the Ottoman Empire extended "protection" against death (or, at least, forced conversion) at the hands of the Muslim faithful to its Christian and Jewish subjects. Based on the traditional Islamic concept that they both constituted "People of the Book" (those who had been chosen by God in the past to receive His divine revelation for mankind and had preserved the message in written form—the Jewish Torah and the Christian Bible) who had strayed from the true religious path over time, the Islamic state could tolerate their existence within its borders so long as they recognized their inferior position vis-à-vis the Muslim "true believers." That recognition was institutionalized in their required acceptance of special additional taxes that were not levied on the Muslim subject population, such as the head tax *(cizye),* and in the imposition of certain cultural, social, and legal restrictions in the areas of religious structures, public rituals, dress, ownership of horses and weapons, and legal testimony in cases involving Muslims. Since in the Balkan lands of the Ottoman Empire Christians predominated in the subject population, and since the empire's Jews played a leading role in commercial endeavors, the special additional taxes collected from them constituted the single most lucrative source of revenues for the state.[18]

It was not in the interests of the Islamic state to eliminate the most important elements in its subject population. In fact, the Ottoman central authorities went to great lengths to preserve them against extinction. Because the empire was a theocratic state ruled by Islamic sacred law, that legal system was valid only for its Muslim subjects. This raised potentially grave administrative problems for the Ottoman sultans. They had to preserve intact for the benefit of the Islamic state a large and financially critical non-Muslim subject population while, at the same time, maintaining over them some sort of administrative control, despite the fact that the judicial framework of the state could not be applied to them. The solution arrived at was the creation of the *millet* system of administration, which was grounded firmly in the theocratic political culture of Islam.

Sultan Mehmed II the Conqueror (1451–81) devised the definitive solution to the problem shortly after his capture in 1453 of Constantinople, the millennium-old capital of the Byzantine Empire that he destroyed. By applying traditional Islamic theocratic reasoning, Mehmed concluded that, if Islamic sacred law governed Muslims, then the ecclesiastical laws of the non-Muslims could serve the same purpose for them. He divided his subject population into general groupings called *millets* (loosely, nations), which were based solely on religious affiliation, and he delegated internal administrative responsibilities for each to its highest religious authorities. The religious leaderships of the *millets* represented their respective memberships before the Ottoman court. They were granted the rights to tax, judge, and order the lives of their members insofar as those rights did not conflict with Islamic sacred law or impinge on the sensibilities of the Muslim ruling establishment. They also were charged with seeing that their members paid all requisite state taxes and fulfilled all obligations to the central authorities and their provincial representatives. In creating the *millets,* Mehmed endowed their respective religious establishments with civil responsibilities beyond their traditional ecclesiastical duties. Each *millet,* through its religious authorities, became a veritable department of the Islamic central government's domestic administration, with its chief cleric held accountable directly to the sultan. In return for ensuring the smooth internal administration of his non-Muslim subjects, the sultan granted each *millet* a considerable amount of autonomy in the spheres of religious devotion, cultural activity, judicial affairs not involving Muslims, and local self-government.

By 1461 three non-Muslim *millets* were in effective operation: the Orthodox Christian (founded 1454), headed by the Greek patriarch of Constantinople and representing the single largest, and therefore most financially important, group of non-Muslims in the empire; the Armenian Christian (1461), headed by the patriarch *(Katholikos)* of the Armenian Monophysite church, whose seat was located in Istanbul and who also came to represent all Roman Catholic Ottoman subjects as well; and the Jewish (for all practical purposes in 1453, but officially designated as such only in 1839), headed by an elected representative of the rabbinical council in Istanbul.[19]

Two aspects of the *millet* system can be considered significant for Ottoman Balkan history, especially after Western European nationalist cultural influences came into play starting in the early nineteenth century. One was the fact that, despite the loose translation of the Turkish word *"millet"* as "nation" in English, ethnicity played no role whatsoever in the term's definition, as it did in the West. Religious affiliation alone was the sole criterion for membership in any given *millet*. For example, no matter if a particular individual was Bulgarian, Serbian, Greek, or Romanian, so long as she or he was an Orthodox Christian that person belonged to the Orthodox *millet* administered by the Orthodox church hierarchy headed by the Greek patriarch of Constantinople. The Turks made no ethnic distinctions among the general Orthodox subject population as far as the *millet* was concerned, even though it is certain that the Turks fully were aware that ethnic differences among them existed. In the Islamic theocratic scheme of things, religious belief was fundamental in distinguishing separate groups of people, while ethnicity was of little account in such a spiritual reality.

The second important aspect of the *millet* was linked to the first. Since ethnicity held small value to the Muslims in identifying human groups, the sense of territoriality associated with traditional ethnic group existence in Western conceptions was lacking completely in the *millet* concept. No matter where one lived within the borders of the empire, no matter where one moved, no matter how mixed in religious terms the population of a particular region might be, *millet* affiliation governed one's life. Each *millet* possessed its own, self-contained administrative organization that was complete unto itself, with no claims whatsoever on any of the other *millets* or their memberships. One's neighbors, therefore, could be Muslims, Orthodox Christians, Jews, or Armenian (or Roman Catholic) Christians in any combination without that fact bringing on territorial disputes or animosities spawned by envy of the others' rights or privileges. For all the subjects of the Ottomans, the *millet* system meant that their homeland literally could be anywhere within the confines of the empire.

Such was the general nature of sociopolitical conditions in the Ottoman Empire by the time the Bosnians were incorporated into it after 1463. Apparently the nature of the Ottoman system itself, more than any Bogomil heretical factor, interacting with centuries-old unique Bosnian sociopolitical conditions accounted for the inordinately large number of conversions to

Islam among the Bosnian aristocracy that occurred shortly after Bosnia fell to the Turks.

As noted throughout the brief overview of medieval Bosnian developments, the king-bans almost never managed to consolidate central authority over their powerful regional aristocracy. In the very few cases where a Bosnian ruler did acquire a measure of central control (Tvrtko I, Kotromanić), such success was brief and incomplete. Moreover, the regional lords tended to keep Bosnia in a state of endemic instability through their continuous family rivalries and frequent civil wars. They used religious affiliation as a political tool in those internal struggles, gaining support from or assisting in forming alliances with Bosnia's powerful foreign neighbors—Catholic Hungarians and Croats or Orthodox Serbs. In general, the regional nobility of Bosnia were more concerned about retaining or expanding as much individual wealth and power as possible in any given situation than with maintaining a united Bosnian state. The only apparent reason for their continued acceptance of a titular king-ban until the Ottoman conquest seems to have been the fact that they believed they could better preserve their individual positions and interests in a state independent of their powerful neighbors. Otherwise, they would have been swallowed by the more numerous foreign aristocracies and their wealth and power reduced. It was among the regional aristocracy that conversions to Islam predominated within the Bosnian population following the fall of the state to the Ottomans.

In the Ottoman conquests in the Balkans, the Turks commonly made their initial inroads into a particular region by first acquiring military vassal allies from among the native Christian aristocracy. These were easy to find, given the burning rivalries that existed among the various Christian Balkan states, especially Byzantium, Serbia, and Bulgaria, throughout the fourteenth and into the fifteenth centuries. Moreover, each of those states was plagued by internal discord and often civil war, which facilitated Ottoman inroads through the Turks allying themselves to one or more of the warring Christian factions. Vassalage to the Ottoman sultan swiftly became the basic condition for the Christians forging such alliances. Although those Christian military vassals at first retained a certain measure of autonomy, as time passed and the Turkish presence solidified, they were increasingly assimilated into the Ottoman revenue-fief system, with all of the responsibilities to the Turkish central authorities that the system entailed. Thus, the Christian vassals' continued privileged military-lord status was made directly dependent on the will of the Ottoman sultan. In the second quarter of the fifteenth century, nearly a third of all Ottoman provincial cavalry troops in the Balkans were Christian revenue-fief holders.[20]

By the close of the fifteenth century, however, that situation had changed drastically. No Christians still ranked among the Ottoman provincial cavalry. Over the span of less than fifty years, the Christian vassal forces of the Turks melted into the dominant Muslim military fold. No application of direct force on the part of the Turks was necessary for this assimilation process. The Christian warriors' frequent direct exposure to Islamic influences within the military ranks of the Muslim Ottoman forces alongside whom they fought played an important role. In addition, while Christian military vassals were required to pay increasing amounts of tribute to the Turks and suffered the usual discriminatory effects of membership in a second-class religious faith in the Islamic theocratic state, the Muslim warriors enjoyed the legal and fiscal advantages that accompanied membership in the dominant religious element. The Christian military vassals of the Turks steadily converted to Islam after the fall of Constantinople demonstrated that the Ottomans were in the Balkans to stay—the act made their lives simpler and less taxing (in every sense of the word).[21]

A characteristic of the Ottoman Turks was their willingness to preserve much of the old institutions and administrative organizations in the territories they conquered by adapting them to their own administrative and organizational framework. Ottoman provinces and their various territorial subdivisions tended to mirror those of the states that existed before the conquest. Much the same held true for the revenue-fiefs granted the Christian military vassal converts. Their revenue parcels often included much, if not all, of the converts' former feudal possessions. That fact, combined with the unique extreme centrifugal, turbulent nature of the self-interested Bosnian regional nobility, explains the swift and widespread Islamic conversions that took place among them soon after the Turks overran Bosnia in 1463.

The nature of the Ottoman sociopolitical system, with or without the additional factor of Bogomilism, also goes a long way toward explaining the conversions to Islam of numerous common Bosnians. Muslims in the Islamic state were free of the special taxes levied on Christian subjects but remained subject to general taxation. At the time Bosnia was conquered by the Turks, however, the additional taxes paid by Christian subjects were more symbolic of their second-class status within the Islamic state than actually onerous. In fact, the relatively low level of taxation and the measure of local self-government provided by the *millet* system served to make the lot of the Christian commoner in the Ottoman Empire significantly better than that of her or his counterpart in neighboring Christian European states—at least until the Ottoman system began to break down in the late sixteenth century. Interestingly, Bosnian Muslim converts asked for and received (sometimes officially, oftentimes through bribery) permission to contribute youths to the special child levy *(devşirme)*, which technically could be levied only on Christians. Such being the case, tax relief may have played a role in the extensive conversions of common Bosnian Christians to Islam shortly after the conquest but it probably was a subsidiary benefit more than a primary contributing factor in the process.

Far more important in bringing about the rapid and widespread conversions among the common Bosnian population were the nature of the *millet* system itself and the presence of Islamic *sufi* (mystical) sects.

As we have seen, medieval Bosnia was a meeting ground for three Christian faiths—Roman Catholicism (which enjoyed predominant popularity, especially in the western and central portions of the region), Orthodoxy (which flourished mostly in the east and southeast [Hercegovina] but had made a few inroads into other areas of the region), and the Bosnian schismatic church (which was relegated mostly to monasteries in the central portion of the region and was limited in its general popularity). Orthodox Bosnians had little trouble joining the Orthodox *millet*—it was the largest and most important in the empire. On the other hand, Catholic Bosnians who wished to remain Christian were forced to enter the Armenian *millet* administered by an ecclesiastical organization that, while it vaguely acknowledged the pope as the supreme head of all Christianity, held to a heretical system of belief in Roman Catholic eyes—monophysitism. Rather than submit to the authority of heretics, a number of Bosnian Catholics preferred conversion to Islam as the more morally correct road of action. As for the few members of the Bosnian church, neither of the two choices available was attractive, given past history. They converted to Islam almost to a man.

Islamic conversions of Christians belonging to all three faiths, but most especially among the monastic members of the Bosnian church, were eased further by the appearance in their midst of *sufi* sects—*derviş* orders that bore a certain outward resemblance to Christian monastic orders—that commonly accompanied Ottoman military forces on campaign. Although those orders technically were considered orthodox *(sunni)* in their Islamic faith, their attachment to the mystical branch of Islam often spawned a syncretic approach in matters of religion. For instance, some *derviş* orders incorporated Christian or Zoroastrian elements of popular belief into their governing Islamic ideologies, elements such as the veneration of saints and of holy shrines, the Christian concept of confession, and, in some more extreme cases, the Christian sacrament of holy communion. One *derviş* order—the Bektaşi—not only adopted Christian confession and communion but took to making the Christian sign of the cross as a gesture of respect.

On entering a new region opened by Ottoman military invasion, members of those wandering mystical orders confiscated Christian churches, adopted

Christian saints held as patrons by local inhabitants, and generally blended their brand of folk Islam, which recognized "saints" or holy men and considered certain locales sacred in the eyes of God for one reason or another, with the similar folk Christianity that flourished among the generally illiterate rural population in the region. Often there existed no discernible overt differences in religious expression between *derviş* Muslims and poor Christian villagers. The flexibility, eclecticism, and pragmatism exhibited by the Muslim *derviş* sects in their systems of belief were virtually boundless, and a place often was found for the most un-Islamic rituals and practices. As a result, the wandering *dervişes* scored numerous victories in winning converts to their particular form of Islamic belief from among rural populations in the Balkans. Bosnia was one of their most fruitful fields of endeavor.[22]

The accounts of late fifteenth- and sixteenth-century Western travelers through Bosnia noted that as many as three-fourths of the inhabitants were Muslims. The rest were Catholics or Orthodox. But more accurate were the data from an Ottoman census of 1520–30, which indicated that 46 percent of the Bosnian population was Muslim. (Only some thirty years previous [1489], a similar census listed Muslims in Bosnia at 18.4 percent.)[23]

Widespread conversions to Islam among the Bosnians transformed Bosnia into a stronghold of Ottoman Islamic culture. The urban landscape was soon dotted with the material expressions of a flourishing Islamic society— mosques, caravansaries, fountains, baths, *derviş* lodges *(tekkes)*, charitable houses for the poor and the destitute *(imarets)*, Islamic schools *(medreses)*, and covered marketplaces *(bedestans)*, among others—which were usually supported by financial endowments *(vakıfs)* drawn from all or part of the income from revenue-producing land parcels that were set aside by pious Muslim landholders, and registered as such with the central government. In the sixteenth century the cities of Sarajevo (Bosna Sarayı, in Turkish) and Mostar (originally, Gost Radina in Slavic) were literally transformed from small villages into the two most economically and culturally important urban centers in Bosnia and Hercegovina, respectively, largely through the building and sociocultural activities funded in them by *vakıf* foundations granted by the local Muslim (formerly Christian) notables *(beys)*. Both became the administrative, cultural, and social hubs for the Muslim officials-warriors in their regions, who came to monopolize the Ottoman provincial administrations in Bosnia and Hercegovina.

Sarajevo, located on a bowl-like plateau in the mountains of central Bosnia, lay on the main Ottoman overland trade route linking the capital at Istanbul to Florence in Italy by way of Dubrovnik on the Dalmatian Adriatic coast. A *bedestan,* where merchants traveling the route could congregate and where goods could accumulate, was built in the Bosnian village sometime during the

1480s or 1490s and served as the commercial core around which the city swiftly grew. Trading ties were established with the Dalmatian ports of Split and Šibenik, as well as with Dubrovnik, which led to Sarajevo's development into one of the largest and wealthiest merchant and crafts centers in the Ottoman Balkans. Local Muslim *beys* quickly grew attracted to the flourishing activity in the city and lavished on it rich endowment monies in support of numerous Islamic institutions and foundations. Sarajevo's naturally beautiful surroundings led them also to construct luxurious residences in and around the thriving center. So renowned did the city become that the sultans took to adopting Sarajevo as one of their more important provincial residences (hence the name *Sarayı,* which means "palace" in Turkish, and the source of the current Slavic name for the city). In 1520–30, the urban population was listed as completely Muslim (100 percent) in the Ottoman census, although we know that large numbers of Dubrovnik and Jewish merchants were active in the city and that many of them maintained permanent or semipermanent residences there. So firmly was Sarajevo under the control of the local Bosnian Muslim *beys,* and so important was the economic life of the city, that Ottoman military forces were banned from entering Sarajevo's limits.[24]

The commercial value of the Istanbul-Dubrovnik-Florence overland trade route also led to the rapid development of Mostar, in Hercegovina, as a significant Ottoman urban center. Prior to the coming of the Turks, Mostar was a minor appendage of Herceg Vukčić, lying on the Neretva River near his capital at Blagaj. A fortified bridge spanning the river provided the small settlement with its name, which in Slavic meant "the bridge-keeper." The settlement and its bridge were captured by the Turks sometime in the late 1460s. Owing to its strategic importance as a primary river crossing on the main overland trade route, Mostar quickly developed into a town of some size in a fashion very similar to the process experienced by Sarajevo. By the mid-1550s the city sported a number of large and impressive Islamic architectural monuments (mosques, baths, and the like), and the new picturesque bridge spanning the Neretva that served as the focus for Mostar's civic pride and city emblem (until, regrettably, it was completely destroyed in the recent vicious fighting between Muslims and Croats that virtually levelled the old city center) was completed by the stonemason Haireddin. Crafts and Islamic arts thrived in Mostar until the Ottoman Empire's slide into economic decline grew pronounced by the early eighteenth century.[25]

◄═   ═►

For a number of reasons, the efficient centralized Ottoman sociopolitical system began to break down by the early seventeenth century. One crucial factor was the system's dependency on a strong, effective, and competent absolute ruler for its stability and cohesiveness. Military, administrative, and social organization required the oversight of a sultan who understood their natures and purposes and who took an active interest in their operations. The Turks had been blessed with a series of ten consecutive gifted, or at least competent, sultans whose reigns stretched from that of the empire's founder, Osman I (1281–1324), through that of Süleyman I the Magnificent (1520–66), who was recognized as perhaps the most powerful ruler in Europe by his Western contemporaries. Those sultans had formed and shaped the Ottoman system into the highly effective centralizing sociopolitical structure on which their state was based. Beginning with Süleyman's son and successor, Selim II the Sot (1566–74), the reigning sultans progressively deteriorated in governing abilities and interests, with only a few notable exceptions, until the empire came to an end after World War I.

The destabilizing effects on the state of the growing ineptness of its linchpin—the sultan—simultaneously were magnified by external events in the West that led to disruptive internal developments. The West's forging of direct naval commercial contacts with the spice and luxury markets of Far East Asia and its opening of the Western Hemisphere in the sixteenth century had profound impacts on the Ottoman Empire. The former development for the most part removed the Turks "from the loop" in the European-East Asian spice trade that was so crucial for the West. They lost their lucrative position as middlemen in such transactions. The latter event had, as one of its results, an adverse effect on Ottoman silver-based currency, since an increased volume of South American-mined silver eventually found its way into the Levantine markets of the empire. That flood of silver currency caused rapid inflation within the empire, since, by the end of the sixteenth century, the Turks had already devalued their silver coins in response to the decline in revenues they experienced because of the shift in European-Asian trade from overland to sea routes.

While those international economic factors worked at undermining the Ottoman monetary system, Western technological developments in the military sphere led to progressively improved gunpowder weapons and equipment, resulting in the formation of more effective military tactics and command structures. These Western military improvements brought the string of Ottoman military successes in Europe to an end by the middle of the seventeenth century. The Turks, bound by an Islamic cultural perspective that considered tradition an essential element of human reality, were slow to respond to the new technological challenge posed by their Western enemies. Their failure to do so resulted in the end of Ottoman military preeminence in Europe and the onset of near-continuous defeat on the battlefield. The empire ceased to expand, but the Turks' ability to maintain and enlarge their military forces through the revenue-fief system depended on new territorial acquisitions.

Both developments, in conjunction with the decline in central control caused by the increasingly ineffective capabilities of the sultans, had adverse repercussions on the Ottoman sociopolitical system. Cancerous monetary inflation permeated Ottoman society so that, as the value of the currency decreased, the need for more drastically increased. The efficient slave household bureaucracy was disbanded in favor of selling government posts to the highest bidders. Taxes were constantly raised and the imposition of "extraordinary" taxes multiplied, while the methods of their collection grew more aggressive and, thus, oppressive. Privately owned land held by the sultans and their family, friends, and associates in high offices was sold off to wealthy individuals able to pay, without regard for the buyers' military or administrative abilities. The new owners swiftly discovered that the central authorities were more interested in acquiring immediate cash than in ensuring conditional services tied to the property transactions, so they converted the new holdings to privately owned, income-producing estates virtually at will, and with no effective government reaction. Provincial cavalrymen, also taking advantage of the decline in central control, cast off their military obligations in increasing numbers and illegally transformed their formerly conditional revenue-fiefs into private estates. Provincial governors, finding themselves increasingly free of central oversight, began ruling their provinces as if they were their own autonomous domains. Levels of banditry rose among Ottoman troops who either lost the lands of their revenue-fiefs to more powerful warrior-administrator neighbors or, as retainers of a former fief-holders, could no longer expect to win similar grants from newly conquered territories. Competition among provincial governors, cavalrymen, and bandits for land and cash intensified the crisis in central authority, and anarchy became the norm in Ottoman domestic conditions by the mid-eighteenth century.

To counter the collapse of the traditional provincial military-administrative structure based on conditional revenue-fief holdings, the sultan's central government attempted to fall back on its once-invincible salaried Janissary standing forces. When the empire was in the ascendant, those troops—slaves of the sultans all, recruited primarily through the child levy on Christians—constituted the most highly disciplined, effectively organized, and well-trained military units in Europe. They had been forbidden to marry, to live off barracks, or to take up trades in an effort to guarantee that their existence was dedicated completely to performing unquestioningly the military duties they owed their lord and master, the sultan. With the provincial military forces declining in numbers and growing less effective, the central government was forced to depend more on its paid Janissary troops. Their numbers increased drastically over the course of the seventeenth century, but not through means controlled strictly by the government. The Janissaries were not spared the breakdown of central authority that undermined the other critical military sectors of Ottoman society. Janissary troopers began living off barracks with impunity, marrying, raising families, and taking up crafts to support their new lifestyles. Later, their male children were enrolled in the ranks. Born Muslims, who sought only the lucrative pay and had little inclination for military discipline, bribed their way into the units. As inflation worsened, the Janissary troops, exploding in numbers while plummeting in military effectiveness and dependability, commonly took to rebelling for higher salaries, often making and breaking sultans in the process.

The bill for the internal Ottoman decline ultimately was footed by the non-Muslim subject populations in the empire. Taxes multiplied and their rates grew exorbitant, causing the level of indebtedness among the non-Muslims to rise. Most of the lenders were Muslims in the process of transforming themselves into wealthy capitalist landowners at the state's expense, so loans to the formerly self-governing and free non-Muslim peasants or artisans were increasingly secured by property collateral. The rampaging inflation resulted in numerous loan defaults, upon which the debtors were forced to lose both their property and personal freedom to the lender. Indebtedness and movement restrictions on the *reaya* increased along with the rise of private land ownership among the former provincial Muslim warriors. Moreover, as their Christian enemies in Europe emerged militarily dominant and Ottoman victories in battle dried up, the Muslims readily vented their frustrations on the non-Muslim subjects close at hand. Discriminatory and violent acts against Christians in the empire became common, exacerbated by the endemic banditry and anarchy that swept through the provinces. By the end of the eighteenth century the lot of the non-Muslim subjects of the Ottoman Empire had deteriorated to such a point that they were a ready audience for the new Western European nationalist culture that began filtering into the Balkans from across the borders with the Turks' Western enemies or by means of commercial contacts with the Western European and Russian worlds.[26]

If viewed from a broader perspective than merely one focusing on the Balkans alone, the dissolution of the Ottoman system of provincial revenue-fiefs resulted in bringing sociopolitical conditions in the empire more into line with those holding in most of eighteenth-century Western Europe. Land was now in the possession of large, usually absentee, estate owners who operated their holdings as capitalist, cash-crop enterprises. There existed some small peasant holdings alongside the larger estates, but most of the peasantry worked lands owned by the large landowners, for which they paid either rent or tithes, or both. The Ottoman landlords enjoyed less direct power over the peasants than in most other areas of Europe at the time, but they often could rival their Western counterparts in acts of oppression and arbitrariness. Only the breakdown of civil administration that accompanied the agrarian transformation into the realm of capitalist development probably prevented the empire's rural sector from evolving in the more positive direction taken by landlord-peasant relationships in Western Europe during the nineteenth century. Therefore, the crucial crisis in Ottoman society lay in the political-administrative sphere.

The collapse of effective government can be blamed for the progressive deterioration in the situation of the non-Muslims inside the Ottoman Empire that led them eventually to espouse Western nationalist ideals. Ultimately, the importation of nationalism led to the disappearance of the empire from Europe and, in its place, to the rise of adamantly nationalistic and mutually antagonistic "nations" in the Balkans. As a result of the disappearance of central control, power in the empire's provinces was contested among the old traditional leadership elements (officeholders, landowners, members of the legal professions, merchants, and artisans), the armed Janissary and lesser warrior element (who owned little or no land or other property but who possessed or claimed certain legal privileges and sinecures), and armed bandits (known as *haiduts* among the Slavs or *klephts* among the Greeks, who usually hailed from the non-Muslim populations, possessed no legal privileges that could form the basis for claims to rights within the establishment, and slowly acquired a *millet* consciousness). Throughout the eighteenth century members of the first two groups involved in the power struggle within the empire conducted a veritable civil war between themselves, while they both fought against the third.

As the internal conflict among the contenders for power within the Ottoman Empire intensified during the eighteenth century, the Balkan provinces tended to become increasingly fragmented among local power bases controlled by one or the other of the two primary groups of contestants—we will call them officeholders and Janissaries for convenience sake. In a generalized scenario, either an official administrative officeholder, the members of a prominent local family, or a strong, charismatic individual would succeed in gathering enough land, offices, and privileges to attract the loyalties of other leading sociopolitical figures in a particular region, who then coalesced into a core for a political-military power base controlling and defending the region. In the conditions prevailing by the late eighteenth century, such local power centers often were able to exert so much administrative authority and military might within their regions that the presence of the sultan's central government became nominal at best. Such was the case in the example of Osman

Pasvanoğlu (1799–1807), technically an officeholder *(paşa)* of the central government who transformed the northwest Bulgarian region of Vidin into a personal domain, from which he raided other regions of the empire for his personal benefit. So too was the case of Ali, *paşa* of Ioannina (1788–1822), who transformed his Albanian and Epirote administrative territory into a veritable state within the Ottoman state, from which he dealt virtually as an independent sovereign with the British, Russian, and French forces that operated in the Adriatic region during the Napoleonic wars.[27]

While Ali may have created the largest single regional power base in the Ottoman Empire, neither it nor any of the other similar creations rivaled that of Bosnia in longevity and stability. Ever since their noble ancestors' swift conversion to Islam following the Ottoman conquest in 1463, the Muslim *beys* of Bosnia had enjoyed a monopoly on administrative-military power in the region. Although they had been active and enthusiastic contributors to the sultan's imperial administration—they supplied the central government of the empire with numerous high officials (even when the bureaucracy was staffed by child-levy slaves, since the Bosnians had won the right to have their Muslim youths voluntarily collected)—they had remained fiercely attached to their old local and regional loyalties. When the decline of central authority set in during the seventeenth century, the Bosnian *beys* banded together to maintain order in their land. In return, the grateful central government turned to appointing only native Bosnians to official posts in the region below that of provincial governor, the holder of which thereafter functioned as little more than a figurehead administrator. By the end of the eighteenth century the Bosnian *beys* ran the region as they pleased—taxes collected in the region were not sent to Istanbul but remained in the hands of the *beys;* the increasingly disruptive Janissaries were not permitted to gain a toehold in Bosnia (witnessed by the prohibition of troops in Sarajevo); and even the centrally appointed provincial governor of Bosnia was forced to reside in the small town of Travnik rather than in the provincial capital at Sarajevo. As far as Bosnia was concerned, the sultan's government held no authority.[28]

Bosnia did not escape the socioeconomic changes that occurred during the period of decline in central authority. The Muslim *beys* wholeheartedly joined in the process of transforming their conditional revenue-fiefs into privately owned landed estates and reducing the Bosnian non-Muslim peasantry to restricted renters almost completely at their mercy. A new element appeared among the ranks of the traditional *beys,* comprised of *nouveau riche* tax farmers and land speculators, adventurers, and warriors expelled from Croatia and Hungary by successful Habsburg military advances during the late seventeenth century, who, in one way or another, managed to acquire land in

Bosnia. They played a minor role relative to the numerous native *beys,* but they took a leading part in oppressing the non-Muslim peasantry. With the expansion of privately owned landed estates, the peasantry lost its former security and protection, taxes and tithes continuously rose, and confiscations of peasant holdings grew commonplace. Thus, the status of the non-Muslim peasants in Bosnia approached that of serfs. No serious challenge was raised to the rule of the *beys* because they enjoyed the support of the Muslim free peasantry, who it is estimated made up about a third of the region's population at that time, and because religious-cultural differences kept the remaining two-thirds divided.[29]

Beginning in the late eighteenth century and continuing with ever-increasing force during the nineteenth, religious-cultural identity among the non-Muslims of the Ottoman Empire was translated into ethnonational identity under powerful outside influences from the West. In Bosnia, however, that transition process was slow in developing. The most probable reason for that was the fact that the Muslim *beys,* who in other regions of the empire came to be viewed by the non-Muslims as ethnically "foreign" oppressors—mostly Turks—in Bosnia were recognized as fellow Slavs. They spoke the same native Slavic language as did the general population; they understood the same local traditions; they believed in the same superstitions; they exhibited the same mores and customs; and, because of those factors of commonality, they tended to be more tolerant of non-Muslim religious cultures than were the average Turkish overlords. Common ethnic cultural ties and understanding between the *beys* and the *reaya* population tended to make general relations between them more acceptable in Bosnia than elsewhere in the declining Ottoman Empire. With such acceptance, religious-cultural differences among the non-Muslims faced a more difficult road than elsewhere in spawning truly anti-Turk ethnonational awakenings, since, in a strange way, they all felt themselves a part of a natively controlled society.[30]

Not until the modernizing Sultan Mahmud II (1808–39) succeeded in imposing a modicum of central control over Bosnia in the 1830s were the *beys* forced to relinquish their monopoly on the internal affairs of the region (although ultimate success required a decade-long suppression of the Bosnian *beys'* resistance through military force that ended only in 1850). By that time, strains of Western-style nationalism were beginning to emerge within both the religious-cultural sectors of the non-Muslim population, serving to broaden further the cultural chasm that divided them. As the nationalist process matured, religious affiliation assumed an ethnonational connotation—the Catholics acquired the identity of Croats and the Orthodox that of Serbs; both came to claim Bosnia as part of their respective greater nation-states.

⊠ ⊠

Croat and Serb nationalism shared a number of things in common. Both were born within the borders of the Habsburg Austrian Empire and both eventually claimed primacy of place in a "Yugoslav" (South Slav, in Slavic) nationalist movement that aimed to unite all of the Slavs in the Balkans under their respective leadership. As the nineteenth century progressed, the Yugoslav ideal served as a motivation for both common action and for fierce antagonism.

The very idea of a "Yugoslav" ethnic identity, ultimately leading to its corollary nationalist objective of a Yugoslav nation-state—"Yugoslavia"—first emerged among the Croats in the Habsburg Empire. As members of the Western European world since medieval times, when they adopted Catholicism in the ninth century and formed a Croatian kingdom recognized by the pope and other Western states in the early tenth, the Croats lay in the mainstream of Western cultural development. In the early twelfth century their kingdom was joined to that of Hungary when they accepted the Hungarian monarch as hereditary ruler out of military necessity in struggles against the Venetians and Serbs for control of Dalmatia and its hinterlands—primarily Bosnia. The partnership with Hungary was not always harmonious—Croat nobles often were forced to exert their continued rights of local political autonomy against attempted Hungarian encroachments—but neither was it antagonistic. Under mostly loose Hungarian oversight, the Croats enjoyed local autonomy within the territories of their historic kingdom, and many of them came to play roles of importance within Hungary itself. Croats were prominent players in Hungarian efforts to win control of Bosnia throughout the pre-Ottoman medieval period.[31]

Croatian forces under general Hungarian command determinedly fought the advancing Ottoman Turks throughout the fifteenth century. By the end of that period, territories considered part of the Croatian lands included all of Slavonia (a region generally bounded by the Drava River on the north and the Sava River on the south, with historically shifting eastern and western borders) as far east as Belgrade, most of northern Dalmatia to the town of Omiš, and northern portions of Bosnia that extended as far south as Jajce and included Tuzla. After Hungary was crushed by the Turks at the Battle of Mohács in 1526, the Habsburg Ferdinand I was elected king of Hungary in a disputed election. The Croats voted to accept the rule of Ferdinand on condition that he protected Croatia against the Ottoman threat and that he recognized the continued rights and privileges of the Croat nobility.

Pledges of Habsburg royal protection did not spare the Croats continued suffering at the hands of the Turks. By the 1540s all of Slavonia, northern Bosnia,

and much of northern Dalmatia were lost to the Muslim enemy. Worse, the
Ottomans managed to capture territories running deep into Croatia proper itself,
which were then placed under the general authority of the Turks' provincial
governor of Bosnia. But the pressures of Turkish invasion proved to have a
silver lining for the Croats—it resulted in the Habsburgs' establishing the
Croatian Military Border in 1538 along the frontier with the Ottoman Empire
in the Balkan northwest. Manned by settled military colonists commanded by
the local Croatian aristocracy, the border zone—called "Krajina" in Croat—
was removed from Hungarian jurisdiction and placed directly under the
authority of the Habsburg emperor and his imperial military establishment. Only
that part of Croatia proper that lay north of the border around Zagreb remained
officially bound to Hungary. When Slavonia was retaken from the Turks by
Habsburg forces in the late seventeenth century, it too was designated a military border region and organized along lines similar to the Croatian Krajina.
The border system also was extended into the Vojvodina (Banat) region,
which lay across the Danube north of Belgrade, by Emperor Leopold I following
the Treaty of Sremski Karlovci, signed with the Turks in 1699, which essentially confined the Ottoman Empire south of the Danube and signaled the beginning of a prolonged Turkish withdrawal from most of the territories they held
in Europe.

The Habsburg creation of the Croatian Military Border, with its later extensions into Slavonia and Vojvodina, was probably inspired by a similar frontier organization founded earlier in the sixteenth century by the Turks in the
northern Bosnian and Slavonian lands under their control that fronted
Hungary-Croatia. The Turks established strong garrisons in towns and
fortresses along the border with the Habsburgs from which continuous raids
could be launched against the Christians and defense made against similar
attacks from the enemy's side. To support the regular Ottoman forces man-
ning the border region, the Turks settled military colonists in those territories.
As Ottoman fortunes rose, their military border institution was extended
deeper into Croatian regions to the north and northwest of Bosnia.[32]

An interesting consequence of the rise of military border colonies on both
sides of the Christian-Muslim frontier was the impact that development made
on the demographic picture in the northwestern areas of the Balkans. On the
Turkish side, the military colonists settled in the border zones facing the
Croats were predominantly Orthodox Serbs, which demonstrated that the
Muslim authorities recognized the usefulness of the centuries-old cultural
animosity that prevailed between the two branches of Christianity for furthering
their own interests in the war against the West. The noticeable presence of large
Serbian habitation in Bosnia, especially in its northwestern areas around

Bihać (which the Serbs today designate as Krajina), and in Slavonia dated to the sixteenth-century creation of the Turkish military borders in those regions. Interestingly, the Croats who faced constant battles and skirmishes with Ottoman frontier forces along the military border did not recognize the ethnicity of their enemy's non-Muslim allies (the Croats called them Vlahs); they were, however, well aware that the non-Muslims who fought in the Turkish ranks were Orthodox Christians.[33]

On the Habsburg side of the military frontier, while Croatian troops at first predominated in the border forces, mounting casualties and the need to increase the numerical strength of the frontier troops over time led the Habsburgs to settle as colonists any available and willing peoples. Among the more numerous non-Croatian border recruits were Orthodox Serbs who, unlike their compatriots who willingly served as Ottoman vassals, had fled Muslim domination for perceived freedom within the borders of the Turks' Christian enemy—the Habsburg Empire. The most famous incident of Serbian settlement in Habsburg border territories was the mass exodus of Serbs out of the Ottoman Empire in 1690 led by their Orthodox archbishop-patriarch of Peć, Arsenije Černojević, and their subsequent settlement in Vojvodina, which was designated a military border zone by the Habsburgs in 1699. In that same year, recently reconquered Slavonia received similar status, and, again, Serbs were among the most numerous elements in the region's population. Serbs originally colonized in the Turks' frontier zone in northern Dalmatia were left inside the Habsburg Empire as the Croatian Military Border expanded into the region as a result of the successful late seventeenth-century campaigns against the Turks.

The military frontier in northern Bosnia remained rather stable throughout that late seventeenth-century period of transformation in surrounding Slavonia, Vojvodina, and northern Dalmatia, and the Serbian presence on either side of it continued. So numerous did the Ottoman Serb border population become that, by the late eighteenth century, Orthodox Christians outnumbered Catholics in Bosnia's non-Muslim population by about two to one, and the proportional disparity widened during the nineteenth.[34]

Because the Habsburg military border system was both anational (it was removed from any historic regional authority—such as the state of Hungary—and placed directly under imperial oversight from Vienna) and essentially nonethnic (the border colonists were a veritable hodgepodge of ethnicity—Croats, Germans, Serbs, Hungarians, Italians, and others— although Croats predominated in the former Croatian region and in Dalmatia, and were numerous in Slavonia; Serbs and Hungarians predominated in Vojvodina, and Serbs were numerous in Slavonia), it became the spawning ground, either directly or indirectly, for the national movements of both Serbs and Croats.

Modern Serb nationalism coalesced among the emigré military border colonists who had followed Černojević in his flight from the Ottoman Empire. The Habsburgs granted them religious autonomy and other privileges in return for their military frontier duties. The Vojvodina Serbs enjoyed a century of autonomous Orthodox cultural development and continuous contacts with Enlightened Western and traditional Orthodox Russian intellectual advances, which eventually crystallized into full-blown Serb cultural and political nationalism by the early nineteenth century. Fostered by the linguistic-cultural efforts of Dimitrije (Dositej) Obradović and Vuk Karadžić, the Vojvodina Serbs managed to transform an 1804 local Ottoman Serb uprising against unruly Janissaries in the Belgrade region into a full-blown, successful Serbian national revolution against Turkish rule by 1815. An autonomous Serbian state was created in 1830, and the Serbs emerged as the first Christian Slavic people in the Ottoman Empire to win virtual independence. (The formality of full independence came only at the Treaty of Berlin in 1878.)[35]

Between the establishment of the autonomous Serbian nation-state and the reign of Serb prince Mihail Obrenović (1860–68), a radical Serb nationalist agenda arose that called for the incorporation of Balkan territories that had once formed part of medieval Serbia. The ideal epitome was the mid-fourteenth-century state of Tsar Stefan Dušan. But the European Great Power balance, which saw England and France propping up an increasingly decrepit Ottoman Empire as a useful pawn against Russian expansion into the Balkans, militated against the Serbs actively attempting to put their Greater Serbian nationalist program into action. Ironically, an 1875 anti-Muslim revolt in Bosnia—a region that Dušan had never managed to incorporate into his state but, as a result of past pro-Ottoman Serbian military colonists, then housed a population with a Serb majority—provided them with their first opportunity for nation-state expansion.[36]

Regarding the growth of Croat nationalism, the military border played a less direct role for them than it did for the Serbs. After all, the Croats were full-fledged members of Western European civilization from their medieval origins, so they had been active participants in and receptors of every development that shaped the culture of the West. The birth of national consciousness among them was an organic process that emerged in all Western European societies by the opening of the nineteenth century. The military border provided the Croats with a taste of independence from general Hungarian control during the sixteenth and seventeenth centuries, but that period was followed by a sense of disappointment and growing discontent over the Hungarians' gradually reestablishing their authority in Croatia throughout the eighteenth. Having experienced the relative autonomy granted by the Habsburg authorities to local Croatian leaders within the framework of the military border administration, the Croats found it difficult to swallow Hungarian attempts to exert a more direct sociopolitical presence in Croatian affairs, based on rights received by the Hungarians in the medieval union of the two kingdoms.[37]

The Napoleonic wars fanned Croat discontent with increasing Hungarian authority into an authentic Croat nationalist movement. As a result of military victories over the Habsburgs, the French acquired possession of all Dalmatia and Istria, much of Croatia proper as far inland as the outskirts of Zagreb, and most of Slovenia, including Ljubljana. Napoleon organized those territories into what he called the "Illyrian Provinces" and incorporated them directly into France (1809–13). Because of that fortuitous arrangement, French administration, French law, and French language were imported into the new provinces. The French instituted public works projects (road and bridge building, reforestation, land reclamation) and social reforms (serf emancipation, land redistribution). Most important, direct French rule not only brought the ideas of liberal democracy, nationalism, and the nation-state to the provinces, it put them into actual practice. Although the French interlude lasted only a few short years, and its thrust was essentially anti-Croat and anti-Slovene (since the provinces were considered *French* and not Croatian or Slovenian), the Croats and Slovenes gained a heightened awareness of their own ethnonational identities and briefly experienced firsthand the sociopolitical benefits of the new liberal, nationalist political culture that France heralded for the other member societies of the West.[38]

While the Croats may have been happy to see the end of France's direct rule in 1813—taxes had been heavy and conscription into the French army odious— the national self-identity that they had developed as a result of their exposure to the French left them decidedly joyless over being reincorporated into Habsburg Austria once again as an appendage of Hungary, where nationalism noticeably also was beginning to rear its head. By that time, Romantic concepts of ethnic and cultural values were infiltrating the political and military nationalist precepts sparked by the French Revolution and the Napoleonic wars. Language and religion—that is, ethnicity—tied to history were emerging as the definitive factors in defining groups of people and their worth. Those factors served to validate the claims of peoples to possess the right to specifically located, liberal-democratic nation-states of their own.

The Croats found themselves in a good position regarding the newly emerging Romantic ethnic nationalism. They possessed a literary language traceable back in time to the thirteenth century. During the seventeenth century the Croat poet from Dubrovnik Dživo (or Ivan) Gundulić had elevated Croatian written

in Latin letters to a high level of literary sophistication. Yet in the early nineteenth century Latin dominated as the official administrative language in
Croatia, as it did also in Hungary. Although the use of Latin may have been useful in emphasizing the Western cultural affinities of Croats and Hungarians in
the past, it rapidly grew anachronistic in a Western world that was fast becoming permeated with ethnonational consciousness. The Croats were aware that
their native literary language needed modernizing and that the administrative
use of Latin had to be abandoned. Their opportunity to move in those directions
came in the 1820s when, in reaction to the Hungarians' use of their vernacular
Magyar in the Hungarian National Diet, the Croats decided to do the same.[39]
      Linguistic ethnic expression soon led to political national aspirations. The
Croats were ripe for the move. They possessed their own literary language and,
furthermore, they had maintained some sort of continuous autonomous position within first Hungary and then the Habsburg Austrian Empire since the early
twelfth century. The Croatian aristocracy was socially powerful and enjoyed
a modicum of political influence and experience through the Croatian national
diet that met in Zagreb. It was members of the nobility that fomented the nineteenth-century Croatian nationalist movement, a movement that, in their eyes,
held as its goal a great South Slav state in the Balkans, which would be led by
the highly developed, sophisticated—Westernized—Croats.
      The "Illyrian Movement," as the Croat-spawned Yugoslav nationalist pro-
gram was called, arose soon after the fall of Napoleon in 1815, though it did
not reach full maturity until the 1830s and 1840s. Heavily patronized by the
Croatian nobleman Count Janko Drašković, the movement received its definitive philosophical and intellectual framework from the publications of
Ljudevit Gaj, a prolific journalist and publisher. Despairing of the return to
"despotic" Hungarian control following the end of the Napoleonic wars, the
Croat movement idealized the brief period when parts of Croatia and Dalmatia
formed components of the French "Illyrian Provinces"—from which the
movement received its name. But instead of crediting the freedom, prosperity, and creativity that had characterized that episode to enlightened, liberal
French rule, the Croat nationalists focused on the unification of Slavs from
Croatia proper, Dalmatia, and Slovenia as the primary contributing factor in
those achievements. There emerged out of that perspective the dominant idea
that the future of the Balkan Slavs depended on their unification in a greater
Balkan Slavic state—"Illyria." The nationalists bolstered their concepts by creating a specious mythological historical foundation for the proposed Illyria,
which maintained that the ancient Illyrians mentioned in classical Roman
and medieval Byzantine texts as inhabiting the Adriatic coastline of the
Balkans and its hinterlands were actually Slavs. Furthermore, since the Croats

were culturally Western and they possessed an unbroken political tradition that stretched back in time to the tenth century, their cultural and political superiority over all other existing Slavic peoples in the Balkans placed them in the best position to lead the greater South Slavic state once it was established.[40]

The Croatian Illyrianists faced a choice between two potential roads toward their goal—by gaining Habsburg support for realization of their aims within the Habsburg Empire, or by breaking with the empire completely and forging alliances with other South Slavs, especially with the Serbs (who by the 1830s possessed an autonomous nation-state of their own centered on Belgrade). The Croats chose the former route at first, especially since it appeared that the Habsburgs were sympathetic to their hopes. While Illyrianism grew among the Croats in the 1830s and '40s, a parallel great Slavic intellectual and cultural movement appeared among the Czechs and the Slovaks in the empire. Known as Panslavism, it called for the creation of a huge greater Slavic state in Europe that would encompass within its borders all of the Slavic peoples, who were considered close blood kin, in a single, universal, extended Slavic family. Since at the time, of all the European Slavs, only the Russians possessed a state of their own, they were seen as the core around which the rest of the Slavic peoples could be united. Of course, given the nature of European Great Power politics in the mid-nineteenth century and the realities of significant ethnic diversity among the Slavic peoples, the ideals of the Panslavs were pie in the sky. No Western Great Power would tolerate the aggrandizement of Russia on such a vast scale, since that would reduce them to insignificance on the European and world stages. And centuries of historical circumstance had led to innate cultural differences among the Slavic peoples that precluded any realistic commonality binding them all harmoniously together. In the 1840s, however, with Romantic nationalism riding its crest, the dangers of Panslavism for the multicultural-multiethnic Habsburg Empire seemed all too real to its imperial rulers. So the Habsburgs fostered the Croats' more benign ideas of uniting the South Slavs within the context of the Austrian Empire as a useful counterpoise to threatened dismemberment by pro-Russian Panslavism.

The Habsburgs used the Illyrian Movement as the core around which they sought to unite Slavs within, and some outside of, the empire under the overall umbrella of their rule—a policy that became known as Austroslavism. Stress was placed on Catholicism and its cultural animosity toward Orthodox Christianity. The intent was to stop the extension of Orthodox Russia's influence among the Slavs of the Habsburg Empire and among those on its borders to the south by installing a substitute for the popular Panslav movement in Bohemia and northern Hungary. The Revolution of 1848 in the empire, however, undermined Austroslavism to the point of irrelevancy—Panslavism collapsed under the weight of its own delusions at the Prague Panslav Congress, and the shortsightedness of the Habsburgs in dealing with its loyal Slavic subjects was demonstrated for all to see by the way they treated the Croats.[41]

When the Hungarians precipitated the Revolution of 1848–49 in the Habsburg Empire, the Croat nationalists declared their independence from Hungary and their continued loyalty to the emperor in Vienna. Croatian troops under the command of the Croat ban Josip Jelačić fought long and hard against liberal revolutionaries in Vienna and, especially, against the radical Hungarian nationalists who had declared Hungary's complete independence from Habsburg control. Instead of being rewarded for their loyal efforts on behalf of the Habsburg cause by being granted their expected national independence from Hungarian authority once the revolution was successfully crushed, the Croats found themselves still tied to Hungary. Then, in 1867, the Habsburgs were forced to reorganize their empire along new lines to preserve their Great Power position in Europe after being expelled from German affairs by Bismarck. They turned to their most ardent nationalist enemies within the empire—the Hungarians—for a power-sharing partnership, which handed over to Hungarian control more than half of the state's territories, including Croatia. The new imperial partners-allies of the Habsburgs immediately proceeded to govern their share as if it were a Hungarian nation-state. That development both weakened Croat faith in the Habsburg monarchy and awakened a new strain of Croat nationalist aims to win a completely independent Yugoslav state.[42]

Yet even after the 1867 Compromise, many Croat nationalists continued to conceive of a Croat-led greater South Slav nation-state under some sort of Habsburg aegis. Among the most influential of these was the Catholic bishop Josip Strossmayer, who strove to create an autonomous Croatia within the Austro-Hungarian Empire that would serve as the core for a future "Yugoslav" (Strossmayer popularized the term, and considered it an identification of a real nationality) state that was to encompass all of the South Slavs, no matter their religious cultures. (Such differences would cease to matter, he thought, once the Orthodox Slavs accepted a Uniate compromise with Roman Catholicism.) To further his goals, during the 1870s Strossmayer patronized intellectual and cultural efforts through building schools, subsidizing scholars, and founding in Zagreb a number of important institutions, including a national university and a Catholic seminary. With its schools, galleries, libraries, academies, bookstores, and other such cultural endeavors, Zagreb under Strossmayer's influence became one of the leading Slavic cultural centers in the Balkans.[43]

◄※ ※►

In 1875 a revolt erupted in Bosnia that would eventually precipitate a European international crisis, transform the map of the Balkans, turn Bosnia into the focal point of Croat-Serb nationalism, and, in the course of the latter process, spark World War I.

Centuries of social and fiscal exploitation of the non-Muslim peasantry by the wealthy, landowning Bosnian Muslim *beys* came to a head in July 1875, when the Christians of Bosnia took up arms against the Islamic oligarchy that controlled the region. Perhaps their actions were in response to a tour of Dalmatia made by Habsburg emperor Francis Joseph earlier that spring, during which he received a number of petitions from Bosnian Christians requesting Habsburg protection, and following which the emperor was convinced that Bosnia-Hercegovina had to be occupied by the empire. He conducted the tour at the urgings of his military officers, many of whom were Croats who subscribed to the Yugoslav ideals of Gaj and Strossmayer and who sought to further transform the Dual Monarchy (as Austria-Hungary often was called) into a triune state, with Croat-led Slavs as the new third partner in power. In any event, the military felt that possession of Bosnia-Hercegovina was essential for the defense of Habsburg Dalmatia, and they hoped that the emperor's tour would stir up anti-Turkish unrest in those provinces. In that they succeeded.

As the insurrection, which began in Hercegovina and quickly spread into Bosnia, flared into outright warfare, Croat Habsburg officials in Dalmatia aided the rebels as best they could short of direct intervention. So too did the Russians through their consular representatives in Dalmatia. While both powers worked behind the scenes to support the rebellion, they outwardly called for a mediated settlement. The Turks made promises of reform, but the rebels considered them valueless and countered with demands for either political autonomy under a Christian prince or foreign occupation until all of their grievances were redressed. With the breakdown of mediation, the fighting grew more widespread and vicious. By early 1876 over 150,000 refugees had fled the carnage in Bosnia and Hercegovina, flooding into the surrounding states. While both Austria-Hungary and Russia were anxious that the Bosnian situation did not cause a rift between themselves by upsetting the delicate balance of power in the Balkans should either actively seek to intervene, the Serbs held no such reservations. Despite the unwillingness of Prince Milan Obrenović (1868–89) to become involved in the Bosnian fighting, rabidly nationalist Serb public opinion, headed by Jovan Ristić, forced Milan to give way, and in June 1876 Serbia declared war on the Turks in support of the Bosnian rebels. Serbian troops invaded Bosnia while Prince Nikola I Petrović of Montenegro (1860–1918), not to be outdone by Milan in a rivalry to lead a Serb-dominated greater South Slav movement, declared war on the Turks in July and promptly invaded Hercegovina.[44]

Russian Slavophile assistance came to the Serbs' aid in the form of money, weapons, and volunteers, but the expected Russian declaration of war against the Turks did not materialize. Despite a mass Serb mobilization of the population (a sixth was called to arms) and command by Russian Slavophile officers on leave from their duties at home, the Turks inflicted a series of defeats on the Serbs and then invaded the territory of their stunned enemy, where their victories continued. In desperation, the Serbs begged the Great Powers for a mediated armistice, but the Turks were intransigent. Only a Russian ultimatum in October, made possible by the impact on public opinion in England of news of Turkish massacres of Bulgarians involved in another uprising (1876) that tied the pro-Turkish Disraeli government's hands, forced the Turks to agree to a six-week cease-fire in Bosnia and Serbia. The break in the fighting permitted representatives of England and Russia to meet in Istanbul, at English insistence, to hammer out an acceptable joint plan for ending the crisis that could then be imposed on the Turks.[45]

Although the two powers worked long and hard at finding a comprehensive solution to the complex Balkan problem and its many international ramifications, their efforts came to naught when the Turks publicly rejected their reform terms and, instead, announced a new liberal constitution that made Great Power plans for reforms in the disturbed provinces ostensibly unnecessary. The English-Russian conference then closed, with both parties realizing that the proposed constitution was worthless, since it was doubtful that the Turks would actually implement its terms. Russia then brokered an arrangement with Austria-Hungary that stipulated the latter's neutrality in case of war with the Turks and its implied acquiescence of a Russian presence in the eastern Balkans in return for the right to occupy Bosnia-Hercegovina. With Habsburg neutrality secured and English resistance muzzled by public opinion at home, Russia declared war on the Turks in April 1877.[46]

The war itself was not the most important factor in determining Bosnia-Hercegovina's future. What mattered were the results of the Berlin Treaty of 1878, which stemmed from the West's unwillingness to accept the Russian-imposed Treaty of San Stefano that ended the actual fighting earlier in March by giving the victors virtual control of the strategically crucial Bosphorus and Dardanelles straits. The representatives of the European Great Powers who met at Berlin essentially undid all of the gains made by Russia in the war. The most important of those gains—the creation at San Stefano of a large, Russian puppet-client state of Bulgaria controlling all of the eastern and central Balkans (which would have handed Russia free access to the eastern Mediterranean through the straits and thus the ability to threaten both England's maritime lifeline to its important Indian colony and France's aspirations to gain Syria and political dominance in the Levant)—was dismantled to deprive Russia of its strategic advantages. But in a decision that demonstrated the deep-seated but unspoken cultural animosity that separated the two European civilizations, the Western power brokers at Berlin, while punishing East European Russia, rewarded West European Austria-Hungary by honoring the Austrian portion of the deal it had made with Russia just prior to the war. The Habsburgs were given the right to occupy Bosnia-Hercegovina. Serbian protests over Austria's obstruction of their nationalist expansion into that region were muffled only slightly by the Western powers declaring Serbia a completely independent kingdom.[47]

Austria-Hungary implemented its right to occupy Bosnia-Hercegovina almost immediately. Along with the troops, there arrived an organized and efficient administrative system that initiated a civic works regime not seen in the Balkans since the French Illyrian episode earlier in the century. Railroads and bridges were constructed; flourishing industries (primarily mining, chemical, and timber) were developed; reforestation projects and agricultural research were undertaken. By all Western standards, Habsburg occupation should have been a boon for the inhabitants of the region. Unfortunately, such was not the case.[48]

At the time of the occupation, the Bosnian population was divided among three component elements, each of which represented a culture of a separate civilization. The largest single element was the East European Orthodox (some 43 percent), followed by the Muslim (39 percent), and then the Western European Catholic (18 percent). Both of the Christian components had developed ethnonational self-identities through influences that had infiltrated into Bosnia from its neighbors—the Orthodox espoused a Serb identity and the Catholics a Croat. Given the traditional theocratic culture of Islam, the Muslims, though ethnically Slavic and speaking the same language as the Christians (but writing it in either Latin or Cyrillic form, as the case might be), held no ethnonational affiliation. They maintained an Islamic cultural self-identity alone.[49]

The Habsburgs' mistake in their occupation policy lay in the fact that, despite the modernization efforts initiated, they did not dismantle the old landholding regime that had evolved in Bosnia after the disintegration of the Ottoman revenue-fief system in the seventeenth century. A few thousand Muslim *beys* continued on as large estate owners wielding immense local power over tens of thousands of Christian peasants. The estates were run in the age-old fashion, which was inefficient and unproductive in Western terms because of outdated methods of land use and outmoded equipment and techniques. Thus agriculture, in which the majority of the Bosnian population was engaged, remained backward, and the peasants remained poor. Their poverty mitigated against their taking extensive advantage of Austrian laws that permitted still-enserfed peasants to purchase their release from the authority of the powerful landholding *beys*. So despite all of the other benefits that Austrian occupation brought to Bosnia-Hercegovina, the majority of the population—Christians of both stripes—remained downtrodden and grew increasingly discontented. Their unrest often found release in revolutionary activity directed culturally against the powerful Muslim oligarchy and politically against continued Austrian occupation. The Bosnians looked to their coreligionists-nationals across the borders for help.[50]

Meanwhile, developments within the Croat nationalist camp had proceeded apace. A more radical movement that rejected the moderate Gaj-Strossmayer Yugoslav concepts emerged among the Croats in the final decades of the nineteenth century. Founded by Ante Starčević, the radicals sought a blatantly independent greater Croatian nation-state rather than a Yugoslavia composed of a federation of equals in which the Croats' perceived intrinsic cultural superiority would bring them leadership. Included within Starčević's ideal Greater Croatia were all of Croatia proper, Dalmatia (with Istria), Slavonia, and Bosnia, and it left little room for toleration of any Serb nationalist aspirations that might exist within its borders. Near the end of his life in 1896, Starčević gravitated toward the Trialist position that looked for a reshuffling of Habsburg Dualism in favor of making the Croats a third ruling partner in the empire, with a status equal to that of the Hungarians. At his death, Starčević's followers fragmented. The largest of the offshoots—called the Party of Pure Right ("right" in terms of "righteous" and not of political conservatism)—led by Josip Frank, advanced a more extreme Greater Croatia program that emphasized Croatian Catholicism and denigrated the Serbs as degenerated Croats who had sold out to Orthodoxy and Byzantine culture in the medieval past.[51]

The Hungarian administrators who governed Croatia as part of their share of the Habsburg Empire, understanding the cultural divide that separated Croats and Serbs, played the Serbs living in the Croatian regions off against the various Croat nationalists. They founded and patronized Serbian schools, bestowed privileges on the Serbian Orthodox church, appointed Serbs to civil offices, and generally showed ostensible favor to the Serbs that riled the sensibilities of the native Croats. By the end of the nineteenth century, Croat and Serb nationalists commonly fought publicly in the streets throughout Croatia. But as time went on, the pro-Serb actions of the Hungarian authorities grew transparently specious to the Serb nationalists in Croatia, who came to realize that no Serbian future lay in Hungarian support.[52]

Their realization was aided by the fact that in 1903 the pro-Austrian Serb king Aleksandr I Obrenović (1889–1903), who had felt constrained to pursue a policy of friendship with Austria-Hungary in hopes of winning future support for Serbia regarding nationalist expansion to the south and southwest, was brutally murdered by a group of ultranationalist military conspirators. The assassins installed the anti-Austrian Petr I Karadjordjević in his place (1903–21), who appealed for the loyalty of the Slavs in the Habsburg Empire by linking Yugoslav aspirations to Greater Serbian nationalist claims. Both the Habsburg Serbs and Croats were encouraged to look to Belgrade for their nationalist future in a Serb-created Yugoslav state. Such efforts increased the nationalist agitation among both ethnic groups within Austria-Hungary. A group of nationalist Croats devised a program in 1905 calling for reforms that would liberalize the political administration in Croatia in favor of free Croat elections, Croat voting rights, and Croat civil liberties. Serbs in Croatia joined the Croat protest, and there emerged for the first time a Serbo-Croat political coalition, to which all of the Croatian opposition parties except the extreme radicals of Frank and a new Peasant party headed by the Radić brothers, Stjepan and Antun, subscribed. A year later the new coalition won a plurality in elections for the Croatian diet, and the Hungarian authorities grew genuinely concerned. The diet was closed in early 1908, and the Hungarians proceeded to govern Croatia by decree.[53]

Later in 1908, a group of Turkish nationalist military officers, known as the Young Turks, overthrew the government of Ottoman sultan Abdul Hamid II (1876–1909) and installed themselves as the empire's new liberal-national leaders, supposedly governing under the terms of the old constitution of 1876 but seeking to transform the old Islamic empire into a modernized, Western-style Turkish nation-state. The revolutionary change of government in the Ottoman Empire threw Europe into turmoil, as the Great Powers hastily convened foreign policy meetings with one another in a flurried attempt to reshuffle the balance of power in the Balkans should the Ottoman state fall apart completely over conflicting nationalisms. In September, such a meeting between the foreign ministers of Austria-Hungary and Russia took place at Buchlau in Austria, at which the Austrians managed to finesse the Russians into accepting the Habsburgs' outright annexation of Bosnia-Hercegovina in exchange for—essentially nothing—merely empty words regarding future Austrian support among the Great Powers for Russia's claim to free access to the straits. In October 1908 Austria-Hungary announced its intention to acquire Bosnia-Hercegovina permanently.

The announcement was met by frenzy and rage among the Serbs, who viewed the region as a rightful nationalist legacy. Serbia and Montenegro prepared for war in the hopes of Turkish and Greek assistance. The Russians protested loudly that they had been duped. Germany supported its ally Austria, while the French and English stood by their ally Russia. Though the Great Powers strongly voiced their concerns over Austria's territorial coup, none acted, since all feared that a general European war would result (given the existence of the Central Powers-Entente alliance system that was then in place). In early 1909 the Turks agreed to accept the annexation in return for compensation from Austria, and the crisis ended. Thereupon, the annexation of Bosnia-Hercegovina was implemented.[54]

Reaction to the annexation among Croat and Serb nationalists in both Croatia and Bosnia-Hercegovina was strong. The more moderate, traditional Croat Yugoslavs saw it as opening a bright future, in which their Trialist dreams for the Habsburg Empire would be fulfilled. The heir to Emperor Francis Joseph's throne, Archduke Francis Ferdinand, had made it known that he was considering favorably such a restructuring of the empire once he attained power. The radical Croat nationalist Party of Pure Right considered the annexation the first concrete step on the road toward creating Greater Croatia. But the recently founded, powerful Serbo-Croat coalition considered the event a catastrophe, for the same reasons that the others found it so promising. To them, Francis Ferdinand's Trialistic sympathies marked him as the personification of the Austro-Hungarian threat to their future aspirations. Nurtured by Belgrade, the Serbo-Croats bewailed the annexation as an insulting blow to Yugoslavism (by which they meant, whether the Croat partners realized it or not, Serb nationalism).[55]

Hungarian attempts to clamp down on the Serbo-Croat nationalists resulted in trumped-up show trials of supposed anti-Austrian, pro-Serbian "traitors" and in libelous charges of sedition and pro-Serbian activities against members of the coalition. In 1912, following elections that once again returned a Serbo-Croat majority to the Croatian diet, the Hungarians again dissolved the assembly and closed Zagreb University, which had become a breeding ground of anti-Hungarian sentiment. Such repressive actions failed in their immediate objective to squelch the Serbo-Croats, and succeeded only in discrediting Austro-Hungarian administration even further in the eyes of most Croats and Serbs within the empire and in intensifying the discontent of the Belgrade-looking faction.[56]

In Bosnia-Hercegovina itself, similar reactions to the annexation elicited similar responses from similar nationalist groups. But by 1909 a new, more dangerous element to Austro-Hungarian rule in the region was beginning to make itself felt among the Serb population. Until the turn of the century, the number of Serb intellectuals in Bosnia-Hercegovina had been small and limited almost exclusively to members of the professional middle class. In 1902 a cultural society called *Posveta* (Enlightenment), funded in part by money from

Serbia, was established for the express purpose of educating peasant and lower-class Serb children. Within a decade of its founding, the society spawned a new type of Bosnian Serb intellectual—poor, often jobless with no vested interest in the Austrian-imposed establishment (the Habsburg administration tended to hire Croats over Serbs), and with a chip-on-the-shoulder attitude because of firsthand experience of the inequitable existing social system.

That younger generation of Bosnian Serbs formed the cadres of a nationalist movement known as "Young Bosnia," an amorphous but widespread association that sought independence from the Habsburgs and social reforms within a Bosnian Serb nation-state. There was little agreement among its members as to how their objectives were to be attained, but a general affinity among them for Russian revolutionary literature led them to think mostly in similar terms. Turning their backs on evolutionary political reform tactics, the Young Bosnians embraced terrorism, which they elevated into a veritable cult. Terrorist acts and the "martyrs" that such actions invariably created inflamed their blood and inspired their efforts. By 1912 members of Young Bosnia were in direct contact with a secret Serb ultranationalist revolutionary organization, commonly known as the "Black Hand" but correctly named "Union or Death" (Ujedinjenje ili Smrt). The Black Hand was controlled by Serbian military officers holding high positions in the Belgrade government—the very officers who had conspired to kill King Aleksandr in 1903—and led by Colonel Dragutin Dimitrijević, known as "Apis." While King Petr disliked the Black Hand leadership personally (they were, after all, regicides) and they, in turn, operated beyond his control and often at variance with his policies, he tolerated the organization's existence because of its anti-Habsburg and Greater Serbia stance. Through its Young Bosnia contacts, the Black Hand engineered and armed terrorist activities inside Bosnia.

In the five years preceding the outbreak of World War I, the Habsburg authorities in Bosnia came down hard on Young Bosnian agitation, making hundreds of arrests for treason and espionage and mostly winning convictions. In turn, the youthful Bosnian Serb revolutionaries intensified their propensities for violent action. When in the early summer of 1914 it was announced that Archduke Francis Ferdinand would make a tour of inspection in Bosnia and that he would visit Sarajevo on 28 June—Vidovdan (St. Vitus' Day)—the anniversary of the Battle of Kosovo Polje (1389), at which medieval Serbia went down to bloody defeat to the Turks, and which Serb nationalists considered sacred in a morbid sort of way ("Remember our defeat so that we will never let it happen again"), neither the Young Bosnians nor the Black Hand could let pass the opportunity to murder that personification of the Habsburg threat to Greater Serb national aspirations. In a comedy of errors that would have been humorous if it were not so fatefully tragic, the Young Bosnian tool of the Black Hand, Gavril Princip, managed to shoot the Habsburg heir to the throne (and his wife to boot). Princip's handgun shots on a Sarajevo street-corner and the two bodies of their victims proved to be but the first of a thunderous barrage and millions of corpses spanning four years, as the Central Powers-Entente alliance system refused to permit Austria-Hungary to punish Serbia for the Sarajevo crime by means of a limited, localized military drubbing. Within a month of the outbreak of the Habsburgs' war of retribution, begun in July 1914, the struggle mushroomed into all-out, total world war.[57]

⊰⧓ ⧓⊱

The Greater Serbia concept held by the nationalists of Belgrade, led by Nikola Pašić, envisioned a future Serbian nation-state built around the Kingdom of Serbia and including all territories inhabited by ethnic Serbs. Bosnia-Hercegovina played a particularly important role in the Greater Serbia approach since it offered an opening on the Adriatic Sea to a state that otherwise essentially would be landlocked. Greater Serbia was to be cemented together by the common cultural glues of Orthodox Christianity and the Serbian language. Room was made in the minds of the nationalists for the possible acquisition of other, non-Serb-inhabited South Slavic territories—Croatia, Slovenia, Dalmatia, Vojvodina—but they were not considered essential. No matter what the ultimate extent of the state might be, the Serb nationalists strongly demanded that it be centralized under their native Karadjordjević rulers and that Serbs dominated politically and culturally.

The Croat nationalists in the Habsburg Empire, who constituted the major force in pushing the "Yugoslav" ideal, as well as many members of the Serbo-Croat coalition, were opposed to most, if not all, of the Greater Serbia program espoused by the Belgrade nationalists. They sought a truly all-inclusive South Slavic state organized along fundamentally federalist lines and structured so as to preserve the individual political, religious, and ethnic cultural identities of all its member peoples. The Karadjordjevićes were acceptable to them as rulers only so long as they renounced their exclusively Serbian identity and agreed to reign as "Yugoslav" monarchs.[58]

The disparities in nationalist ideology that separated the two South Slav movements were evident as soon as World War I began in earnest. It took three years of fighting, and the consequent growing realization that, by mid-1917, Austria-Hungary was likely to lose the war and be dismantled as a result, before the two sides were able to bridge their differences. In July 1917 Ante Trumbić, the leader of a Serb-leaning Serbo-Croatian faction from Dalmatia, and Pašić met on Corfu and signed a pact that called for the establishment of a Yugoslav state following the war. Pašić agreed to accept Croat demands for a constitutional monarchy responsible to a democratically elected national assembly as the governing framework for the proposed state. He did so, however, only because of political circumstances holding at the time of the meeting: the Serbs lacked the customary Russian support for their Greater Serbia claims (the revolution had overthrown the tsar); the Americans, newly involved in the war, favored the Croat-inspired Yugoslav idea; and Serbia was occupied by Austrian and Bulgarian enemy forces.

Despite the apparent compromise in the Serbian nationalist stance made on Corfu, the Serbs continued to act along lines commensurate with their old Greater Serbia approach for the duration of the war, much to the apprehension of the Croat Yugoslavs. As the fighting ground to a close in 1918 and the Habsburg Empire disintegrated, a series of declarations proclaiming South Slav independence by the various "Yugoslav" nationalists of Serbia, Croatia, Montenegro, and Slovenia culminated in a final joint pronouncement in December 1918 from Belgrade formally establishing the Kingdom of the Serbs, Croats, and Slovenes. The United States was the first Great Power to recognize the new state in February 1919, and the victorious Entente mapmakers at Versailles swiftly followed suit by stamping their approval into the treaties signed with their defeated enemies.[59]

From the beginning, the Radić Croat Peasant Party opposed vesting political power in the hands of the Serb king-regent Aleksandr I (of the new state, II of Serbia) Karadjordjević, ostensibly until a constitutional assembly met to create the agreed-upon liberal-democratic constitution. Croat fears were justified. Pašić and the Serb nationalists refused to relinquish their centralizing program, and elections for representatives to the assembly were delayed. In the meantime, a land reform program was passed by the Serb-dominated interim government, which became a political football used by the Serbs to win support for their centralizing platform in the future constitutional assembly. The numerous Muslim landowners of Bosnia-Hercegovina played an important role in aiding the Serb nationalists to defeat the federalizing program of the Croats. Those Bosnians, along with their coreligionists from Macedonia, had organized a Muslim party and controlled a significant number of seats in the National Assembly. By mitigating the effects of the land reform through overly generous compensation payments to the dispossessed Muslim landlords, the Serbs won their firm support when the constitutional assembly met in 1921. Backed by the bloc of Muslim representatives, the Serb nationalists triumphed by passing into law a constitution creating a strongly centralized state governed under the authority of the Serbian monarchy—essentially, the prewar constitution of Serbia. (One major change was apparent: The old constitution gave the Orthodox church privileged status; the new one accorded equality and toleration to all religions, as reward to the Muslims for their support.) With that development, the breech between Serbs and Croats in the new state was solidified.[60]

From the moment when the centralist constitution was passed in 1921 until 1941 and the fall of Yugoslavia to the Germans in World War II, the Serb nationalists dominated the state in every way—most important, the top government ministries and offices, the military officer corps, and the police. King Aleksandr exerted complete control over the army, which guaranteed that the Serbs managed to maintain their position of dominance even though the 1920 elections for the constitutional assembly had demonstrated that the majority of the population opposed their centralist program by voting for federalist candidates. Before the end of World War I, Aleksandr had crushed the Black Hand, which acted as a rival to royal authority over the military, by having its leaders tried and executed on trumped-up charges of treason. He then had installed a group of trusted and loyal officers, whom he called the "White Hand," in its place. The White Hand existed as a favored group of officers during Aleksandr's reign, and they placed the military unquestioningly behind the king at all times.

Besides military backing, the Serbs were able to count on the disparate ethnocultural differences that fragmented the non-Serb population of the state to the point that no truly effective unified majority opposition to them could be mounted. Moreover, the Croat nationalists behind Stjepan Radić, who constituted the only large, cohesive opposition to the Serbs, committed numerous political mistakes (boycotts of the National Assembly at the wrong times, erratic "waffling" in their political tactics) that lessened their effective clout. The Serbs could buy off smaller political interest groups, such as the Bosnian and Macedonian Muslims, with minor political concessions. And if keeping the opposition divided was not enough, the Serbs could always fall back on tried and true Ottoman Balkan extralegal political tactics—bribery, police coercion, election-rigging, patronage, manipulating the legal system—when necessary.[61]

The Croats responded to the constant Serb repression of their federalist Yugoslav program by maintaining blatant and continuous opposition. When in 1928 Radić was murdered in the National Assembly by a radical Serb nationalist from Montenegro, the Croats declared all-out political war against the Serbs. A Croat ultranationalist revolutionary terrorist organization—the *Ustaše*—was formed, which promptly established ties with the similar Bulgaro-Macedonian IMRO, with revisionist Hungary, and with fascist Italy. A separate Croat "parliament" was set up in Zagreb, and King Aleksandr, raised in the Orthodox authoritarian culture of the Russian tsarist court, felt compelled to declare a royal dictatorship resembling a police state to stave off the dissolution of the kingdom. In an effort to mollify the Croats and to unite the disparate non-Serb peoples under his rule, Aleksandr changed the name of the state to Yugoslavia in 1929, but the Croats remained adamant in their opposition, after which the royal dictatorship acquired noticeable anti-Croat overtones. Under Aleksandr's heavy-handed methods, the term "Yugoslav" appeared to mean "Serb" in most non-Serb minds, and thus the royal dictatorship was discredited. By eliminating all party politics, Aleksandr lost even Serb nationalist support, and in 1931 he was forced to issue a new constitution that superficially lent a measure of political respectability and representative government to what remained a centrally run authoritarian monarchical state. By 1934 the king came to realize that his dictatorship had failed to solve the Croat-Serb political conflict, but before he could end it he was assassinated on a visit to Marseilles, France, by an *Ustaše*-connected Macedonian revolutionary in the pay of Italian fascists.[62]

Fear of Italian ambitions in Dalmatia briefly united more level-headed Croats with the Serbs behind the regency of Prince Pavel, who governed in the name of the young heir, King Petr II (1934–41) in continuing dictatorial fashion. It was a brief honeymoon. By 1935 the Croats were once again boycotting the National Assembly after having received no concessions from the Serbs regarding their federalist claims. The Bosnian Muslims remained staunch Serb political allies in maintaining the centralist structure of the state. Continuing adamant Croat opposition finally led the Serb-dominated government to try cultural bribery on them—a concordat with the Vatican, which would give Roman Catholics wider privileges in Yugoslavia (the Orthodox and Muslim faiths already possessed written legal definitions of their official standing), was signed in 1937. Orthodox opposition to the move was so swift and widespread that the government was forced to treat the deal as a dead letter.

The rift separating the two contesting nationalities remained as wide as ever following the concordat fiasco, and, in the rising tide of fascism that permeated European politics at the time, both Croat and Serb nationalists began assuming German and Italian political techniques—youthful uniformed paramilitary units, mass public chanting of short, simple, authoritarian-tinged slogans, and the like. As Hitler's Nazi Germany began swallowing independent, Versailles-created states in East-Central Europe in 1938 and 1939, Regent Pavel felt constrained both to draw closer to the Nazi strongman and to settle his state's internal divisions before Hitler might take an inkling to turn his greedy attention to Yugoslavia. Thus on the brink of World War II, in August 1939, the Croats were granted an autonomous Croatian territory within the state and their leading spokesperson, Vladko Maček, was offered a position within the government as vice-premier. The extremists on both sides were unhappy with the new arrangement, and the two other politically powerful elements in the state—the Slovenes and the Bosnian Muslims, who until that time had been allies of the centralist Serbs—immediately demanded rights of autonomy similar to those granted the Croats. The internal turmoil created by the compromise with the Croats continued up to the moment that German troops invaded Yugoslavia in April 1941.[63]

Once Hitler successfully overran Yugoslavia, he dismantled it into a number of territorial and ethnonational parts. Slovenia was divided between Germany and Italy. Vojvodina was divided between Hungary and local German residents. Most of Macedonia went to Bulgaria. The Italians acquired the rest of Macedonia, the Kosovo region of Serbia, most of Dalmatia, Montenegro, and slices of Bosnia-Hercegovina. The largest area of the latter region was placed into the hands of an ultranationalist neofascist Croatian puppet state ruled by Leader-Dictator *(Poglavnik)* Ante Pavelić, head of the *Ustaše* terrorist organization, who ostensibly served as the viceroy for an Italian absentee king. What was left of Serbia was placed under full and direct German military control, with Serb general Milan Nedić serving as the Serbian marshal Pétain.

Following the fascist conquest, the ethnocultural situation within the various parts of the divided former Yugoslav state rapidly grew atrocious. Albanians, Hungarians, and Vojvodina Germans set about indiscriminately massacring Serbs in the vicinities under their control. Bulgarians pressured Slavs in Macedonia to adopt Bulgarian identities. But Pavelić's Croatia was the worst culprit in perpetrating ethnonational atrocity. Supported by some Roman Catholic clerics, the *Ustaše* regime set out either to exterminate all Serbs and Jews living within Croatia or to force them to convert to Catholicism. A veritable litany of massacres occurred. In Bosnia, the Muslims, having for so long been the Serbs' political allies, turned on them with a vengeance and joined in the bloodletting, now that political power had shifted to the Croats. By 1942 the situation in Bosnia resembled a virtual religious-cultural war, with Catholics and Muslims pitted against the Orthodox and Jews. The Serbs retaliated as best they could, and Bosnia was turned into a vicious cultural battleground.

It was in Bosnia that the first organized antifascist resistance was formed under the leadership of a Hercegovinian Serb colonel, Draža Mihailović, whose headquarters were located in Serbia. His followers assumed the name of *četniks*, from the word *četa*, the old name of Serb guerilla bands who fought the Turks in Ottoman days. Mihailović's movement avidly espoused the traditional Greater Serbia nationalist program. Communist resistance forces also were fielded, led by party boss Josip Tito, a Croat forced out of

Zagreb by the *Ustaše* and into Serbia. Instead of cooperating against their common fascist foes, the two resistance camps fought a civil war between themselves while simultaneously resisting the enemy. Tito's Communists, with their superior organization and unity of purpose, won out over the loosely organized, essentially regional forces of Mihailović. The more militarily effective Communist partisans eventually earned the bulk of support and supplies given to the resistance fighters in the former Yugoslavia by the anti-Hitler Western allies, who between 1942 and 1944 were more concerned about military success than about political ideology.[64]

Tito fostered and used nationalist sentiments of all stripes to whip together a unified resistance force. By embracing every nationalist concept, his partisans enjoyed a continual stream of reinforcements from inhabitants seeking to escape the increasing acts of retribution inflicted on them by the fascists in response to guerilla activities. Tito publicly proclaimed a policy of toleration for the various nationalist movements and the right of all people to national self-determination. No other political movement in the Balkans did so. That Communist policy placed Mihailović and his Greater Serbia program at a distinct disadvantage among the overall population of the former Yugoslav state. Tito deftly linked the war against the fascists with the old national problem by considering the two as one—his partisans were not only fighting to expel the fascists but to create a truly federal Yugoslavia. With that, he won significant success among the inhabitants of Croatia and Bosnia.

Tito's ideological flexibility in the area of nationalism, in conjunction with a strong grassroots political organization grounded in that flexibility, guaranteed that the Communist partisans emerged politically victorious at the end of World War II. His transfer of partisan main headquarters to the mountainous regions of Bosnia-Hercegovina and Montenegro helped him win militarily. The terrain there provided Tito's partisans with protection, freedom from any constant fascist presence, and the strategic advantage of interior lines, since it lay squarely between the three main foci of German-fascist interest in the Balkans—the Dalmatian coast, the cities and agriculture of the northern Danubian Plain, and the Vardar-Morava river valley line of Balkan communications. Within his Bosnian stronghold, Tito began the organization of the future Communist Yugoslav state by holding congresses of partisan representatives from every region of the former Yugoslavia at Bihać in 1942 and Jajce in 1943, at which were stressed his effective slogan regarding nationality—"Brotherhood and Unity."[65]

In May 1945 World War II ended in the northwest Balkans. Partisan and Soviet troops had swept the Germans out of the region, and Tito capped the military victory by finally crushing both of his remaining armed competitors for postwar power—the Croatian *Ustaše* and the Serbian *četniks*. In 1945 Tito massacred tens of thousands of Croats he suspected of involvement in the *Ustaše* and its atrocities, although certainly many of his victims were innocent of any direct participation. In the next year, 1946, Mihailović was captured and executed and his *četniks* suppressed. At the same time, the Communists methodically eliminated all other sources of possible opposition by wide-ranging intimidation and arrests. Socialist Yugoslavia thus became a reality.[66]

The new Yugoslavia was reconstituted once again within the old state's prewar boundaries. The triumphant Tito, Yugoslavia's military and political master, and his Communist apparatus generated a federalist constitution, in keeping with the decisions and resolutions made during the war. Socialist Yugoslavia was divided into six federated, supposedly autonomous and equal republics, each considered territorially representative of a major ethnonational component of the population. Orthodox Serbia housed the largest single ethnonational component in the state, though not an outright majority. Serbia also housed two autonomous provinces that were created to satisfy the nationalist sensibilities of the Hungarians in Vojvodina and the Albanians in Kosovo. Second largest of the Yugoslav republics was Catholic Croatia, which was handed all of the territories in Dalmatia and Slavonia to which Croat nationalists had traditionally laid historical claim, perhaps to make amends for the vicious conclusion of the war inflicted on them but more probably to keep them tied to the socialist state. Catholic Slovenia, in the extreme northwest, represented a relatively well-off, Germanized, and industrious Slavic population. Montenegro preserved the identity of a Serbian people who long rivaled their conationals in Serbia proper for leadership in the Serb nationalist movement. Macedonia appeared as an official national entity for the first time in its long, tortured history. It was thus in the sticky position of creating a unique national language, history, and culture by any means (real or artificial) to justify its separate existence from the neighboring Bulgarians.

The sixth republic in federated socialist Yugoslavia was Bosnia-Hercegovina. In ethnonational terms, it presented an exceptional case. Its inhabitants were divided among three religious cultures (civilizations) and, simultaneously, two ethnic groups (microcultures). But religious culture separated out one of the demographic components—the Muslims—from strict ethnic considerations— they were a mixed ethnic bag of Slavic "Serbo-Croats" (one is hard pressed to be more specific, since both of those two ethnic groups were [and are] primarily defined by their Christian religious affiliation). History had created a distinct region within which the three groups had shared in a certain common overall regional experience since medieval times, though the participation of each in that experience had often been unique. Both the Serbs and the Croats of Bosnia fully bought into the Western ethnonationalist culture, while the Muslims essentially adhered to their traditional theocratic identity.

Following the establishment of Habsburg rule in Bosnia, beginning with the occupation and continuing through the first Yugoslav state and into World War II, the Muslims had been forced to adapt to modern European secularized political realities. They had formed political parties to represent their interests within the nationalist, pseudoliberal political culture of that period, and they had played that game adroitly—always managing to keep themselves on the side of whichever group predominated politically in matters affecting them. They, of the three elements in Bosnia's population, maintained an awareness of Bosnia as a unique political entity. It is not surprising that Serbs, Croats, and virtually all Westerners, by taking account only of the Muslims' necessary outward adaptations to the political culture within which they were forced to live, came to consider them as an ethnonational group similar to the others.

Such was not the case at the time World War II ended. Three years after the creation of socialist Yugoslavia, the official census of 1948 contained an ethnonational category for respondents labeled "Muslims, nationally undeclared." The label demonstrated the Yugoslav government's complete misconception of the Islamic religious concept of self-identity. Tito's government assumed that Muslims eventually would see themselves as either ethnic Croats or Serbs who happened to hold to the Islamic faith, so those who had yet to decide on that issue were given the opportunity to notify the government of that fact. By 1961 the socialists had grown more convinced that the Muslims' persistent and pronounced cultural differences from the Christian populations within the state had to reflect some sort of ethnonational self-identity. The census for that year listed an ethnic identity category of "Undefined Yugoslavs [Muslims in the *ethnic* sense]" specifically for the Muslims of Bosnia-Hercegovina. If the approach taken by the socialist authorities is viewed in a truly historical perspective, the ambiguity in terminology applied to Bosnian Muslims smacked of the old Ottoman *millet* approach to a somewhat similar problem of governing a multicultural state. In essence, the Muslims were being defined as a unique "nationality" by the socialist authorities on the sole basis of their religion. The issue was not clarified when in 1968 the Bosnian wing of the Yugoslav Communist party came right out and said so exactly—Muslims constituted a distinct nation. If that were so, then "nation" could be defined only in Ottoman *millet* terms and not in those of Western ethnonational culture.[67]

Only the strong hand of Tito's autocratic leadership, a unitary Marxist ideology, and the partisan legacy kept the socialist state of Yugoslavia peacefully
together by providing an umbrella of commonality, imposed by the
Communist party, that overrode the long-standing ethnic and religious differences that separated the various groups of inhabitants in the state. For that
condition to be maintained, it was necessary for all four of those critical factors to function optimally and indefinitely. But that, of course, was impossible.
In 1980 Tito, perhaps the most crucial factor of all, died, leaving both the socialist rulers and the state leaderless. So dominating had been the presence of Tito,
and so dependent on his presence had the political leadership become, that no
other individual within the party structure could fill his vacant shoes. Soon
after the leader's death, certain innate flaws in the supposedly flawless, scientific Marxist ideology began to emerge as the economy of the state worsened in spite of all socialistic efforts to fix the perceived problems. By that
time as well, the partisan generation, who spearheaded the socialist effort, were
far down the road to their graves, and the younger ones had little, if any, sincere attachments to the common bond of righteous struggle against fascist evil
that World War II resistance had created in their elders. In the minds of the
young, individual and regional materialism meant more than the common
struggle. And the very economic policies that won such positive acclaim in
the West—mixed socialist-market economics, with their emphasis on local self-
management—undermined the centralized control of the Communist party itself,
as self-management in industry steadily was applied to local, regional, and eventually republic-level politics. With the demise of the most crucial unifying factors in socialist Yugoslavia, the door was opened for the reemergence of old
national-religious differences among the population that were grounded in the
innate divisiveness of the presocialist nationalist nation-state political culture.
    In 1991 those differences reappeared with devastating consequences.
    There is little need here to describe in detail the disturbing, violent, and dehu-
manizing chain of events that characterized the bloody collapse of socialist
Yugoslavia that followed Slovenia's secession from that bankrupt state in 1991,
continued in the Croat-Serb warfare in Slavonia and "Krajina" during
1991–92, and culminated in the catastrophic violence of the bloodletting in
Bosnia-Hercegovina since 1992. The day-to-day details of that struggle have
appeared regularly in our news media. What needs pointing out regarding the
Bosnian fighting is the fact that, from the beginning, it involved much more
complicated issues and human realities than our Western cultural preconcep-
tions led most of us to believe. While analysts expounded on the purely
nationalist political and economic factors involved—factors that are products
of Western culture—they failed to appreciate the more fundamental forces that

led to the fighting in the first place and that maintained it, despite all Western efforts at mediating a peace, into the present. Those forces were the products of human history in the region.

Bosnia-Hercegovina is one of those places on the face of the earth where innately different human realities—that is, cultures—meet. In classical Roman times, Greek East met Latin West in the territory of present-day Bosnia-Hercegovina. When Roman emperor Diocletian (284–305) administratively divided the empire into two halves at the end of the third century, he did so along the invisible cultural frontier that separated the Greek and Latin worlds in the Balkan northwest. That boundary line ran through Bosnia. As Europe evolved two separate civilizations out of the dying loins of the Greco-Roman civilization, Diocletian's Bosnian line of demarcation became their most intimate and continuous meeting ground. Throughout the medieval period in Bosnia's history, the region was a focal point of contention between Catholic Western and Orthodox Eastern Europe. The standard-bearers of both sides were Slavs who spoke languages almost indistinguishable from one another but who wrote it in two different alphabets, thus expressing their two fundamentally separate cultures. In using Latin, the Catholic Croats demonstrated not only their Christian faith but the entire gamut of human reality that medieval Catholicism represented—a practical, legalistic world in which the spiritual and secular authorities governed in uneasy competition for supreme, divinely ordained power, with the spiritual leadership of Rome (the papacy) in the ascendant. The Orthodox Serbs, on the other hand, by using Cyrillic expressed their belief in a mystical, ritualistic world in which the spiritual and secular worlds were partners in power, with the secular ruler recognized as God's direct representative on earth and, therefore a divinely ordained autocrat. The Catholic Croats' practical expression of reality was born in the Holy Roman Empire of Charlemagne; the Orthodox Serbs' was rooted in the Byzantine Empire. Over time, the elements of overt expression changed for both but the bedrock cores of their different realities did not.

A third factor was added to the traditional East-West European confrontation in Bosnia when Islamic civilization entered the region in the fifteenth century in the guise of the Ottoman Empire. Its culture expressed a human reality that shared much of the ritualism, mysticism, and authoritarianism of the Orthodox East, but it cloaked them in terms that made no worldly differentiation between the spiritual and secular spheres—they were one and the same, and that was spiritual. The Muslim Turks and their numerous Bosnian converts found their practical cultural underpinnings in the original Islamic state established in Arabia by the prophet Muhammad.

By the nineteenth century both the Catholics and Orthodox Christians of Bosnia had developed strong senses of ethnonational self-identity that they projected into the political realm—the Croats organically as members of Western European civilization, the Serbs through adaptation of cultural influences from the West—while they retained their separate civilizational characters. The Muslims developed the *millet* approach to human identity, which recognized only religious differences among groups of people and labeled them as such; ethnicity was of no importance in the *millet* context.

In Bosnia, the key to comprehending the driving forces in the recent fighting lies in comprehending the cultural realities of the peoples involved. Both the Croats and the Serbs are struggling for nationalist goals, but, as we have seen in our brief historical survey, those goals, while appearing similar, are intrinsically at odds. The Orthodox, authoritarian Serbs seek a centralized, Greater Serbia-type objective (along the model of the Orthodox Russian or, even more pertinent, Byzantine Empire), while the Catholic Croats are willing to accept a partnership in a federated Bosnian state in loose confederation with independent Croatia (à la a workable Habsburg Empire). Both the Serbs and the Croats in Bosnia have demonstrated remarkable consistency in their respective historical political cultures. So too have the Bosnian Muslims, who, of the three societies involved in the conflict, have unswervingly envisioned Bosnia as a unitary state encompassing all of the region's inhabitants, no matter their ethnonational identities. Theirs is a logical stance, given their traditional Islamic *millet* approach to human reality, in which ethnicity, the basis for nationalistic divisiveness, is meaningless.

It was the Muslims' attempt to implement an updated and liberal-democratically modified version of the *millet* through their proposed 1992 constitution for the newly independent Bosnian state that sparked the conflict itself. The ultra-nationalist Serbs would accept no such anational existence and resisted the Muslim efforts by force. The Croats, succumbing to their historical sense of federalism, at first sided with the Muslims; broke with them when it appeared as if the Muslims would be utterly defeated by the Serbs; and then realigned themselves with the Muslims in a new federal approach once the latter weathered the worst of the military-political storm. In no case, even during that dark period when they turned against their allies to gain as much territory as possible before the war ended in a seeming Muslim defeat, did the Croats attempt to forge a workable alliance with their traditional cultural enemies—the Serbs.

In that last fact lies a warning for the future in Bosnia. Should the Muslims ultimately go down in defeat, with them would disappear the only force to consistently uphold a sense of a unitary Bosnian state (be it *millet* in Islamic terms or federated in Croat). The innate ethnonationalist cultures of the surviving Serbs and the Croats, when related to their past histories, appear to leave little doubt that, barring determined and effective outside intervention, the region would experience a new round of conflict over territorial acquisition for their respective nation-states. Should that occur, the Muslim inhabitants would be relegated to second-class status (if not worse) in whichever aggrandizing state they might find themselves.

⬛ NOTES TO READINGS ⬛

Marriages and Divorces

1. For the Versailles peace conference, see: Ferdinand Czernin, *Versailles, 1919: The Forces, Events, and Personalities That Shaped the Treaty* (New York: Putnam, 1964); and Edward M. House and Charles Seymour, *What Really Happened at Paris: The Story of the Peace Conference, 1918–1919, by American Delegates* (New York: Scribner, 1921).
2. Regarding President Wilson and the peoples of Eastern Europe, see Victor S. Mamatey, *The United States and East Central Europe, 1914–1918: A Study in Wilsonian Diplomacy and Propaganda* (Princeton, NJ: Princeton University Press, 1957).
3. See Dennis P. Hupchick, *Culture and History in Eastern Europe* (New York: St. Martin's Press, 1994), 87–91, 94–96, 114–18, for a discussion of East European historical political culture and its Russian expression.
4. Among useful general studies of the Habsburg Empire are: Robert A. Kann, *The Habsburg Empire: A Study in Integration and Disintegration* (New York: Octagon, 1973), and *A History of the Habsburg Empire, 1526–1918* (Berkeley: University of California Press, 1974); Victor-L. Tapié, *The Rise and Fall of the Habsburg Monarchy*, trans. Stephen Hardman (New York: Praeger, 1971); and A.J.P. Taylor, *The Habsburg Monarchy, 1809–1918: A History of the Austrian Empire and Austria-Hungary* (New York: Harper & Row, 1965).
5. Some useful general studies of the Ottoman Empire are: Halil Inalcik, *The Ottoman Empire: The Classical Age, 1300–1600* (London: Weidenfeld & Nicolson, 1973); Norman Itzkowitz, *Ottoman Empire and Islamic Tradition* (Chicago: University of Chicago Press, 1980); Lord [John P.D.B.] Kinross, *The Ottoman Centuries: The Rise and Fall of the Turkish Empire* (New York: Quill, 1977); Stanford J. Shaw, *History of the Ottoman Empire and Modern Turkey*, 2 vols. (Cambridge: Cambridge University Press, 1976–77); and Wayne S. Vucinich, *The Ottoman Empire: Its Record and Legacy* (Huntington, NY: Robert E. Krieger, 1979 [reprint]).
6. Friedrich Heer, *The Holy Roman Empire*, trans. Janet Sondheimer (New York: Praeger, 1968), provides interesting details on the early Habsburg emperors. One of the most useful studies of premodern East European political developments is Francis Dvornik, *The Slavs in European History and Civilization* (New Brunswick, NJ: Rutgers University Press, 1962), although by concentrating on the Slavs, he gives the Hungarians short shrift.
7. Given in Tapié, 43.
8. The seminal role of Ferdinand's elections to the crowns of both Hungary and Bohemia for cementing the Habsburg Empire in Eastern Europe is detailed in R.J.W. Evans, *The Making of the Habsburg Monarchy, 1550–1700: An Interpretation* (Oxford: Clarendon Press, 1991).
9. For the Hussites, see: Peter Brock, *The Political and Social Doctrines of the Unity of Czech Brethren in the Fifteenth and Early Sixteenth Centuries* (The Hague: Mouton, 1957), for the Hussites' program; and Josef Macek, *The Hussite Movement in Bohemia*, trans. Vilém and Ian Milner, 2nd ed. (Prague: Orbis, 1958).
10. See C.V. Wedgwood, *The Thirty Years War* (Garden City, NY: Anchor/Doubleday, 1961), 78–80, 79n.
11. The standard work on Bohemia during the eighteenth century is Robert J. Kerner, *Bohemia in the Eighteenth Century: A Study in Political, Economic and Social History; with Special Reference to the Reign of Leopold II, 1790–1792* (New York: Macmillan, 1932).
12. For Hungary during the two centuries preceding Mohács, see: Joseph Held, *Hunyadi: Legend and Reality* (Boulder, CO: East European Monographs, 1985); and Domokos Varga, *Hungary in Greatness and Decline: The 14th and 15th Centuries*, trans. Martha Szacsvay Lipták (Atlanta, GA: Hungarian Cultural Foundation, 1982), a popular but informative general overview.

13. On Hungarian-Habsburg relations during the eighteenth century, see: Ladislas Hengelmüler von Hengervár, *Hungary's Fight for National Existence; or, the History of the Great Uprising led by Francis Rákóczi II, 1703–1711* (London: Macmillan, 1913); Béla K. Király, *Hungary in the Late Eighteenth Century: The Decline of Enlightened Despotism* (New York: Columbia University Press, 1969); and Henrik Marczali, *Hungary in the Eighteenth Century* (Cambridge: Cambridge University Press, 1910). For the War of the Austrian Succession, see Reed Browning, *The War of the Austrian Succession* (New York: St. Martin's Press, 1993).

14. For Vienna and its reactionary regime, see Harold Nicolson, *The Congresses of Vienna: A Study in Allied Unity, 1812–1822* (New York: Harcourt, 1946). Regarding Metternich and his role, see: Arthur G. Haas, *Metternich, Reorganization and Nationality, 1813–1818: A Story of Foresight and Frustration in the Rebuilding of the Austrian Empire* (Wiesbaden: Franz Steiner, 1963); Paul W. Schroeder, *Metternich's Diplomacy at Its Zenith, 1820–1823* (Austin, University of Texas Press, 1962); Henry F. Schwarz, ed., *Metternich, the "Coachman" of Europe* (Boston: D.C. Heath, 1962); and Peter Viereck, "New Views on Metternich," *Review of Politics* 13, no. 2 (April 1951): 211–28.

15. Surveyed in Robert A. Kann, *The Multinational Empire: Nationalism and National Reform in the Habsburg Monarchy, 1848–1918*, 2 vols. (New York: Columbia University Press, 1950).

16. For Széchenyi, see: George Barany, *Stephen Széchenyi and the Awakening of Hungarian Nationalism, 1791–1841* (Princeton, NJ: Princeton University Press, 1968). For Kossuth, see István Deák, *The Lawful Revolution: Louis Kossuth and the Hungarians, 1848–1849* (New York: Columbia University Press, 1979), which is also the best study in English of the Hungarians' 1848 revolution itself.

17. The standard work in English on Panslavism is Hans Kohn, *Pan-Slavism: Its History and Ideology*, 2nd ed.(New York: Vintage, 1960). For the rise of Czech national consciousness, see: Peter Brock and H. Gordon Skilling, eds., *The Czech Renascence of the Nineteenth Century* (Toronto: University of Toronto Press, 1970); and Joseph F, Zacek, *Palacký: The Historian as Scholar and Nationalist* (The Hague: Mouton, 1970). For Šafařík, see Joseph M. Kirschbaum, *Pavel Josef Šafařík and His Contribution to Slavic Studies* (Cleveland, OH: Slovak Institute, 1962).

18. See Elinor M. Despolatović, *Ljudevit Gaj and the Illyrian Movement* (Boulder, CO: East European Monographs, 1975).

19. Among the many studies of 1848, of particular interest are: Lewis B. Namier, *1848: The Revolution of the Intellectuals* (London: G. Cumberlege, 1944); Priscilla Robertson, *Revolutions of 1848: A Social History* (Princeton, NJ: Princeton University Press, 1952); and Peter N. Stearns, *1848: The Revolutionary Tide in Europe* (New York: W.W. Norton, 1974).

20. Kohn, 75–82.

21. On the issue of German nationalism in the Habsburg Empire, see: Peter J. Katzenstein, *Disjointed Partners: Austria and Germany since 1815* (Berkeley: University of California Press, 1976); and Walter C. Langsem, *The Napoleonic Wars and German Nationalism in Austria* (New York: Columbia University Press, 1930).

22. There is little on the 1867 Compromise in English. An interesting study is Péter Hanák, "Hundred Years of *Ausgleich*," *New Hungarian Quarterly* 8, no. 27 (1967): 17–31.

23. See F.R. Bridge, *From Sadowa to Sarajevo: The Foreign Policy of Austria-Hungary, 1866–1914* (London: Routledge & Kegan Paul, 1972). For the Habsburgs' Balkan policy, see R.W. Seton-Watson, *The Southern Slav Question and the Habsburg Monarchy* (New York: H. Fertig, 1969).

24. General European Great Power politics is comprehensively treated in A.J.P. Taylor, *The Struggle for Mastery in Europe, 1848–1914* (London: Oxford University Press, 1971). For Russian policy in the Balkans, see Virginia Cowles, *The Russian Dagger: Cold War in the Days of the Czars* (New York: Harper & Row, 1969); and Michael B.

Petrovich, *The Emergence of Russian Panslavism, 1856–1870* (New York: Columbia University Press, 1966). For the diplomacy surrounding the Crimean War, Ann P. Saab, *The Origins of the Crimean Alliance* (Charlottesville: University of Virginia Press, 1977), is useful.

25. See William N. Medlicott, *The Congress of Berlin and After: A Diplomatic History of the Near Eastern Settlement, 1878–1880* (London: Metheun, 1938). Of much use is Benedict H. Sumner, *Russia and the Balkans, 1870–1880* (Hamden, CT: Archon, 1962).

26. For political liberalization in Austria-Hungary, see William A. Jenks, *The Austrian Electoral Reform of 1907* (New York: Columbia University Press, 1950).

27. For the web of developments that led to the outbreak of World War I, see: Laurence LaFore, *The Long Fuse: An Interpretation of the Origins of World War I*, 2nd ed. (Philadelphia: J.B. Lippincott, 1971); and vol. 1 of Luigi Albertini, *The Origins of the War of 1914*, 3 vols., trans. Isabella M. Massey (New York: Oxford University Press, 1952–57).

28. A useful general study of the Habsburgs from the 1867 Compromise to their fall is Arthur J. May, *The Habsburg Monarchy, 1867–1914* (Cambridge, MA: Harvard University Press, 1951).

29. For the Czechs, see: Bruce M. Garver, *The Young Czech Party, 1874–1901* (New Haven, CT: Yale University Press, 1978); and Paul Vyšný, *Neo-Slavism and the Czechs, 1896–1914* (Cambridge: Cambridge University Press, 1977).

30. On the position of the Slovaks in Hungary, see Thomas Čapek, *The Slovaks of Hungary, Slavs and Panslavism* (New York: Knickerbacher, 1906); Gilbert L. Oddo, *Slovakia and Its People* (New York: R. Speller, 1960); and Peter P. Yurchak, *The Slovaks: Their History and Traditions* (Whiting, IN: John J. Lach, 1946).

31. See Stanko Guldescu, "Croatian Political History, 1526–1918," in Francis H. Eterovich and Christopher Spalatin, eds., *Croatia: Land, People, Culture*, vol. 2 (Toronto: University of Toronto Press, 1970), 3–118, esp. 43–64.

32. An excellent study of the Sarajevo assassination and the circumstances that led to it is Vladimir Didijer, *The Road to Sarajevo* (New York: Simon & Schuster, 1966). Joachim Remak, "Sarajevo—Design and Accident," *Journal of Central European Affairs* 21, no. 2 (July 1961): 165–75, treats with the fortuitous character of the affair.

33. For Czech and Slovak emigré political efforts, especially the role of Masaryk and Beneš, see: Edvard Beneš, *My War Memoirs* (London: Allen & Unwin, 1928); Tomáš Masaryk, *The Making of a State* (New York: Frederick A. Stokes, 1927); and Zbynek A.B. Zeman, *The Masaryks: The Making of Czechoslovakia* (New York: Barnes & Noble, 1976).

34. See Dimitrije Djordjević, ed., *The Creation of Yugoslavia, 1914–1918* (Oxford: Oxford University Press, 1980).

35. For the Romanian nationalist view, see Miron Constantinescu and Ştefan Pascu, eds., *Unification of the Romanian National State: The Union of Transylvania with Old Romania* (Bucharest: The Academy, 1971).

36. See: Josef Korbel, *Twentieth Century Czechoslovakia: The Meaning of Its History* (New York: Columbia University Press, 1977); Jozef Lettrich, *A History of Modern Slovakia* (New York: Frederick A. Praeger, 1955); Victor S. Mamatey and Radomir Luža, eds., *A History of the Czechoslovak Republic, 1918–48* (Princeton, NJ: Princeton University Press, 1973); and Eugen Steiner, *The Slovak Dilemma* (Cambridge, MA: Cambridge University Press, 1973).

37. See: Josef Chmelař, *Political Parties in Czechoslovakia* (Prague: Orbis, 1926); and Karel Hoch, *The Political Parties in Czechoslovakia* (Prague: Orbis, 1936).

38. See the chapter on Ruthenia in Macartney, *Hungary and Her Successors* (London: Oxford University Press, 1937).

39. For the Hungarian minority, see Ibid. as well as Stephen Borsody, *Czechoslovak Policy and the Hungarian Minority, 1945–1948* (New York: Brooklyn College, 1982). For the Bolshevik episode at the end of the war, see: Andrew C. Janos and William B. Slottman,

eds., *Revolution in Perspective: Essays on the Hungarian Soviet Republic of 1919* (Berkeley: University of California Press, 1971); Oszkar Jaszi, *Revolution and Counter-Revolution in Hungary* (New York: H. Fertig, 1969); and Ivan Volgyes, *The Hungarian Soviet Republic, 1919: An Evaluation and a Bibliography* (Stanford, CA: Hoover Institute Press, 1970).

40. For the Sudeten Germans and their expulsion from Czechoslovakia, see: J.W. Bruegal, *Czechoslovakia Before Munich* (Cambridge: Cambridge University Press, 1973); and Radomir Luža, *The Transfer of the Sudeten Germans: A Study of Czech-German Relations, 1933–1962* (New York: New York University Press, 1964).

41. The unified Danubian economic system of the Habsburgs is examined in: David F. Good, *The Economic Rise of the Habsburg Empire, 1750–1914* (Berkeley: University of California Press, 1984); and John Komloss, *The Habsburg Monarchy as a Customs Union: Economic Development in Austria-Hungary in the Nineteenth Century* (Princeton, NJ: Princeton University Press, 1983).

42. For a general survey, see: Stephen Clissold, ed., *A Short History of Yugoslavia: From Early Times to 1966* (Cambridge: Cambridge University Press, 1966); and Vladimir Didijer, et al., *History of Yugoslavia*, trans. Kordija Kveder (New York: McGraw-Hill, 1974).

43. See Dragisa N. Ristić, *Yugoslavia's Revolution of 1941* (University Park: Pennsylvania State University Press, 1966).

Transylvania: The Undead Question

1. For the early Magyars, see C.A. Macartney, *The Magyars in the Ninth Century* (Cambridge: Cambridge University Press, 1968). Some useful general studies of Hungary and the Hungarians are: Dominic G. Kosáry and S. Béla Várdy, *History of the Hungarian Nation* (Astor Park, FL: Danubian Press, 1969); Emil Lengyel, *1,000 Years of Hungary* (New York: John Day Co., 1958); C.A. Macartney, *Hungary: A Short History* (Chicago: Aldine, 1962); Denis Sinor, *History of Hungary* (London: Allen & Unwin, 1959); and Peter F. Sugar, Péter Hanák, and Tibor Frank, eds., *A History of Hungary* (Bloomington: Indiana University Press, 1990).

2. See: R.W. Seton-Watson, *A History of the Roumanians* (New York: Cambridge University Press, 1934), 19; and Constantine C. Giurescu, *Transylvania in the History of the Romanians* (Bucharest: Meridiane, 1968), 40.

3. For the Székelys, see Benedek Jancsó, *The Székelys: A Historical and Ethnographical Essay* (Budapest: V. Hornyánszky, 1921). For examples of various hypotheses regarding their origins, see: Seton-Watson, *A History of the Roumanians*, 20; John M. Cabot, *The Racial Conflict in Transylvania* (Boston: Beacon Press, 1926), 8; and C.A. Prothero, ed., *Transylvania and the Banat* (London: British Foreign Office, Historical Section, 1920), 10.

4. Complete 1910 census figures for Transylvania are given as an appendix in Cabot, 182–88. Cabot gives Székely figures on p. 126. Though the census generally may have been flawed by Magyar bias, the figures for the Székelys are probably least so, given their compact habitation pattern in specific counties.

5. For the Transylvanian Saxons, see John Foisel, *Saxons Through Seventeen Centuries: A History of the Transylvanian Saxons* (Cleveland, OH: Central Alliance of Transylvanian Saxons, 1936).

6. For the Teutonic Knights in Eastern Europe, see Hermann Schreiber, *Teuton and Slav: The Struggle for Central Europe* (New York: Knopf, 1965).

7. For the "Sibin Burg" theory, see Seton-Watson, *A History of the Roumanians*, 22. For the Jewish merchants, see Alan Palmer, *The Lands Between: A History of East-Central Europe since the Congress of Vienna* (New York: Macmillan, 1970).

8. Transylvanus [pseud.], *The Ethnical Minorities of Transylvania* (London: Eyre & Spotteswoode, 1934), 11–12.

9. Ştefan Pascu, *A History of Transylvania*, trans. Robert Ladd (New York: Dorset, 1990), 60–61; Anne F. Sanborn and Géza Wass de Czege, eds., *Transylvania and the Hungarian-Rumanian Problem: A Symposium* (Astor Park, FL: Danubian Press, 1979), 106.

10. The 1804 figures are given in the published travel account of John Paget, *Hungary and Transylvania; with Remarks on Their Condition, Social, Political and Economical*, vol. 2 (Philadelphia, PA: Lea & Blanchard, 1850), 213n. See Cabot, appendix, for the 1910 figures.
11. A concise explanation of the development of the Transylvanian "nations" can be found in Peter F. Sugar's introductory summary of conditions in the region just prior to the coming of the Ottoman Turks in his *Southeastern Europe under Ottoman Rule, 1354–1804* (Seattle: University of Washington Press, 1977), 144–49.
12. For Hunyadi, see Joseph Held, *Hunyadi: Legend and Reality* (Boulder, CO: East European Monographs, 1985).
13. For Matthias, see Domokos Varga, *Hungary in Greatness and Decline: The 14th and 15th Centuries*, trans. Martha Szacsvay Lipták (Atlanta, GA: Hungarian Cultural Foundation, 1982), 89–123.
14. See Sugar, 147–67, for Transylvania from 1526 to 1699.
15. Pascu, 114–18.
16. Walter Kolarz, *Myths and Realities in Eastern Europe* (London: Lindsay Drummond, 1946), 96.
17. For the Reformation in Transylvania, see János G. Bauhofer, *History of the Protestant Church in Hungary from the Beginning of the Reformation to 1850; with Special Reference to Transylvania*, trans. J. Craig (New York: J.C. Derby, 1854).
18. Paraphrased from C.A. Macartney, *Hungary and Her Successors* (London: Oxford University Press, 1937), 260–61.
19. For the position of the Romanians and their Orthodox church organization in the late seventeenth and early eighteenth centuries, see Keith Hitchins, *The Rumanian National Movement in Transylvania, 1780–1849* (Cambridge, MA: Harvard University Press, 1969), 11–14.
20. The classic study of unionist efforts from their beginning at Florence until the Union of Brest is Oskar Halecki, *From Florence to Brest (1439–1596)* (Rome: Sacrum Poloniae Millennium, 1958). For the efforts at church union in Transylvania, Hitchin's study is the standard in English.
21. Hitchins, 19–20.
22. Ibid., 30–32.
23. See Ibid., 22–32, for the life of Micu.
24. For the Latinist School's nationalist role, see Stephen Fischer-Galati, "Romanian Nationalism," in Peter F. Sugar and Ivo J. Lederer, eds., *Nationalism in Eastern Europe* (Seattle: University of Washington Press, 1969), 373–95.
25. For Joseph II, see Derek E.D. Beales, *Joseph II* (New York: Cambridge University Press, 1987); and Saul K. Padover, *The Revolutionary Emperor, Joseph II of Austria* (Hamden, CT: Archon, 1967).
26. For the *Supplex* and events leading up to it, see D. Prodan, *Supplex Libellus Valachorum; or, The Political Struggle of the Romanians in Transylvania during the 18th Century*, trans. Mary Lăzăescu (Bucharest: The Academy, 1971).
27. See George Barany, *Stephen Széchenyi and the Awakening of Hungarian Nationalism, 1791–1841* (Princeton, NJ: Princeton University Press, 1968), for Széchenyi.
28. For Kossuth, see István Deák, *The Lawful Revolution: Louis Kossuth and the Hungarians, 1848–1849* (New York: Columbia University Press, 1979).
29. For Deák, see Béla K. Király, *Ferenc Deák* (Boston: Twayne, 1975).
30. Useful for the 1848 revolutions are: Lewis B. Namier, *1848: The Revolution of the Intellectuals* (London: G. Cumberlege, 1944); Priscilla Robertson, *Revolutions of 1848: A Social History* (Princeton, NJ: Princeton University Press, 1952); and Peter N. Stearns, *1848: The Revolutionary Tide in Europe* (New York: W.W. Norton, 1974).
31. See Hitchins, 181–279, for the Transylvanian Romanians' nationalist activities during 1848–49.

32. For post-1848 developments, see: Robert A. Kann, *The Multinational Empire: Nationalism and National Reform in the Habsburg Monarchy, 1848–1918*, 2 vols. (New York: Columbia University Press, 1950); and A.J.P. Taylor, *The Habsburg Monarchy, 1809–1918: A History of the Austrian Empire and Austria-Hungary* (New York: Harper & Row, 1965). For the reign of Francis Joseph, see Anatol Murad, *Franz Joseph I of Austria and His Empire* (New York: Twayne, 1968).

33. See Péter Hanák, "Hundred Years of *Ausgleich*," *New Hungarian Quarterly* 8, no. 27 (1967): 17–31.

34. For Eötvös, there are: Paul Bödy, *Joseph Eötvös and the Modernization of Hungary, 1840–1870* (Boulder, CO: East European Monographs, 1985); and Steven B. Várdy, "Baron Joseph Eötvös: The Political Profile of a Liberal Hungarian Thinker and Statesman," (Ph.D. diss., Indiana University, 1967).

35. For conditions of the Transylvanian Romanians in the post-1867 era, see: Cabot, 82; and Oszkar Jaszi, *The Dissolution of the Habsburg Monarchy* (Chicago: University of Chicago Press, 1929), 331–34, 346.

36. Quoted in Palmer, 98.

37. For the events surrounding the Alba Iulia resolution of union with Romania, see Miron Constantinescu and Ştefan Pascu, eds., *Unification of the Romanian National State: The Union of Transylvania with Old Romania* (Bucharest: The Academy, 1971).

38. Fischer-Galati, 376–87.

39. See Eugene Horvath, *Transylvania and the History of the Roumanians* (Budapest: Sarkany, 1935), 74–80.

40. For Kun's Bolshevik republic, see: Andrew C. Janos and William B. Slottman, eds., *Revolution in Perspective: Essays on the Hungarian Soviet Republic of 1919* (Berkeley: University of California Press, 1971); Oszkar Jaszi, *Revolution and Counter-Revolution in Hungary* (New York: H. Fertig, 1969); and Ivan Volgyes, *The Hungarian Soviet Republic, 1919: An Evaluation and a Bibliography* (Stanford, CA: Hoover Institute Press, 1970).

41. See R.W. Seton-Watson, "The Little Entente," *Contemporary Review* (December 1927): 1–16.

42. The Hungarian arguments began at Versailles and have continued into the present. They range in tenor from the scholarly to the emotionally frantic. A representative sampling might include: J. Ajtay, B. Jancsó, and A. Kovács, *The Transylvanian Question* (New York: Steiger, 1921); Horvath; Pal Teleki, *The Evolution of Hungary and Its Place in European History* (New York: Macmillan, 1934); Sanborn and Wass de Czege; Viator Transylvanus [pseud.], *In Transylvania* (New York: Steiger, 1921); and Gyula Zathureczky, *Transylvania: Citadel of the West* (Astor Park, FL: Danubian Press, 1964).

43. The same overall evaluation made of the Hungarian arguments made in note 42, stands for the Romanian as well. A sampling might include: Sylvius Dragomir, *The Ethnical Minorities in Transylvania* (Geneva: Sonar, 1927); Giurescu; Pascu; Pavel Pavel [pseud.], *Transylvania and Danubian Peace* (London: New Europe, 1943); and Transylvanus [pseud.]. The Romanian position was avidly supported by the renowned English historian, R.W. Seton-Watson. Besides his *History of the Roumanians,* see his *Transylvania: A Key-Problem* (Oxford: Classic Press, 1943). A more modern expression of the Romanian position is Cornelia Bodea and Virgil Candea, *Heritage and Continuity in Eastern Europe: The Transylvanian Legacy in the History of the Romanians* (Boulder, CO: East European Monographs, 1982).

44. See: Elemér Illyés, *Ethnic Continuity in the Carpatho-Danubian Area* (Boulder, CO: East European Monographs, 1988); and Louis L. Löte, ed., *Transylvania and the Theory of Daco-Roman-Rumanian Continuity* (New York: Committee of Transylvania, 1980). Though both studies are decidedly pro-Hungarian in bias, they do manage to present much useful material. A Western work supporting the Hungarian contentions is Louis Cornish, *Transylvania: The Land Beyond the Forest* (Philadelphia, PA: Dorrance, 1947). Also see Kolarz, 171–88.

45. Given in Kolarz, 184; Cabot, 122.
46. For a general study of the rise of neofascism in Eastern Europe, see Anton Polonsky, *The Little Dictators: The History of Eastern Europe since 1918* (London: Routledge & Kegan Paul, 1975). For Hungarian and Romanian neofascism, see Nicholas M. Nagy-Talavera, *The Green Shirts and Others: A History of Fascism in Hungary and Rumania* (Stanford, CA: Hoover Institute Press, 1970).
47. For Hungary's relations with the European Powers and Nazi Germany during the 1930s, and for Hitler and the Second Vienna Award, see: Gabor Baross, *History of Hungary: Hungary and Hitler* (Los Angeles: University of Southern California Press, 1964); and Thomas L. Sakmyster, *Hungary, the Great Powers, and the Danube Crisis, 1936–1939* (Athens: University of Georgia Press, 1980).
48. Figures given in *The Minority Question in Transylvania* (Bucharest: Government Press, 1925).
49. Quoted in Louis C. Cornish, *Transylvania in 1922* (Boston: Beacon Press, 1923), 6.
50. Macartney, *Hungary and Her Successors,* 289.
51. Francis Deák, *The Hungarian-Rumanian Land Dispute* (New York: Columbia University Press, 1928), offers a useful analysis of the agrarian reform.
52. One of the most objective, scholarly examples is Stephen Borsody, ed., *The Hungarians: A Divided Nation* (New Haven, CT: Yale Center for International and Area Studies, 1988). One might also see Elemér Illyés, *National Minorities in Romania: Change in Transylvania* (Boulder, CO: East European Monographs, 1982).

Macedonian Mischiefs

1. See Halil Inalcik, *The Ottoman Empire: The Classical Age, 1300–1600,* trans. Norman Itzkowitz and Colin Imber (London: Weidenfeld & Nicolson, 1973), for the Ottomans in their ascendancy.
2. For the Ottoman decline, see Alan Palmer, *The Decline and Fall of the Ottoman Empire* (New York: M. Evans, 1992).
3. For general studies of the Greeks under Ottoman rule, see: Apostolos E. Vakalopoulos, *The Greek Nation, 1453–1669: The Cultural and Economic Background of Modern Greek Society,* trans. Ian and Phania Moles (New Brunswick, NJ: Rutgers University Press, 1976); Speros Vryonis, "The Byzantine Legacy and Ottoman Forms," *Dumbarton Oaks Papers* 23–24 (1969–70): 251–308; and Dionysios A. Zakythinos, *The Making of Modern Greece: From Byzantium to Independence* (Totowa, NJ: Rowman & Littlefield, 1976). For the Greek Orthodox church and the Orthodox *millet,* see: N.J. Pantazopoulos, *Church and Law in the Balkan Peninsula during the Ottoman Rule* (Thessaloniki: Institute for Balkan Studies, 1967); Theodore H. Papadopoullos, *Studies and Documents Relating to the History of the Greek Church and People under Turkish Domination* (Brussels: Bibliotheca Græca ævi posterioris, 1, 1952); and Steven Runciman, *The Great Church in Captivity: A Study of the Patriarchate of Constantinople From the Eve of the Turkish Conquest to the Greek War of Independence* (London: Cambridge University Press, 1968).
4. See: Richard Clogg, ed. and trans., *The Movement for Greek Independence, 1770–1821: A Collection of Documents* (London: Macmillan, 1976); and G.P. Henderson, *The Revival of Greek Thought, 1620–1830* (Albany: State University of New York Press, 1970).
5. See: Stephen G. Chaconas, *Adamantios Koraïs: A Study in Greek Nationalism* (New York: Columbia University Press, 1942); William P. Kaldis, *John Capodistrias and the Modern Greek State* (Madison: State Historical Society of Wisconsin, 1963); and Christopher M. Woodhouse, *Capodistria: The Founder of Greek Independence* (London: Oxford University Press, 1973).
6. For the Greek War of Independence, see: Richard Clogg, ed., *The Struggle for Greek Independence: Essays to Mark the 150th Anniversary of the Greek War of Independence*

(Hamden, CT: Archon, 1973); Douglas Dakin, *The Greek Struggle for Independence, 1821–1833* (London: Batsford, 1973); and Christopher M. Woodhouse, *The Greek War of Independence: Its Historical Setting* (London: Hutchinson's University Library, 1952).

7. For foreign philhellene and military intervention in the Greek war, see: Douglas Dakin, *British and American Philhellenes during the War of Greek Independence, 1821–1833* (Thessaloniki: Institute for Balkan Studies, 1955); William St. Clair, *That Greece Might Still Be Free: The Philhellenes in the War of Greek Independence* (London: Oxford University Press, 1972); and Christopher M. Woodhouse, *The Battle of Navarino* (London: Hodder & Stoughton, 1965).

8. For Greek domestic politics, see John A. Petropulos, *Politics and Statescraft in the Kingdom of Greece, 1833–1843* (Princeton, NJ: Princeton University Press, 1968). For the Byzantinistic "Great Idea" in Greece, see: George G. Arnakis, "Byzantium and Greece," *Balkan Studies* 4, no. 2 (1963): 379–400; Cyril Mango, "Byzantinism and Romantic Hellenism," *Journal of the Warburg and Courtauld Institutes* 28 (1965): 29–43; Theodore G. Tatsios, *The Megali Idea and the Greek-Turkish War of 1897* (Boulder, CO: East European Monographs, 1984); Arnold J. Toynbee, *The Greeks and Their Heritage* (Oxford: Oxford University Press, 1981); and Apostolos P. Vakalopoulos, "Byzantium and Hellenism, Remarks on the Racial Origin and Intellectual Continuity of the Greek Nation," *Balkan Studies* 9, no. 1 (1968): 101–26.

9. See Peter F. Sugar, *Southeastern Europe under Ottoman Rule, 1354–1804* (Seattle: University of Washington Press, 1977).

10. There are no English-language studies of the Serbian church available. The best Western-language study is László Hadrovics, *Le peuple serbe et son église sous la domination turque* (Paris: Presses universitaires de France, 1947).

11. See James F. Clarke, *The Pen and the Sword: Studies in Bulgarian History*, ed. Dennis P. Hupchick (Boulder, CO: East European Monographs, 1988), 214–17.

12. For Obradović, see his autobiography, *The Life and Times of Dimitrije Obradović*, trans. and ed. George R. Noyes (Berkeley: University of California Press, 1953).

13. The classic study of the Serbian revolution and the early Serb autonomous state is Leopold Ranke, *The History of Servia and the Servian Revolution; with a Sketch of the Insurrection in Bosnia*, trans. Mrs. Alexander Kerr (London: Bohn, 1853). Karadžić receives due treatment. Also see Wayne S. Vucinich, ed., *The First Serbian Uprising, 1804–1813* (Boulder, CO: East European Monographs, 1982).

14. For Karadžić, see Duncan Wilson, *The Life and Times of Vuk Stefanović Karadžić, 1787–1864: Literacy, Literature, and National Independence in Serbia* (Oxford: Clarendon Press, 1970).

15. For Serbia from its war of independence to the end of World War I, see Michael B. Petrovich, *A History of Modern Serbia, 1804–1918*, 2 vols. (New York: Harcourt Brace Jovanovich, 1976).

16. See the relevant Serbian passages in Ivo J. Lederer, "Nationalism and the Yugoslavs," in Peter F. Sugar and Ivo J. Lederer, eds., *Nationalism in Eastern Europe* (Seattle: University of Washington Press, 1969), 396–438.

17. The Great Power diplomatic crisis sparked by the uprising is commonly categorized under the term "Eastern Question." Among the many studies available, useful are: M.A. Anderson, *The Eastern Question, 1774–1923* (New York: Macmillan, 1966), which takes a broad perspective; Barbara Jelavich, *The Ottoman Empire, the Great Powers, and the Straits Question, 1870–1887* (Bloomington: Indiana University Press, 1974); William L. Langer, *European Alliances and Alignments, 1870–1890* (New York: Vintage, 1964); Mihailo D. Stojanović, *The Great Powers and the Balkans, 1875–1878* (Cambridge: Cambridge University Press, 1939); and, very important, Benedict H. Sumner, *Russia and the Balkans, 1870–1880* (Hamden, CT: Archon, 1962).

18. For the Berlin Congress, see William N. Medlicott, *The Congress of Berlin and After: A Diplomatic History of the Near Eastern Settlement, 1878–1880* (London: Metheun, 1938).

19. For the position of the Bulgarians under Ottoman rule, and for the significance of their religious culture, see Dennis P. Hupchick, *The Bulgarians in the Seventeenth Century: Orthodox Society and Culture under Ottoman Rule* (Jefferson, NC: McFarland, 1993), esp. part 1. For a general overview of the Ottoman period in Bulgaria, see Mercia MacDermott, *History of Bulgaria, 1393–1885* (New York: Frederick A. Praeger, 1962).

20. For the Bulgarian national revival, see Clarke, *The Pen and the Sword*, 79–111 (for Paisii), 171–205 (for educational and literary activity). Also see Thomas A. Meininger, *The Formation of a Nationalist Bulgarian Intelligentsia, 1835–1878* (New York: Garland, 1987).

21. Clarke, *The Pen and the Sword*, 271–85.

22. For the Bulgarian church question and the Exarchate, see: Ibid., 328–44; Richard von Mach, *The Bulgarian Exarchate: Its History and the Extent of Its Authority in Turkey* (London: n.p., 1907); and Thomas A. Meininger, *Ignatiev and the Establishment of the Bulgarian Exarchate, 1864–1872: A Study in Personal Diplomacy* (Madison: State Historical Society of Wisconsin, 1970). For American Protestant missionary involvement, see James F. Clarke, *Bible Societies, American Missionaries, and the National Revival of Bulgaria* (New York: Arno, 1971).

23. For Ottoman reform efforts, see Roderic H. Davison, *Reform in the Ottoman Empire, 1856–1876* (Princeton, NJ: Princeton University Press, 1963).

24. For Levski and the Bucharest revolutionaries, see Mercia MacDermott, *The Apostle of Freedom: A Portrait of Vasil Levsky Against a Background of Nineteenth Century Bulgaria* (Sofia: Sofia Press, 1979).

25. For a firsthand account of the uprising, see Zaharii Stoyanov, *Extracts from Notes on the Bulgarian Uprisings,* trans. Mariya Rankova (Sofia: Sofia Press, 1976).

26. Regarding the "massacres" and the American role in leaking news of them to the West, see Clarke, *The Pen and the Sword,* 392–401, 421–57. For MacGahan, see: James F. Clarke and George A. Tabakov, eds., *MacGahan and Bulgaria, 1878–1978: A Centennial Commemoration* (New Lexington, OH: MacGahan-Bulgarian Centennial Commemoration Committee, 1979); and Dale L. Walker, *Januarius MacGahan: The Life and Campaigns of an American War Correspondent* (Athens: Ohio University Press, 1988). For Schyler, see Michael B. Petrovich, "Eugene Schyler and Bulgaria, 1876–1878," *Bulgarian Historical Review* 7, no. 1 (1979): 51–69. For the public furor in England, see: David Harris, *Britain and the Bulgarian Horrors of 1876* (Chicago: University of Chicago Press, 1939); and R.W. Seton-Watson, *Disraeli, Gladstone and the Eastern Question* (London: F. Cass, 1962).

27. San Stefano is treated in Sumner.

28. For Russia's Balkan policy and its effect on the young Bulgarian state, see Charles Jelavich, *Tsarist Russia and Balkan Nationalism: Russian Influence in the Internal Affairs of Bulgaria and Serbia, 1879–1886* (Berkeley: University of California Press, 1958).

29. For Ferdinand and his imperialist ambitions, see: Stephan Constant, *Foxy Ferdinand, 1861–1948, Tsar of Bulgaria* (London: Sidgwick & Jackson, 1979); John Macdonald, *Czar Ferdinand and His People* (New York: Arno, 1971); and Hans R. Madol, *Ferdinand of Bulgaria: The Dream of Byzantium* (London: Hurst & Blackett, 1933).

30. Some general studies of Macedonia include: Henry N. Brailsford, *Macedonia: Its Races and Their Future* (London: Metheun, 1906), slightly pro-Bulgarian in its slant; Lovett F. Edwards, *Macedonia* (London: David Harvey, 1971); Tihomir R. Georgevitch, *Macedonia* (London: Allen & Unwin, 1918), pro-Serbian in slant; Alan G. Ogilvie, "A Contribution to the Geography of Macedonia," *Geographical Journal* 55 (January 1920): 1–34; and Stoyan Pribichevich, *Macedonia: Its People and History* (University Park: Pennsylvania State University Press, 1982), pro-Macedonian in slant. The study by Apostolos E. Vakalopoulos, *History of Macedonia, 1354–1833,* trans. Peter Megann (Thessaloniki: Institute for Balkan Studies, 1973), provides the historical basis for the current Greek position on Macedonia.

31. See Leften S. Stavrianos, *Balkan Federation: A History of the Movement toward Balkan Unity in Modern Times* (Hamden, CT: Archon, 1964), for relations among the contenders (despite the title!).
32. For the brothers, see Larry Koroloff, et. al., eds., *The Miladinov Brothers: A Miscellany* (Toronto: Macedonian Historical Society of Canada, 1982).
33. See the coverage given in Wayne S. Vucinich, *Serbia Between East and West: The Events of 1903–1908* (Stanford, CA: Stanford University Press, 1954).
34. A general survey of the struggle that ensued is provided by Christ Anastasoff, *The Tragic Peninsula: A History of the Macedonian Movement for Independence Since 1878* (St. Louis, MO: Blackwell & Wielandy, 1938).
35. For Stambulov, see A. Hulma Beaman, *M. Stambuloff* (London: Bliss, Sands & Foster, 1895).
36. For IMRO, see Anastasoff.
37. See Laura B. Sherman, *Fires on the Mountain: The Macedonian Revolutionary Movement and the Kidnapping of Ellen Stone* (Boulder, CO: East European Monographs, 1980).
38. For Delčev, IMRO, and EMRO developments, see Mercia MacDermott, *Freedom or Death: The Life of Gotsé Delchev* (London: Journeyman Press, 1978).
39. See Vucinich, *Serbia Between East and West*, 25, for the Serbian Society of St. Sava. For stepped-up Greek activity in Macedonia, see: Jerry Augustinos, "The Dynamics of Modern Greek Nationalism: The 'Great Idea' and the Macedonian Problem," *East European Quarterly* 6, no. 4 (January 1973): 444–53; Douglas Dakin, *The Greek Struggle in Macedonia, 1897–1913* (Thessaloniki: Institute for Balkan Studies, 1966); and George B. Zotiades, *The Macedonian Controversy* (Thessaloniki: Institute for Balkan Studies, 1954).
40. For Ilinden, see Pribichevich, 127–36.
41. See Walter Kolarz, *Myths and Realities in Eastern Europe* (London: Lindsay Drummond, 1946), 241–45.
42. See Douglas Dakin, *The Unification of Greece, 1770–1923* (London: Ernest Benn, 1972).
43. For a good general overview of Greek nationalism, see Stephen G. Xydis, "Modern Greek Nationalism," in Sugar and Lederer, 207–58.
44. The ethnic turmoil of the medieval Balkans is aptly described in: two studies by John V.A. Fine, Jr., *The Early Medieval Balkans: A Critical Survey from the Sixth to the Late Twelfth Century* (Ann Arbor: University of Michigan Press, 1983), and *The Late Medieval Balkans: A Critical Survey from the Late Twelfth Century to the Ottoman Conquest* (Ann Arbor: University of Michigan Press, 1987); and Dimitri Obolensky, *The Byzantine Commonwealth: Eastern Europe, 500–1453* (New York: Praeger, 1971).
45. For the first medieval Bulgarian state, see: Robert Browning, *Byzantium and Bulgaria: A Comparative Study Across the Early Medieval Frontier* (Berkeley: University of California Press, 1975); and Steven Runciman, *A History of the First Bulgarian Empire* (London: G. Bell & Sons, 1930). No specialized study for the second medieval Bulgarian state exists in English. For it, see the pertinent passages in Fine, *The Late Medieval Balkans*.
46. Kolarz, 213–45. For American missionary pro-Bulgarian statements, see: Clarke, *The Pen and the Sword*, 311–20; and Vladimir A. Tsanoff, comp. and ed., *Reports and Letters of American Missionaries Referring to the Distribution of Nationalities in the Former Provinces of European Turkey, 1858–1918* (Sofia: n.p., 1919).
47. For the Orthodox conversion of the Bulgarians, the creation of the Cyrillic alphabet, and its cultural dispersion among the Balkan and Russian Slavs, see: Ivan Duichev, ed., *Kiril and Methodius: Founders of Slavonic Writing* (Boulder, CO: East European Monographs, 1985); Francis Dvornik, *Byzantine Missions Among the Slavs: SS. Constantine-Cyril and Methodius* (New Brunswick, NJ: Rutgers University Press, 1970); and A.P. Vlasto, *The Entry of the Slavs into Christendom: An Introduction into the Medieval World of the Slavs* (Cambridge: Cambridge University Press, 1970).

48. For Bulgarian nationalism, see Marin V. Pundeff, "Bulgarian Nationalism," in Sugar and Lederer, 93–165.
49. For medieval Serbia, see the relevant passages in Fine's two studies, noted previously.
50. See Nicholai D. Velimirovich, *The Life of St. Sava* (Libertyville, IL: Serbian Eastern Orthodox Diocese for the USA and Canada, 1951), for Sava and his illustrious father.
51. Dušan's state is treated in detail in most studies of the later Byzantine Empire and of the rise of the Ottoman Empire in the Balkans. For the Serb nationalist view, see: Kolarz, 189–212; Lederer, 415n. The impossibility of territorially reconciling the nationalist claims of the three major contenders—Greece, Bulgaria, and Serbia—and their respective Western supporters within the context of the Western European nation-state political culture is aptly demonstrated in H.R. Wilkinson, *Maps and Politics: A Review of the Ethnic Cartography of Macedonia* (Liverpool: University Press of Liverpool, 1951), which is a work that should be studied closely by all current foreign policymakers in their efforts to deal with the emerging national crises in Eastern Europe during the post-cold war era. Although restricted to one specific problem, its lessons are relevant globally.
52. The "Macedonian" nationalist idea is expounded in: Anastasoff; and in Ivan Mihailoff, *Macedonia: A Switzerland of the Balkans,* trans. Christ Anastasoff (St. Louis, MO: Pearlstone Publishing, 1950).
53. The approach used in Pribichevich.
54. For the key contributions to the artificial creation of Macedonian linguistic cultural consciousness, see the two works by Blaže Koneski: *The Macedonian Language in the Development of the Slavonic Literary Languages,* trans. Ivana Kovilovska-Popska and William Reid (Skopje: Nova Makedonija, 1968); and *Towards the Macedonian Renaissance* (Skopje: Nova Makedonija, 1968). Also see the following works by Horace Lunt: *A Grammar of the Macedonian Literary Language* (Skopje: State Publishing House, 1952); and "A Survey of Macedonian Literature," *Harvard Slavic Studies,* vol. 1 (Cambridge, MA: Harvard University Press, 1953), 363–96.
55. See Ernest E. Ramsaur, Jr., *The Young Turks: Prelude to the Revolution of 1908* (Princeton, NJ: Princeton University Press, 1957).
56. See Feroz Ahmad, *The Young Turks: The Committee of Union and Progress in Turkish Politics, 1908–1914* (Oxford: Clarendon, 1969).
57. See Andrew Rossos, *Russia and the Balkans: Inter-Balkan Rivalries and Russian Foreign Policy, 1908–1914* (Toronto: University of Toronto Press, 1981).
58. The standard study of the diplomatic "niceties" involved in the alliances of the Balkan states, and of their bastardizations, is Ernst C. Helmreich, *The Diplomacy of the Balkan Wars, 1912–1913* (Cambridge, MA: Harvard University Press, 1938). Also see Edward C. Thaden, *Russia and the Balkan Alliance of 1912* (University Park: Pennsylvania State University Press, 1965).
59. For the two wars, see Jacob G. Schurman, *The Balkan Wars, 1912–1913* (Princeton, NJ: Princeton University Press, 1914).
60. For dealings with Bulgaria, see Harry N. Howard, *The Partition of Turkey: A Diplomatic History, 1913–1923* (New York: H. Fertig, 1966), 152–66.
61. See George P. Genov, *Bulgaria and the Treaty of Neuilly* (Sofia: Danov, 1935).
62. Regarding Stamboliiski, see John D. Bell, *Peasants in Power: Alexander Stamboliski and the Bulgarian Agrarian National Union, 1899–1923* (Princeton, NJ: Princeton University Press, 1977).
63. For the assassination, see Allen Roberts, *The Turning Point: The Assassination of Louis Barthou and King Alexander I of Yugoslavia* (New York: St. Martin's Press, 1970).
64. See Joseph Swire, *Bulgarian Conspiracy* (London: Hale, 1939).
65. On the reign of Boris, see Stephane Groueff, *Crown of Thorns: The Reign of King Boris III of Bulgaria, 1918–1943* (Lanham, MD: Madison, 1987).

66. See Elisabeth Barker, *Macedonia: Its Place in Balkan Power Politics* (London: Royal Institute of International Affairs, 1950).

67. For the Greek Civil War, see: Evangelos Kofos, *Nationalism and Communism in Macedonia* (Thessaloniki: Institute for Balkan Studies, 1964); D. George Kousoulas, *Revolution and Defeat: The Story of the Greek Communist Party* (London: Oxford University Press, 1965); Edgar O'Ballance, *The Greek Civil War, 1944–1949* (New York: Praeger, 1966); Stephen E. Palmer, Jr., and Robert R. King, *Yugoslav Communism and the Macedonian Question* (Hamden, CT: Shoestring Press, 1971); and Christopher M. Woodhouse, *The Struggle for Greece, 1941–1949* (London: Hart-Davis, MacGibbon, 1976).

68. See Stavro Skendi, *The Albanian National Awakening, 1878–1912* (Princeton, NJ: Princeton University Press, 1967). Two general studies of Albania are: Stefanq Pollo and Arben Puto, *The History of Albania: From Its Origins to the Present Day* (London: Routledge & Kegan Paul, 1981); and Joseph Swire, *Albania: The Rise of a Kingdom* (London: William & Ungate, 1929).

69. For Zog, see: Bernd J. Fischer, *King Zog and the Struggle for Stability in Albania* (Boulder, CO: East European Monographs, 1984); Vandeleur Robinson, *Albania's Road to Freedom* (London: Allen & Unwin, 1941); and Joseph Swire, *King Zog's Albania* (London: Robert Hale, 1937).

Between Warsaw and Moscow

1. For Mieszko, see Zygmunt Wojciechowski, *Mieszko I and the Rise of the Polish State* (Toruń-Gdynia: Baltic Institute, 1936).

2. See Pawel Jasienica, *Piast Poland,* trans. Alexander T. Jordan (New York: Hippocrene, 1985), for developments.

3. For Kiev, see George Vernadsky, *Kievan Russia* (New Haven, CT: Yale University Press, 1948).

4. For this complex period, see the relevant passages in Francis Dvornik, *The Slavs in European History and Civilization* (New Brunswick, NJ: Rutgers University Press, 1962), esp. chap. 1 and 2.

5. For Poland at this time, see Paul Knoll, *The Rise of the Polish Monarchy: Piast Poland in East Central Europe, 1320–1370* (Chicago, IL: University of Chicago Press, 1972). For the establishment of the first Polish university, see Kazimierz Lepszy, *Jagiellonian University of Cracow: Past, Present and Future* (Cracow: Jagiellonian University Press, 1964).

6. See: Charlotte Kellogg, *Jadwiga, Poland's Great Queen* (New York: Macmillan, 1931); and Oskar Halecki, *Jadwiga of Anjou and the Rise of East Central Europe* (Boulder, CO: East European Monographs, 1991).

7. For Louis and aspects of his reign, see S. Béla Várdy, G. Grosschmid, and L.S. Domonkos, eds., *Louis the Great, King of Hungary and Poland* (Boulder, CO: East European Monographs, 1986).

8. See Pawel Jasienica, *Jagiellonian Poland,* trans. Alexander T. Jordan (Miami, FL: American Institute of Polish Culture, 1978).

9. The "Jagiellonian System" is expounded by Oskar Halecki in his *A History of Poland,* trans. Monica M. Gardner and Mary Corbridge-Patkanowska (New York: Roy, 1943), 95–105.

10. See Ivo Banac and Frank E. Sysyn, eds., *Concepts of Nationhood in Early Modern Eastern Europe* (Cambridge, MA: Harvard University Press, 1986).

11. See: Tadeusz Cyprian, *Nazi Rule in Poland, 1939–1945* (Warsaw: Polonia, 1961); and Jan T. Gross, *Polish Society under German Occupation* (Princeton, NJ: Princeton University Press, 1979).

12. See Norman Davies, *Heart of Europe: A Short History of Poland* (Oxford: Oxford University Press, 1984), 81–82.

13. See Gale Stokes, *The Walls Came Tumbling Down: The Collapse of Communism in Eastern Europe* (New York: Oxford University Press, 1993), 181–84, 186, 210–11.
14. See S.C. Rowell, *Lithuania Ascending: A Pagan Empire Within East-Central Europe, 1295–1345* (Cambridge: Cambridge University Press, 1994).
15. For Lublin, see Harry E. Dembkowski, *The Union of Lublin: Polish Federalism in the Golden Age* (Boulder, CO: East European Monographs, 1982).
16. See Andrzej Kamiński, "The *Szlachta* of the Polish-Lithuanian Commonwealth and Their Government," in Ivo Banac and Paul Bushkovitch, eds., *The Nobility in Russia and Eastern Europe* (New Haven, CT: Yale University Press, 1983), 14–45.
17. For the Reformation in Poland, see: Paul Fox, *The Reformation in Poland: Some Social and Economic Aspects* (Baltimore, MD: Johns Hopkins University Press, 1924); Stanisław Kot, *Socinianism in Poland: The Social and Political Ideas of the Polish Antitrinitarians in the XVIth and XVIIth Centuries* (Boston: Starr King Press, 1957); Antony Polonsky, ed., *The Jews in Old Poland: Jewish Communities in the Polish-Lithuanian Commonwealth, 1000–1795* (New York: St. Martin's Press, 1993); and Janusz Tazbir, *State Without Stakes: Polish Religious Toleration in the Sixteenth and Seventeenth Century* (New York: Kościuszko Foundation, 1973).
18. See Pawel Jasienica, *The Commonwealth of Both Nations*, trans. Alexander T. Jordan (Miami, FL: American Institute of Polish Culture, 1990).
19. See George Vernadsky, *Russia at the Dawn of the Modern Age* (New Haven, CT: Yale University Press, 1959), for Ivan III and his Lithuanian problems.
20. For Ivan IV, see: Ian Grey, *Ivan the Terrible* (Philadelphia, PA:: Lippincott, 1964); Sergei Platonov, *Ivan the Terrible*, trans. Joseph L. Wieczynski (Gulf Breeze, FL: Academic International Press, 1974); and A. Yanov, *Ivan the Terrible in Russian History*, trans. S. Dunn (Berkeley: University of California Press, 1981).
21. For the "Third Rome" theory, see: D. Stremooukhoff, "Moscow, the Third Rome: Sources of the Doctrine," *Speculum* 28 (1953); Constantine Toumanoff, "Moscow the Third Rome: Genesis and Significance of a Politico-Religious Idea," *Catholic Historical Journal* 40 (1955): 411–47; and Robert L. Wolff, "The Three Romes: The Migration of an Ideology and the Making of an Autocrat," *Daedalus* (Boston, 1959), 291–311.
22. See J. Pelensky, *Russia and Kazan: Conquest and Imperial Ideology (1438–1560)* (The Hague: Mouton, 1974).
23. See William Urban, *The Livonian Crusade* (Washington, DC: University Press of America, 1981).
24. For the papal peace mediation, see Antonio Possevino, *The Moscovia*, trans. Hugh F. Graham (Pittsburgh, PA: University of Pittsburgh Press, 1977).
25. See Oskar Halecki, *From Florence to Brest (1439–1596)* (Rome: Sacrum Poloniæ Millennium, 1958).
26. For the pretender and surrounding events, see Philip Barbour, *Dimitry, Called the Pretender, Tsar and Great Prince of All Russia, 1605–1606* (London: Macmillan, 1967).
27. For the "Time of Troubles," see: S. Platonov, *The Time of Troubles*, trans. J. Alexander (Lawrence: University of Kansas Press, 1970); and George Vernadsky, *The Tsardom of Moscow, 1547–1682* (New Haven, CT: Yale University Press, 1969).
28. See Vasili Klyuchevsky, *A Course in Russian History: The Seventeenth Century*, trans. Natalie Duddington (Chicago, IL: Quadrangle, 1968).
29. For a general survey of the Baltic warfare in the seventeenth century, see Jill Lisk, *The Struggle for Supremacy in the Baltic: 1600–1725* (Portsmith, NH: Minerva, 1968).
30. See M. Hrushevsky, *A History of Ukraine*, ed. O.J. Frederikes (London: Oxford University Press, 1941).
31. See Linda Gordon, *Cossack Rebellions: Social Turmoil in the Sixteenth-Century Ukraine* (Albany: State University of New York Press, 1983).

32. See Maurice Hindus, *The Cossacks: The Story of a Warrior People* (Westport, CT: Greenwood, 1970).
33. See George Vernadsky, *Bohdan, Hetman of Ukraine* (New Haven, CT: Yale University Press, 1941).
34. See: John Basarab, *Pereiaslaval 1654: A Historical Study* (Edmonton, Alberta: University of Alberta Press, 1982); and C. Bickford O'Brien, *Muscovy and the Ukraine: From the Pereiaslavl Agreement to the Truce of Andrusovo, 1654–1667* (Berkeley: University of California Press, 1963).
35. See: Robert I. Frost, *After the Deluge: Poland-Lithuania and the Second Northern War, 1655–1660* (Cambridge: Cambridge University Press, 1993); and John Stoye, *Europe Unfolding, 1648–1688* (New York: Harper & Row, 1969).
36. See Peter J. Potichnyj, "The Cossack Experiment in Szlachta Democracy in the Polish-Lithuanian Commonwealth: The Hadiach (Hadziacz) Union," *Harvard Ukrainian Studies* 1, no. 2 (1977): 178–97.
37. For Poland in decline, see Pawel Jasienica, *Calamity of the Realm*, trans. Alexander T. Jordan (Miami, FL: American Institute of Polish Culture, 1992). Also see the relevant studies in J.K. Fedorowicz, ed. and trans., *A Republic of Nobles: Studies in Polish History to 1864* (Cambridge: Cambridge University Press, 1982).
38. See John B. Morton, *Sobieski, King of Poland* (London: Eyre & Spotteswoode, 1932).
39. See the relevant passages in Lisk.
40. For the role of the tsar in Russian history and culture, see Michael Cherniavsky, *Tsar and People: Studies in Russian Myths* (New York: Random House, 1969). For Peter, see: Vasili Klyuchevsky, *Peter the Great*, trans. Liliana Archibald (New York: Vintage, 1958); and Benedict H. Sumner, *Peter the Great and the Emergence of Russia* (New York: Collier, 1968).
41. See Andrzej Walicki, *The Enlightenment and the Birth of Modern Nationhood: Polish Political Thought from Noble Republicanism to Tadeusz Kościuszko* (Notre Dame, IN: University of Notre Dame Press, 1989). No adequate work in English is available for the *liberum veto*. The best Western-language study is Władysław Konopczynski, *Le Liberum veto: étude sur le développement du principe majoritaire* (Paris: Champion, 1930).
42. For the final century prior to the partitions, see Pawel Jasienica, *The Tale of an Agony*, trans. Alexander T. Jordan (Miami, FL: American Institute of Polish Culture, 1992).
43. For Poniatowski, see Robert N. Bain, *The Last King of Poland and His Contemporaries* (New York: Arno, 1971).
44. See Herbert H. Kaplan, *The First Partition of Poland* (New York: Columbia University Press, 1962).
45. See Jerzy Łojek, "The International Crisis of 1791: Poland Between the Triple Alliance and Russia," *East Central Europe* 2, no. 1 (1975): 1–63.
46. See Robert H. Lord, *The Second Partition of Poland: A Study in Diplomatic History* (Cambridge, MA: Harvard University Press, 1915).
47. For Kościuszko, see Miecislaus Haiman, *Kościuszko: Leader and Exile* (New York: Polish Institute of Arts and Sciences in America, 1946). For the final partition, see Robert H. Lord, "The Third Partition of Poland," *Slavonic and East European Review* 3 (March 1925): 481–98.
48. See the relevant passages in Hannah A. Straus, *The Attitude of the Congress of Vienna Toward Nationalism in Germany, Italy and Poland* (New York: Columbia University Press, 1949).
49. For Czartoryski, see Marian Kukiel, *Czartoryski and European Unity, 1770–1861* (Princeton, NJ: Princeton University Press, 1955).
50. For the Congress Kingdom of Poland under Alexander I, see Frank W. Thackeray, *Antecedents of Revolution: Alexander I and the Polish Kingdom, 1815–1825* (Boulder, CO: East European Monographs, 1980).
51. See Roy F. Leslie, *Polish Politics and the Revolution of November 1830* (London: Athlone, 1956).

52. For the emigration nationalists, see Peter Brock, "Polish Nationalism," in Peter F. Sugar and Ivo J. Lederer, eds., *Nationalism in Eastern Europe* (Seattle: University of Washington Press, 1969), 310–72.

53. See: Arthur P. and Marion M. Coleman, *The Polish Insurrection of 1863 in the Light of New York Editorial Opinion* (Williamsport, PA: Bayard, 1934); and Roy F. Leslie, *Reform and Insurrection in Russian Poland, 1856–1863* (London: Athlone, 1963).

54. See Jerzy Jedlicki, "State Industrial Economy in the Kingdom of Poland in the 19th Century," *Acta Poloniæ Historica* 18 (1968): 221–37.

55. For the separate development of the Poles dispersed among the three partitioning powers during the nineteenth century, see Piotr Wandycz, *The Lands of Partitioned Poland*, 2nd ed. (Seattle: University of Washington Press, 1984). Also see Roy F. Leslie, ed., *The History of Poland Since 1863* (Cambridge: Cambridge University Press, 1980). For Poles in the Habsburg Empire, see Andrei S. Markovits and Frank E. Sysyn, eds., *Nationbuilding and the Politics of Nationalism: Essays on Austrian Galicia* (Cambridge, MA: Harvard University Press, 1982). For Poles in Germany, see: Richard Blanke, *Prussian Poland in the German Empire, 1871–1900* (Boulder, CO: East European Monographs, 1981); and Richard W. Tims, *Germanizing Prussian Poland: The H-K-T Society and the Struggle for the Eastern Marches in the German Empire, 1894–1919* (New York: Columbia University Press, 1941).

56. See Brock, 328–50.

57. See Walter Kolarz, *Myths and Realities in Eastern Europe* (London: Lindsay Drummond, 1946), 99–117.

58. For Piłsudski, the single most influential figure in interwar Poland, see: Wacław Jedrzejewicz, *Pilsudski, A Life for Poland* (New York: Hippocrene, 1982); and William F. Reddaway, *Marshal Pilsudski* (London: Routledge, 1939).

59. See Titus Komarnicki, *Rebirth of the Polish Republic: A Study in the Diplomatic History of Europe, 1914–1920* (London: William Heinemann, 1957).

60. See: the relevant passages in W. Bruce Lincoln, *Red Victory: A History of the Russian Civil War* (New York: Simon & Schuster, 1989); Piotr S. Wandycz, *Soviet-Polish Relations, 1917–1921* (Cambridge, MA: Harvard University Press, 1969); and Adam Zamoyski, *The Battle for the Marchlands: The Russo-Polish Campaign of 1920* (Boulder, CO: East European Monographs, 1981).

61. See Anna M. Cienciala and Titus Komarnicki, *From Versailles to Locarno: Keys to Polish Foreign Policy, 1919–1939* (New York: Praeger, 1962).

62. For the economic aspects of the partition legacy, see Roman Gorecki, *Poland and Her Economic Development* (London: Allen & Unwin, 1935); for the political, see Antony Polansky, *Politics in Independent Poland, 1921–1939: The Crisis of Constitutional Government* (Oxford: Clarendon, 1972); and for the ethnic, see Stephen Horak, *Poland and Her National Minorities, 1919–1939: A Case Study* (New York: Vantage, 1961).

63. For the military aspects of Polish national politics, see Jerzy Wiatr, *The Soldier and the Nation: The Role of the Military in Polish Politics, 1918–1985* (Boulder, CO: Westview, 1988).

64. Regarding French-Polish relations, see the relevant passages in two studies by Piotr Wandycz: *France and Her Eastern Allies, 1919–25* (Minneapolis: University of Minnesota Press, 1962) and *The Twilight of French Eastern Alliances, 1926–36* (Princeton, NJ: Princeton University Press, 1988). Also see Jan Karski, *The Great Powers and Poland, 1919–1945: From Versailles to Yalta* (Lanham, MD: University Press of America, 1985). For relations with Germany, see Harold von Riekhoff, *German-Polish Relations, 1918–1933* (Baltimore, MD: Johns Hopkins University Press, 1971). And for relations with the Soviet Union, see: Bohdan B. Budurowycz, *Polish-Soviet Relations, 1932–1939* (New York: Columbia University Press, 1963); and Josef Korbel, *Poland Between East and West: Soviet and German Diplomacy Toward Poland, 1919–1933* (Princeton, NJ: Princeton University Press, 1963).

298   CONFLICT AND CHAOS IN EASTERN EUROPE

65. See: Bernadotte E. Schmitt, ed., *Poland* (Berkeley: University of California Press, 1945); and Ferdynand Zweig, *Poland Between Two Wars: A Critical Study of Social and Economic Changes* (London: Secker & Warburg, 1944).
66. In A.J.P. Taylor's controversial but highly logical study, *The Origins of the Second World War,* 2nd ed. (New York: Atheneum, 1961), he disputes the commonly held notion that Hitler possessed such a premeditated plan.
67. See Gerald Freund, *Unholy Alliance: Russo-German Relations from the Treaty of Brest-Litovsk to the Treaty of Berlin* (London: Chatto & Windus, 1957).
68. See Leonard Mosley, *On Borrowed Time: How World War II Began* (New York: Random House, 1969), for a detailed account of the negotiations.
69. See: Jan Ciechanowski, *The Warsaw Rising* (Cambridge: Cambridge University Press, 1975); Tadeusz Bór-Komorowski, *The Secret Army* (New York: Macmillan, 1950); and Stefan Korbonski, *Fighting Warsaw: The Story of the Polish Underground State, 1939–1945* (New York: Funk & Wagnalls, 1968).
70. See: Herbert Feis, *Between War and Peace: The Potsdam Conference* (Princeton, NJ: Princeton University Press, 1960); Wenkel Jakisch, *Europe's Road to Potsdam* (New York: Praeger, 1963); and John L. Snell, ed., *The Meaning of Yalta: Big Three Diplomacy and the New Balance of Power* (Baton Rouge: Louisiana State University Press, 1956).

Bosnia: Shots Heard 'Round the World

1. For post-Versailles Yugoslavia, see Stephen Clissold, ed., *A Short History of Yugoslavia from Early Times to 1966* (Cambridge: Cambridge University Press, 1966).
2. See the pertinent passages in "Macedonian Mischiefs" herein.
3. For the nature of culture, as viewed in this context, see Dennis P. Hupchick, *Culture and History in Eastern Europe* (St. Martin's Press, 1994), 5–8, 13–14, 26–28, 32–34.
4. For useful geographical descriptions, see the pertinent passages in the Yugoslav sections of: Monica and Robert Beckinsale, *Southern Europe: A Systematic Geographical Study* (New York: Holmes & Meier, 1975); and R.H. Osborne, *East-Central Europe: An Introductory Geography* (New York: Frederick A. Praeger, 1967).
5. There are no general English-language studies treating specifically with medieval Bosnia. For our essay, we have depended heavily on: Francis Dvornik, *The Slavs in European History and Civilization* (New Brunswick, NJ: Rutgers University Press, 1962); and, especially, John V.A. Fine, Jr., *The Late Medieval Balkans: A Critical Survey from the Late Twelfth Century to the Ottoman Conquest* (Ann Arbor: University of Michigan Press, 1987).
6. For Croatia during this period, see Stanko Guldescu, *History of Medieval Croatia* (The Hague: Mouton, 1964).
7. For Bogomilism and its offshoots, see: Dimitri Obolensky, *The Bogomils: A Study in Balkan Neo-Manichæism* (Cambridge: Cambridge University Press, 1948); Steven Runciman, *The Medieval Manichee* (Cambridge: Cambridge University Press, 1967); and Victor N. Sharenkoff, *A Study of Manichæism in Bulgaria; with Special Reference to the Bogomils* (New York: Columbia University Press, 1927).
8. See Fine, *Late Medieval Balkans,* 143–45.
9. For the Bosnian church, see John V.A. Fine, Jr., *The Bosnian Church: A New Interpretation* (Boulder, CO: East European Monographs, 1975).
10. See Fine, *Late Medieval Balkans,* 142–43, 266–68.
11. For Kotromanić, see Ibid., 275–85.
12. For Tvrtko, see Ibid., 368–70, 392–95. For Dubrovnik and its role in the Balkan northwest during this period, see B. Krekić, *Dubrovnik in the Fourteenth and Fifteenth Centuries* (Norman: University of Oklahoma Press, 1972).
13. See Fine, *Late Medieval Balkans,* 453–84 (for political developments), 481–88 (for religious). For Hungary after Sigismund and for the battles against the Turks, see Joseph Held, *Hunyadi: Legend and Reality* (Boulder, CO: East European Monographs, 1985). For the

rising tide of Ottoman conquest, see Franz Babinger, *Mehmed the Conqueror and His Time*, trans. Ralph Manheim (Princeton, NJ: Princeton University Press, 1978).

14. See Fine, *Late Medieval Balkans*, 578–80.
15. See Ibid., 581–90.
16. Of some interest is Vaughn Cornish, "Bosnia: The Borderland of Serb and Croat," *Geography* 20 (December 1935): 260–70.
17. This is the interpretation advanced by Fine in *The Bosnian Church*.
18. For brief overviews of Ottoman state structure, see: Norman Itzkowitz, *Ottoman Empire and Islamic Tradition* (Chicago: University of Chicago Press, 1980); and Wayne S. Vucinich, *The Ottoman Empire: Its Record and Legacy* (Princeton, NJ: Van Nostrand, 1965).
19. For the *millets*, see: Theodore H. Papadopoullos, *Studies and Documents Relating to the History of the Greek Church and People under Turkish Domination* (Brussels: Bibliotheca Græca ævi posterioris, 1, 1952); Steven Runciman, *The Great Church in Captivity: A Study of the Patriarchate of Constantinople From the Eve of the Turkish Conquest to the Greek War of Independence* (London: Cambridge University Press, 1968); and Peter F. Sugar, *Southeastern Europe under Ottoman Rule, 1354–1804* (Seattle: University of Washington Press, 1977).
20. See Halil Inalcik, "Ottoman Methods of Conquest," *Studia Islamica* 2 (1954): 103–30.
21. For the process of Islamization within the Ottoman military, see Dennis P. Hupchick, *The Bulgarians in the Seventeenth Century: Slavic Orthodox Society and Culture under Ottoman Rule* (Jefferson, NC: McFarland, 1993), 61–62.
22. For the role of the *dervişes*, see: the relevant passages in Sugar, *Southeastern Europe;* Halil Inalcik, *The Ottoman Empire: The Classical Age, 1300–1600*, trans. Norman Itzkowitz and Colin Imber (London: Weidenfeld & Nicolson, 1973), esp. chap. 19. The latter work is particularly valuable for all aspects of Ottoman society during the period that it examines. Also see Mark Pinson, ed., *The Muslims of Bosnia-Herzegovina* (Cambridge, MA: Harvard University Press, 1994), which is the first attempt in English to treat with the entire history of the Bosnian Muslims.
23. Sugar, *Southeastern Europe*, 50–52.
24. Ibid., 51.
25. See Inalcik, *Ottoman Empire*, pt. 3.
26. For the Ottoman decline and its consequences, see: Hupchick, *The Bulgarians*, 31–37; Lord [John P.D.B.] Kinross, *The Ottoman Centuries: The Rise and Fall of the Turkish Empire* (New York: Quill, 1977); Alan Palmer, *The Decline and Fall of the Ottoman Empire* (New York: M. Evans, 1992); and Sugar, *Southeastern Europe*, pt. 4.
27. See Sugar, *Southeastern Europe*, chap. 11 (Pasvanoğlu and Ali are treated on pp. 238-40). For Ali, see William F. Plomer, *Ali the Lion: Ali of Tebeleni, Pasha of Yanina, 1741–1822* (London: J. Cape, 1936).
28. Sugar, *Southeastern Europe*, 236–37.
29. L.S. Stavrianos, *The Balkans Since 1453* (New York: Holt, Rinehart & Winston, 1958), 236–37.
30. Sugar, *Southeastern Europe*, 236–37.
31. See Stanko Guldescu, *The Croatian-Slavonian Kingdom, 1526–1792* (The Hague: Mouton, 1970).
32. See Gunther E. Rothenburg, *The Austrian Military Border in Croatia, 1522-1747* (Urbana: University of Illinois, 1960).
33. See Stanko Guldescu, "Croatian Political History, 1526–1918," in Francis H. Eterovich and Christopher Spalatin, eds., *Croatia: Land, People and Culture*, vol. 2 (Toronto: University of Toronto Press, 1970), 9.
34. Stavrianos, *The Balkans*, 236.
35. See Michael B. Petrovich, *A History of Modern Serbia, 1804–1918*, vol. 1 (New York: Harcourt Brace Jovanovich, 1976).

36. For the philosophical nationalist framework for Greater Serbia, see Walter Kolarz, *Myths and Realities in Eastern Europe* (London: Lindsay Drummond, 1946), 189–212.
37. See Gunther E. Rothenburg, "The Croatian Military Border and the Rise of Yugoslav Nationalism," *Slavonic and East European Review* 43 (December 1964): 34–45.
38. See George J. Prpić, "French Rule in Croatia, 1806–1813," *Balkan Studies* 5, no. 2 (1964): 221–76.
39. See Ante Kadić, *From Croatian Renaissance to Yugoslav Socialism* (The Hague: Mouton, 1969).
40. For Gaj and the "Illyrians," see Elinor M. Despalatović, *Ljudevit Gaj and the Illyrian Movement* (Boulder, CO: East European Monographs, 1975).
41. See Hans Kohn, *Pan-Slavism: Its History and Ideology,* 2nd ed (New York: Vintage, 1960).
42. See Oszkar Jaszi, *The Dissolution of the Habsburg Monarchy* (Chicago, IL: University of Chicago Press, 1929).
43. See the relevant passages in: Robert A. Kann, *The Multinational Empire: Nationalism and National Reform in the Habsburg Monarchy, 1848–1918,* 2 vols. (New York: Columbia University Press, 1950); Arthur J. May, *The Habsburg Monarchy, 1867–1914* (Cambridge, MA: Harvard University Press, 1951); and R.W. Seton-Watson, *The Southern Slav Question and the Habsburg Monarchy* (New York: H. Fertig, 1969).
44. Stavrianos, *The Balkans,* 397–403.
45. For the Russian Panslav role, see David MacKenzie, *The Serbs and Russian Pan-Slavism* (Ithaca, NY: Cornell University Press, 1967).
46. For the Great Power diplomatic efforts, see: Barbara Jelavich, *The Ottoman Empire, the Great Powers, and the Straits Question, 1870–1887* (Bloomington: Indiana University Press, 1973); Mihailo D. Stojanović, *The Great Powers and the Balkans, 1875–1878* (Cambridge: Cambridge University Press, 1939); and Benedict H. Sumner, *Russia and the Balkans, 1870–1880* (Oxford: Oxford University Press, 1937).
47. See William N. Medlicott, *The Congress of Berlin and After: A Diplomatic History of the Near Eastern Settlement, 1878–1880* (London: Metheun, 1938).
48. See Peter F. Sugar, *Industrialization of Bosnia-Hercegovina, 1878–1918* (Seattle: University of Washington Press, 1963). For the position of the Bosnian Muslims under Habsburg rule, see Robert J. Donia, *Islam under the Double Eagle: The Muslims of Bosnia and Hercegovina, 1878–1914* (Boulder, CO: East European Monographs, 1981).
49. Stavrianos, *The Balkans,* 462.
50. Ibid., 462–63.
51. See Ivo J. Lederer, "Nationalism and the Yugoslavs," in Peter F. Sugar and Ivo J. Lederer, eds., *Nationalism in Eastern Europe* (Seattle: University of Washington Press, 1969), 420–22.
52. For Hungary's divide and rule approach, see Guldescu, "Political History," 51–55.
53. For the Serbo-Croat alliance, see the relevant passages in: L.S. Stavrianos, *Balkan Federation: A History of the Movement toward Balkan Unity in Modern Times* (Hamden, CT: Archon, 1964); and Wayne S. Vucinich, *Serbia Between East and West: The Events of 1903–1908* (Stanford, CA: Stanford University Press, 1954).
54. For the Young Turks, see: Feroz Ahmad, *The Young Turks: The Committee of Union and Progress in Turkish Politics, 1908–1914* (Oxford: Clarendon, 1969); and Ernest E. Ramsaur, Jr., *The Young Turks: Prelude to the Revolution of 1908* (Princeton, NJ: Princeton University Press, 1957). For the international repercussions, see: Andrew Rossos, *Russia and the Balkans: Inter-Balkan Rivalries and Russian Foreign Policy, 1908–1914* (Toronto: University of Toronto Press, 1981); and Bernadotte E. Schmitt, *The Annexation of Bosnia, 1908–1909* (Cambridge: Cambridge University Press, 1937).
55. See Guldescu, "Political History," 63–64.
56. Stavrianos, *The Balkans,* 463–64.

57. For Serb and Bosnian Serb nationalist activities, and for events leading up to the Sarajevo assassination, see Vladimir Didijer, *The Road to Sarajevo* (New York: Simon & Schuster, 1966).
58. Lederer, "Nationalism," 428–32.
59. See: Dimitrije Djordjević, ed., *The Creation of Yugoslavia, 1914–1918* (Oxford: Oxford University Press, 1980); and Ivo J. Lederer, *Yugoslavia at the Paris Peace Conference: A Study in Frontier-Making* (New Haven, CT: Yale University Press, 1963).
60. See Ivo Banac, *The National Question in Yugoslavia: Origins, History, Politics* (Ithaca, NY: Cornell University Press, 1993).
61. See Charles A. Beard and George Radin, *The Balkan Pivot: Yugoslavia. A Study in Government and Administration* (New York: Macmillan, 1929).
62. For Alexander, see Stephen Graham, *Alexander of Yugoslavia* (New Haven, CT: Yale University Press, 1939).
63. For events in the last decade before Hitler's invasion, see: Jacob B. Hoptner, *Yugoslavia in Crisis, 1934–1941* (New York: Columbia University Press, 1962); Vladko Maček, *In the Struggle for Freedom*, trans. Elizabeth and Stephen Gazi (New York: R. Speller, 1957); and Rebecca West, *Black Lamb and Grey Falcon: A Journey Through Yugoslavia* (New York: Viking, 1943).
64. For conditions in partitioned Yugoslavia and the resistance movements, see: Matteo J. Milazzo, *The Chetnik Movement and the Yugoslav Resistance* (Baltimore, MD: Johns Hopkins University Press, 1975); Walter R. Roberts, *Tito, Mihailović and the Allies, 1941–1945* (New Brunswick, NJ: Rutgers University Press, 1973); and Jozo Tomasevich, *The Chetniks: War and Revolution in Yugoslavia, 1941–1945* (Stanford, CA: Stanford University Press, 1975).
65. See Paul Shoup, *Communism and the Yugoslav National Question* (New York: Columbia University Press, 1968).
66. See Stephen Clissold, *Whirlwind: An Account of Marshal Tito's Rise to Power* (New York: Philosophical Library, 1949).
67. For Tito's Yugoslavia and Bosnia's place in it, see: Stevan K. Pavlowitch, *Yugoslavia* (New York: Praeger, 1971); Dennison Rusinow, *The Yugoslav Experiment, 1948-1974* (Berkeley: University of California Press, 1977); and Duncan Wilson, *Tito's Yugoslavia* (Cambridge: Cambridge University Press, 1979).

◙ SELECT BIBLIOGRAPHY ◙

The titles that follow are presented to supplement those cited in the notes to the individual essays in this collection. For the most part, they represent general studies that can be applied to particular essays or to more than one. While some have been listed in the notes, they have been included here because their usefulness is broader than any single topic, or because it is believed that they are of intrinsic interest to the general reader or student.

Barker, Elisabeth. *Macedonia: Its Place in Balkan Power Politics*. London: Royal Institute of International Affairs, 1950.

Bogdan, Henry. *From Warsaw to Sofia: A History of Eastern Europe*. Translated by Jeanie P. Fleming. Santa Fe, NM: Pro Libertate, 1989.

Borsody, Stephen, ed. *The Hungarians: A Divided Nation*. New Haven, CT: Yale Center for International and Area Studies, 1988.

_____. *The Tragedy of Central Europe: The Nazi and Soviet Conquest of Central Europe*. New York: Collier Books, 1962.

Clarke, James F. *The Pen and the Sword: Studies in Bulgarian History*. Edited by Dennis P. Hupchick. Boulder, CO: East European Monographs, 1988.

Clogg, Richard. *A Short History of Modern Greece*. Cambridge: Cambridge University Press, 1979.

Crampton, Richard J. *A Short History of Modern Bulgaria*. Cambridge: Cambridge University Press, 1987.

Davies, Norman. *God's Playground, A History of Poland*. 2 vols. New York: Columbia University Press, 1982.

_____. *Heart of Europe: A Short History of Poland*. Oxford: Oxford University Press, 1986.

Dedijer, Vladimir. *The Road to Sarajevo*. New York: Simon & Schuster, 1966.

Dedijer, Vladimir, et al. *History of Yugoslavia*. Translated by Kordija Kveder. New York: McGraw-Hill, 1974.

Djordjević Dimitrije, ed. *The Creation of Yugoslavia*. Santa Barbara, CA: Clio, 1980.

Dvornik, Francis. *The Slavs in European History and Civilization*. New Brunswick, NJ: Rutgers University Press, 1962.

Eterovich, Francis H., and Christopher Spalatin, eds. *Croatia: Land, People and Culture*. 2 vols. Toronto: University of Toronto Press, 1964–70.

Fine, John V.A., Jr. *The Early Medieval Balkans: A Critical Survey From the Sixth to the Late Twelfth Century*. Ann Arbor: University of Michigan Press, 1983.

_____. *The Late Medieval Balkans: A Critical Survey from the Late Twelfth Century to the Ottoman Conquest*. Ann Arbor: University of Michigan Press, 1987.

Fischer-Galati, Stephen, et al., eds. *Romania Between East and West: Historical Essays in Memory of Constantin C. Giurescu*. Boulder, CO: East European Monographs, 1982.

Florescu, Radu, and Raymond T. McNally. *Dracula, Prince of Many Faces: His Life and His Times*. Boston: Little, Brown, 1989.

Gazi, Stephen. *A History of Croatia*. New York: Philosophical Library, 1973.

Guldescu, Stanko. *History of Medieval Croatia*. The Hague: Mouton, 1964.

Halecki, Oskar. *Borderlands of Western Civilization: A History of East Central Europe*. New York: Ronald Press, 1952.

_____. *A History of Poland*. Translated by Monica M. Gardner and Mary Corbridge-Patkaniowska. New York: Roy Publishers, 1943.

_____. *The Limits and Divisions of European History*. Notre Dame, IN: University of Notre Dame Press, 1962.

Hoensch, Jorg K. *A History of Modern Hungary.* London: Longman, 1988.

Hupchick, Dennis P. *Culture and History in Eastern Europe.* New York: St. Martin's Press, 1994.

Inalcik, Halil. *The Ottoman Empire: The Classical Age, 1300–1600.* Translated by Norman Itzkowitz and Colin Imber. London: Weidenfeld & Nicolson, 1973.

Itzkowitz, Norman. *Ottoman Empire and Islamic Tradition.* Chicago: University of Chicago Press, 1980.

Jelavich, Barbara. *History of the Balkans.* 2 vols. Cambridge: Cambridge University Press, 1985.

Jelavich, Charles, and Barbara Jelavich. *The Establishment of the Balkan National States, 1804–1920.* Seattle: University of Washington Press, 1977.

Jelavich, Charles, ed. *The Balkans in Transition: Essays on the Development of Balkan Life and Politics Since the Eighteenth Century.* Berkeley: University of California Press, 1963.

Kann, Robert A. *A History of the Habsburg Empire, 1526–1918.* Berkeley: University of California Press, 1974.

Kaplan, Robert. *Balkan Ghosts: A Journey Through History.* New York: St. Martin's Press, 1993.

Lang, David M. *The Bulgarians: From Pagan Times to the Ottoman Conquest.* Boulder, CO: Westview Press, 1976.

Lendvai, Paul. *Eagles in Cobwebs: Nationalism and Communism in the Balkans.* Garden City, NY: Doubleday, 1969.

Kinross, Lord [John P.D.B.]. *The Ottoman Centuries: The Rise and Fall of the Turkish Empire.* New York: Quill, 1977.

Kohn, Hans. *Pan-Slavism: Its History and Ideology.* 2nd rev. ed. New York: Vintage Books, 1960.

Kolarz, Walter. *Myths and Realities in Eastern Europe.* London: Lindsay Drummond, 1946.

Korbel, Josef. *Twentieth Century Czechoslovakia: The Meaning of Its History.* New York: Columbia University Press, 1977.

Macartney, C.A. *Hungary: A Short History.* Chicago: Aldine, 1962.

———. *Hungary and Her Successors.* London: Oxford University Press, 1937.

Macartney, C.A., and A.W. Palmer. *Independent Eastern Europe: A History.* London: Macmillan, 1966.

MacDermott, Mercia. *A History of Bulgaria, 1393–1885.* New York: Praeger, 1962.

Malcolm, Noel. *Bosnia: A Short History.* London: Macmillan, 1994.

May, Arthur J. *The Habsburg Monarchy, 1867–1914.* Cambridge, MA: Harvard University Press, 1951.

Mikuš, Joseph A. *Slovakia: A Political History, 1918–1950.* Milwaukee, WI: Marquette University Press, 1963.

Obolensky, Dimitri. *The Byzantine Commonwealth: Eastern Europe, 500–1453.* New York: Praeger, 1971.

Oddo, Gilbert L. *Slovakia and Its People.* New York: Robert Speller & Sons, 1960.

Okey, Robin. *Eastern Europe 1740–1985: Feudalism to Communism.* 2nd ed. Minneapolis: University of Minnesota Press, 1986.

Osborne, R.H. *East-Central Europe: An Introductory Geography.* New York: Frederick A. Praeger, 1967.

Palmer, Alan. *The Decline and Fall of the Ottoman Empire.* New York: M. Evans, 1992.

———. *The Lands Between: A History of East-Central Europe Since the Congress of Vienna.* New York: Macmillan, 1970.

Petrovich, Michael B. *A History of Modern Serbia, 1804–1918.* 2 vols. New York: Harcourt Brace Jovanovich, 1976.

Pollo, Stefanaq, and Arben Puto. *The History of Albania: From Its Origins to the Present Day.* London: Routledge & Kegan Paul, 1981.

Pribichevich, Stoyan. *Macedonia: Its People and History*. University Park: Pennsylvania State University Press, 1982.

Ramet, Pedro. *Nationalism and Federalism in Yugoslavia, 1963–1983*. Bloomington: Indiana University Press, 1984.

Reddaway, William F., et al., eds. *Cambridge History of Poland*. 2 vols. Cambridge: Cambridge University Press, 1941–50.

Rothenberg, Gunther E. *The Military Border in Croatia, 1740–1881: A Study of an Imperial Institution*. Chicago: University of Chicago Press, 1966.

Rothschild, Joseph. *East Central Europe Between the Two World Wars*. Seattle: University of Washington Press, 1974.

_____. *Return to Diversity: A Political History of East Central Europe Since World War II*. 2nd ed. New York: Oxford University Press, 1993.

Runciman, Steven. *The Great Church in Captivity: A Study of the Patriarchate of Constantinople From the Eve of the Turkish Conquest to the Greek War of Independence*. London: Cambridge University Press, 1968.

Seton-Watson, Hugh. *The East European Revolution*. 3rd ed. New York: Praeger, 1956.

Seton-Watson, R.W. *A History of the Roumanians*. New York: Shoe String Press, 1934.

Shaw, Stanford J. *History of the Ottoman Empire and Modern Turkey*. 2 vols. Cambridge: Cambridge University Press, 1976–77.

Stavrianos, L.S. *The Balkans Since 1453*. New York: Holt, Rinehart & Winston, 1958.

Stoianovich, Traian. *A Study in Balkan Civilization*. New York: Alfred A. Knopf, 1967.

Stokes, Gale. *The Walls Came Tumbling Down: The Collapse of Communism in Eastern Europe*. New York: Oxford University Press, 1993.

Sugar, Peter F. *Southeastern Europe under Ottoman Rule, 1354–1804*. Seattle: University of Washington Press, 1977.

Sugar, Peter F., and Ivo J. Lederer, eds. *Nationalism in Eastern Europe*. Seattle: University of Washington Press, 1969.

Swain, Geoffrey, and Nigel Swain. *Eastern Europe Since 1945*. New York: St. Martin's Press, 1993.

Tapié, Victor-L. *The Rise and Fall of the Habsburg Monarchy*. Translated by Stephen Hardman. New York: Praeger, 1971.

Taylor, A.J.P. *The Habsburg Monarchy, 1809–1918: A History of the Austrian Empire and Austria-Hungary*. New York: Harper & Row, 1965.

Thomson, S. Harrison. *Czechoslovakia in European History*. Hamden, CT: Archon, 1965.

Vakalopoulos, Apostolos E. *The Greek Nation, 1453–1669: The Cultural and Economic Background of Modern Greek Society*. Translated by Ian Moles and Phania Moles. New Brunswick, NJ: Rutgers University Press, 1976.

_____. *History of Macedonia, 1354–1833*. Translated by Peter Megann. Thessaloniki: Institute for Balkan Studies, 1973.

Vucinich, Wayne S. *The Ottoman Empire: Its Record and Legacy*. Reprint ed. Huntington, NY: Robert E. Krieger, 1979.

Walters, E. Garrison. *The Other Europe: Eastern Europe to 1945*. Syracuse, NY: Syracuse University Press, 1988.

Wandycz, Piotr S. *The Price of Freedom: A History of East Central Europe from the Middle Ages to the Present*. London: Routledge, 1992.

West, Rebecca. *Black Lamb and Grey Falcon: A Journey Through Yugoslavia*. New York: Penguin, 1982.

Wilkinson, H.R. *Maps and Politics: A Review of the Ethnographic Cartography of Macedonia*. Liverpool: University Press of Liverpool, 1951.

Wolff, Robert L. *The Balkans in Our Time*. Cambridge, MA: Harvard University Press, 1956.

Woodhouse, Christopher M. *A Short History of Modern Greece*. New York: Praeger, 1968.

◼ INDEX ◼

Enver Pasha, 144
Eötvös, József, 81, 82
Epiros, 106, 135, 141, 147, 253
Essad Pasha, 156
Estonia, 1, 218
Estonians, 92
Esztergom, 41, 69, 70
"ethnic cleansing," 43-44
ethnicity, 4, 5, 7, 13, 22, 42, 54, 55, 57,
 58, 78, 85, 97, 98, 100, 101, 105,
 106, 108, 111, 114-118, 125-126,
 127, 133, 136-137, 142, 143, 152,
 155, 156, 158, 177, 187, 188, 224,
 226, 227, 243, 254, 257-258, 259-
 260, 265, 270, 276-277
Eurasia, 1, 2, 21, 163, 173, 174, 190, 210,
 219
Europe, Eastern (geographic;
 "Orthodox"), 1, 3-4, 5, 16, 24, 40, 41,
 42, 47, 49, 50, 51, 53, 61, 64, 85, 90,
 91, 94, 100, 101, 104, 105, 122, 125,
 140, 157, 158, 163, 164, 167, 168,
 169, 170, 173, 175, 180, 190, 196,
 201, 215, 216, 218, 220, 237, 273,
 279; political culture of, 6, 196, 203,
 273, 279
Europe, Western (geographic; "the
 West"), 1-6, 8, 13, 15, 16, 19, 20, 21,
 24, 38, 51, 54, 56, 58, 70, 83, 88, 94,
 98, 102, 104, 105-106, 108, 109, 110,
 111, 121, 136, 152, 159, 165, 166,
 167, 169, 171, 173, 175, 179, 195,
 201, 203, 204, 213, 217, 221, 223,
 225, 226, 230, 235, 237, 240, 243,
 249, 251, 252, 254, 257, 258, 259,
 278, 279, 280; political culture of, 2-
 6, 7, 8-10, 13, 19-21, 25, 28, 29, 40-
 41, 53, 59, 76-77, 78, 85-86, 88, 92,
 100-101, 102, 107, 165, 166, 169,
 176, 196-198, 200-201, 202, 203,
 208-209, 212, 215, 217, 223-224,
 225-227, 239, 243, 259, 267, 277,
 278, 279
European Union (EU), 47, 157, 158, 159,
 160
Exarchate, Bulgarian, 99, 117-119, 122,
 126-129, 130, 135, 149
External Macedonian Revolutionary
 Organization (EMRO), 131-132

F
fascism (Nazism), 3, 42, 43, 45, 51, 90,
 156, 171-172, 214-215, 216-217,
 221, 273-275, 278
faults, macrocultural, 92; Eastern-
 Western European, 50, 51, 64, 66,
 69, 74, 91, 164, 173, 203, 206, 219,
 226, 237, 257, 261, 265, 266, 273,
 279; East European-Islamic, 97, 98,
 99-100, 226; Western European-
 Islamic, 226, 256
federalism, 45, 46, 112, 142, 151, 153,
 154, 157, 224, 266, 270, 271, 272,
 275, 276, 281
Fedor I, Russian tsar (1584-98), 180
Ferdinand and Isabella, Spanish joint
 monarchs (1474-1504), 12
Ferdinand I of Habsburg, Bohemian and
 Hungarian king (1526-64), Holy
 Roman emperor (1556-64), 12-13,
 15, 16, 61, 169, 255
Ferdinand I, Habsburg emperor (1835-
 48), 25, 77, 78-79
Ferdinand I of Saxe-Coburg, Bulgarian
 prince and tsar (1887-1918), 125,
 129, 131, 132, 145, 148, 150
Ferdinand II of Styria, Holy Roman
 emperor and Bohemian king (1619-
 37), 14
Florence, 248; church council of (1439),
 66, 181-182
France, 2, 3, 4, 11, 12, 19, 20, 22, 23, 24,
 27, 29, 30, 31, 37, 38, 77, 83, 86, 90,
 104, 106, 112, 150, 172, 176, 198,
 199, 202, 203, 204, 208, 210, 213,
 215, 217, 218, 219, 230, 239, 253,
 258, 259, 260, 265, 268, 273
Francis I, Habsburg Holy Roman
 emperor (1792-1835), 22
Francis Ferdinand, Habsburg archduke,
 35-36, 84, 223, 268, 269-270
Francis Joseph, Habsburg emperor (1848-
 1916), 25, 33, 35, 38, 79, 80, 263, 268
Frank, Josip, 266, 267
Frankfort, 24, 26, 27
Frederick, Elector Palatine, Bohemian
 king (1619-20), 14
Frederick II the Great, Prussian king
 (1740-86), 18, 171, 199

Jagiełłos, Lithuanian ruling dynasty, 9, 11, 16, 61, 169, 175, 176, 197
Jajce, 255, 275
Janissaries, 110, 240, 250-251, 252-253, 258
Jelačić, Josip, 24, 77, 262
Jesuits, 13, 64, 67-68, 70, 176, 180, 181, 182, 183
Jews, 57, 64, 92, 103, 107, 125, 155, 172, 176, 181, 212, 214, 241-242, 248, 274
Joanna, daughter of Ferdinand and Isabella and wife of Philip the Fair, 12
Joseph I, Habsburg Holy Roman emperor (1705-11), 66
Joseph II, Habsburg Holy Roman emperor (1780-90), 22, 70, 72-74, 75

K
Kálmán, Hungarian and Croatian king (1095-1119), 229
Kalocsa, 231
Karadjordje, Djordje (Petrović), 110-111
Karadjordjević, Aleksandr I, Serb-Yugoslav king (1921-34), 6, 45, 151, 271, 272, 273
Karadjordjević, Pavel, Yugoslav prince-regent (1934-41), 45, 46, 273
Karadjordjević, Petr I, Serb-Yugoslav king (1903-21), 32, 145, 267, 269
Karadjordjević, Petr II, Serb-Yugoslav king (1934-41), 45, 46, 273
Karadjordjevićes, Serbian ruling house, 39, 132, 145, 224, 270
Karadžić, Vuk, 110-111, 226, 258
Karavelov, Lyuben, 119, 120
Karl I, Romanian king (1866-1915), 84
Kavalla, 148, 150
Kemal (Atatürk), Mustafa, 9, 144, 145, 158
Kettler, Gothard, 179
Khmelnitsky, Bogdan, 192, 193
Kiev, 166, 167, 173, 174, 187, 188, 194, 210
Kliment (Ohridski), 139, 142-143
Klyuchevsky, Vasili, 188
Kollar, Jan, 23
Kollonics, Lipot, 67-68
Komnenos, Manuel I, Byzantine emperor (1143-80), 229
Koneski, Blaže, 144, 154
Königgrätz (Sadowa), battle of (1866), 27

Konstantin, Russian regent of Poland, 203
Kopitar, Jernej, 111
Koraïs, Adamantios, 104
Kościuszko, Tadeusz, 200
Košica Program, 43
Kosovo, 97-98, 125, 139, 146, 156, 159-160, 274, 276. *See also* Raška
Kosovo Polje: first battle of (1389), 36, 141, 234, 269; second battle of (1448), 61
Kossuth, Lajos, 23, 25, 76, 77, 79, 80
Kotor, 233, 236
Kotromanić, Stjepan, Bosnian *ban* (ca. 1318-53), 231-232, 233, 234, 244
Krajina, 231, 256, 278. *See also* military borders, Croatian
Kruševo, 133
Kuber, Bulgar *han,* 138, 142
Kulin, Bosnian *ban* (ca. 1180-1204), 229, 230
Kun, Béla, 43, 84
Kurbskii, Andrei, 179

L
Ladislas (Ulászó) of Angevin Naples, 234
languages, 14-15, 22-24, 34-35, 52-53, 58, 65, 70, 71, 73-74, 75, 76, 78, 82, 89, 93, 104, 105, 106, 110, 111, 115, 116, 117, 118, 119, 126, 127, 130, 132, 138-139, 142, 143-144, 151, 154, 157, 174, 206, 225, 226, 258, 259, 260, 265, 270, 276, 279
Latvia, 1, 218
Latvians, 92
Lazar, Serbian prince-ruler (1371-89), 141
Lazarović, Stefan, Serbian prince-despot (1389-1427), 234
League of Nations, 2, 4, 86, 90
Lech, battle of (955), 54
Lenin, Vladimir, 2, 209, 210
Leopold I, Habsburg Holy Roman emperor (1658-1705), 17, 65, 66-67, 68-69, 109, 256
Leopold II, Habsburg Holy Roman emperor (1790-92), 22, 74, 83
Leszczyński, Stanisław, Polish king (1704-9), 195-196, 198
Levski, Vasil, 119, 120
liberal democracy (liberalism), 2, 7, 19-21, 23, 25, 28, 31, 41, 45, 75-78, 81, 82, 93, 113, 116, 124, 201, 202, 203,

318 CONFLICT AND CHAOS IN EASTERN EUROPE

Poles, 63, 163, 164-166, 167-168, 169,
170-173, 174-175, 177, 179, 183,
184, 189, 192, 199, 200, 201-206,
207-215, 215-216, 217, 220, 221;
culture of, 168, 174, 175-176, 182-
183, 185, 186, 188, 189, 190, 191,
193-194, 194-196, 196-198, 202, 204
Polish corridor, 171, 210, 211, 218, 219
Polish Home Army, 220. *See also* partisans
Polish nationalist emigration, 204
Polish partitions (1772; 1793; 1795), 18,
31, 171, 199, 200, 201, 202, 207,
208, 211
Polish revolutions (1830-31; 1863-64),
203-204, 205-206
Polish Socialist party, 207-208
Polish Succession, War of (1733-35), 198
Polotsk, 173, 180
Poniatowski, Stanisław II, Polish king
(1764-95), 199, 200
pope, 54, 56, 61, 67, 140, 180, 230, 231,
236, 246, 255. *See also* papacy;
Rome; Vatican
Possevino, Antonio, 180
Posveta (Enlightenment) Society, 269
Potockis, Polish aristocratic family, 198-
199
Potsdam conference (1945), 172, 221
Pragmatic Sanction, 17
Prague, 13, 14, 15, 17, 23, 24, 41, 42, 44,
167, 173
Přemysl, Otakar II, Czech king (1253-
78), 10
Přemysls, native Czech ruling dynasty,
165, 167, 175
Preslav, 139
Princip, Gavril, 36, 270
Prussia, 19, 20, 26, 27, 29, 30, 80, 170-
171, 179, 194, 198, 199, 200, 201,
202, 207, 212, 213, 239;
Brandenburg, 171, 199; East, 26, 55,
56, 171, 199, 211, 218. *See also*
Germany
Prussians, 56, 112, 163-164, 170-171,
176, 200
Pumnul, Aron, 78

R
Radić, Antun, 267

Radić, Stjepan, 45, 267, 272
Rákoczi, Ferenc II, Transylvanian *vajda*
(1704-11), 75
Rákoczi, György I, Transylvanian *vajda*
(1630-48), 62
Rákosz, 197-198
Rakovski, Georgi, 119
Raška, 97, 139-140, 141, 232. *See also*
Kosovo
reaya, 107, 114, 241, 254
Reformation, 7, 8, 13, 57, 62-64, 171,
176, 197, 226, 239
Regat, 92, 93. *See also* Romanian
(Danubian) Principalities
Renaissance, 61, 197
Revolutions of 1848, 20, 24-26, 28, 75,
77-80, 204, 262
Ribbentrop, Joachim von, 91, 217-218
Ribbentrop-Molotov pact (1939), 1, 90,
218
Riga, 179, 210, 211, 218; treaty of
(1921), 210, 211, 212, 218
Ristić, Jovan, 263
Roman Empire, 51-52, 88, 89, 135, 136,
158, 236, 261. *See also* Byzantine
Empire
Romania, 4, 5, 30, 33, 34, 40, 47, 49, 50,
51, 83-84, 86, 90, 91-95, 113, 119,
122, 132, 137, 148, 149, 150, 218;
"Greater," 40, 83
Romanian (Danubian) Principalities, 29,
30, 32, 65, 75, 83-84, 89, 92, 101,
104, 105. *See also* Moldavia;
Wallachia
Romanians, 5, 25, 32, 34, 36, 39-40, 43,
46, 50, 51, 53, 54, 57-59, 60, 62, 64-
66, 66-69, 70-72, 74-75, 77-80, 82-
84, 86, 88-90, 91-95, 103, 105, 132,
147, 148, 153, 224; culture of, 243.
See also Vlahs
Romanov, Alexis, Russian tsar (1645-
76), 193
Romanov, Filaret, father of Tsar Mihail I,
185
Romanov, Konstantin, brother of Tsar
Alexander I and Polish viceroy, 203
Romanov, Mihail I, Russian tsar (1613-
45), 185-186, 193
Romanovs, Russian imperial dynasty, 29,
186, 187, 188, 203, 211

Romanticism, 19-20, 22, 75, 100-101, 106, 111, 134, 207, 213, 259, 261
Rome, 54, 58, 66-67, 68, 70, 71, 89, 164, 165, 166, 181, 182, 231, 232, 233, 238, 279. *See also* papacy; pope; Roman Empire; Vatican
Roosevelt, Franklin D., 220
Rudolf I, Habsburg Holy Roman emperor (1273-91), 10
Rudolf II, Habsburg Holy Roman emperor (1576-1612), 14
Ruriks, Russian imperial dynasty, 166, 180, 183, 186
Russia, 2, 19, 21, 23, 25, 29-32, 37, 104-105, 106, 109, 112, 114, 116, 117, 118, 120, 121, 122, 123, 124, 129, 138, 145, 146, 148, 149, 160, 170, 173, 177, 178, 180, 183, 184, 185, 186, 187, 192, 193, 194, 196, 198, 199, 200, 201, 202, 205, 206, 208, 209, 211, 212, 213, 214, 217, 221, 223, 251, 253, 261, 263, 264-265, 267-268, 273, 280; empire of, 1, 4, 6, 21, 29, 31, 171, 203, 205, 206; Kievan, 1, 165, 166, 173, 174, 178, 187-188; Muscovite (Muscovy), 174, 175, 177-179, 181, 182, 183-184, 185-186, 187, 188, 189, 190, 192, 193. *See also* Soviet Union
Russian civil war (1918-21), 209, 210, 211, 214
Russian revolutions (1917), 39, 208, 209, 214, 271
Russians, 21, 29, 31, 32, 37, 79, 92, 113, 118, 122-123, 125, 137, 147, 149, 163-164, 166, 170, 173, 177, 179, 182, 183-184, 185, 186, 187-188, 189, 190, 193, 198, 200, 201, 202-203, 204, 205-206, 210, 219, 224, 258, 261, 263-264, 267, 269, 271; culture of, 21, 108, 114, 124, 137, 166, 174, 177, 182, 183, 185, 191, 196, 202, 203, 258, 269, 280
Russo-Polish war (1920-21), 210
Russo-Turkish wars, 110-111; (1828-29), 112; (1877-78), 30, 113, 122, 135, 264
Ruthenians, 42-43, 92, 192
Ryngoldas, Lithuanian ruling family, 173

S

Šafařík, Pavel, 23
Samuil, Bulgarian-Macedonian tsar (976-1014), 138, 140, 143
San Stefano, treaty of (1878), 113, 118, 122-123, 124, 125, 126, 149, 264
Sandanski, Jane, 130, 131, 133
Sandjak of Novi Pazar (Sandjak), 29, 123, 146, 159
Sarajevo, 36, 37, 98, 161, 223, 228, 236, 247-248, 253, 269-270
Sava (Rastko Nemanja), Serbian saint, 140, 235-236
Saxons, 53, 56-57, 58, 59, 60, 62, 63, 74, 79, 83, 87, 164, 232
Schmalkaldic War (1546-47), 13
Schuyler, Eugene, 121
Schwarzenberg, Felix, 79, 80
sejm, 175, 194, 197, 200, 202
Selim II the Sot, Ottoman sultan (1566-74), 249
Serbia, 1, 29, 30, 32, 33, 36, 37, 45, 52, 101, 112, 113, 117, 120, 122, 123, 124, 126, 129, 132, 134, 139, 140-141, 145, 146, 147, 148, 149, 150, 151, 157, 159, 160, 224, 225, 229, 231, 233, 234, 235, 236, 237, 244, 258, 263-264, 267, 269, 270, 271, 272, 274, 275, 276; "Greater," 112, 113, 123, 153, 258, 267, 269, 270-271, 275, 280
Serbian revolution (1804-30), 110-112, 117, 119, 258
Serbo-Croat coalition, 267, 268, 270-271
Serbs, 17, 25, 29, 32, 36, 37, 39, 44-46, 79, 92, 97, 100, 102, 103, 105, 106-108, 108-113, 114, 115, 116, 119, 123, 124, 125, 126-127, 128, 130, 132-133, 135, 136, 138, 139-142, 146, 147, 148, 149, 150, 151, 153, 155-156, 158, 160, 223-224, 225-226, 227, 229, 230, 231, 232, 233, 234, 235, 236, 244, 255, 256, 257-258, 261, 263-264, 265, 266, 268-270, 270-274, 276-277, 278, 279-280; culture of, 226, 243, 244, 255, 256, 257, 258, 265, 266-267, 270, 279-281
Seven Years War (1756-63), 72, 199
Shatorov, Sharlo, 153